The Araucana

Alonso de Ercilla

The Araucana

A New Translation
With Annotations and Introduction

Cyrus Moore

Eikonica Press

Published by Eikonica Press
New York, New York
© 2022 Cyrus Moore
All rights reserved.

Publisher's Cataloging-in-Publication data

Names: Ercilla y Zúñiga, Alonso de, 1533-1594, author. | Moore, Cyrus (Professor), translator.
Title: The Araucana : a new translation with annotations and introduction / Alonso de Ercilla; [translated and edited by] Cyrus Moore.
Description: Includes bibliographical references and index. | New York, NY: Eikonica Press, 2022.
Identifiers: LCCN: 2022900764 | ISBN: 9798985432534 (hardcover) | 9798985432503 (paperback) | 9798985432510 (Mobi) | 9798985432527 (Epub)
Subjects: LCSH Ercilla y Zúñiga, Alonso de, 1533-1594. Araucana. | Spaniards--Chile--Poetry. | Araucanía (Chile)--History--Poetry. | Mapuche Indians--Wars--Poetry. | Chile--History--1565-1810--Poetry. | Colonies in literature. | BISAC POETRY / European / Spanish & Portuguese | POETRY / Subjects & Themes / Places | POETRY / Epic
Classification: LCC PQ6389 .A2013 2022 | DDC 861/.39--dc23

Front cover: *Lautaro in Front of his Army* (Gaspar & Roig, 1852); frontispiece: Alonso de Ercilla (Antonio Carnicero, 1791). Images are in the public domain.

For Isaías Lerner:
scholar, teacher,
friend.

Table of Contents

Introduction	xix
Additional notes	xli
Translator's Preface	xliii

Part I (1569)

Prologue — 3

Canto 1 — 7
   The first canto describes the province of Chile and the state of Arauco, as well as the natives' customs and ways of waging war. It also briefly recounts the arrival and conquest of the Spanish prior to the Araucan rebellion.

Canto 2   20

>   This canto tells of the discord that arose among the Araucan caciques over the selection of a commander and of the resolution they reached with the advice of the cacique Colocolo. It also describes the cunning that gained them entry to the Tucapel fort and the battle they fought there with the Spanish.

Canto 3   36

>   Accompanied by a few Spanish troops and Indian allies, Valdivia makes his way to the Tucapel fort to punish the attackers. At a narrow pass the Araucans first kill his scouts, then engage him in a battle where the great valor and determination of Lautaro result in Valdivia being slain with all his men.

Canto 4   52

>   Coming from La Imperial to join Valdivia at the Tucapel fort, the fourteen Spaniards are ambushed by Indians who engage them in a bitter fight. Lautaro arrives with reinforcements, and seven of the Spanish die, along with all their allies. Through great good fortune the rest of them escape.

Canto 5 — 69
> This fifth canto describes the hard-fought battle between the Spanish and Araucans on the hill at Andalicán, where Lautaro's shrewdness and the great obstacles facing the Spanish resulted in their rout, with more than half of them killed, along with three thousand of their Indian allies.

Canto 6 — 79
> The battle continues with the strange and varied deaths the Araucans inflicted upon the defeated and the little pity they showed the women and children, all of whom they put to the blade.

Canto 7 — 89
> The Spanish arrive badly battered at Concepción, where they tell of their losses and defeat. Considering the great number of women, children, and elderly, and seeing how few are left to resist the powerful enemy, they decide to withdraw to Santiago. This canto also describes the sacking and burning of Concepción.

Canto 8 — 101
> The caciques and principal warriors gather in the valley of Arauco for a general council, during which Tucapel kills the cacique Puchecalco. Caupolicán approaches La Imperial in the Cautén valley with a powerful army.

Canto 9 113

> The Araucans come within three leagues of La Imperial with a sizable army, but lacking divine sanction their plans have no effect and they return to their homes. Learning that the Spanish are rebuilding the Penco fort and city of Concepción, they move to attack them, engaging in a bitter battle.

Canto 10 131

> Proud of the victories they've won, the Araucans organize public festivities attended by people from near and far, who compete in great contests.

Canto 11 141

> In this eleventh canto the festivities and disagreements come to an end, and Lautaro marches against the city of Santiago. Before arriving there he builds a stronghold where the Spanish attack him, leading to a bitter battle.

Canto 12 156

> Safe in his fort, Lautaro decides against trying to defeat the Spanish in battle. He and Marcos Veaz have a conversation from which Pedro de Villagrán realizes the danger the Spanish are in and retreats. The Marquis of Cañete arrives at the City of Kings in Peru.

Canto 13   173

    Following the Marquis of Cañete's punishment of the Peruvian rebels, envoys arrive from Chile requesting his assistance, and recognizing the importance and justice of their petition, he sends them abundant aid by land and sea. This canto also describes how Francisco de Villagrán, guided by an Indian, comes upon Lautaro.

Canto 14   184

    Villagrán reaches the enemy stronghold during the night without being detected. At dawn he suddenly attacks, Lautaro is killed in the initial skirmish, and a bloody battle is fought.

Canto 15   193

    In this fifteenth and final canto of Part I the battle ends, and none of the Araucans being willing to surrender, all are killed. Also recounted here is the sailing of the ships from Peru to Chile and the great storm they encountered between the Maule river and the port of Concepción.

Part II (1578)

To the Reader   211

Canto 16   213

    In this canto the storm subsides, and the Spanish arrive at the island of Talcahuano in the bay of Concepción. The council held by the Indians in the valley of Ongolmo is described here as well, along with the argument that arose between Peteguelén and Tucapel and the agreement they reached.

Canto 17   227

    Millalauco conducts his embassy. The Spanish leave the island and build a fort on the hill at Penco, where the Araucans attack them at the same time Phillip II is attacking Saint Quentin in France.

Canto 18   238

    King Philip attacks Saint Quentin and enters it in triumph. The Araucans attack the Spanish fort.

Canto 19   252

    This canto describes the Araucan attack on the Penco fort, Gracolano's rushing of the rampart, and the battle on the seashore between the enemy and those who stayed behind to guard the ships.

Canto 20   261

    The Araucans retreat with the loss of many men; Tucapel, badly wounded, breaks through the enemy and escapes. Tegualda tells Alonso de Ercilla her strange and pitiable story.

The Cantos

Canto 21 — 275
Tegualda finds her husband's body and returns home with it, lamenting. Spanish cavalry from Santiago and La Imperial arrive at Penco; Caupolicán reviews his troops.

Canto 22 — 285
The Spanish enter the State of Arauco, meeting the Araucans in a hard-fought battle in which Rengo gives great proof of himself. Courageous Galbarino is sentenced to having his hands cut off.

Canto 23 — 294
Galbarino appears before the Araucan senate and makes a speech that upsets many. The Spanish set out in search of the enemy. The cave and many marvels of the sorcerer Fitón are described.

Canto 24 — 310
This canto is devoted to the great naval battle of Lepanto, the rout and destruction of the Turkish armada, and the flight of Ochalí.

Canto 25 — 329
The Spanish make camp in Millarapué, where Caupolicán sends a messenger to challenge them. A bloody battle follows in which Tucapel, Rengo, and many Spanish distinguish themselves.

The Araucana

Canto 26 — 343
> This canto describes the end of the battle and Araucan retreat, together with the obstinacy and death of Galbarino. Described here as well are the garden and residence of Fitón.

Canto 27 — 352
> This canto describes the many cities, provinces, and natural features within Fitón's sphere, famous either for their beauty or for events associated with them. It recounts as well how the Spanish raised a fort in the Tucapel valley and how Don Alonso de Ercilla came upon the beautiful Glaura.

Canto 28 — 368
> Glaura recounts her misfortunes and explains how she came to be here. The Araucans attack the Spanish at the Purén ravine, and a pitched fight follows in which the enemy is routed but left content at having sacked the baggage train.

Canto 29 — 380
> The Araucans enter a new council at which they propose burning their homes. Tucapel asks that his dispute with Rengo be allowed to resume, and the two have a spirited fight in the arena.

Part III (1598)

Canto 30 — 393
This canto recounts the end of the fight between Tucapel and Rengo, as well as what transpired between Pran, an Araucan, and Andresillo, a *yanacona* of the Spanish.

Canto 31 — 404
Andresillo tells Reynoso what was agreed upon with Pran. He then deceives Caupolicán, who attacks the Tucapel fort expecting to find the Spanish asleep.

Canto 32 — 413
The Araucans attack the fort and are repelled in a terrible slaughter. Caupolicán disbands the army and retreats to the sierra. Soldiers ask Don Alonso de Ercilla to tell them the life and true history of Dido.

Canto 33 — 429
Don Alonso continues with Dido's voyage and arrival at Bizerte, telling how she founded Carthage and explaining the reason she took her own life. Caupolicán's capture is also described.

Canto 34 — 444
Caupolicán speaks to Reynoso, and learning he is to be executed, converts to Christianity before bravely dying a miserable death. The Araucans gather for the

election of a new general; King Philip raises an army to enter Portugal.

Canto 35 — 455

The Spanish set out to explore the new territory. Tunconabal meets them and advises them to return, but realizing they will not, provides them with a guide who leads them into rugged wilderness where they suffer terrible hardships.

Canto 36 — 464

A cacique comes ashore and offers the Spanish all they need for their journey, but the route ahead is soon blocked by a great channel of water. Don Alonso crosses this in a piragua, accompanied by ten soldiers, after which they return to their camp and follow a different road back to La Imperial.

Canto 37 — 473

In this final canto war is discussed as a nation's right, and the war King Philip waged against the kingdom of Portugal is explained along with the warrants he provided the Portuguese justifying his armies.

Ercilla's Index of Notable Events in the Poem	487
Index of Extended Similes	495
General Index	499

D. ALONSO DE ERCILLA.
Caballero de Santiago, nació en Madrid á 7 de
Agosto de 1533: Poeta Heroico tan dulce como va-
leroso Soldado: compuso el Poema de la Araucana,
y falleció despues del Año de 1596.

Introduction

Generations of Chilean students have memorized the following lines from Alonso de Ercilla's sixteenth-century epic poem of Spanish conquest:

> Chile, fértil provincia y señalada
> en la región antártica famosa,
> de remotas naciones respetada
> por fuerte, principal y ponderosa;
> la gente que produce es tan granada,
> tan soberbia, gallarda y belicosa,
> que no ha sido por rey jamás regida
> ni a estranjero dominio sometida.
>
> (1.6.1-8)[1]

(Chile is a large and fertile province in the famous region of Antarctica, respected by distant nations for

---

[1] Citations refer to canto, octave, and line.

its prominence and power. The people it produces are so remarkable and proud, so courageous and warlike, that it has never been ruled by kings nor subject to foreign domination.)

These proud, warlike people, Ercilla's Araucans, eventually forced the Spanish to withdraw with the treaty of Quillín in 1641, after which they remained autonomous in their southern homelands. In the early eighteenth century the history of their fierce resistance proved an irresistible symbol in Chile's fight for independence, and the names of Ercilla's heroic warriors began to grace everything from streets and plazas to newspapers, proving popular for children as well. In the fledgling nation's first decades these quintessential freedom fighters—Lautaro, Caupolicán, Colocolo, and Galbarino—paragons of courage, fortitude, and martial skill, were joined by their female counterparts from the poem, the equally memorable Guacolda, Tegualda, Glaura, and Fresia, all these denominating civic organizations, business ventures, and more than a dozen Navy vessels. The poem inspired musical, dramatic, and literary works during these years, as well, including an early twentieth-century opera, *Caupolicán*, and the later twentieth-century poetry of Chile's Nobel laureates Gabriela Mistral and Pablo Neruda. The *Colo Colo* soccer club, begun in 1925, is still one of the most popular. In the twenty-first century the *Araucana* has already been the source of two rock operas and a video game.

Such a romantic melding of racial and national identity was never destined to be straightforward. Forty years into independence, pursuing economic expansion and nationalist integration, the state set out to incorporate the territory of the Araucans—properly known as the Mapuche—by means of a military "pacification" program modeled on the United States's forced resettlement of indigenous populations to reservations and the seizure of their lands. To justify the process, these previous epitomes of independence were transformed into their opposites, now no longer heroes, but *flojos*, *borrachos*, and *pobres*—lazy, drunk, and poor. The outcome was great loss of life and the eventual displacement of most of the Mapuche to the outskirts of metropolitan areas. The country's military dictatorship (1973-1990) escalated the assault with "terrorist" legislation (an early example of this popular maneuver against political adversaries). Mirroring their ancestors' defiance of the Spanish, however, Mapuche resistance to the process never ended, and by the late twentieth century efforts at recuperation of their homelands and preservation of their language (Mapudungun) and identity had developed into one of the most vital movements for social justice and indigenous rights on the continent.

For Gabriela Mistral, champion of the downtrodden, Ercilla's glorification of the Araucans had humanized them, suggesting a reconciliation of the country's dual patrimony. For Pablo Neruda, the poem's inscription of the origins of Chilean history made its author Chile's inventor and true liberator. Few examples better illustrate art's role not merely in reflecting reality but in helping shape it.

What is this work that 450 years after composition continues to permeate the country's imagination and who was its author, a Spaniard who wrote for the glorification of Spain?

When Alonso de Ercilla first set foot in Chile in June of 1557, he was a 23-year-old member of a Spanish force sent to confront a rebellion among the native population. His background was privileged, but not without misfortune. His father, a jurisconsult to the Holy Roman Emperor and king of Spain, Charles V, had died within a year of his birth. His mother, left with six children, eventually entered service as a lady-in-waiting to Charles's daughter, the princess Maria, and at age fifteen Alonso himself entered service as a page to Charles's son, the future Philip II. Among the many advantages the position offered were travel to centers of European culture and a humanist education under the tutelage of the court classicist and historian. Travel began immediately with a six-month progression of Philip's retinue from Spain to the Habsburg court in Brussels, passing through cities that vied in entertaining their royal guests. Following a lengthy stay in the Low Countries, Ercilla joined his mother and the princess on a visit to Vienna, and in 1554 he accompanied Philip to England for his marriage to Queen Mary.

It was in London that news reached the court of a rebellion among Spanish soldiers in Peru and of an uprising by the Araucan Indians farther south, the latter responsible for the death of the region's military commander. Ercilla sought and was granted permission to join those responding to these threats, and the following year he embarked for the New World. Spain had been in South America for a generation at this point, and many of the early conquistadors were settled on grants of land with the forced labor of local inhabitants. Commercial activity was growing and the mining of silver was beginning to swell the wealth that would underpin Spain's far-flung empire and sixteenth-century wars. By the time Ercilla reached Lima the rebellion by Spanish renegades had been suppressed. The Araucan uprising was gaining strength, however, and shortly thereafter the poet was part of a small

INTRODUCTION

armada that made landfall near Concepción. The Araucans had seen the ships approach and were waiting to attack.

———

As we learn from the poem, the idea of capturing his experience in verse occurred to the young soldier soon after his arrival. For the rest of his time in the New World he pursued the project as conditions allowed—"now with my pen in hand, now with my lance" (20.24.8)—composing, as he tells us in the Prologue to Part I, on scraps of paper or even leather. Ercilla determined that the key strength of his work would be its accuracy and fairness, guaranteed by his unbiased testimony as an eyewitness participant, "[. . .] neither blinded by passion, which I shun, nor depriving anyone of their due" (12.70.7-8). While the poem's early verses stress its documentary character—"My account comes straight from the truth and is cut to its measure" (1.3.5-6)—the narrative quickly took on literary attributes, from elevated language to elements of classical epic. In sixteenth-century Spain this most prestigious of genres was associated primarily with the Latin poets Lucan and Virgil, the former's *Pharsalia* a model of rhetoric and military history, the latter's *Aeneid* beginning where Homer's *Iliad* had ended, with a few survivors of Troy escaping to heroically overcome adversity and lay the foundations of the future Roman empire. Many participants in Spain's colonizing of the Americas saw themselves as inhabiting an equally epic age.

A year later, with the Araucan rebellion contained, Ercilla began a slow return to Spain, where he collated the verses he'd written in the field ("no small effort" the Prologue says) and continued composing new ones. He wrote in the era's most prestigious verse form, the *octava real*, stanzas of eight lines, each with eleven syllables and linked by an *abababcc* rhyme. This difficult format, recently adapted into Spanish from Italian, had a density associated with heroic subjects and elevated speech. Ercilla embellished it with a notably Latinate vocabulary, as in *indómito* (indomitable), a favored term for the Araucan spirit. He also employed a full range of poetic devices and rhetorical figures, from intricate patterns of sounds to complex figures of speech, all contributing to the highly prized sense of richness or abundance—*copia*—associated with the era's best writing.

The *Araucana* was further enriched with a wide variety of literary imagery. Much of this was traditional to classical epic, including certain well-known scenes that following antiquity became set-pieces or clichés of the genre: descriptions of harsh combat between armies and one-on-one fights between mighty champions, rousing speeches by commanders to their troops, stately reviews of armies before battle, athletic contests among soldiers during lulls in the fighting. Other epic elements include extended (Homeric) similes, references to gods and mythology, and anthropomorphism, or the attributing of human emotions to the natural world. A description of the terrifying novelty of Spanish cannons, combining the latter two, includes the first encounter many European readers had with American wildlife: "Alpacas and vicuñas, jaguars and pumas ran terrified here and there; dolphins, Nereids, and Tritons hid deep within their caverns, while swift rivers and springs, confused, restrained their flow" (16.37.3-8). The presence of gods, prophecy, and other supernatural paraphernalia, uncontroversial in the ancient world, was problematic in a Christian one. Readers had long enjoyed these features, however, and rather than deprive them of such pleasures modern authors devised a variety of explanations for their continued use. In the *Araucana* the Roman goddess of war, Bellona, and a goddess-like figure identified as Reason appear to the narrator in an exhaustion-induced vision or dream, while a powerful Araucan sorcerer, Fitón, possesses a magical sphere in which he is able to see the future. A celestial appearance by the Virgin Mary is described as a modern Christian miracle (9.13 ff.).

Ercilla drew on a wide variety of sources in addition to epic. Erotic passion, a frequent theme of ancient lyric, pastoral, and drama, had been idealized in the medieval traditions of courtly love and spiritualized in the poetry of Petrarch. Pastoral's bucolic world, far from the concerns of city life and exemplified in the *locus amoenus* or beautiful place, with meadow, stream, and rustling trees, offered a welcome respite from epic's battles. References to Roman history abound in the *Araucana*, along with others to the Bible and to the history of medieval and early-modern Spain. Early-modern authors are important sources of inspiration and emulation, as well, from the lyric poetry of Garcilaso de la Vega, who introduced the 11-syllable line from Italian to Spanish, to Baldassare Castiglione's popular book on courtly etiquette, *The Courtier*, and Ludovico Ariosto's *Orlando Furioso*, an interweaving of epic and chivalric romance which was a sixteenth-century bestseller. All these components, from Latinate lexicon to elements of other genres and allusions to specific authors, were employed by Ercilla to elevate and ennoble his narrative, affiliating it with illustrious predecessors in a process of competitive imitation through which he paid tribute to them while showcasing his own ability. By the time he died in 1594—all the while serving Philip II on diplomatic missions, marrying and raising a son, and being made an official examiner of books—the work had grown to more than 2600 octaves or 21,000 lines, divided into 37 cantos or chapters. Regarding his initial proposal for a historical account, he says, in Canto 12: "If weakness leads me beyond this, I ask that it be indulged in light of my worthy intention, which is only to be accurate while giving pleasure" (12.73.7-8).

Part I of the poem, which was published in 1569, six years after Ercilla returned to Spain, opens with a declaration distinguishing it from popular romance. "I do not sing of ladies, love, and gallant, enamored knights," the poet says, promising to focus instead on the "those valiant Spaniards and their daring deeds, whose swords forced untamed Arauco to its knees" (1.1.5-8). The first canto proceeds with an introduction to Chile's geography and the social organization of the Araucans, whose homeland lies below the mighty Biobío river in the south. We learn of an unsuccessful attempt by Incas to invade the area years earlier and are given a summary of Spain's early forays into the region culminating in the Araucan uprising, which the narrator attributes to Spanish greed and complacency, hinting darkly at heavenly chastisement to come. Once the Araucans have chosen a general by means of a contest based on who can support an immense log on their shoulders the longest (an apparent frivolity later shown to be a clever ploy), the rest of Part I recounts a series of bloody skirmishes, ambushes, and battles during which the Araucans maintain the upper hand, all prior to the poet's arrival on the scene. Near the end of Part I the narrative momentarily shifts to Peru, where Spanish reinforcements are preparing to travel south. Back in Chile, the Spanish have secretly surrounded the main Araucan encampment in the middle of the night and are preparing to attack when the canto ends. The following canto opens on an intimate scene between the foremost Araucan warrior, Lautaro, and his lover, Guacolda, who's had a terrifying premonitory dream and tearfully urges him to arm himself. The abrupt shift in topic and tone is utterly unexpected, but for the remainder of the poem, amidst the narrator's assertions of the need for relief from so much violence, the themes of love and erotic passion assume key roles.

Part II of the *Araucana*, which appeared a decade later, in 1578, begins with Spanish troops, including the poet, arriving from Peru. From this point forward the Spanish gain the upper hand, and the range of topics expands. Especially notable is the way events in this remote outpost of the New World are now magnified by contextualizing them within Spain's larger imperial program in the Old. Bellona spirits the narrator to the top of a celestial mountain from which he witnesses Spain's victory over France at the battle of Saint Quentin in August of 1557, the very day of an important battle with the Araucans. A few cantos later, thanks to an encounter with Fitón and his magical sphere, he's given a bird's eye view of the famous naval battle of Lepanto, in which the Holy League, made up of the Papal States, Venice, and, predominantly, Spain, defeat the Ottoman Turks. The battle occurred in 1571, its inclusion in the day-to-day narration of events in 1557 made possible through the venerable device of epic prophecy. Shortly thereafter Fitón uses the sphere to give the narrator a worldwide geography lesson, beginning at the heart of the ancient western world and circling the globe to eventually arrive at the current, Chilean one. The theme of love reappears when Reason shows the poet a vision of his future wife and is further explored in encounters between the narrator and a series of Araucan women. Two of these tell tragic stories of falling in love, only to have their husbands killed by the Spanish. A third recounts an adventurous tale inspired by Boccaccio and the ancient genre of Greek romance in which she and her beloved are separated in a Spanish attack and lose track of each other, only to be miraculously reunited much later. These stories of chaste, conjugal love awaken the narrator's own romantic sensibility, and their emphasis on loyalty inspires his spirited defense of the classical heroine Dido as a paragon of the virtue, in contrast to her portrayal in Virgil's *Aeneid*.

It's not until near the end of Part III, which appeared after another ten years, in 1589, that we learn of an incident that deeply affected the poet's experience in Chile. Referred to in the sparest of terms, this arose from an altercation between Ercilla and another soldier, which progressed to a duel. Unfortunately, the governor of the region, an impulsive young nobleman, was nearby, and any unauthorized resort to weapons was strictly proscribed. Ercilla was subject to capital punishment, and his sentence was only narrowly commuted to banishment and a period of confinement in Peru. This was what precipitated the poet's departure from Chile, and it seems likely that the public humiliation of having been over-hastily condemned underlies, in part, the poem's emphasis on honor, including Dido's. It is also responsible for an oft-noted structural anomaly, the absence of a unifying hero, which the governor, as the highest ranking Spanish official, would traditionally have embodied.

Part III opens with an Araucan attack on the Spanish fort at Ongolmo. This was supposed to result in a war-ending victory for the Araucans, a spy of theirs having been assured by one of the

Spaniards' Indian workers that the fort was defenseless at midday when its soldiers took their siesta. The worker, who promised to alert the Araucan army to the best moment for attack, was loyal to the Spanish, however, and having betrayed his countrymen he alerted the Spanish, who pretended to be asleep until the last possible moment, when they suddenly arose and dealt the Araucans a devastating defeat. Many of the best-known chieftains or caciques only survive because they refused to take part in the attack, considering it beneath their dignity to engage in such a ruse against an unarmed, sleeping enemy. With the brutality of the Spanish victory and cruelty of their subsequent execution of the Araucan general, Caupolicán, the focus on the conquest of Arauco falters and the narrative veers toward a precipitate end. The last edition of the poem published during Ercilla's lifetime begins describing the election of a new Araucan leader, only to suddenly question the point of pursuing the subject in light of contemporary unrest in Europe. Then comes a canto explaining Philip II's role in the Portuguese War of Succession, a military conflict between Christians requiring every legal justification the conquest of the Americas and Araucans had not, and then the poem abruptly ends, halfway through Part III's expected length, on a note of somber reflection and personal failure. This final gesture is largely rhetorical, since in addition to being a widely-admired author, Ercilla had acquired a sizable fortune through his marriage and skilled business dealings.

Three years after the poet's death in 1594, his editors issued a longer version of the poem (used for the present translation) incorporating more than 100 octaves devoted to an expedition Ercilla joined to Chile's unknown south, after events at Ongolmo, during which the Spanish discover "another New World" (35.6.1) and quasi-paradise of innocence and good will. This material holds considerable interest and may have been intended for a Part IV, but does little to alter the poem's awkward truncation.[2]

———

Key themes help unify the poem's wide range of topics. Courage, honor, and glory, core values of the martial ethos of ancient epic, are ever-present and personified by heroic figures on both sides of the conflict. The Christian virtues of mercy and forgiveness, by contrast, become more important as the narrative continues and by its end are clearly elevated above their pagan counterparts, while honor, detached from glory, is internalized as moral rectitude and right behavior. The importance of justice and of Stoic persistence in the face of the ever-changing Fortune are repeatedly emphasized, as is rational control of the emotions, notably anger and lust (whether erotic or for wealth), control symbolized in the recurring image of the bridle. The friction between wise old age and hot-headed youth and the age-old adages of "might making right" and history's being written by the winners, the wisdom of which the narrator reluctantly acknowledges, become leitmotifs, while the providential role of imperial Spain in world history and the exemplary Christian rectitude of Philip II are never far from view.

Indictments of the failures associated with these themes function as additional unifying elements. The most sustained critique is of excessive, that is, irrational, violence, associated with both sides in the conflict, although that of the Spanish has more serious ramifications. The Araucans are notorious for

---

[2] For additional discussion, see "Esta edición" (pp. 52-53) of the Spanish edition of the poem discussed below in the Translator's Preface.

their ferocity, but Spain's brutality against a people defending its homeland leads the narrator to claim that "[. . .] our invasions and conquests caused enormous and heretofore unseen cruelties" (32.4.7-8). Spanish aggression is also said to provoke retaliatory violence and the threat of perpetual war (34.36.5-8), a prescient observation considering the persistence of the Araucan/Mapuche conflict into the present. The poem's denunciation of greed is similarly evenhanded and its effects similarly disproportionate, the avarice of the invaders described as that which "[. . .] led to so much war and to the ruin of the entire land" (3.3.7-8). In the decades prior to the poem's appearance the nature of just war had been extensively debated in Spain, influenced, among other things, by Erasmian pacifism, and the wars it waged against France and Portugal are defended by Ercilla in considerable detail. Aggression beyond European borders required less justification. The one most frequently invoked was the conversion of barbarians, but the issue of greed was never far from view.

The evenhandedness of the poem's critiques is among its most striking features. The Araucans are a formidable enemy, but many of the *caciques* are vain, impulsive, and argumentative, qualities that seriously impede their cohesion and effectiveness. They meet in a council or senate to consider important issues and plan military strategy, but such sessions are traditionally inaugurated with bouts of drinking, which on more than one occasion lead to serious fights. The exemplary bravery and skill of Spanish soldiers, fighting for God and king, are repeatedly emphasized, but their excesses are also denounced, as when, upon killing men who had surrendered, the narrator describes them as "Christians until then" (26.7.1). After the sack of Santiago there's a vivid description of the Araucans pillaging the town in a swarming horde (7.45.1-7.53.8). Following Spain's victory at San Quentin the town's ransacking by Spanish troops is described in much the same way (18.17.1-18.21.8).

———

The poem's cantos frequently open with moral exhortations or *exordia*, a narrative device Ercilla borrowed from Ariosto's *Orlando Furioso*. Another Ariostan technique is that of ending a canto at the height of a dramatic scene, a device that assumed bravura dimensions when Ercilla applied it to the poem's three parts, the first ending at the climax of a violent storm in which the ships bearing Spanish reinforcements are threatened with sinking, the second halting just as a sword descends in a bitter duel between two champions. In both instances the poem's initial readers had to wait more than ten years to read of the outcomes. The *Furioso* was famous for its narrator's witty commentary, which regularly pierced the veil of fiction to speak directly to the reader. While Ercilla's narrative is historical and his tone usually earnest, he employed a similar technique. Most of his comments are addressed to Philip II, his dedicatee and ideal reader, to whom he regularly appeals for favor and forbearance. To the rest of us he directs pro forma claims of weariness and the need for rest (before proceeding further) or pleas for patience (for going on so long). Once the theme of love is introduced, narratorial comments become more personal. Petrarchan clichés of emotional turmoil expressed by the Araucan women eventually become those of the poet himself, reflected in his complaint of "perfidious and tyrannical love" (22.1.1) hampering his focus on war. At times disconcerting, such remarks, as in his comments on the mix of hatred and pity he feels during a bloody Spanish victory and assertions that had he been present he would have prevented the worst excesses of his fellow soldiers, create a clear image of Ercilla as an honorable and conscientious young man. As the expedition to the south, near the end of the poem, is forced back by the approach of winter, there's a scene in which he carves the following in the bark of a tree:

> *Reaching this point, where no one had ever come before, don Alonso de Ercilla was the first to cross this channel in a small, unballasted boat with only ten men, in the year fifteen fifty-eight, on the last day of February at two o'clock in the afternoon [. . .]*
>
> (36.29.1-7)

The poem's descriptive passages have long been admired for their vividness and detail. The most dramatic are brutal scenes of combat, as when "[. . .] heads hacked from bodies and containing vital spirit go spinning across the bloody field, their eyes rolled back and lips still moving" (3.31.5-8), or "[. . .] chunks of flesh raining down far and wide, livers and intestines, broken bones, palpating entrails, heaving lungs" (32.8.6-8). The Spanish are typically armored and the Indians not (unless with equipment they've captured), resulting in a deadly disparity: "Accustomed to meeting steel, when the swords come into contact with soft, naked flesh they need little force to strew arms and legs on all sides" (14.32.1-4). It's a distinction that's audible: "The sounds made by the blows of the fighters differ, some cutting through flesh and bone, others leaving dents in tempered armor" (14.35.5-8). Spanish breastplates and bucklers are not always sufficient protection against clubs of the enraged

Indians: "Embossed armor is crushed, bursts open, and falls apart; battered bucklers come undone; pieces of broken pikes and helmets roll on the ground [. . .]" (4.33.5-7). The Araucans face terrifying cannons, but "blind fear does not perturb or slow them even for a moment. Instead, if a shot takes off someone's arm, he immediately grips his sword with the arm that remains [. . .]" (5.28.1-4).

In contrast to such straightforward descriptions of violence, others are more stylized, as when an Araucan warrior is described as "[. . .] splattering blood and fresh brains like fine rain before the wind" (8.51.5-6), or when a Spanish swordsman leaves a victim "standing on one leg like a crane" (25.48.8). Many of the poem's similes offer more elaborate stylization, as in one based on the frightening American alligator or *caiman*:

> Like a hungry alligator that sees a school of fish noisily darting through the water, churning the clear current all around, and opens its great maw to carefully gather them in, clamping its cavernous jaws together and crushing them, satiating its insatiable belly, / just so the small squadron [of Spaniards] was drawn in by the killers and quickly consumed without a single man escaping alive.
>
> (3.24.1-3.25.4)

Long recognized for their powerful imagery, Ercilla's similes typically conjoin human and natural worlds, as when comparing the Araucan hero Lautaro to "a shaggy Libyan lion bursting through a timid mob of closely- packed men"

(19.31.5-7), or the Spanish champion Andrea to " [. . .] a valiant bear harassed by hunters, which feeling itself injured becomes enraged and shatters their knotty javelins, clearing a path through a mountain gorge with furious impatience while pitiful, wounded dogs, chastised, give it wide berth" (14.49.1-8). Ercilla's hunting similes are among the most admired, along with those based on bullfighting: "Like someone who dreams of being inside a vast arena with a furious bull approaching, and distraught with terror, tries to flee the violence and run faster but cannot move at all, just so the riders try to spur their horses to greater speed" (6.53.1-8). Similes that invoke the natural world are equally effective:

> But like some mighty river that bursts its floodgates and goes spreading through woods, tearing out deep-rooted trees as its roaring, rampant flood carries off everything it meets, even solid, sunken boulders borne away on its furious waters, / with just such violence the Indians uprooted our soldiers, and with nothing ahead to stop them, carried them along in a raging torrent [. . .]
>
> (11.66.1-11.67.5)

At times the descriptions of violence become ironic, as in references to battle as a *dance* (2.22.2) or *game* (5.6.7). Blow-by-blow accounts of swordfights or deadly wrestling matches, upon repetition, verge on parody. Other descriptions are lightly mocking, as when panicked Spaniards fleeing Indian pursuers make "[. . .] vows and promises of fasts and pilgrimages, along with other things the Pope alone can fulfill, if only God will save them from the peril" (6.51.5-8). The amassing of descriptive terms becomes hyperbole, as when the Araucan hero Tucapel "[. . .] smashes, bruises, grinds, and tortures, dislocating and dismembering, ravaging and exterminating" (8.50.5-6). In other passages the hyperbole is darkly humorous, as when following a rout of the Spanish, three soldiers on horseback are being pursued on foot by a formidable Araucan fighter named Rengo:

> "Whoa, whoa!" he cried. "Wait! Wait!" This was the extent of his Spanish, but impudent insults continued in his own tongue. For three leagues he ran like this, right on the tails of their horses, however hard they drove them, calling them infamous and despicable names. / High in the air he held a weapon the likes of which no one had ever seen, a massive, ill-trimmed beech branch the size and weight of a rafter, its head tipped with iron. The youth wielded this with less effort than an expert fencer a slender foil, / and whenever he overtook the horses with this mighty truncheon the blow was so brutal it almost broke their backs. Thus chastened each mount sped forward with no need of spurs, nor was a racing crop ever dreaded as much
>
> (9.95.1-9.97.8).

At times the humor is sardonic, as when we're told of Indian women widowed by a battle that, "One of these will call on heaven for vengeance, the rest will leap with joy" (4.30.5-6), and of Indian men placing bets on a wrestling match that "[. . .] some, not wanting to win, wagered old wives" (29.21.7-8).

In the few formal battles the poem describes the number of Spanish rarely exceeds a few hundred, and in many skirmishes they are often no more than a few dozen. As previously in Mexico and Peru, they exploited tensions among indigenous populations, and in Chile were sometimes joined by several thousand Indian allies. The Araucans, in the thousands themselves, were joined by allies, as well. The novelty of horses and of "[. . .] men mounted on tamed beasts, as though descended by some miracle from celestial regions" (1.64.2-4) was initially an enormous advantage. The Indians eventually learned to counter the danger of meeting cavalry on open ground by retreating into low-lying marshes where horses were useless and their riders forced to dismount. Some of the most bitter fighting takes place in such locales:

> Germans [notoriously brave mercenaries] never fought so stubbornly, face to face and one on one, dealing and receiving unending and ferocious double-handed blows, as the two sides here, who became so firmly stuck in the mud they couldn't take a single step back, and promptly striking, were promptly struck. / One man, up to his waist in the sodden mire, was fighting two or three at a time. Another, wanting to move to gain more mobility, became more entrapped. Still another, testing his strength and luck,

>   assaulted the enemy next to him by biting
>   and blinding him with mud, seeking to win
>   however he could.
>
>   (22.30.1-22.31.8)

The *Araucana* quickly became one of early modern Spain's most popular works, reaching 23 editions by 1632. An important source of information on the geography and people of Chile, its account of the Araucan conflict was soon substantiated by contemporary historians and Ercilla's fellow soldiers, many of whom the text identifies by name, as it does the most prominent Araucans. The poem's impact on subsequent Spanish literature was substantial. In *Don Quijote* it's famously identified as one of the best poems ever written in Spanish (1.6), and Cervantes memorably adopts the device of ending a chapter in the middle of a swordfight (*Don Quijote*, Chap. 8). While lukewarm in his overall assessment of the poem, Voltaire favorably compared a speech by Colocolo (2.28.1-2.35.8) to a similar one delivered by Homer's Nestor and subsequently wrote a drama, *Alzire*, inspired in part by Ercilla's text. Popular ballads, romances, and theatrical works in Spain were based on the poem's characters, and numerous neologisms (primarily the Latinate vocabulary mentioned earlier) and a few indigenous terms Ercilla employed to convey the uniqueness of his New World experience were absorbed into the Spanish language (he explains a number of these in a brief glossary at the end of the poem).

Ercilla's commingling of genres and themes resulted in an anomalous, hybrid text. A dedicated royalist, the ethical and moral values of his Christian humanism, as evidenced in his frequent criticism of Spanish conduct and empathy for the Araucans, produced a work sufficiently nuanced to be taken, on the one hand, as a glorification of Spain's worldwide empire and, on the other, as a foundational work of Chilean nationalism, which it remains to this day.

Contemporary readers will surely be struck by the relevancy of many of its concerns: the challenges of asymmetrical warfare and the deploying of traditional force against an untraditional foe; the frequent inconclusiveness of military encounters despite the clear materiel superiority of one side over the other; the unforeseen consequences of excessive violence and unintended strengthening of adversaries through the very means meant to suppress them; the corrupting influence of endless war. Having his hands cut off to terrorize his compatriots, Galbarino warns that "[. . .] there remain many others who can skillfully wield a sword" (22.47.7-8), and Caupolicán, about to be brutally executed, tells the Spanish, "Don't think that if I die here at your hands the State will lack a leader, for there will instantly be a thousand other Caupolicáns, none as unlucky as I!" (34.10.1-4) From the intensity of early cantos to the disillusionment of later ones, the *Araucana* is frequently engrossing and unexpectedly moving, its author's lively intellect and ready compassion always apparent.

Cyrus Moore

Additional notes

The use of proper names in the poem is potentially confusing. The two most important Araucans are sometimes referred to by epithets (another trait of ancient epic): Caupolicán, the Araucan commander, is called "the son of Leocán," and the heroic warrior, Lautaro, "the son of Pillán." Other names designate places as well as individuals, as with Tucapel, Purén, and Ongolmo. Of seven Spanish towns the narrator identifies (1.66.7-8), three are alternately referred to by the names of the valleys in which they're located: Santiago – Mapochó; Concepción – Penco (Penco also designates the Spanish fort at this location); and Imperial – Cautén. A fourth town, Del Lago, became better known as Valdivia, after its founder. In several passages, notably the voyage by ship from Peru to Chile (cantos 15 and 16) and Fitón's global tour (canto 27), winds are identified by their mythological names: Boreas (north), Caurus (northeast), Eurus (east), Vulturnus (east or southeast), Notus or Auster (south), Garbino (southwest), Zephyr (west), and Thrasias (northwest).

Araucan troops were frequently accompanied by wives and children (e.g., 10.7.1), while larger Spanish contingents would be joined by servants and other attendants, Spaniards and mestizos, as well as allied Indians, some of whom had converted to Christianity (e.g., 7.35.2). As exemplified by Lautaro, Araucans themselves might be *yanaconas* or Spanish servants. This complex mix underlies the Araucan exhortation to fight "without regard to friend or relative" (e.g., 5.25.8).

As elsewhere in the Americas, the Spanish in Chile were accompanied by slaves of African origin, whom they continued to import into the continent and who regularly accompanied the Spanish army, as the poem notes on several occasions. References to them are casually racist, in keeping with Ercilla's class and era.

The use of *barbaro(a)* or "barbarian" is best understood as a designation of non-Christian or pagan status rather than a term of ignorance or crudity.

To facilitate reference to the Spanish text, octaves are separated by virgules [/] and numbered at the beginning of paragraphs with Canto and Octave, e.g., (3.13): Canto 3, octave 13.

Additional reading:
For further discussion of the poem see the present author's: *Love, War, and Classical Tradition in the Early Modern Transatlantic World: Alonso de Ercilla and Edmund Spenser* (Tempe, Arizona: Arizona Center for Medieval and Renaissance Studies, 2014).

Translator's Preface

The following translation is based on the finest modern edition of the *Araucana*, edited and annotated by Isaías Lerner (Catedra: 1993), who worked with the 1597 Madrid exemplar of the poem held by the New York Public Library. I have included several paratexts from this edition, notably Ercilla's Prologues to Parts I and II and indexes of "*cosas notables*" or notable events, published individually with each installment of the poem and here combined. I have added a first-line index of Ercilla's remarkable extended similes, and, for printed versions of the work, a general index.

Among previous translations I have consulted, the most illuminating has been Alexandre Nicolas's prose one into French, *L'Araucana: poême épique espagnol*, of 1869. I never envisioned a verse translation, lacking the skill for such an undertaking, and the prose one attempted here is no more than a faint reflection of Ercilla's richly complex, sonorous creation.

Isaías Lerner, with whom I had the great good fortune to study at the Graduate Center of the City University of New York, introduced me to the *Araucana* and helped guide my subsequent comparative study of it. His untimely death in 2013, prior to my undertaking the present work, was a great loss to scholarship and to all who knew him. A rigorous but gracious scholar, any felicity in what follows owes much to his instruction, while all errors are entirely my own.

Part I of La Araucana

Don Alonso de Ercilla

1569

Prologue

Had I realized the effort I spent on this work would do so little to relieve my fear of publishing it, I would never have had the courage to see it through. Yet being a true history and dealing with war, which interests so many, I've resolved to have it printed, prompted by the insistence of numerous participants who find themselves in so much of it as well as by the offense to Spanish soldiers had their achievements remained forever unknown for lack of someone to record them. That would never have been from their insignificance, but rather from where they occurred, in the most distant part of Peru the Spanish ever reached, so remote there was hardly any news of it, as well as from how little support and opportunity there was for writing about a war while fighting it. Whatever time I was able to steal I therefore devoted to this book, which to be more authentic and truthful I composed in the midst of the war itself, in its very locations and locales, frequently writing on leather for lack of paper, and on scraps of letters, some so small they hardly held six lines and which cost me no small effort to reassemble afterwards. Considering this and the modesty of a work emerging from such constrained circumstances, I hope the zeal and purpose with which I wrote it will help readers endure its faults. If it seems to some that I've been partial to the Araucans, spending more time on their deeds and valor than required for barbarians, once we take into account their upbringing, customs, and methods and practice of war, we see that few have ever surpassed them in defending their land with such tenacity and conviction against enemies as fierce as the Spanish. It is certainly admirable, considering they possessed no more than twenty leagues of territory and no settled town, rampart, or stronghold in which they might take shelter, nor had weapons, at least not defensive ones, which the protracted war with the Spanish had depleted, and were living in an area accessible to three Spanish towns and two forts, that with all this they still were able to redeem and sustain their freedom through sheer courage and stubborn determination, sacrificing so much blood, their own as well as Spanish, that one can truly say there were few places not stained by it and covered with bones. Nor did their dead lack for those to come afterward and carry on their cause, for their children, eager to avenge dead parents and moved by natural rage and inherited valor, accelerated the passage of years and took up arms before their time, offering themselves up to the rigors of war. The lack of warriors became so acute, due to all those who died in the endeavor, that in order to increase their numbers and swell their battalions women also joined in the hostilities, some fighting like men and facing death with great bravery. All this I have wanted to describe in testament to and validation of the courage of this people, deserving of greater praise than I can offer with my verses. And since, as I noted earlier, there are now a number of people in Spain who once found themselves in the events I describe, to them I entrust the defense of my work, commending it as well to all others who may read it.

CANTO 1

The first canto describes the province of Chile and the state of Arauco, as well as the natives' customs and ways of waging war. It also briefly recounts the arrival and conquest of the Spanish prior to the Araucan rebellion.

I do not sing of ladies, love, and gallant, enamored knights, nor of love's tender tokens and delights, but of those valiant Spaniards' daring deeds, whose swords forced untamed Arauco to its knees. / I will speak as well of a remarkable people who obey no king, of memorable feats of theirs deserving celebration, and of their rare ingenuity, all of which further exalt the Spanish since the more the vanquished are esteemed the more the victor will be. /

[1.3] I entreat you, mighty Philip, that having considered this work you will accept it, for lacking all favor it is enough if it be favored by you. My account comes straight from the truth and is cut to its measure. Do not disdain this gift, however modest, denying my verses your authority. / My boldness in dedicating them to such a lofty lord has been to sustain them, ennobling the work so that those who see it may deem it more worthy. If this does not stop some from criticizing it, at least they may hesitate, thinking that since it is addressed to You it must contain some hidden merit. / Being raised in your household has proved a merit, as well, making my dull style delicate and that which is disordered full of art. Encouraged by thoughts like these, I entrust my pen to the fury of Mars. Lend your ear to what I say, my Lord, since for much of it I have been a reliable witness.[3] /

[1.6] Chile is a large and fertile province in the famous region of Antarctica, respected by distant nations for its prominence and power. The people it produces are so remarkable and proud, so courageous and warlike, that it has never been ruled by kings nor subject to foreign domination. / The country is very long from north to south and measures a hundred miles where widest from east to west. With a coast on the New or South Sea, it extends from 27° beneath the antarctic pole to where the Ocean and Chilean seas mingle their waters in a narrow strait.[4] / These two great seas, struggling to breach their boundaries and unite, send

---

3 Ercilla entered the royal household in 1548, at age fifteen, as a page to prince Philip, son of Charles V; Mars is the Roman god of war.

4 The Southern Sea (the *Mar del Sur*) refers to the Pacific, as does the Chilean sea; the Ocean sea, to the Atlantic; 27°, i.e., the 27th parallel south; the border between sixteenth-century Peru and Chile was further south than today.

forth their waves to batter the rocks, but their union is denied until this point at which they finally cleave the land and can connect. Magellan, my Lord, was the first to open this route and give it a name, / but due to an error of our pilots or to some other cause the route remained hidden from us. Perhaps its precise location was mistaken, or perhaps some small island, roused by tempestuous seas and angry winds, had run aground and blocked its entrance. /

[1.10] Chile, as I said, runs north to south and is bathed by the sea on the west, while along the eastern side are mountains that stretch a thousand leagues.[5] In the center of this is where warfare, through custom and practice, is most advanced, for here Venus and Ammon have no place and angry Mars alone is master.[6] / Here, at 36°, the State that has spilled so much blood, its own as well as others', is manifest in all its grandeur, its fierce, untamed people placing Chile in great peril while making every land around them tremble through their sheer valor in waging war. / Arauco had long dominated most of this great region, its fame and reputation extending from one pole to the other. As my account will soon show, it threatened the Spanish as well. The State's twenty leagues of territory are controlled by sixteen powerful men.[7] / These caciques or chieftains, the finest offspring of barbarian mothers when it comes to military skill, lead the proud state and form the bulwark of its defense. None of them have preference in governing,

---

5   A league is approximately 3½ to 4 miles.
6   That is, love, whether pure or impure, has no place here: Venus, the goddess of beauty and love, is associated with the former; Ammon, the incestuous son of Lot, the latter (Genesis 19.38).
7   In brief notes at the end of the text Ercilla describes the Araucan state as twenty leagues in length and seven in width.

and while there are additional chieftains, owing to their valor these sixteen are preeminent.[8] / Each cacique is served by vassals, whose duty he can compel at any time. In return he instructs them in the art of war, doing so with careful discipline until they master it. / To develop strength and agility in their children, the Araucans make them run up steep, rocky slopes, and upon returning they give the winner some reward, thereby engendering in them the speed and stamina of deer. / From childhood on they make them exercise, and as they grow they encourage and train them in the hard work of war. Any who show signs of weakness are disqualified from military service, and those who prove adept with weapons are granted rank equal to their ardor. /

[1.17] Military command among the Araucans is not casually decided nor assigned according to status, inheritance, or wealth. Valor and the excellence of a man's arm are what win him preference, for these are what ennoble and perfect him, determining his value as a person. / Those dedicated to war are not required to do anything else, but are exempt from work and cultivation. The common folk support them, while the warriors are obliged by law to be ready with their weapons and conduct themselves skillfully when called to fight. / The weapons they use most often are pikes, halberds, and short, broad lances; long-handled knives made like poniards; axes, mallets, and reinforced cudgels; darts, javelins, arrows, and clubs; lassos made of tough willow and vine, slingshots, and catapults.[9] / They've adopted some of these weapons from Christians, for constant practice

---

8   Caciques often take the name of the area they control, as do their successors, which can lead to confusion.
9   The Araucans attached a type of lasso to their spears with which they were able to pull riders from their horses.

instructs and improves them every hour. Others they've invented according to their needs, for necessity is a great inventor and hard work the master of ingenuity. / Their warriors wear strong, doublets, the common armor of soldiers, as well as a kind of short coat, more modern and widespread. They also have greaves, brassards, and gorgets, along with various fitted headgear made of tanned skin and hard, uncured leather, which even fine steel cannot penetrate.[10] / Each soldier is required to study and practice with only one weapon, the one he favors in childhood, which is the only one he seeks to master. An archer does not practice with the pike, nor a pikeman with club or arrows. /

[1.23] When assembling as an army the Araucans arrange themselves in distinct battalions, in rows of more than a hundred soldiers. Between the pikemen they place archers who can wound at will from a distance, marching shoulder to shoulder with their protectors until able to measure the enemy with their shafts. / If the first battalion to attack is routed, a second comes to assist so quickly there's scarcely time to notice. If this one is driven back, another attacks, and even if the first battalion has reformed by this time, it doesn't leave its position until it sees how the other has fared. / To frighten and injure our horses they defend themselves with marshes, where they sometimes take refuge if forced to flee. From here they can safely regroup and harm us without our being able to retaliate, since the danger of unstable terrain prevents our men from approaching. /

[1.26] The most outstanding of the barbarians precede their battalions, arrogantly scorning heaven and earth and eager to distinguish themselves by their valor. Trailing their pikes by the

---

10 Greaves, brassards, and gorgets are pieces or armor protecting the shins, arm, and throat, respectively.

point, they strike bold stances, calling out, "If there's any brave Christian here, let him come forward right now, one on one!" / Assembled in companies of thirty to forty, they advance with great pride and boldness to the rapid beat of drums, ambitious for praise and renown. They outdo one another in painting their weapons bright colors, adorning their heads with bunches of feathers, and in leaping all about. / If they believe a site advantageous they build a stronghold on it, either to occupy the area or in response to some predicament or peril. From such places they defend themselves with great safety, making sudden sallies and timely withdrawals. The design and construction of these forts is as follows: / a location being chosen and lines laid out, they enclose a broad, square space with great, trimmed tree trunks secured by large stakes. This prevents anyone outside from entering to fight, and protected by such a wall a few can easily defend against many. / Formerly, they used to build another wooden structure inside of this. Supported at intervals by great timbers, it had four tall towers rising above the outer enclosure and its walls were filled with small openings from which they could safely and fearlessly fire their weapons. / Encircling their forts a short distance from the walls are closely-spaced pits, some long, some broad, and some narrow, aligned so that any brave but careless young man hurrying his horse after some cunning barbarian is lured within their dangerous ring. / They also dig deeper holes with sharpened stakes at the bottom and cover them with rushes, grass, or flowers to make our men spur ahead even more heedlessly. Unwary riders fall into these pits and are buried there, impaled on the sharp points with only heaven to help them. /

[1.33] The Araucans have a council or assembly, customary since ancient times, at which they gather to eat and drink whenever anything important occurs. The cacique who first hears of such an event quickly dispatches envoys to all the others, / informing them that the time has come for them to convene, since the matter affects them all and requires prompt attention. The need for speed and the danger of delay is stressed according to the situation, and recognizing their common benefit no one who can attend does not. / When the caciques of the senate have gathered, the case is presented, and after they have examined and pondered it a fitting remedy is discussed. Once they issue their collective decision, anyone who disagrees cannot excuse himself from what it requires, for among them the opinion of the majority must be followed. / If nothing is found to oppose it, the new decree is announced to the anxiously waiting commoners. If battle is called for, a great cry arises, with loud horns and drums, so that the word reaches everyone. / A certain period is set aside for reviewing their decisions, and once a decree has been ratified for three days without retraction and this open period has passed, it cannot legally be revoked. Thus faced with unforeseen challenges they ready their response. / These councils are held in one of many pleasant groves, places made even more alluring by the abundance of flowers and of trees rustling in cool, caressing breezes. Frequently there's a limpid stream weaving its way across a meadow, / the broad clearing artfully surrounded by refreshing stands of lofty poplars. Spacious enough for any great meeting or festivity, such places invite repose, shielded from the hot afternoon sun and filled with the sweet, harmonious songs of birds. /

[1.40] The Araucans are a godless, lawless people, although they revere the one cast down from heaven, forever celebrating him in their chants as a great and powerful prophet. Invoking his fury in their false religion, they call on him in all their activities and consider whatever he says about auspicious or ominous portents to be true. / They consult him in rites when preparing for battle, and if his response is unfavorable they restrain themselves however much they may want to proceed. No serious matter or situation arises where the accursed one is not summoned. They call him Eponamón, a name they frequently apply to someone courageous. / Relying on the fraudulent services of sorcerers, a science to which they naturally incline, they take heed of signs and auguries, according to which they determine their affairs. They venerate foolish fortune-tellers who divine the future, omens increasing their audacity or instilling them with fear and dread. / Some of those who exhort them are held in sacred reverence, living lives of strict abstinence and supported by their acclaim. It's these who lead the frivolous public astray with their eloquence, their inanities considered as true as we take Holy Scripture to be. / Those adhering to this order have neither God nor law nor believe in sin, but living like this are taken as wise. Soldiers, on the other hand, take the sword, lance, and bow and arrow to be a higher science and maintain that good or bad omens consist in strength and courage. / Finally, when it comes to what the planets foretell, the lot and destiny of this land is for contention, furor, discord, and war, for to this last alone the people aspire.[11] All its good and evil are contained herein, for its men are quick to anger, ferocious in temperament, and enjoy

---

11   Ancient observers divided the world into seven latitudinal zones believed to be governed by specific planetary influences.

dominating others. / They have strong, beardless faces, large, well-proportioned bodies, broad backs, deep chests, sturdy limbs, and powerful muscles. They are agile, confident, robust, courageous, and daring, accustomed to hard work and inured to mortal cold, hunger, and heat. / No king has ever subjugated this proud, bold people, nor any foreign nation boasted of invading their territory. No neighbor would dare raise a sword or move against them, for they have always been independent, indomitable, and feared, free of laws, their heads proudly erect. /

[1.48] The mighty king of the Incas, renowned throughout the Antarctic region, was a ruler exceedingly eager to conquer new nations, and hearing enticing reports of the Araucan state, he dispatched his *Orejones* to Chile. In spite of the widespread fame of its people, which tempered their ardent spirits, / these valiant Incan nobles made their way across the harsh wilderness. Here they forcibly enslaved some of the warlike Chilean tribes and imposed burdensome laws and edicts with a heavy, armed hand, their ruinous statutes forcing people to pay enormous subsidies and tributes.[12] / Once established, with the territory reorganized beneath their powerful army, the troops pushed on in pursuit of the realm they desired, but they had not marched far when they discovered that the valor of the Araucans matched the fame of their weapons. / The Promaucaes of Maule, hearing of the presumptuous Incas' vain intentions, advanced to meet them in a fierce encounter, no less well-organized than spirited, and when the two groups fought, countless *Orejones* were killed, losing the battlefield and all their standards. / The Promaucaes live a hundred miles before the Araucan state and are a proud, robust, and valiant people, as the Spanish well

---

12 *Orejones* or "big ears," so-called for the disks inserted in their ear lobes, were Incan military nobility.

know.[13] This being said, they are different from the fierce Araucans, compared with whom there is a great contrast and superiority among the latter both in courage and excellence with weapons. / The Incas, seeing the strength embodied in that invincible province and realizing how little they stood to gain by fighting, brought the war they had started to an end. Acknowledging their misguided intentions, they abandoned the territory they had won and returned to the regions they had left, where they remained. /

[1.54] Don Diego de Almagro, the *Adelantado* considered so wise in many previous conquests, then came to Chile. Admired for his boldness, valor, and generosity, he was determined to extend and deepen the Christian faith, but having reached his destination he soon found it necessary to return. / To Valdivia alone the victory was finally granted and rightly so, and it is fitting his memory be celebrated for advancing his sword so far.[14] He achieved a glory in Arauco that no one had before him, placing its proud people beneath a heavy yoke and reducing their liberty to subjugation. / With sword and cape alone, aided by singular perseverance, he assembled a large, splendid company and with a bold plan and spirit made directly for Chile, resolved to arrive at the goal of his efforts or the end of his life.[15] / On the long and arduous march he was sorely

---

13 The Promaucaes lived in the Maipo river area, south of Santiago; they were one of a number of Indian groups in northern Chile, between the Incas and the Araucans, who lived below the Bíobío river, south of Concepción.
14 Pedro de Valdivia was an associate and later rival of Francisco Pizarro in Peru.
15 To fight by "sword and cape" alone, which implies a high level of skill, refers to a technique of draping a cape or cloak over the left arm and using it in various defensive and offensive movements.

distressed by hunger, thirst, and cold. Yet setting his ardent breast against these privations with the necessary resolve, a benign fate and prosperous destiny led him to Chile in spite of all those who tried to thwart him, taking up arms to their own injury. / Upon entering the region, he faced many dangerous battles with its inhabitants, the outcomes of which were often in doubt. But in the end, vigorously pursuing the war and their destiny with strong, valiant arms, the courageous Spanish occupied a great part of the land. / Not without great peril and loss of life did they maintain themselves here, under siege, for six years, sustaining their exhausted bodies on unpalatable wild roots. Yet with extraordinary effort and unflinching bravery they overcame the barbarians and their weapons, bringing them under Spanish control and gaining new strength through the struggle. / Afterwards Valdivia went farther, courageously subduing the Promaucaes with his brutal sword, then subjugating the Curios and the Cauquenians, both bellicose peoples. Crossing the swift Maule and Itata rivers he came to Andalién, where he founded that famous city surrounded by high ramparts, shortly to be both so fortunate and so ill-starred.[16] / Here he was on the point of losing a bloody battle when God came to his aid, just as He had in every previous encounter. Others to whom the task is entrusted will provide a fuller account of these events. It was here that the barbarian Ainavillo, leader and glory of the Penconians, was taken prisoner. / Valdivia then came to the famous Biobío, which is joined by the broad Nivequetén and other rivers as it runs to the sea, separating Penco from Arauco. With renewed strength and enthusiasm, he crossed the rocky

---

16 Andalién denotes a province that includes the "famous" city of Concepción.

slopes of Andalicán mountain and with his squadrons in well-ordered ranks set foot on fertile Araucan soil. /

[1.63] Not wishing to be tiresome I will say no more about this, but instead proceed quickly to avoid annoyance. Such is my plan, for there were so many battles before the Araucans were subdued that I'm forced to refrain from recounting them all. / The Spanish were helped a great deal by the naive misconceptions that arose among the natives when they saw our men mounted on tamed beasts, as though descended by some miracle from celestial regions, and once they experienced the sudden roar and terrible injuries of gunpowder, they feared those who fought with such lightning bolts as immortal gods. / The error of being taken for immortals was reinforced by our soldiers' heroic exploits, and the most superstitious among the Indians foretold future evils from their present troubles. Thus cowed and confused, and seeing clear signs of their subjugation, the Araucans professed their brotherhood and swore loyalty, offering the Spanish an obedience they had never offered anyone before. / Leaving sufficient garrisons, our men pressed south, where seeing Arauco subdued, all the other regions surrendered. A great number of people following their lead, seven flourishing cities were founded: Coquimbo, Penco, Angol, and Santiago; La Imperial, Villarrica, and del Lago.[17] / This happy outcome, together with the victories, fame, and wealth the Spanish acquired, induced such vanity and arrogance among them that ten men could not fit within a thousand leagues, never mind that in the end all their vanity

---

[17] Strictly speaking, Penco denotes the narrow coastal valley where Concepción was founded but is used interchangeably for the town; Del Lago became better known as Valdivia, after its founder.

and arrogance would have to fit in seven feet of earth. / Self-interest and malice grew at the cost of others' sweat and misery, and ravenous, wretched greed, freely fed, advanced unbridled. Legality, rights, and justice became whatever was thought best by Valdivia, who was lenient in cases of serious wrongdoing and rigorous in trivial ones. / The wickedness and self-regard of the ungrateful Castilians continued to grow, chasing after prosperous fortune in pursuit of their arrogant, vain designs. Cutting short their advance, however, the heavenly Father permitted those on whom Valdivia had placed the yoke to become the blade of his own pitiless execution. / The Araucan state, accustomed to dictating laws, ruling, and being feared, finding itself toppled from power and subjugated by mortal men, determined to regain its liberty, and rejecting the impositions from which it had suffered, it once more took up the sword, idled until then by indolent peace. / To see how seriously they would be taken, the Indians first tested us with two of our soldiers, whom they tortured to death without reason or cause. That impudence being overlooked, their audacity grew, and waiting no longer they openly began to assemble their men. / The origin of this unexpected ill was Valdivia's not taking prompt corrective action against the State with an exemplary punishment, but no one was ever punished. Fearless and shameless in their new freedom, the people soon burst the reins of their promised obedience, as the second canto will show. /

CANTO 2

This canto tells of the discord that arose among the Araucan caciques over the selection of a commander and of the resolution they reached with the advice of the cacique Colocolo. It also describes the cunning that gained them entry to the Tucapel fort and the battle they fought there with the Spanish.

Fortune helps many to an illusory pinnacle in life, aiding their rise so that afterwards it can hurl them down when least expected, making the shock of their fall even worse. / Not realizing that happiness is the source of sorrow, they never think about the sudden changes of all-devouring time, but with a proud and futile faith believe their luck will last. Fortune's wheel continues to turn, however, and with its customary cruelty / and a single reversal it wins everything back. It doesn't like anyone testing it and always recoups more than it bestows, exempting nothing old or new, including honor and reputation. The proof of this comes at life's close, when all must be judged, including those with an auspicious start. / And once what is good is lost, what remains other than pain, unhappiness, and grief? As for believing that Fortune is constant, the sun will first cease to give us light, for it is not in Fortune's nature to stay its wheel nor change its habits, and its best benefit is to never enjoy it. / This will be seen in what follows, where riches and honor and glory, together with every imaginable blessing, were not enough to ensure a Spanish victory, since in the end blue skies grew turbulent and Fortune turned destiny's prosperous course into bitterness. /

[2.6] The ungrateful Spanish were enjoying the prosperity I spoke of earlier, along with another, greater good I forgot to mention, contentment, something rarely attained. Yet they were so heedless—a sure sign of sad things to come—that in a single hour they lost the honor and position they'd won through countless years of struggle. / The Indians, as I said, had regarded our people as gods, but eventually they realized we were born of man and woman and began to take note of our weaknesses. Finding themselves in miserable servitude, they recognized their ignorant mistake and burned with terrible rage and shame at having been conquered by mortals. / Unwilling to endure this any longer, they began to consider how best to organize their revenge, and coming together in council, they soon reached their harsh decision in favor of an exemplary and irrevocable judgment spreading terror far and wide. / With this the caciques and their men began to fill the countryside, nor was any general proclamation required, for the thirst for war drew them on without any need of promises or pay. Everyone was waiting for that longed-for moment, so slow to arrive, when the brutal punishment would be delivered, ensuring the enemy's death and destruction. /

[2.10] It's fitting that the names of some of the caciques attending this council be remembered, for these uncouth barbarians soon gained well-deserved fame, achieving great victories over notable adversaries. Those still living will testify to this, as do the dead where they lie. / The first to arrive at the chosen location was Tucapel, stubborn in his hatred and a butcher of Christians, leading three thousand vassals who obeyed him like a king. Next came Ongol, a courageous young man who commanded four thousand fine soldiers. / Cayocupil was not slow to depart his home and was third to arrive. A famous and troublesome cacique, he was ready to make war on the whole world by himself and had three thousand vassals accustomed to chasing wild beasts in the mountains. Millarapué, in charge of five thousand men, was fourth to appear in spite of his great age. / Paicabí arrived the same day, leading three thousand experienced soldiers, and Lemolemo came shortly thereafter with six thousand of his own. Mareguano, Gualemo, and Lebopía, each wanting to be first in everything, hastened to the site, each bringing three thousand men, / nor was tall, robust Elicura slow to appear at the appointed time. He was reputed one of the most courageous chieftains and said that being a subject was sheer folly for someone with six thousand warriors. The venerable Colocolo arrived next, commanding as many men and more, / and after him Ongolmo with four thousand. Purén, who led six thousand soldiers, was close behind him, and more than six thousand accompanied the haughty, fierce Lincoya, who was agile, brave, and gigantic in height and proportions. / The renowned cacique Peteguelén was obeyed as their natural lord by those who lived in the great valley of Arauco. It is from here the State appears to have taken the name it still uses today, just as vibrant Venice, excelling all others in governance, gave its name to the Seigniory. / Peteguelén himself did not attend the assembly, having been imprisoned by the Spanish, but of his six thousand men, all natives of the valley, a large number arrived to offer their help. The formidable Caupolicán, obeyed by all Pilmaiquen, was also not present. / Tomé and Andalicán, members of the Araucan leadership, came with many other caciques I don't mention to avoid being tiresome. Showing great pleasure at seeing themselves assembled, they greeted each other and once the welcomes were exchanged, a splendid banquet began. /

[2.19] The drinking among the caciques had reached a fever pitch, with the wine jugs the worse for wear, when little by little a great commotion began to rage until no one was listening to anyone else. The dispute was over who was bravest and most worthy of leading the people, / and the furor grew to the point that men toppled the tables covered with food and rushed to their weapons, ripping off the tree limbs on which they were hung. Menacing, offensive words kept coming as they armed themselves, further fanning the anger set ablaze by the heat of the wine and food. / Audacious Tucapel loudly claimed that the authority of command was his, since the entire universe knew that when it came to valor he deserved it. "No one is as brave as I," he haughtily declared, "which I'm ready to prove to any and all who would deny it. . ." / Not letting him finish, Elicura cried, "The leading of this dance belongs to me, and any fool attempting some other madness will taste the steel of my lance!" Ongolmo, eager to be first among them, said, "I still have hope in my arm's ability to wield this ironclad mace!" / Insane with rage, Lincoya replied, "To talk like this is folly, for as long as I brandish my club, being lord of the world is in my hands!" "No one," shouted Angol, "should be so vain as to think themselves my equal, since the fear they would be forced to face is greater than the glory they would gain!" / Furious Cayocupil, arrogantly shaking his cudgel, made room for himself. "I'll see who can best carry through on such claims," he said. "Let the pretenders step forward right now and we'll soon find out to whom the position belongs! I'll prove that I merit it more than all of you combined!" / "Stop! That's enough!" Lemolemo answered; "I accept your challenge and am happy to put what's mine to the test, which I prefer to resolve by the sword. I'll prove the truth of my claims against two, four, or six of you, and if all of you pick a quarrel with me, I'll still make good on what I say!" / Purén had been standing apart, but hearing this exasperating talk and great outcry he made his way into their midst, saying that no one in his presence should be impertinent. "Is anyone brazen enough to imagine that where Purén is present they should command?" he asked. The shouting and furor increased. One man grabbed his club, another his pike. / Tomé and the other caciques quickly placed themselves in the middle of the dispute and finally managed to separate everyone, which was no small matter. Once the danger of their harming each other had passed, Colocolo, the eldest, raised his angry voice and fearlessly began to speak: /

[2.28] "Caciques and defenders of the State, a desire to command is not what prompts me to object upon watching you claim what so clearly belongs to me! As you see by my age, I'm ready to depart this world for the next, and it's the love I've always shown you that spurs me to give you sound advice. / Why are you laying claim to a position of such honor and prestige, when all the world knows we were overthrown and defeated? And yet still oppressed by the Spanish, you don't want to see reason! How much better it would be to discharge this fury in battle against our fierce enemy! / What rage is this, men of Arauco, that leads you toward destruction without even realizing it, raising your hands against each other instead of resisting the tyrant, and with the Christians so near at hand, turning your knives against yourselves? If it's the desire for death that moves you, let it not be in such a base and abject way. / Turn your weapons and furious courage against the chests of those who've placed you in such cruel bondage and insulting conditions, so obvious to all the world! Throw off the shameful yoke of servitude, thus proving your bravery and strength, instead of spilling the blood of the State, which we've yet to redeem! / Your ardent spirits do not trouble me, but offer me hope. Yet I fear that your ill-governed valor will veer from the right path, and that turning this dispute against yourselves you'll use the fatherland's own strength to behead it! If that's how it must be, then cut my aged throat first of all! / My frail body, still standing after such misery and tormented by fortune's blows, longs for nothing more than the sharp blade of a sword, and fortunate is the life assured an early death! When it comes to the public good, however, I must say what I think best in this situation. / You are peers in valor and strength, and heaven has made you equals in birth. In lineage, status, and wealth it has given each of you an equal share, and any one of you alone, with your fortitude and courage, could rule the world. This is the precious but unappreciated gift that has brought us to the present moment. / I'm hoping the power of your arms will shortly remedy our situation, but first there must be one captain by whom all agree to be governed. Let this be the man who can bear a mighty log on his shoulders the longest, and since fortune has made you all equals, let each of you strive to be the strongest!" / No one was inattentive to the elder's words, and once the speech ended opinions among them differed. Finally, by general consent, thinking of what was best, the caciques all accepted Colocolo's proposal. /

[2.37] Some may find it implausible that such a powerful province, so practiced in the art of war and abundant in laws and statutes, could not have appointed a leader and endowed him with authority without recourse to such a ploy. / My response is that the land had never been without a leader elected by the senate until our men defeated Ainavillo at Penco, as I noted earlier, following which it is said, although it's not certain, that having been brought to one of our strongholds he was poisoned, ending his leadership along with his life.[18] /

[2.39] At this point a great tree trunk was quickly brought. I dare not say what it weighed, for it was an enormous, stout cedar that a man could scarcely get his arms around. Paicabí impatiently seized it, settling it on his stout shoulders, and for six hours that brawny warrior held it up but could not last a seventh. / Cayocupil immediately stepped forward, confident of being the strongest, but having kept it aloft for only five hours let it fall from weariness. A well-built youth, Gualemo, tried but lasted no longer, and once he was finished, Angol took up the massive beam and stayed six long hours at the sport. / Following him, Purén carried it for half a day, and the formidable Ongolmo for more than half. Lebopía reached four hours and a half, but couldn't bear

---

18   See Canto 1:61.

it any longer. For seven hours it was sustained by Lemolemo, who during all that time never ceased walking and leaping about, here and there, until his strength began to fail. / Elicura then prepared himself for the test and strove to support the great cedar. At nine hours he was forced to put it down and could not have tolerated it a moment longer had it been a straw. Tucapel shouldered it for fourteen hours, with everyone proclaiming his superiority, but when they caught sight of Lincoya their clamor turned to silence. / Throwing off his mantle and exposing his massive frame, Lincoya hoisted the rough, weighty log, and after settling it on this sturdy base began to run lightly back and forth, showing how little the burden bothered him. The day progressed from sunup to sundown, and still unwearied he sustained the weight. / Odious night arrived, but Diana soon brought light, shining brightly down on the scene.[19] Even as morning broke Lincoya did not seek help with his burden, and it was not until the sun arrived at mid-heaven that he finally let it fall to the ground. / No one among the crowd was not astonished, for none believed any man strong enough to endure the heavy weight so long. They unanimously acknowledged his superiority and granted him governance, command, and whatever else was due such a worthy general, so justly merited until that point. / The barbarian was proudly striding about, pleased with having distinguished himself above all the others, when Caupolicán appeared at the assembly, alone and traveling light. Since birth he had been sightless in one eye, which was the color of fine garnet, but whatever he lacked in vision he made up for in strength and courage. / An imposing and noble young man of natural authority, Caupolicán

---

19   In Roman mythology Diana is the goddess associated with the moon.

was grave, severe, and while respectful of rights, a rigorous and exacting judge. Large in stature and broad-chested, he was shrewd, extremely strong, and agile, as well as intelligent, determined, and calm in unforeseen circumstances. / The senate welcomed him with signs of joy—although I can't confirm that everyone was pleased—and the conditions of the test were explained to him in every detail. Since Apollo had hidden himself deep within the sea by this point, the contest was deferred until the return of day. /

[2.49] The caciques spent the night in a great dispute over the new arrival. Some sided with Lincoya, some said Caupolicán was stronger, and bets were placed for and against each man. Others, uncertain and not wagering, looked to the east, waiting for Apollo's steeds to reappear.[20] / Now rosy-fingered dawn began to adorn the clouds with a thousand frills, awakening wretched laborers to their daily toil. New light was already brightening the valley, restoring color and lost freshness to the faded fields, when Caupolicán stepped forward. / With a confident, disdainful attitude he took hold of the stout, knotty tree trunk as though it were a delicate twig and placed it across his powerful shoulders. The people fell silent, marveling to see such a strong, muscular body, and Lincoya turned pale, beginning to doubt his victory. / Bright day rapidly advanced as the shrewd barbarian walked slowly about; the sun shortened long shadows, but his perseverance never lagged; the light withdrew at dusk, yet not for this did he show any weakness; the stars shone clearly above, and still the valiant warrior revealed no frailty. / A brilliant moon emerged from its gloomy, wet abode to watch the festivities, ridding the woods and fields of their dismal black veil. Caupolicán did not relent in his efforts, but instead with greater strength and growing energy

---

20   I.e., the horses that pull the chariot of the sun god, Apollo.

walked about as though he bore no weight at all. / Tithonus's wife appeared between two towering peaks, shaking cool frost from her scattered, golden tresses as she revived the wilted meadows with refreshing dew, which lay encrusted on the flowers like pearls on colored stones.[21] / Phaeton's chariot came rushing from the sea on its customary course, the mountains withdrew their shadows at sight of the sun, and still the formidable man moved here and there, sustaining the heavy weight without fatigue, even when thick, black darkness again hastened forward.[22] / The moon delayed its longed-for appearance until much later, but finally, troubled and inflamed, it slowly revealed the faint light of its face and then halted mid-course, more beautiful, to watch the strange ordeal. Seeing that nothing had changed, it plunged into the arctic hemisphere, / while the barbarian, balancing the great beam on his shoulders, gave no sign of change or distress, overcoming fatigue with fortitude as his strength continued to grow. Following his companion, Apollo sent forth his rays of light, and the son of Leocán's expression was still steady and even more determined than at the start.[23] / The sun had fully appeared by the time Caupolicán threw the enormous weight from his back, and he gave an exorbitant leap as he tossed it away, to show that he still retained more strength. With one voice the encircling crowd proclaimed the outcome: "Upon these firm shoulders we now place the great burden and weight we all share!" /

---

21 Tithonus is the husband of Aurora, the dawn.
22 Phaeton is the son of Helios, the god of the sun, but sometimes stands for the sun itself. Aurora, the dawn, makes her appearance in the sun's chariot.
23 Apollo, the sun, follows Aurora, the dawn, considered his sister or daughter. The "son of Leocán" is Caupolicán.

[2.59] The unusual test decided, Caupolicán was invested as the people's supreme leader in the most solemn ceremonies, and everyone submitted to his command. His reputation now enhanced, the fear and renown in which they held him grew so great that even many miles away the people trembled, respecting him almost as a king. / These events have raised doubts among a great number of people, many of whom remain unconvinced to this day whether what I have described is simply poetry or some fiction. Reason cannot accept that an orderly, well-disciplined senate would base an election of such importance on strength rather than judgment. / Know then that it was all an artifice and prudent measure of wise Colocolo, who seeing such harmful discord, realized the great risk his fatherland was facing. He also knew of the bravery and competence of Caupolicán, who was absent from the assembly, as well as his exceptional physical strength and gifts of rare skill and valor. / He therefore astutely proposed the apparently irrelevant contest in order to prolong the election of a commander, using this delay to alert Caupolicán to make an appearance, and by conducting the matter in this roundabout way was able to achieve his worthy goal. / Once the senate had celebrated Caupolicán's election with suitable pomp and festivities, the new commander, already intent on some great enterprise, instructed Palta, his lieutenant, to quietly assemble eighty tested fighters from among the most spirited and agile men, keeping them ready for his orders. / With the eighty chosen from those known to be most courageous, two outstanding soldiers were selected to lead them, both skilled fighters accustomed to danger and ready for any peril. One was named Cayeguano, the other Alcatipay of Talcaguano. /

[2.65] Our soldiers maintained three garrisons in this area to ensure security, thick-walled constructions with encircling ditches to protect them. Each was furnished with experienced troops accustomed to the work of war, along with horses, provisions, and cannons set in broad embrasures. / One of the forts was close to where the Araucans had gathered, and their exuberant army, defying the entire world, wanted to raze it to the ground. Prudent Caupolicán had a more effective response in mind. / Some of the caciques thought they should surround the closest fort; others that they should head in orderly battalions for Penco. Each group gave its reasons, but the general, agreeing with neither, withdrew to his tent and summoned the eighty warriors. / After explaining a clever subterfuge for easy entry to the fort, he gave explicit orders that it and its people be put to flame and sword, while he came behind to secure the entrance and other approaches. Thoroughly aroused, the men immediately put the plan into action. / Among the Indians, access to the fort's interior and buildings was restricted to those serving its Spanish defenders, dedicated to fierce Bellona.[24] The cunning barbarians set off carrying hay, grass, and firewood, / deaf to any questions as they pursued their plan along the road, bearing their burdens in an orderly file. With their iron-tipped spears hidden among their bundles, they approached the stronghold, its soldiers unaware of the ruse, and entered the proscribed area. / Looking like miserable wretches, they crossed the bridge and passed through the wall and gate with woebegone expressions, some limping with fatigue and seemingly exhausted and cowed. Once inside, however, they untied the bundles and boldly seized their weapons with the menacing arrogance of long-awaited vengeance. /

---

24 Bellona is the Roman goddess of war.

[2.72] Surprised at seeing angry death so close, the stalwart Spanish rush to arm themselves. Dismayed by such singular cunning, but determined to defeat their attackers or die, they dash forward, some with no more than a helmet or breastplate, to repel the insane fury of the audacious Araucans. / The clash of steel resounds from one side of the fort to the other as they violently assault each other, bloody Mars revealing his raging might as never before. Each man, wanting to win, seeks some new way to guide the strokes of his sword, striving through skill and art to open a pathway for death. / Rage and courage surge anew, as does the blood drawn by cruel blades. Now the Spanish press the Indians until their backs are against the rampart. Now the infidel battalion recovers its strength and lost ground, and the disputed space between them is littered with the weapons of those disarmed by powerful blows. / Finding themselves in such straits, the Christians grip their swords more tightly, and driven by fear and shame and consumed with rage, mount a furious charge against the Araucans, who fall back at the new assault. Penetrating their ranks, our soldiers wound and topple them, depriving many of their lives and cares / as they pursue their advantage, sowing bloody, horrifying havoc among their brave opponents. The barbarians now pay for their great but imprudent audacity and can hardly defend themselves, giving up their position only to gain their punishment. In the end, the Spanish fight so fiercely they force the attackers beyond the walls. /

[2.77] Cayeguano and Talcaguano had just managed to escape when Caupolicán appeared at a run with his battalions, thinking the operation had been a success. Seeing the fort's raised bridge and realizing his expectations had been in vain, he had his warriors encircle the walls, vowing not to leave a single stone in place. / There was one young Spaniard who felt our troops were too fearful, and with more temerity than courage he fearlessly lowered the bridge by himself and advanced to the middle of it, loudly calling out, "Come on then! Let the bravest man step forward! I challenge thirty of you, one after the other, and won't say no to a thousand!" / Wild beasts never ran as quickly to the bellowing of an abandoned calf, seeing it separated from its flock and shepherd, as the Araucans when they heard the brave Spaniard's bold words. More than a hundred quickly drew near, avid for the fight and certain victory. /

[2.80] The approach of so many does not frighten the valiant Spaniard nor cause him the slightest dismay. To better receive the dense squadron he strides forward to meet them, and the stream of fierce adversaries is checked as he fearlessly throws himself into their midst with such fury that some are sent tumbling to the ground. / Circling his sword on all sides, he strikes down two with two strokes, now sending a group scattering, now attacking where he sees them massing together. He is holding his own in the unequal fight when his well-armed companions suddenly open a large postern gate and emerge to defend him. / With their opponents advancing from the other side, the bands of Spaniards and Araucans settle down to Mars's bloody work in the middle of a broad clearing. The initial encounter, a hundred Indians to a single Castilian, breaks apart as the attackers turn their pitiless, unstained blades against those coming from the fort. / With heedless fury the two sides are joined, hurling themselves forward amidst the keen-edged weapons, testing with hardened tips where they can do each other the most harm. Like Cyclops beating tirelessly on Vulcan's anvils they hammer and cleave, making the hollow caverns of the mountains resound.²⁵ / Victory hangs in the balance, for Spanish courage makes up for the great difference in numbers. Seeing one of our soldiers resisting a hundred of theirs, the proud barbarians, with raging, diabolical force, drive the Christians from the field. / Unable to withstand them, the Spanish abandon the clearing in a headlong rush and dash for the fortress. Raising the bridge and lowering the portcullis to block the barbarians' entry, they ready their defenses, and fearful of the enemy's fierce assault, carry cannons and fire to the rampart.²⁶ / Soon, realizing that all is lost and that there is nothing they can do to save themselves, by unanimous decision, foreseeing certain destruction, the soldiers abandon the fort, and in the darkness of night, when the world appears most peaceful, they leave. / The moment the gates are opened they are ready and mounted, and throwing down the bridge and spurring their swift horses, they attack the Indian battalion head-on, wounding and trampling as they force their way forward. Fortunately, shrouded by night's deep shadows, they reach the fortress at Purén without losing a single man. /

[2.88] At the time this was happening in Arauco, captain Valdivia was residing in the nearby town of Penco, flourishing during that period from the richness of its mines of pure gold. When news arrived confirming the Araucan uprising and mobilization, / the Indians who served the town, always fond of trouble, longed for liberty and war. Agitating and inciting each

---

25 Vulcan, the Roman god of fire, is frequently depicted as a blacksmith who forges armor for the gods, assisted by the mythological giants known as Cyclopes.
26 The portcullis is a wooden grill lowered to block access through the walls.

other, they lifted their voices at these reports and refused to work, shirking their duties and shamelessly raising their arrogant heads in denial of the obedience they had sworn to Charles V.[27] /

[2.90] Valdivia, who was skeptical, indolent, and careless, had plentiful troops in Concepción, but trusted more in his own good luck than in them. Had he exercised a little diligence, the Tucapel fort with its soldiers, munitions, and six pieces of artillery, including two cannons, would still be standing. / He ordered La Imperial to send armed troops directly to the stronghold, where he would meet them to deliver an exemplary punishment to the rebels, one that would resound so far and wide they would never provoke another war. / He abandoned this prudent course, however, and instead altered his route, taking a different road that led to a gold mine he owned. Greedy to see the magnificent bounty of its rich veins, it was here he was waylaid by avarice and here that the prosperous thread of his fate was severed. / Had he left earlier he would have arrived at the rendezvous at the agreed upon time, but gluttony for the metal he mined intoxicated him, and although he later hastened on, by then it would have been better had he not left at all. Now I must end this canto and address what remains to be said about greed. /

---

27 Charles the Fifth, Holy Roman Emperor, father of Philip II.

CANTO 3

Accompanied by a few Spanish troops and Indian allies, Valdivia makes his way to the Tucapel fort to punish the attackers. At a narrow pass the Araucans first kill his scouts, then engage him in a battle where the great valor and determination of Lautaro result in Valdivia being slain with all his men.

Incurable evil, so carefully nourished! Universal, seductive vice, obsession unchecked by reason, enemy of the public good! Thirsty, bloated beast, the beginning and end of all our ills: man's insatiable greed! / We see lords of high estate unhappy with their positions and lowly laborers who suffer the same disease. The desire and ambition for more have no end nor limit, and riches and status only swell but do not satisfy even the most modest. / Consider Valdivia and whether or not his status was insignificant: once a simple foot soldier, fifty thousand vassals now brought him twelve marks of gold a day.[28] But this and even much more were not enough, and thus his avarice delayed him. Greed was what led to so much war and to the ruin of the entire land. / Greed is what prompted the discovery of Antarctica's remote Indians and is why they were worked so harshly in such cruel conditions. Once their endurance had been exceeded, however, they sought new ways to free themselves and to wreak cruel revenge, their hardships inspiring their hopes. / How often we see ourselves, when healthy, offering advice to the sick we wouldn't follow ourselves, taking pride in lecturing them! How easily we speak of cruel war in the midst of peace and offer counsel when far from peril! / How harshly those safe within a harbor criticize the seaman who loses his way, and how well they issue directions, offering advice at every turn! How easily they make decisions, seeing danger and safety so clearly, whereas faced with such perils themselves, God knows who among them would take the right route! /

[3.7] Valdivia was pursuing his journey in accordance with cruel fate, yet not with his usual fervor, for he had a foreboding and feared some coming ill. Suspecting an ambush, he sent some men ahead to check the road and secure it, but they never returned. / When these scouts did not come back as expected, some of the soldiers thought the danger obvious, while others said they were only delayed. After considering the matter, they finally decided to press ahead, all offering themselves to the same fate, same chances, and same death. / Even though afraid, they

---

28 A mark represents approximately eight ounces.

trusted in their valiant arms, commending the uncertain future to their auspicious destiny and good luck, but they had not traveled two leagues when they came upon the bloody heads of their companions, severed from their bodies and atop tall poles. / The horrifying spectacle causes no change in their steadfast spirits, instead their anger and impatience burn even brighter, and thirsting for revenge and incited with new rage they curse any delay. Valdivia alone is quiet, fearing the decisive moment, but then he breaks his troubled silence. / "Companions," he says, "in whom all bravery, valor, and judgment are combined! Here you see the shamelessness of this land, unfurling its banners to the wind against us! Here you see trust violated, war begun, and the violation of all our pacts. My ears hear the sounds of harsh trumpets, and my eyes see the fires of a diabolical conflagration! / The power of the Araucan State, confirmed by such great injury, you know very well. Yet do not forget how Fortune has always helped you, guiding your swords with her hand, and remember the hardship and blood this land has cost and with which it is nourished! As we still have time, it is best we take new counsel. / Who these warriors are you surely recall, having come to know them. If we aren't victorious and can't defeat them in the field, their arrogance and presumption will be so great the whole world won't be able to contain them! But now I'm uncertain how best to satisfy our honor and our cause." /

[3.14] The lack of experience of the impulsive young soldiers was seen in the foolish temerity typical of such moments. "Oh, captain!" they said, "Give the word, and ten of us alone will ravage this band of Araucans and clear our way forward! / Doing other than what we've always done in such situations would be bad for our honor, and retreating a single step will tarnish all we've accomplished. Let's set our brave chests against the danger, for this is the way to the glory we seek!" Valdivia, stung by their response, fell silent in rage and shame. / Oh, Valdivia, acclaimed leader, how deeply you felt such naive talk! Unused to feeling fear as a soldier, now as a skilled captain you were afraid, going forward condemned to certain death. Intelligent and experienced, you knew all this, but would rather have lost your life than show any weakness. / A friendly Indian approached at this point, and kneeling at Valdivia's feet cried out, "Oh, Captain! Heed what I say and do not press beyond forbidden limits! I can confirm that twenty thousand rebels await you in Tucapel, fearlessly vowing to endure an honorable death rather than live a shameful life!" / This friendly advice instantly created a commotion, sending a cold chill among the men as a vision of sad death appeared among them. But the captain, who until then had been confused, spoke boldly. "Gentlemen," he said, "why do we hesitate? And why, without even seeing the enemy, are we afraid?" / Eagerly prodding his horse and with no further exhortation he then sprang forward, and the courageous company, shaking fear from their limbs, set out after him. Soon the Tucapel valley came into view and in the distance the fort, once tall and imposing but now razed to its foundations. / Valdivia stopped and cried, "Oh, steadfast and courageous Spanish nation! The powerful stronghold on which all our hopes depended lies in the dust! Ahead you see the treacherous enemy and threatening lances of your adversaries. I've no more advice to give you, for fighting alone can save you now!" /

[3.21] He was speaking as I describe and had not even finished his words when the enemy began to surround them on all sides in dense formations, brandishing their broad-bladed spears: "Deceivers and thieves," they cried, "today you'll leave your lives upon this earth, paying us a debt long overdue!" / Valdivia, seeing it inevitable that courage and fortune would be tested, instead of waiting to be attacked, ordered Bobadillo to charge the closest and least numerous formation. With no further admonishment the man did so, furiously assaulting Mareande's battalion with great bravery but few men. / The barbarian pikemen awaited the Spanish with their weapons leveled, but at the moment of impact they raised them and turned aside, offering no resistance as they opened a wide passage. Gathering them into their midst, the open ranks then closed, and the Christians were buried deep within. / Like a hungry alligator that sees a school of fish noisily darting through the water, churning the clear current all around, and opens its great maw to carefully gather them in, clamping its cavernous jaws together and crushing them, satiating its insatiable belly, / just so the small squadron was drawn in by the killers and quickly consumed without a single man escaping alive. Now the orderly ranks of the Araucan army, incited by raucous horns and raising a great roar, attacked from all sides. / Emboldened, Mareande's bloodied troops picked up their pace. Seeing them advance, Valdivia, unchastened, ordered his sergeant to choose the most experienced men and attack, but only ten Spaniards dared set their courageous faces toward death. / Reins flying, they fearlessly charged the threatening battalion, and in the collision none failed to redden his lance. Only one was unseated, his breast torn open to the ultimate agonies of rabid death as he fell lifeless to the ground on his wound. /

[3.28] After this the other nine fell, performing remarkable feats that deserve to be exalted by eternal fame, for all ten died cut to pieces, having first avenged themselves of their deaths. At this point the trumpet was heard giving the final signal to attack. /

Canto 3

Gritting their teeth as they grip their lances, the Spanish rush forward, forcing the largest of the four battalions to retreat a good distance, wounding and trampling as they deal out death, lopping off arms and legs and heads. The barbarians are not shaken, but instead recover the field and drive back their opponents. / Now the struggle is for life or death—may God have mercy on those who fall—and the fighting so fierce from group to group that many die on both sides. Every inch of ground is prized and defended, nor is anyone willing to retreat a single step. Crimson blood covers the entire meadow, turning it from green to red. / Well-tempered armor resounds at the assault of murderous weapons, and cruel blows expose hidden, throbbing entrails. Heads hacked from bodies and containing vital spirit go spinning across the bloody field, their eyes rolled back and lips still moving. / The enemy's brutal blades are all stained by blood. The attack grows more furious, and even where the fighting is less intense no one aspires to any respite beyond the ultimate one of death, the most fearful striving mightily to only die avenged. / Their rage at death and the end awaiting them results in such extraordinary strength among our men that the Araucans, to their dishonor and injury, lose the field. In the end they turn their backs, and voices loudly ring out: "Victory! Spain! Spain!" But then cruel, inflexible Fate gave a strange beginning to what was ordained. /

[3.34] Serving Valdivia as a page at that time was the son of a well-known cacique, a young man the Spaniard cherished and favored. Seeing his people's retreat and moved by love of his fatherland, the youth now loudly began to rouse and encourage them with the following words: / "Oh, blind people, guided by fear, where are you running in such terror? The fame won over a thousand years is perishing along with all your accomplishments!

Today you lose a power never previously profaned, as well as all your laws and rights as free and feared men, only to become abject slaves and vassals! / You stain your noble heritage and your descendants, grafting onto illustrious stock the plague of perpetual shame and dishonor! Behold the impotence of your adversaries, their failing strength, and the violent trembling of their horses, whose flanks are bathed in sweat and blood. / Don't abandon the customs of our ancestors, which we've sustained until now, nor cast the Araucan name from its pinnacle to such low infamy! Why show the enemy your broad backs, so accustomed to danger? Flee bondage and its oppressive yoke instead, offering your brave breasts to the cruel swords! / Think about what I'm saying, for blind, shameful fear has confounded you. Leave behind an everlasting story of how you liberated your subjugated homeland! Turn back, do not refuse such a great victory, for a felicitous fate is calling you! At least slow down long enough to see me die in your defense!"

[3.39] With this he made a great show of brandishing a weighty lance against his lord, Valdivia, offering the other barbarians new hope. To better convince them he then attacked, hurling himself amidst Spanish steel like a stag on a simmering summer day that throws itself into cool waters to temper the fierce heat of the sun. / With his first thrust alone he transfixes one man and pierces another below the chest, and even though the cruel lance is very thick its bloody iron tip emerges from the other side. He then leaps and turns with sudden speed, and boring into another soldier's thigh the sturdy lance breaks off, a great piece of it remaining in the wound. / The dangerous shaft now ruined, he seizes a heavy cudgel from the ground and begins to kill, maim, and crush, soon clearing a large space. Now the Spanish forget about everyone else and all focus on him, but he moves so quickly this way and that they only strike empty air trying to wound him. / Who has ever heard of anything so amazing, not even read about in ancient texts, where a victor changes sides to join the vanquished? Where the courage of a single barbarian youth was enough to snatch a great victory from Christian hands? / Neither the two Decii, who sacrificed their lives for their beloved fatherland, nor Curtius, Horatius Cocles, Scaevola, or Leonidas gave such a remarkable show of themselves,[29] nor those who achieved great fame with their swords in such bitterly-fought wars: Furius Camillus, Marcelus, Fulvius Flaccus, Quintius Cincinnatus, Marcus Sergius, Publius Philo, Cassius Scaevus, and Curius Dentatus.[30] / Tell me: what did these famous

---

29 The figures cited here are drawn from Roman history: Publius Decius Mus and his son both gave their lives to save Rome; Marcus Curtius was reported to have thrown himself in sacrifice into a great fissure that had opened in the Roman Forum, causing it to close; Publius Horatius Cocles defended a bridge leading into Rome from the Etruscans; Gaius Mucius Scaevola, having been taken prisoner, held his arm over a flame to demonstrate how little the Romans feared pain, inducing the enemy to sue for peace; Leonidas, king of the Spartans, died leading the Battle of Thermopylae against Xerxes and the Persians.

30 Marcus Furius Camillus was celebrated for saving Rome from the Gauls; Marcus Claudius Marcellus defeated the Carthaginians at Syracuse; Quintus Fulvius Flaccus captured Capua, which had allied with Hannibal; Lucius Quintius Cincinnatus, named dictator in order to help defeat Rome's enemies, left office immediately after completing the task; Marcus Sergius fought heroically against Hannibal; Quintus Publius Philo was Rome's first plebeian dictator and responsible for numerous victories; Cassius Scaevus was a centurion of Caesar's who held a fort against Pompey during the Civil War; Manius Curius Dentatus was a Roman consul who won numerous important victories.

men do to equal the deeds of this barbarian? What enterprise or battle did they undertake which was ever in doubt? What peril did they face not driven by a thirst for command, or by all-consuming self-interest, which makes even timid men bold? / In their greed for fame and vanity for glory, many who are incapable of withstanding a forceful blow undertake heroic feats, offering themselves courageously to death. They show their fortitude until their luck begins to change, but once fortune's fragile thread is broken, valor and resolve both fail them. / This youth confounded the fatal sentence against his fatherland, forced its reconsideration, and in the end was able to revoke it. He fought back Fortune and the fates, constraining their explicit will, and stood up to the fury of the conquerors, granting victory to the fearful. /

[3.47] The ground was strewn with weapons and the unequal combat well advanced before Caupolicán turned back, slowed by the friendly words. His men had also stopped, embarrassed ardor mixed with anger at seeing a single youth resist what so many of them together could not. / This frequently happens to honorable men suddenly caught off guard, or to those in difficult situations, who thinking they are unobserved flee dangerous encounters, only to turn around ashamed and furious, constrained by honor, when recognized by those who come behind. / Thus the Araucans now turn back to attack the victors, and brandishing the weapons they had earlier relinquished they all promise with loud cries to die. The ground trembles and moans from the horrendous fury with which both sides assault each other, spilling what little blood they have left with ferocious rage. / Diego Oro brings down Paynaguala, piercing his chest with the point of his sword, but Caupolicán marks the Spaniard out, leaving him little time to enjoy his accomplishment. The blow from his iron-plated club falls at an angle but still strikes solidly, leaving the inside of his helmet sprinkled with steaming brains. / After this Caupolicán brings down another, so disfigured he was never recognized again, for his armored head and all the side where the blow landed were crushed. Valdivia and Ongolmo then meet and attack each other, and Valdivia wounds Ongolmo in the hand while the Araucan delivers his blow in vain. / Impetuous Valdivia furiously presses on, troubling himself no further with Ongolmo, and comes to where the young, intrepid Leucotón is in a hotly-fought contest with Juan de Lamas and Reynoso. All alone the barbarian is maintaining his side of the dispute, using his skill and good sense to keep the engagement on equal footing. /The struggle breaks up when Valdivia arrives, as other Araucans rush to aid their companion, and the carnage and destruction begin anew. Men fight from one side to the other, and a great clamor rises up to the stars as sparks fly from iron. / For a long time victory remains uncertain. The air is filled with a deafening uproar, and the earth, soaked with blood, turns red. One man seeks nothing more than an honorable end; another grapples hand to hand with his enemy, probing the point at which his dagger can most quickly deliver cruel death. / Considering himself a master at combat did Juan de Gudiel little good. He closed on Guaticol, no less shrewd, in an untimely and vain effort, for just at that moment the Indian's brother, Purén, was next to him and used his dagger to open a wound in the Spaniard's side through which death entered as life departed. / Andrés de Villarroel, already weakened by the blood he had lost, made his way through the midst of the barbarians, seeking out the most dignified death. Juan de las Peñas, badly wounded as well, broke through the tightly-packed warriors and came alongside him, and at the same moment fate made them equals in death. /

[3. 57] The difference in the numbers of infidels and baptized was incalculable, one forming an immense battalion, the other amounting to no more than sixty. And now capricious Fortune, which had remained ambivalent until then, sanctioned evil, justifying a cause until then unjust. / Two thousand barbarian allies who fought for Valdivia, all expert bowmen, added to the bloody havoc, spilling more blood. Courageous in the face of death, they stayed with the Spanish soldiers, who as long as they remained alive remained undefeated. / First in one place and then another the good Valdivia demonstrated his courage and skill, doing everything with his sword that mighty Mars could have done, but he alone could not make up for the many men lost. Those who remained at his side sought no pact or truce, even in the face of destruction. / Two by two and three by three they fell, drained of blood, and as the end approached the barbarians' momentum kept growing. The feeble number of Spanish had been reduced to only fourteen resolute soldiers, who refused to give up until overwhelmed by cruel steel. / Accompanied by a priest who happened to be with them, Valdivia considered his destroyed company and the desperate situation. "Since fighting is hopeless, let's try another way to stay alive!" he said, seeing how few were left, and with this he spurred his horse as fast as he could. The minister of Masses ran after him. / As when two great bristling boars escape from hunters and are pursued by dogs, greedy for wild blood, and noble, fleet-footed wolfhounds join the chase, with no less avid and agile feet the Araucans flew after the two wretched Christians. / The storm of shots they fired, my Lord, was like a squall mixed with hail. A short distance away they caught them, slowed by a marsh, and there the barbarians flung themselves upon them, the last to do so deemed least brave. The priest died immediately. They brought the maltreated Valdivia before the senate. /

[3.64] Caupolicán, exuberant at seeing him alive in such condition, alternately interrogated and threatened him with a victor's arrogance. Valdivia responded like a wretched prisoner, humbly and abjectly begging not to be killed and swearing to leave the territory secure in freedom and peace. / It's said that Caupolicán was inclined to accept Valdivia's contrite proposal, but a hard-hearted kinsman, whom he respected as an elder, said, "Do you mean to lose such an opportunity by trusting a prisoner?" And aiming at Valdivia's skull, he brought down his massive club of hard juniper. / As when a dangerous, bellowing bull, secured to a stake by sturdy rope, is surrounded by a timid crowd of admirers, and the skillful butcher raises his heavy mallet of solid wood and vigorously brings it down on the nape of the bull's neck, laying it out dead with a shudder, / just so the adamant, white-haired elder, who had listened to Valdivia with an evil scowl, used both hands to raise his iron-plated club. Nor did the cruel old man deliver his blow in vain, for he sent Valdivia to eternal sleep, his body falling instantly to the ground as he quivered and died. / This barbarian's name was Leocato. Caupolicán was furious and wanted to punish such open disrespect, but the men implored him otherwise, and in the end the old man emerged from the incident unpunished and the total destruction of the Christians was achieved, for not one of them escaped the ordeal to bear the sad news. / Of their three thousand barbarian allies only two survived, who seeing our soldiers defeated hid in a dense thicket from which they watched the end of the hard-fought battle. Later they recounted how when the stars came out that night they escaped unseen. /

[3.70] By now gloomy night had ascended to the middle of the sky and was quickly covering the earth's vast globe with somber wings. Laying aside their weapons, the triumphant warriors organized great circles of dancers to celebrate their magnificent victory. / The news soon spread through all Arauco, and before the sun rose a great multitude of people had arrived and the field was covered with provisions. Now a general assembly was formed of men both young and old and of women and children, everyone taking part in the festivities. / By the time birds announced dawn's arrival and were repeating their cheerful songs, the barbarians had impaled the Spaniards' severed heads on tall poles encircling a clearing and adorned the branches of nearby trees with their armor. / Within this enclosure, surrounded by a pleasant grove, they began to celebrate and commemorate their victory with cheerful rounds of drinking. Wine augmenting their daring, Spain itself was soon threatened, the lowliest soldier vowing not to leave a single one of its defenses intact. / The general opinion was that a large number of warriors should set off without delay, double their marches, and attack the unprepared towns nearby. Assaulted without warning in such a way, the Spanish would be devastated by fear alone and the fatherland's honor would be restored, with not a single Christian left alive. / Once this was accomplished and their forces were sufficiently organized, in order to fully express their rage they wanted to cross to Spain with a powerful army, placing the country in such straits with their formidable campaign that Iberia's lands would soon be cultivated by other nations. / Leocán's son knew very well how vain this idea was and intended to amend it, for being both wise and shrewd he had a different goal and a better route by which to reach it. Once the festivities had ended and they were more disposed to discussion, he addressed them as follows: / "My lords, no less than you do I aspire to sweet, cherished liberty, nor would I ever deny the restoration of our fatherland's exalted power! But now that you've shown you can win, you must guard against losing, and I'm equally determined not to endanger what's already secure. / Be prudent and accept more reasonable opinions, for returning to your wives and children depends on sound initial steps. Your glory, honor, and domains are all near to being recovered, and time, the father of wise counsel, has put the means to success within our grasp. / You've killed Valdivia and his men and razed an important fort. Once this is known in the cities, vengeance will surely come, so let us offer the enemy free passage, for this is what will best assure our cause. Let them come! Let them come furiously and at full gallop, for their return will be difficult! / Victory is now in our hands! In this land we have thousands of protected places: swamps, quagmires, and marshes, dense ranges of rugged, brutal mountains. This is where we Araucans fight best, while the Spanish do so behind their ramparts, for a man attacked in his home is more knowledgeable, bold, and strong. / I'm telling you this so you grasp how much more likely we are to achieve the right remedy if we await them in locations of our own choosing, where no one can impede our rights and cause. And if they're afraid to seek us out, then we'll visit them in their very homes!" /

[3.82] All of them listened carefully to the general's speech, and finding that it fit with their goal most of them approved of it. When everyone had calmed down, Caupolicán turned to the young man through whom the recent victory, once lost, had with such miraculous effort been won. / As a mark of great favor he took the youth's right hand in his left, saying to him, "Brave warrior, you who've extended the illustrious name and boundaries of Arauco! By you the State has been redeemed, you've wrested it from the tyrant's power, and to you alone is due this victory so worthy of reward and immortal memory! / And, lords," he said, turning to the senate, "our present advantage so clearly being due to Lautaro" (for this was the valiant youth's name), "it's fitting we compensate him in some way, and thus with the authority you've vested in me I make him my captain and lieutenant, although this is far too little for such a debt. / Now that you've witnessed his feats, let him proceed with warriors of his own choosing to take on our enemies wherever he deems best, waiting there until they appear. With my companions and the rest of the men I'll guard the entrance to the valley of Elicura, awaiting a similar encounter." /

[3.86] The grateful youth accepted the rank with which the general favored him. The admiring crowd approved it, and if any were troubled, they didn't show it. Following their traditions, the great Caupolicán then cut the young man's hair, leaving a long plait at the top as the certain sign of his standing. / Lautaro was neither large nor small. He was handsome, mild in disposition, and industrious; intelligent, alert, and prudent; shrewd, determined, and always focused on larger issues. He was strongly-built and well-proportioned, with solid, muscular limbs, a broad back, and powerful chest. / The festivities were prolonged in his honor, with varied contests showing off rarely seen feats of jumping and wrestling. At night there were dances around the fires, and as the games went on there were prizes and splendid jewels, richer and more precious than anything won by Greeks or Trojans. / In the midst of this, Caupolicán was approached by an agitated Indian with a troubled expression, out of breath and covered in dust and sweat. "Lord," he said, "send help at once! Your troops have been overwhelmed and their loss is certain, for most of those who were waiting in ambush are now scattered or dead. / Fourteen heroic warriors have descended upon the land of Elicura, armed with the finest swords and riding swift, agile horses.[31] They've routed two squadrons of pikemen by themselves, and seeing the great carnage I immediately ran to warn you!" / Caupolicán, his expression unchanged, calmed the man's fears, telling him it was impossible that so few armed men would escape in the end. With his usual diligence he then ordered his new lieutenant to set out with the swiftest soldiers, saying he would immediately follow with the others. / Lautaro was not slow to respond and having selected a sufficient cohort marched off with all speed, avid to win fame among the people. But now the loud clamor of Mars is calling and I delay unjustly, for the time has come to speak of the fourteen Spaniards and their bitter, bloody fight. / May their fame spread and become known to all, for their swords excelled superbly, and if ever valor in arms so merits, their memory, as history will testify, should be eternal. With this I bring the canto to an end, for without gaining strength for a new one, I dare not speak of such great deeds. /

---

31 These are the soldiers from La Imperial, whom Valdivia had ordered to meet him at the Tucapel fort; cf. 2.91.

CANTO 4

Coming from La Imperial to join Valdivia at the Tucapel fort, the fourteen Spaniards are ambushed by Indians who engage them in a bitter fight. Lautaro arrives with reinforcements, and seven of the Spanish die, along with all their allies. Through great good fortune the rest of them escape.

How important and beneficial is justice, curing countless ills! If rebellious Arauco was now so powerful, its neighbors alarmed and its fury at such a height, it's because it was not punished in a timely fashion. A wound not treated in the beginning in the end requires a harsher cure, / and it isn't virtue but vice and negligence when one injury leads to another even greater. When necessary, a wound must be mended with iron, although not with such rigor that mercy loses all effectiveness, and he who bravely cuts off a finger to save an arm shows mercy and compassion. / I don't mean that justice should wield a sword at every step, but rather in keeping with the gravity of the case and the severity of the harm. In the present situation justice was clearly corrupted by avarice, which allowed wickedness to take root and overwhelm men's hearts. / We should also not assume that being just means being inhuman or that to be taken seriously means being bloody. Nor should we be like one who unjustly decides, absent any cause or self-control, to leave a memory of his wickedness solely from caprice or conceit. / I could offer other examples but will go no further since doing so would be both perilous and distracting. Time will speak more clearly on the subject than my words, which may raise doubts among some. I will only add that wise men agree that where kings are absent wrongs abound. /

[4.6] Returning to my subject, I will say no more about injustice, which is to labor in vain and cast words to the wind. Instead, I will speak of those who won honor and glory, performing deeds worthy of memory as they fought the enemy's fierce battalions. / Their remarkable achievement, which readers will surely deem among the most impressive, merits the attention of an authoritative account. I will therefore do my best to tell it, although with no more than a brief summary. Here are the names of the soldiers who so rightly deserve to be praised: / Almagro, Cortés, Córdoba, Nereda, Morán, Gonzalo Hernández, Maldonado, Peñalosa, Vergara, Castañeda, Diego García Herrero the fearless, Pero Niño, Escalona, and one more who completes their number, don Leonardo Manrique, last named but equal in valor to the first. / These are the fourteen who were coming to meet Valdivia and who had set out from La Imperial not knowing he had already been killed. They climbed the high hill at Purén and found the trails on its summit littered with branches, a sure sign that warriors had assembled there. / Knowing the land was agitated and that warriors had been summoned did not cause them to alter their route, however, nor did fear affect their determination. A new and refreshing dawn was reddening the sky, gladdening their hearts, and shadows were retreating before the sun when they first caught sight of the valley of Elicura. / This is where the Indians lay in ambush, waiting for our soldiers to proceed so they could attack them in disorder before they realized the danger. To better conceal and protect themselves they were covered with branches, / and the fourteen were descending a steep slope nearby when their enemies suddenly sounded their raucous horns and drums and emerged to block the trails. / A hunter is not filled with such joy, when a terrified hare suddenly bounds into the road between his feet, as our Spaniards were at the clamorous appearance of those previously hidden warriors, and they immediately spurred their horses. / The Indians quickly formed a wall of gleaming spears, but the Spanish did not stop until they had completely breached it, trampling down men, pikes, and clubs. Seeing the strength of their adversaries, however, our soldiers circled back to finish the fight with more courage than hope. / Of the three barbarian squadrons, two had turned aside to close off the road and any chance of escape for our men, who finding themselves surrounded, decided to force an exit through the enemy's midst. Again they attacked shoulder to shoulder, but even though they broke through one squadron, its badly injured members regrouped. / Twice more the Spanish charged like this, overrunning the dense formations. Seeing themselves close to death, however, they set out for the ravaged Tucapel fort, fighting off the Indians mixed among them and attacking from all sides. /

[4.17] The Elicura road narrows along the low skirt of a mountain where it passes a lake that fills the lower valley. This was fortunate for our soldiers, fighting as they went, since one alone in the rear was able to fend off the pursuing barbarians. / Our men had just entered dense woods when they saw an Indian hurriedly descending a steep slope at their side, his countenance pale and his clothing in disarray. Intercepting their path, the man withdrew a sealed message from his breast that Juan Gómez de Almagro himself had written that very day to Valdivia from La Imperial, advising him of his approach with reinforcements. / They now recognized the messenger as the man who had left them that morning, who now tearfully told them of Valdivia's pitiful end. He also reported what else had happened and described how the Indians had ravaged the Tucapel fort to its foundations. Realizing the help they were bringing the fort was in vain, the Spaniards gathered in a clearing / protected by slopes on the north, east, and west. To the south it was open to the well-worn road, which was now covered with a long line of barbarians thirsty for baptized blood. / The Araucans stopped here, as well, regrouping their scattered men into two battalions. The fourteen Spaniards, deeming it best to attack, readied themselves as the orderly formations moved forward, led by the brave Lincoya. /

[4.22] The ferocious barbarians advance shouting insults, accompanied by the shrill uproar of flutes, horns, and other loud instruments. Our soldiers are hoping to change these proud yells to laments, and their courage grows so great they seem to confront no more than a handful of opponents. / There was one unworthy man among them, someone I don't want to name, who seeing his few companions, said, "Alas, if only our squadron were a hundred!" But Gonzalo Hernández, turning his face to heaven, spiritedly responds, "Would it have pleased God we were two men less and only a dozen, since then they could have called us the Famous Twelve!"[32] / With this they ready their horses and, settled firmly in their saddles, loosen their reins. Then, trusting in the blood-honed blades of their sturdy lances, they dig in their spurs and rush forward against the enemy, calling in loud voices upon God in heaven as the ground trembles and groans beneath them. / The barbarians' hard ash pikes, as big as beams, are instantly leveled, like heads of grain bent low by a violent wind. They cannot withstand the Spaniards' impact, however, and our men break through along one side, leaving a breach in the battalion. / Flinging aside their broken lances, they wheel their horses about as one as they turn back to their fierce opponents, unsheathed swords held high, and again they attack, their disadvantage against the infinity of sharp points aimed at their breasts no match for their rage. / One side not knowing what it is to be defeated and the other now accustomed to winning, lead to even more wounds as men's arms come down more heavily. Armor is battered so fast and furiously that a great clamor rises up amidst the flying sparks, and it seems high heaven itself is tumbling to the ground. / Good Gonzalo

---

32 The reference elides two sets of heroes from medieval romances: *Los Nueve de la Fama* or *Famous Nine*, comprising figures embodying chivalric ideals from pagan times through the Christian era, and *les douze pairs de France* or Twelve Peers, Charlemagne's most illustrious knights.

Hernández, striving to emulate the famous Gonzalo of Córdoba, smashes his way through the enemy's ranks, displaying no less skill and strength than bravery. Peñalosa and Vergara, knowing they must win or die, give clear proof of their valor as they risk their lives. / Brave Escalona, brandishing his cruel sword, distinguishes himself in perilous fights, leaving his mark on a thousand brave barbarians. Don Leonardo Manrique, rather than forgive the blows he receives, accelerates his own with greater wrath, punishing, maltreating, and repulsing his opponents. / Another soldier, also named Córdoba, a youth of great fortitude and fearlessness, spills so much Araucan blood that day that he creates a hundred widows. One of these will call on heaven for vengeance, the rest will leap with joy, for in the end women are inconstant and fond of change. /

[4.31] On their side of the fight, Cortés and Pero Niño wreak terrible carnage as they wage cruel war; Morán, Maldonado, and Gómez de Almagro sow the earth with barbarian bodies; Herrera, practiced in dealing skilled blows, kills and tramples; Nereda, equally masterful, chases down and wounds to left and right. / As if destined to die, our men's infuriated swords keep cutting, their brutal strokes falling so forcefully that stout armor makes little difference. What the Araucans' shields cannot withstand their insensible bodies endure, so enraged they feel neither wounds nor death. / Instead, burning with hatred, they hammer away with heavy blows of their own, the impact of which forces horses to their knees. Embossed armor is crushed, bursts open, and falls apart; battered bucklers come undone; pieces of broken pikes and helmets roll on the ground; the air resounds with the clash of swords. / Lincoya's ferocious assault incites his troops, sturdy, tall-crested helmets no match for his powerful club. Cortés, absorbing one of these blows, drops his head to the pommel, and his horse, running for open country, bears him off half-dead, reins trailing. / The horse carries him here and there, slumped over as if asleep, but coming to his senses and filled with shame, he takes up the reins and returns to seek the man who wounded him. The moment he sees him he recognizes him, for Lincoya stood head and shoulders above his countrymen. / He knows him, as well, by the fearlessness with which he inspires his warriors and the agility with which he wields his club. Like a fleet-footed wolfhound, rushing through the undergrowth in pursuit of a ferocious wild boar, Cortés, cruel sword in hand and his shield at his chest, chases and wounds the Araucan / with a slanting stroke to the side. The Indian's solid cuirass avails him little, but the blow affects him no more than it would have a boulder or thick wall. The spurred horse continues on, and Cortés, now safe from Lincoya, cleaves through the middle of the close-packed warriors, laying them out to one side and the other. / Almagro fights hand to hand with a courageous young soldier named Guacón, but the dispute is quickly settled since luck rarely stays neutral for long. A blow from the Spaniard opens a wide portal for death, and a crimson river pours forth as a cold chill overtakes the barbarian's bloodless body. / Castañeda, filled with wrath, assaults and tramples, mutilating, wounding, and killing. Coming upon Narpo on his right, he aims his terrible sword in that direction, and neither the barbarian's coat of fine mail nor breastplate of doubled hides can resist the furious blade, depriving his body of its spirit. /

[4.40] The men grow more enraged with each other, and fervor, courage, and strife keep building. A river of barbarian and Spanish blood continues to swell, and the air is obscured by a dense vapor. Some infernal fury must have run free, instilling them with diabolical hatred, for so many to be carried off in a single day. / The bitter fight lasts so long it's astounding the men can still raise their arms. Here and there corpses are heaped into mounds. The sun had already begun to decline when bereft of strength, torn to pieces, and equally weakened, neither side could proceed. / As when strength and breath begin to fail two great, noble bulls, equals in a fierce, stubborn contest, and they reluctantly back away, facing each other and covered in sweat and lather, their hooves scattering sand to the wind, / just so the two groups now drew apart, drained of strength and blood and breath, face to face and never turning their backs. Both halted at the same moment, no more than an arrow's flight apart. / From their opposing positions they eyed each other, covered with blood and sweat, gasping and unable to catch their breaths as they rested their weary limbs, chests bared and mouths open to a cool breeze that blew in gentle gusts, easing the fierce heat of the sun. / From here, in place of their hands, they wounded each other with malicious tongues, shouting insults and promising each other pitiless deaths. In addition to this, enemy bows launched dangerous arrows, which in the absence of strength and breath were sent flying by ravenous rancor. / I know not whose arm still had the strength to send an arrow cleaving noisily through the air like an impetuous bolt of lightning. Its furious tip brushed past Córdoba's side, not taking hold, then veered toward Morán, where it made its entry, piercing his right eye. / With a steady, ruthless hand the good Morán tore out the arrow with his eye still on it. Gonzalo Hernández rushed to console him, preparing him for the approach of cruel death, but Morán shouted, "I'm not someone of feeble courage, and wounded like this I alone can still defeat all those you see here!" / He boldly spurred his horse, too exhausted to gallop, against that multitude regrouping into a battalion, but diligent Gonzalo quickly got ahead of him and forced him back, for Lincoya was already advancing to attack. /

[4.49] With great spectacle and uproar Lautaro and his ready soldiers now appeared on the crest of a verdant hill, marching rapidly with their banners unfurled to the wind. Just as a famished lion spots its prey from afar and looks joyfully about, roaring ferociously and shaking its matted mane, / even so Lautaro, a good distance ahead of his soldiers, quickly descended the steep slope and made straight for the Spanish, intending to conclude the battle singlehandedly if they didn't abandon the field. Now behold a feat worthy of celebration: there were only fourteen soldiers there, cut to pieces, with broken arms, legs, and heads, / while four thousand victorious warriors approached. Keeping close together our men awaited them, not frightened by the sight of so many since they now hoped to die with even more honor. The arrogant enemy yelled, "Kill them! Kill them!" Lincoya's army, reinvigorated, attacked from the other side. / The Christians spurred their horses, which tramped slowly across the ground toward the rested Araucans, furiously threatening heaven and earth. Sluggish steps led to ready hands, and in the first encounter Pero Niño hit the white sand already cold with death, bathing it in a great rush of blood. / There's no agreement over who was responsible for the wound that traversed his body: some say Angol was the killer, others that it was Leucotón, which is more likely. Whoever it was, after his great fall, pierced by a pike, Pero Niño lay dead on the ground and was swiftly cut to pieces. / Manrique fell dead as well, collapsing at Lautaro's feet. The other twelve broke off, heading for the road through the

Canto 4

densely packed weapons, but Ongolmo, rushing forward, with a skillful blow brought down Nereda, so experienced in warfare. Badly wounded, Cortés fell dead as well. / After him Diego García was brought to earth, his chest torn open by a mortal wound. Another blow, cleanly struck by Tucapel, laid out Escalona. The remaining Spaniards, now on the road—let anyone who has ever been in peril just imagine—desperately lashed the flanks of their horses, which were drained of strength and blood. / Ferocious Tucapel audaciously assaulted them all, and seeing the previous two hit the ground, leapt boldly over their bodies to confront Almagro, whom he quickly attacked. Raised on his toes, he lifted his club high and brought it down with all his might, / but whether through poor aim or excess fury, or perhaps because Almighty God wanted to save him, the blow aimed at the Spaniard's head fell instead on his horse, landing with such force that its haunch was crushed like dough or soft wax and he could no longer ride it. / Seeing the horse maimed, Almagro threw himself to the side, either to his luck and good fortune or to the misfortune of the valiant Maldonado, who was coming behind him and who, covered with blood and dust, arrived just as Tucapel repeated his blow, which came close to knocking him to the ground. / Maldonado's stirrup caught Tucapel's side as he passed, thrusting him four or five strides down the road, and the barbarian bellowed with burning rage. Never did a more venomous snake or scorpion, having been stepped on, turn as fast as Tucapel now turned with a terrible scowl. / Reconsidering the sentence he had passed on Juan de Almagro, he directed his furious bludgeon against the unfortunate Maldonado instead, bringing down his arm with all his might. The Spaniard's quick horse stepped aside, however, and the furious blow went astray, the ironclad cudgel striking the ground. / Maldonado did not escape death, however, for ruthless Lemolemo was instantly there with his knotted club, as long and stout as a thick, curved oar, dealing the Spaniard a blow in which the hard iron tip did not miss, nor did the well-padded helmet prove any use as his brains spilled out on the sand. /

[4.62] At this point an enormous dark cloud suddenly roiled the air and sky, veiling the pale sunlight in its fearsome shadow. Tempestuous Aquilon burst forth in a fury, buckling trees and undergrowth as it mixed wind with great drops of water, which soon began to fall more thickly.[33] / Like a skilled drummer preparing courageous soldiers for battle with measured beats, then hearing the signal to attack sounds his horrible, harsh harmony, just so the turbulent black cloud erupted in a violent deluge. / Covering the heavens with dark gloom, the furious squall grew stronger, letting loose water, hail, and thunder mingled with bolts of lightning. The Araucan army began to scatter in alarm, the gale growing so great it stuck fear into even the bravest. / It was Gómez de Almagro's good fortune that the sky quickly grew dark and night came far earlier than usual. Dazed, he hid himself in the undergrowth until the ferocious barbarians, so greedy for Spanish blood, had passed. / Realizing the violent storm would hide his escape, he then left the thicket, fear showing the way forward, and falling down and getting up, covered with blood, sweat, and mud, he finally came to where the rest of the soldiers were waiting for the furious downpour to abate. / The men were to one side of the road. Hearing the whinny of one of their horses, Almagro was reassured and headed toward the happy sound, arriving just as the six were speaking of him in hushed

---

33   Aquilon, or Boreas, the north wind.

voices. As he gave an account of what had happened, / they looked at him in astonishment, having thought him already dead, and each, moved by pity, offered to die helping him. Astute as he was brave, and knowing nothing could be done, he told them, "Gentlemen, no one should worry about me, but let anyone who can do so save his own life!" / He had no more than uttered these words when he bravely took an uncertain path through the woods, avoiding the road, which was filled with warriors and other barbarians. A greater crisis awaits him, but since there is a reliable history of Chile, anyone who wants to know his story can read of it there.[34] / The historian Estrella writes in Latin with such erudition and accuracy about the history of Chile and Peru that his memory will justly last forever.[35] He has also written a life of the august Charles V, as well as verses celebrating the glory of men in warfare, governance, letters, and justice. /

[4.71] I return to the six soldiers who felt so badly for Almagro's misfortune, but who unable to help him headed back toward La Imperial. The furious storm kept getting worse, and the thunder and lightning did not stop until the sun reappeared the next morning, revealing the Purén fort. / This was the stronghold that Almagro and a few soldiers had been protecting when they were suddenly surrounded one night by a multitude of barbarians, and it was his industry that finally raised the siege and courageously repelled the attackers. Even though the battle

---

34 Two contemporary histories recount much of this material: Alonso de Góngora Marmolejo's *Historia de Chile desde su descubrimiento hasta el año 1575*, and Pedro Mariño de Lobera's *Crónica del Reino de Chile*.

35 The humanist Juan Cristóbal Calvete de Estrella, author of numerous works, was tutor to prince Philip and the court pages, including the poet.

is famous, I'm not going to describe it, in order to avoid being delayed. / Arriving here, the six warriors were warmly welcomed by their friends, who were astonished to see them reduced to such a state: wretched, pale, and afflicted; weak, hoarse, broken, and exhausted; emaciated, dripping with mud and blood, missing their helmets, their armor shattered, their bodies mutilated. / For almost twenty-four hours they had wielded their weapons, not stopping once during all that time as they defended themselves and did everything you have heard here, my Lord. Now they rested at this fort from which they had set out the previous night, the concern of those who had remained behind even greater once they learned what had happened. / A cold fear curdled their blood, and all were deeply shaken when told the details of Valdivia's terrible misfortune. Considering the fort's poor state of readiness and the Indians' strength, they unanimously decided to leave that very day / and head toward the Cautén valley and La Imperial, taking the same road as Almagro, who thanks to the dark night had safely escaped Lautaro's men. Once the stronghold was abandoned, the enemy razed it to the ground, plundering its munitions and food. / The jubilant barbarians, their joyful shouts resounding through the cavernous mountains, then returned to where the main Araucan army was camped, and here in spacious meadows they reveled in the day's victory with songs and games to beguile their weariness. / Once everyone was assembled, grave Caupolicán joyfully welcomed them, then affectionately took the right hand of intrepid Lautaro, his lieutenant, and placed him in charge of a select company of expert warriors. All were fine, valiant men, experienced in weapons and the work of war and ready for any great enterprise or campaign. /

Canto 4

[4.79] Let us leave Lautaro at this point, whose activities have detained me too long, for soon enough I will have to return to him. Now I want to proceed to Penco, since it's important that I speak of the preparations the people there were making for the bloody war that was breaking out and of the understandable distress they were feeling. / Light-footed Fame, bearer of bad news and great misfortune, had been tormenting Penco from hour to hour, her reports reinforced by sinister omens, when two Indians unexpectedly arrived. These were those I mentioned earlier, who seeing Valdivia's downfall had hidden themselves in the brush and who now recounted the sad event. / Hearing the harrowing details from these reliable messengers, the women, children, and elderly all joined in lamentation. New widows, orphaned girls, and young maidens pierced the heavens with shrill cries, filling the wind with sad complaints, a sorrowful thing to see. / Pale faces more lovely than flowers were abused by cruel fists, and handfuls of golden hair were strewn about the ground. Snow-white breasts and delicate necks were stained with blood and heartfelt tears, and rich gowns, jewels, and headpieces were torn apart and cast aside. / With no less turmoil men still robust in age revealed their distress in an entirely different way, for now the clamor of weapons rang out, preparations resounded, and Mars's hoarse trumpet incited them all to war. / Some sharpened dull swords, others polished rusty breastplates, mended coats of mail, or reinforced their lances with iron. Cannons were readied and aimed, flags loosed to the wind, and wherever one looked soldiers busied themselves in valiant displays. / The commander of the troops was Francisco Villagrán, a man of great diligence, considered both wise and capable in matters of war. Pedro de Valdivia's lieutenant, he was the one they now obeyed, and deploring the disaster and terrible events he called for Valdivia's death to be avenged. / The women, seeing their husbands facing such danger and distressed themselves, injure heaven's high dome with new cries. Kneeling in the dust, with tearful eyes and groans they set their little children before their husbands, but this is not enough to dissuade them. / Once preparations are complete, the men set out in search of the barbarians, their resplendent armor gleaming far into the distance. From towers and rooftops the women follow them with fixed and tender gazes, sending forth a thousand benedictions as they turn their prayers and petitions to God. /

[4.88] Saying goodbye to the throng of townspeople who have accompanied them, the soldiers spur their horses in search of the Araucan army. On the left they pass Mareguano; on the right the land belonging to the vassals of Talca, son of Talcaguano, almost entirely surrounded by sea and mountains. / Leaving safe territory behind, they tread the parched sands of Andalicán, and having traversed its vast plain, climb the hills. Not a sound can be heard. At the foot of Andalicán mountain, not knowing what Lautaro is planning, fear of entering the Araucan state tempers their inordinate fury. / Beginning on the north side here, a dangerous pass, difficult and narrow, crosses the rugged, precipitous mountain, the peak of which touches the heavens. Following this there's a brief level area, and then another slope, not as high, but steep, which separates the district of Andalicán from the fertile valley and frontier of Arauco. / Lautaro had chosen this second incline for battle, arranging it so that his entire army was spread out along its exposed summit. Knowing that foot soldiers on level ground are poorly equipped to chase horses across open country, he left the initial route up the mountain unprotected, intending to catch the Spanish out of breath once they had climbed it. / To give an accurate idea of the site, I want to describe it completely. The rise of the road is not severe, but everything around it is precipitous. Just to the west is an immense cliff, its base battered by the stormy sea, while the high ground and summit of the hill is level for the distance of a crossbow shot. / The summit was occupied by the powerful enemy army, while the road, as I said, was left open, with no defense or obstruction. After ascending the first incline, our troops came to the foot of the second, but here Villagrán stopped, uncertain. Slowed by the perilous situation, / he considered anew the dangerous campaign and great enterprise he was undertaking, like Roman Caesar halting his advance and hesitantly putting his foot in the Rubicon. At last, he courageously loosened the reins. "Onward, now the die is cast!" he cried, and thus our Spaniard set forth, giving free rein to his destiny. /

[4.95] Their captain had scarcely taken the first step when the dauntless soldiers eagerly followed him up the lofty, rugged peak. Lautaro, in position and unmoving, let them proceed unchallenged. Commanding ten thousand men, soldiers accustomed to the cruel work of the sword / and now positioned around the summit, he ordered that no one take a single step to begin the cruel festivities until hearing his signal to attack. A severe penalty was promised anyone ignoring these terms, and the men remained as stiff and silent as marble statues. / The Spanish soldiers, eager to exercise their winning skill, advanced on the enemy, approaching the barbarians' left side. The moment he has been waiting for having finally arrived, Lautaro makes a great show for battle with a tremendous clamor of trumpets, drums, horns, and bugles. / Now it seems best, my Lord, being weary from singing, that I bring this long canto to a close, in order that the next be more welcome. Should it appear I proceed too slowly, I pray the delay not displease you, for even though determined to avoid tiresomeness, I still annoy a good many. /

CANTO 5

This fifth canto describes the hard-fought battle between the Spanish and Araucans on the hill at Andalicán, where Lautaro's shrewdness and the great obstacles facing the Spanish resulted in their rout, with more than half of them killed, along with three thousand of their Indian allies.

The loving Lord in his mercy always defers the discipline we deserve until faced with the rebellion of our hardened hearts. Our heedlessness is so great, however, that even seeing our neighbors punished we still are loath to leave the path of wickedness. / I say this because our Spanish soldiers, so eager to fight, had learned nothing from Valdivia's demise nor realized they were following in his steps. Soon they will render a rigorous account of their past and present transgressions, for Lautaro the executioner, burning with rage, has appeared on the field with his men. /

[5.3] Villagrán halted his ready troops on the narrow stretch of open ground, and having positioned six cannons there, ordered whatever else was necessary. For some time he remained like this, waiting to see how Lautaro would respond, for the barbarians covered so much ground that the ardor of more than one Christian was cooled. / Many of them had looked forward to this battle, but God alone knows what their feelings were seeing the entire hilltop covered by organized battalions. Momentarily chilled by fear, their blood soon flowed back to their hearts, and their limbs, briefly deprived of warmth, regained their strength. / Filled with new ardor, not hearing the trumpet to advance they begin to roar, their desire for battle so great that delay is painful. On the other side, the Araucan warriors were raging to attack, but their commander's orders proved a forceful bridle and restraint. / Like a fiery stallion that sees a rival draw near and impatiently snorts and neighs, pawing the earth all around with baleful looks, just so the obedient barbarians, seeing the Castilians so close, howled to see the game begin but did not overstep forbidden bounds. / Thus the situation stood, with both sides eager to come together. Convinced that delay increased his soldiers' fervor, Villagrán drew aside three squads of cavalry eager to test themselves, and at his signal, needing no further encouragement, they vigorously set spurs to their horses. / Swift hooves pound the open ground as they rush forward in furious commotion. At the terrible tumult the Rauco river trembles, and a strange moan escapes the nearby sea. Fearing Lautaro's explicit command, the tightly controlled

Indians, straining to attack, take not a single step forward, / and thus as in the famous Castilian festival where quadrilles advance to cast cane spears at each other and then return, shields at their chests, just so our soldiers, upright in their saddles, come to the crest of the hill and then circle back, unable to advance without falling among the rocks.[36] / In no hurry to leave, they repeatedly attempt to advance, each time enduring a shower of arrows, darts, and stones. Some are well-served by a solid shield, and many come to appreciate their helmets and greaves, for due to the rugged summit they could not employ their swords. /

[5.11] Lautaro remained where he was, with his men encircling the crest, but with his permission some warriors who were eager to distinguish themselves came down to open ground. Wanting to engage the Spanish with pikes or clubs, one on one or in twos or threes, the choice left to those they challenge, / they advance with nonchalant swaggers, grimacing and gesturing as they parade back and forth. More arrogant than high-spirited Germans, they boldly step forward to test themselves against sharp swords, like gallant contenders at a public tourney.[37] / Whoever considers himself a master pikeman now tests his strength and destiny, skillfully probing left and right for advantage. Finding a way forward, one attacks, the Spanish advance to meet him, and he quickly withdraws. This one delivers a blow in vain, that one with such accuracy his enemy lies dead on the ground. / Others

---

36 The image refers to the *juego de cañas* (literally *game of canes*), an intricately choreographed mock battle popular in sixteenth-century Spain, where "gentlemen-soldiers" on horseback cast spears made of cane or reeds.

37 The valor of German troops was a commonplace in the sixteenth and seventeenth centuries.

do not bother with postures nor tarry over attitude and elegance, but only strive to make their blows mortal and remain firmly on their feet. With bold spirits they risk themselves, borne on by bravery and wrath, but at times this leads to futile blows and the adversaries draw close together. / Young Curiomán was distinguishing himself as swiftest on foot, boldly running forward in daring displays, brandishing a formidable lance and fearlessly hurling himself into the fray: a loaded crossbow never shot an arrow with such speed. / He had already wounded seven Spaniards, but no one dared to take revenge since the valiant Araucan was feared for his bravery, skill, and great strength. Chagrined at seeing him cast his eighth lance, Villagrán angrily called out, "Can't anyone punish this insolent barbarian?" / As he spoke he looked at Diego Cano, whose valor was well-known. Cano was ready on his prized, white-tailed stallion, an enormous lance in his right hand, and just as the brawny Araucan drew back his arm with all his might, he spurred his horse, thighs clasped tightly to the saddle. / With a resounding rush the swift charger set off toward the intrepid Indian, who by now had already turned back, but determined he not get away, the stalwart Spaniard loosed the reins and dug in his heels, urging his steed toward the enemy troops. / Neither the fierce Araucan throng, with their heavy pikes leveled, nor the rapid, forceful blows of barbarian clubs and swords could withstand his furious progress as he burst through the tight-packed multitude in pursuit of the nimble Curiomán. / In spite of their numbers, with a steady arm and mighty effort Diego Cano scornfully forced his way through them all, and his lance pierced the chest of one who had only deferred his death in vain. Glorying in this remarkable, brave feat, the Spaniard turned his horse about, opening a way back through the midst of the weapons with skilled aim and great force. / The cavalry immediately rushed forward, calling out to the Araucans, who appeared to await their attack, only to quickly withdraw to the edge of the rocks. One, four, and ten times the Spanish charged to no avail, having yet to stain a single sword with barbarian blood. / The tired horses were laboring to little effect, and our men, harassed and wounded by arrows, goaded them on in vain. Finding themselves in such a predicament, the bravery of some was tempered, since now they were fatigued while their enemies were rested, and all the surrounding roads and trails were blocked. /

[5.23] At this point the fearsome artillery suddenly fired with great violence, battering the Indian formations and flattening anything that stood in its path. Smoke and fire swept up the hill. The air resounded near and far, and with all the uproar the earth appeared to open, giving vent to a new Mt. Aetna. / Lautaro realized it was essential to destroy and be rid of that thundercloud launching lightning bolts among his men, which had already destroyed a good number of them. He ordered the squadron of valiant Leucotón, entrusted to him for his courage, to attack it with all their fury, encouraging them in a loud voice: / "Oh, loyal and victorious companions, whom Fortune calls to such great deeds! Now is the time for your valiant arms to prove our cause and our rights! Charge them! Lower your fierce lances and pierce the enemies' chests with your blades, bringing forth a crimson current with no regard for friend or relative! / Press on to the cannons, for if they be won by your effort your swords will be celebrated by a great victory and your memory on earth will be eternal! The army will follow in your footsteps, but you alone will be the authors of this glory!" Filled with pride, the squadron launches its audacious attack. / Being last is a mark of infamy its men avoid at all costs, the most timid striving to be first to test whether or not his lance will strike home. Seeing a companion killed or a cannonball carry off fifteen or twenty men, cut to pieces and flying through the air, does not frighten them, nor do bodies without their heads. / Blind fear does not perturb or slow them even for a moment. Instead, if a shot takes off someone's arm, he immediately grips his sword with the arm that remains. Never hesitating, they come to the rise where the fire machines stand, which are soon overwhelmed by the barbarian assault. / The rest of the Indians immediately circle and attack, obscuring earth and sky with their blows. No pen or tongue can describe the fury with which they advance. With all the fire, smoke, shouting, and clouds of dust, they can no longer hear or clearly see each other, yet these impediments matter little since being blinded they stay together by touch. / Once engaged, it doesn't take long for the enemy squadrons to coordinate their efforts, and the rapid clashing of swords dominates all else. Both parties do everything they can to distinguish themselves, and one sees heads and helmets severed in great numbers, along with legs separated from their trunks. / Some men defend the artillery being attacked with such violent rage; others fight bitterly to bring their opponents' obstinacy to an end. There are fifty adversaries for every Spaniard, but in spite of the enormous advantage each man resists so bravely that they counter the numbers with valor. / No one wants the standard of the great and glorious Charles V to be forced back. Instead it must always move forward victoriously, in spite of hostile Mars, who was everywhere, terrifying and ferocious, enveloped in rage and bloody dust and giving new vigor to swords that were still not weary after so much fighting. /

As the injuries mount, furor and bravery revive with the same strength and fortitude as if combat had just begun. The death and brutality cannot be described. Lush green grass loses its color, turning blood red. /

[5.34] Villagrán has the battle in hand, not ceding the least part of his position and anticipating everything of importance. Hastening here and there, he does all an experienced captain should and more, for like a daring soldier and good warrior he's the first to throw himself into danger. / Seeing Torbo covered in blood and causing great slaughter among the Christians, he is filled with anger and spurs his horse, gripping his lance in his right hand. Firm in the stirrups, he aims at the chest, but an excess of zeal impairs the hasty effort, and the ill-timed cast is in vain. / His horse cleaves furiously through the crowd of barbarian bodies. The enraged Spaniard turns back to Torbo, and steadying his lance beneath his arm he pierces the Indian's tough, three-layered breastplate and woolen doublet, opening a great wound in his belly through which a lake of blood pours out with his soul. / Villagrán retrieves the lance intact, and drawing back his arm, angrily hurls it forward. The furious spear flies quivering from such force but injures no one, passing between the arm and side of Corpillán, who had stopped to rest, before penetrating the earth where it remains fixed half an arm's length in the ground. / Unsheathing his sword, Villagrán then charges into the middle of the army at great speed, brutally opening a broad path where the mass of men is thickest. To no less a degree, Pedro de Olmos de Aguilera exposes himself to every danger and alone is responsible for the deaths of Guancho, Canio, Pillo, and Titaguano. / Hernando and Juan Alvarado both give remarkable displays of their valor. The old Maldonado, a great horseman, skillfully governs his steed with one hand while wielding his deadly blade with the other. He displays his usual valor, but his strength, weakened by age, makes for feeble blows and light wounds. / Diego Cano, using both hands and no shield, leaves no lance or piece of armor intact, and everything he attacks is cut to pieces and falls to earth in the ferocity of his keen-edged sword. Peña, in spite of the stammer he has when speaking, spins about with the facility of Scaeva amidst Pompey's army or Peleus's fierce son at Troy.[38] / Elsewhere, Reynoso, incited by venomous rage, goes furiously about with his bloody blade, wounding on all sides. Killing Palta with a single blow, he brutally aims the tip of his weapon at the side of mighty Ron, hits a vein, and withdraws it covered in blood. / Bernal, Pedro de Aguayo, Castañeda, Ruiz, Gonzalo Hernández, and Pantoja amass a ring of corpses, turning all the earth around them red. The enemy has not been able to gain a foot of ground, nor has the relentless wounding abated at all, the Christians performing feats that time will deem miraculous. / Their opponents were so numerous and the resources and confidence of our men so depleted, however, that blood, strength, force, and hope failed many altogether, and in the end, carried away by a current whose great force they could not withstand, the Spanish lost a large stretch of the mountain together with their six pieces of artillery. /

[5.44] Never wavering, our soldiers continued to display their ancient valor and fortitude, and not once was weakness witnessed among them until the enemy won the field and cannon emplacement. Finding themselves in such straits at that

---

38   Scaeva was a soldier of Caesar's who fought heroically against Pompey in the civil war (cf. Lucan's *Pharsalia* 6.144 ff.); as told in Homer's *Iliad*, the son of Peleus is Achilles.

hour, for it had been more than five since they began fighting, they began to have doubts about the battle and to lose hope of winning. / Seeing the barbarians so strong when their own strength was waning made them skeptical, and fear, chilling their blood, brought injury and death before their very eyes. Some became so discouraged they withdrew toward the road, not in disarray, my Lord, but facing the enemy and in good order. / But brave Villagrán, making every effort, angrily rushed forward and blocked their way, rallying them with the wise words of an experienced captain. "Gentlemen," he said, "let no one turn away from what honor demands! Don't give in to panic, which I assure you is the great enemy of all our good, / but cast it aside and you will see the manifest indignity and insult awaiting you. Behold how infamous fear, base and blind, hinders us more than the enemy's steel! Do not be troubled, control yourselves, and maintain your calm! Glory, honor, life, and fortune all depend on this single moment, the loss of which is irreparable! / Where are you headed in such confusion, now that the trails are blocked, and with what dishonor and humiliation will our own people receive us? Life and honor lie in winning, death and dishonor in being defeated. Only consider, and you will see that fleeing makes dishonor more certain and life less so!" / This and the other things he said had little effect on the terror brought on by their peril. "What better place is there for me than here?" Villagrán finally cried, attacking as many as he could with reckless audacity so that he might die more honorably. / He was happy to sacrifice his life and avoid the rigors of judgment, with its insults and pointing fingers, which frightened him even more than death, for he had no desire to go about later explaining why he had been forced to retreat. Placing one's honor in question is itself a dishonor and stain, / and how well he avoided such an outcome, for they dragged him stunned from his horse to the ground. One tried to seize and another to kill him, but his good armor served him well. Others shouted, "Disarm him!" Men came running, and the noise... But whoever would like to know how this ends, I ask that they await me at the next canto. /

CANTO 6

The battle continues with the strange and varied deaths the Araucans inflicted upon the defeated and the little pity they showed the women and children, all of whom they put to the blade.

Neither adversity nor the cruel wheel of Fortune can force a noble spirit into shameful conduct. So it was with Villagrán, who having no other means, planned with his death to cut short the harsh road along which his destiny now led him. / Quickening their pace, his soldiers were withdrawing in a confused mass when they heard a new uproar and turned to see their good captain on the ground. Only thirteen of them, disdaining life, pulled up their reins and dug into the flanks of their horses, rushing back to attack all those thousands. / With more courage than I know how to describe, the small squadron quickly closed on their adversaries, opening a breach among them that almost put the battle back into play as they forced their way to where their wretched commander lay stunned by blows, utterly alone, and surrounded by a swarm of enemies. / Each Indian was striving to be first at this remarkable prize and opportunity. With the strident music of their fierce, discordant yells, they were like savage wolves atop a gentle, abandoned lamb, when suddenly the village mastiffs come racing to the commotion. / The tightly-packed barbarians had the unfortunate Villagrán in their midst, some blocking others as they tried to kill him, when the thirteen brave Spaniards suddenly broke through, now covered with the fresh, red blood of those left dead in their wake. / Moved by love of their captain, they hurled themselves forward to where he lay, boldly bloodying their keen-edged blades anew. Wounded Indians abandoned the circle, fearfully retreating this way and that, while others, more fortunate, maintained their positions and honor until they died. / As one dense mob was broken up and fled, thoroughly chastised, a greater horde immediately took its place. Villagrán had not yet emerged from his stupor, but his soldiers employed such skill, spinning about with their agile weapons, that as soon as he returned to himself they set him upon his horse. / Had they delayed any longer he would have been killed, and as it was he emerged in such poor shape that even though protected by armor his body was battered and bruised. Awakening suddenly from his swoon with thirteen Spaniards at his side, he forgot the danger he was still in and rushed amidst the menacing pikes. / Unchastened, he fearlessly cleaved his way through the middle of the enemy, protected by the band of companions wreaking havoc as they advanced, smashing and battering. Traces of the punishment they inflicted exist to this day, and the memory of that slaughter will remain for many years in Arauco. / Passing Mailongo, Bernal wounded him with a mighty slash from top to bottom, the steel helmet availing him little as the blade ran straight down through his chest, and Aguilera, slashing crosswise, left the agile Guamán badly injured. At this point fear opened such a broad path through their adversaries that the Spanish were able to ride away at full speed. /

[6.11] The fourteen headed victoriously to where the rest of the men were milling about in agitated confusion, terrified at the prospect of death. The arrival of Villagrán and the others could not stop what had already begun, however, for by now fear had gained great strength. / Seeing the fierce Araucans so bold and having no hope of victory, their horses exhausted and harassed in vain by vexing spurs, one of the Spaniards shouted at the top of his lungs, "To the plain! Don't let them corner us like this!" And with growing fear and folly some men headed for the road. / Like a herd of mountain goats driven into a narrow ravine by skilled hunters, and finding themselves surrounded and harassed by vexing shots, one suddenly sets off in flight and all the rest follow, just so our men began to flee. / One, two, and then ten and twenty rode wildly toward the foot of the slope, rushing in heedless disorder as if betting on who would finish first. Some courageous soldiers, not realizing their friends are abandoning them, keep fighting with steadfast hearts and ready swords. / They have no intention of running away nor does such a shameful recourse ever occur to them. Instead they continue to fight, disputing the uncertain outcome to the very end, their heroism delaying the Indians' fury and the inalterable decision of Fate, now fixed against them and bent on their destruction. / Thus they keep fighting and killing, opposing their destiny, and it appears the valor of the Araucans is beginning to wane while theirs, so harshly tested, gains strength. But seeing their fleeing friends and everyone disappearing as fast as they can, they, too, are finally forced to follow the same course, for persisting at this point would not have been courage but folly. /

[6.17] Now I want to change my song to a bitter lament more fitting the occasion, for the sorrowful cries of the people and their children still ring in my ears. More than their defeat, I mourn seeing swords so cruelly thrust through young girls, grown women, and servants, whose screams pierce the heavens. / The Spanish infantry and all those accompanying them on foot lost no time rushing away. Fear lent them speed, and more than was helpful for some, since amidst the tumult many lost their footing on the slope. Some went tumbling, breaking ribs; others plunged from steep crags and were torn to pieces. / A thousand were still stretched out along the road, and streams of blood watered the plain. Cries and shouts pierced the air, the clamor rising to the sky. With plaintive pleas and moans, their hands clasped high, they begged in vain for their lives, seeking mercy from the pitiless, inhuman barbarians. / The Indians kept chasing them with agile hands and feet, running down and wounding the wretched, helpless, and disabled, who called in vain on their countrymen for the succor to which friendship entitled them. However compelling these reminders of duty and responsibility, / if some turned back to defend them, seeing how far the others were getting ahead, they also found it best to flee. Neither the men they regarded as friends nor the women to whom kindness indebted them, nor anyone else with whom there had been an attachment or alliance, gained any benefit by calling out, pleading, or weeping. / Not stopping for anything along the road now reddened by their blood, our soldiers rushed ever more furiously on their way, giving free rein to the harried horses. Troubled neither by the voices of tender maidens nor affection's obligations, their only concern was that their mounts could not fly, / and deaf and inured to the cries they measured the verdant plain with rushing hooves. There were a few moved to compassion by this terrible, inhuman spectacle, who consumed by furious rage turned back against the Araucan army, now dispersed across the countryside and mainly burdened by spoils. / Resolved to die, they hastened to protect the timid sex, setting upon the barbarians so fiercely it cost more than ten of them dearly. This did not cause those leading the retreat to reconsider, however, for wanting only to press their advantage they had no desire to risk their lives. The farther they went the safer they felt. /

[6.25] Now the fighting erupts anew and is equally pressed on both sides as men meet lance to lance, sword to sword, and chest to chest. The Spanish are able to hold their own, for the Araucan army has become disorganized, doing what damage it can in confused pursuit. / Like a flock of crows scattered in flight across blue sky, which hearing the cries of a trapped companion feel sorry for it and come together with beating wings, circling down to help it, just so the barbarian battalion now heads toward the commotion. / Seeing the tumult and dust-filled air, those running in different directions abandon their pursuits and converge on the clamor of swords, each rushing to where he can be most useful as they encircle the Christian squadron with bloody blades. / The mass of Indians continues to swell, as does the din of weapons. With no one coming to help them, the number of our soldiers keeps falling, yet still they keep fighting with tremendous courage. No one denies himself to a hundred adversaries, nor can any Spaniard be seen who fails his duty in any way. / Instead, as if assured by heaven of their lives, they rush forward amidst the fury of murderous weapons, attacking without hesitation as they fall to the ground and bring down others, dealing and receiving terrible wounds. The enemy's superior numbers are overwhelming, but our men make up the difference with exceptional valor and courage, and / thus they hold out, fearing neither death nor their opponents' fierce rage as they resist the violence of fighters, fate, and fortune. Finally, unable to withstand so many without reinforcements, they are forced, delaying death, to return to the arduous road. / Waiting any longer seems folly with those in the lead flying off like the wind, which now seems a better option than reckless boldness. Many die along the way for lack of strength or a horse or of blood, the green meadow left stained with its traces. / The barbarians, catching up on foot with weakened, harried horses, test their strength against exhausted riders they knock to the ground. Other horsemen can scarcely trot, hampered by the infantry fleeing among them. / The weary walkers are happy to grasp hold of tails or sturdy stirrups, pitifully but vainly recalling forgotten friendships. When threats prove useless, the riders force them off with thrusts of their swords as they would hated enemies, for this is no time for friends. /

[6.34] An enormous uproar thunders through the valley. Clashing weapons and shouts can be heard, along with the sad cries of the Spanish and those who serve them, perishing at the hands of the Indians. There had never been such a bloody sacrifice, nor such strange and cruel dissections as those inflicted by the savage barbarians upon the twenty-five hundred who died. / Some collapse from horrible wounds, traversed from back to belly, others with their heads cleaved down the middle. Some die honorably of decapitation, while others, beseeching terms and accommodation, have their eyes ripped from their skulls and are forced to run headlong through the perilous crags.[39] / The respect due delicate, grieving women is not honored, instead with even more rigor they ignore their pleas and run them through with their swords. With no consideration for the pregnant, they aim their blows at their stomachs, and tender, unborn legs emerge from the wounds. / Those who are ablest climb the steep slope, while the sluggish and straggling pay, for life is only conceded the agile. Any who are slow or indifferent in the race are forced to remain there, for if they stop, death, coming angrily on their heels, strikes them down. /

[6.38] Although the incline was rugged and steep, many made it to the high summit. Here they found the pass blocked by logs and great stones, nor was there any other way out, since the hill was practically sheer all around, with one side battered by the sea and the other bordered by a high cliff. / The barrier had been hastily constructed of stout tree trunks, partially trimmed and skillfully interlocked to close off the narrow pass. The Indians, their weapons visible above it, were waiting on the other side, so arrogant it seemed they threatened heaven itself instead of other men. / Seeing the road barred and all hope lost, the Spanish were determined to force a way through or die. Placing their trust in God, they were drawing their horses back from the wall and then testing their power to knock it down at a run, while the barbarians tried to defend it. / Thus they were engaged, with

---

39   Decapitation was a punishment typically reserved for the nobility.

none of their efforts succeeding and no hope of escape, when Villagrán arrived, and seeing how little the useless assaults were helping and with no fear of death or any hesitation, made a final test of fortune. / The powerful horse he rode was a chestnut Spanish breed, broad in the haunch, deep-chested, and well-proportioned. It was also agile, high-spirited, and fast on the course, possessing great strength yet obedient to a gentle bit and bridle. / Villagrán raised its head while vigorously kicking its flanks. The horse sprang forward with furious momentum and struck the barrier, taking no more notice of it than a regular road and opening such a breach that all those who had made it this far were able to follow. /

[6.44] The enraged barbarians tried to defend the pass but in the end were unable to do so, for however fiercely they wielded their weapons the courageous Spaniards forced their way forward. Some went to the right, others, choosing a less lucky route, took a treacherous trail to the left that ended at a great cliff. / On this western side were two little-used paths that long ago must have been the way deer went down to the water. I say long ago, for by now they had eroded in a thousand places and ended at a precipice more than a hundred and twenty fathoms high.[40] / Some unknown natural law or the land's great aridity, or perhaps a great flood and inundation, had sliced off the mountain at this point. It was here that these misguided souls, consumed by fear and blindly fleeing death, came face to face with it, / for unsuspecting they tumbled down, and unable to hold back a single step, the one behind pushed the first and the third roughly shoved the second. Their numbers kept multiplying as bodies plummeted with violent fury until hitting the bottom, where

---

40   A fathom is approximately six feet.

they were torn apart. / Like fearsome Typhon straining to throw off the massive mountain that weighs him down, shaking his terrible body and dislodging huge boulders that noisily cascade from the peaks, with growing momentum, to shatter below, even so these wretched, misguided people plunged earthward and were crushed.[41] / Those on the good trail are desperately trying to reach the end of it. No one waits for anyone else, for slowing down would be folly. Rushing faster than they should, some riders and those on foot fall here as well. / Horses run loose across the plain, some of their owners fallen dead, others forced to give up their saddles in exhaustion. Some men ride rapidly, others in such a panic, hampered by the fear of death, that they can't find the stirrups and lose both horse and their advantage. / No one waits for them, instead they dig in their heels and hasten on, always following the one ahead, whom they can never seem to reach however hard they try, making vows and promises of fasts and pilgrimages, along with other things the Pope alone can fulfill, if only God will save them from the peril. / Horses cross the plain with their ears laid back and trembling. Their riders try in vain to spur them on, however brutally they tear at their flanks. Brother does not listen to cherished brother, for all appeals are in vain. Anyone gaining two steps on another is dying to advance another two. / Like someone who dreams of being inside a vast arena with a furious bull approaching, and distraught with terror, tries to flee the violence and run faster but cannot move at all, just so the riders try to spur their horses to greater speed. / The enemy keeps up the chase, always harassing them and creating great carnage. Those with good horses are fortunate, able to get

---

41   Typhon or Typhoeus was a monster imprisoned by Zeus beneath Mt. Aetna.

farther from their fury. One abandons his breastplate, another his lance, another, exhausted, lets himself be overrun, and the ferocious victors slake their savage thirst with his blood. / Those unfortunate enough to fall behind receive no help, not even from a friend. The most fleet-footed move slowly, while anyone whose horse can trot appears to rush ahead. All were afflicted by thirst and fatigue, when God, who comes to our aid when the danger is greatest, checked the enemy's momentum, as I recount in the following canto. /

CANTO 7

The Spanish arrive badly battered at Concepción, where they tell of their losses and defeat. Considering the great number of women, children, and elderly, and seeing how few are left to resist the powerful enemy, they decide to withdraw to Santiago. This canto also describes the sacking and burning of Concepción.

A breast in which fear has never found lodging is something to treasure, for fear diverts us from an honorable death to a life of infamy and dishonor. Courage in the face of calamity is admired by all, and while it is natural that the prudent feel fear, valor consists in overcoming it. / This is what those who kept goading their weary horses must have been telling themselves as they hastened on in such terror, and we'll believe them in spite of their silence since the spurs on their heels, together with their legs, arms, and panting all affirmed it. As for the Araucans, they were also out of breath and losing their fury and momentum, / and exhausted by their enormous exertions they began to slacken in the long, swift race. Finally, after six leagues, winded by their great tenacity, they let the enemy go. Our men, driven on by dread, found themselves as night approached near to where the Biobío reaches the sea, relinquishing its name and existence as a river. / Here on its banks they came upon a great boat secured by chains to an ancient pine, and after placing the worst injured inside, they set out across the water while the rest waited bravely until the coveted craft returned. Thus demonstrating the same diligence they had shown from the beginning, at last they arrived at the city for which all had been yearning. / One can imagine how they must have appeared, covered with wounds and in such great need, some with scarcely any faces left, others swollen by blows. Like some horde from hell they neither spoke nor answered, staring at everyone with burning eyes, their silence the best expression of their affliction. / Afterwards, when fatigue and dull-witted fear allowed them to speak of what had happened, the townspeople were completely stunned. Now sad sounds of shock and lamentation arise, augmenting the great disaster, and a harsh harmony echoes from house to house. / One weeps for a dead father, another for a husband, son, nephew, or brother. Women, crazed with terror, anxiously wring their lovely hands, their moans and vain protests increasing with every fresh grief. Crying children in their mothers' arms ask for their fathers. / Shouts and exclamations spread loudly from door to door announcing those killed in the fighting and the unfortunate ones who fell to their deaths. Young girls, wives, and widows, wailing with clasped hands and eyes raised to heaven, beg God in their terrible grief for the ultimate balm of death. /

[7.9] To such mournful sounds the people passed the bitter night unsleeping, but once day arrived their laments were interrupted by an even greater ill, for the blood-thirsty Araucans, swords in one hand and fire in the other, were said to be nearing the town, now blinded by fear. / Already garrulous Fame is loosening crude, misinformed tongues, exaggerating Lautaro's deeds and sapping the courage of his enemies. Already every Spaniard is practically trembling, a chill running through their spirits as they repeat Fame's reports, elevating the feeblest Araucan to the heavens. / Talk of retreat and of abandoning the sad city begins to spread, for some say they cannot withstand the enemy in battle. Factions begin to form, and general opinion approves abandonment, even as others try to counter feeble reasoning with sound arguments. / Two positions emerge, based on fear or love of wealth. A small number of wounded and dying claim the city cannot be defended. Concern for property and regular revenues restrains rampant fear, which soon reasserts itself, growing so strong it takes over completely. / The principal residents are clearly intending to abandon the town and their homes. The frightened citizens don't realize this yet, but keeping an attentive ear on the dispute, once they see what is happening they wait no longer, but immediately renew their excited cries and laments, their clamor rising to the stars. / One runs to his house, claiming the barbarians are already there; another rushes to cinch a saddle on his fastest horse. Maidens accustomed to seclusion wander back and forth in the streets without shawl or chaperone, lost and desperate for their mothers. / Like bleating lambs separated from loving ewes, hurrying without knowing where and stopping at every sound as they frantically run here and there, just so the delicate, tear-stained maidens seek their mothers with loud cries. / From time to time the sorrow, wails, and weeping resurge and grow louder. At other moments everything suddenly falls silent, and with all their senses focused on listening, people see Lautaro in every shadow and hear his cruel voice in every sound. Some raise a shout and begin to run, knowing only that they see others running. / It was pitiful to hear the sighs, laments, and uproar, which grew with every new detail fear sent winging on the wind. The frightened throng abandon their homes, possessions, and inheritances, their silks and tapestries, canopied beds and embroideries, their treasured bars of gold and silver. / If someone protests, demanding the city not be left defenseless, the leading citizens say it wasn't their decision. Shrugging off fear, an old man shouts, "Vile, cowardly people, disgrace to the honor and dignity of Spain! What are you doing? Where are you running? Who's leading you astray?" / This rebuke has no effect, nor does anything else the old man says. Everyone proceeds in spite of him, and the swiftest have already reached the road. It's only fitting that Fame now sing of a deed that deserves to be celebrated until written memory fades and life as we know it is no more. /

[7.20] Doña Mencía de Nidos, a wise, noble lady of great daring and valor, is a woman who won great fame when men did not. Bedridden and weak from illness, upon hearing the great uproar she boldly seized a sword and shield and set off after her neighbors as best she could. / The fleeing people were already making their way up the mountain, their sorrowful faces turned back to the homes and land they were leaving, accompanied by the sounds of endlessly squawking poultry, horribly mewling cats, and the mournful howls of dogs. Procne and distraught Philomela had once sung such sad songs,[42] / but doña Mencía, her blade unsheathed, followed the people with even greater distress, as her face clearly showed. Reaching their midst on the hillside, she stopped and cried out, "Oh, valiant nation, who through the rigor of keen-edged swords so gloriously won this land at such great cost! / Tell me: where is the bravery you displayed against those you now fear, and what has happened to the lofty ambition and immortal grandeur to which you once aspired? Where is that strength, self-esteem, and bravery, that natural valor on which you prided yourselves? And where are you rushing in such a state, when no one is even pursuing us? / Oh, how many times you were thought haughty, impatient, and reckless, facing perilous situations with no concern for your needs! What multitudes of adversaries we've seen you reduce to the yoke, accomplishing great enterprises meant to be immortal! / Turn a pitying gaze on the town whose foundations you raised with your own hands. Behold the delightfully fertile fields with their ready tribute, the rich mines and deep rivers with their golden sands, the lost cattle that now wander from hill to hill in search of their heedless shepherd! / Even animals bereft of reason understand enough to sympathize and show their sorrow, and savage beasts, their hardened hearts unused to feeling but now softened, pour forth their laments to the wind in an accusing chorus. / You're leaving behind tranquility, property, and an

---

42 In Greek mythology, Procne and Philomela are sisters who take revenge on a rapist, who then pursues them. About to be caught, they pray to the gods and are transformed into a swallow and nightingale.

honorable life acquired through courage and hard work, only to be a burden in someone else's home, where we'll receive a wretched welcome! What could be worse than being a guest for the rest of your lives? Turn back, for a life of honor or swift death is what befits the honorable! / Turn back, don't leave like this, showing how friendly you've become with fear, for I hereby vow to be the first to hurl myself upon the enemy's swords! I'll prove the truth of these words, as you'll soon see! Turn back, turn back!" she cried, but all in vain, for her advice struck none as sound. / Like a father who prudently tries to persuade his son against something harmful, vainly alleging a thousand reasons, his exhortations only annoying and fatiguing the incorrigible youth, just so the people, having already succumbed to fear, would not be counseled. / The Iaculan serpent passed less swiftly through Paul's forehead, losing none of its speed as it took his life, than the brave but odious exhortations of the lady of Nidos passed through the people, scarcely entering one ear before exiting the other.[43] / Deaf to her words and succumbing to impulse, they all walked away, the women without their fine shoes and trailing their skirts through the mud. For twelve days they proceeded like this, at the end of which they came to Mapochó.[44] But Lautaro, now rested, urges me on, for it has been some time since I spoke of him. / Neglecting him so long is unwise since he is not negligent when it comes to doing us harm, and thus let

---

43 Lucan's *Pharsalia* describes a variety of poisonous serpents native to the deserts of Libya, one of which, a flying snake called the *Iaculus*, kills a soldier named Paulus by piercing his temples (*Pharsalia* 9. 822-25).
44 Mapochó, the name of a valley where the Spanish founded Santiago, was also used, as here, to refer to the city itself.

us return to where we left him, where he gave up the stubborn pursuit. What occurred at that point would require many pages to describe in detail, / but exercising the brevity I have already shown I will limit myself to a few pages, lingering as little as possible and doing my best to avoid what's insignificant. I ask to be granted an attentive ear, for the account requires concentration if an inquisitive, agile pen is going to summarize the deeds of these barbarians. /

[7.34] Once the chase had ended the Indians turned back toward Pillán's joyful son, who had remained some distance behind as a matter of rank rather than fear.[45] After dispatching a soldier to the general with news of their victory, the army then made camp in the large, pleasant valley of Talcamávida, which had abundant pasturage and food. / One of the warriors with a farm in that valley happened to encounter a Christianized Indian on the road, and rather than boast of killing him, he took him home as a prisoner, where he began to harangue him as follows: "I'm going to grant you your life, you wretch, even though you don't deserve it! / You came to the battle to benefit from a warrior's honor, so how could you hide among the women and watch your comrades die at the sword? You must be a woman yourself, being so afraid of keen-edged blades, and thus I'd like you to assume that role as my servant." / He then ordered him to undertake the responsibilities of an obedient wife, seeing to the care of the household and food, while overcome by fatigue, he himself rested his weary limbs. Once in his bed, the sun made two full circuits of the earth and still the Araucan did not wake, / for he was buried in a sleep so profound he might well have been dead a thousand years. It was not until the sun

---

45   Pillán is the father of Lautaro.

brought light to the world on its third revolution that he awoke, and having asked for his clothes inquired if his meal was ready. The diligent servant answered that he had cooked it but that now it was cold, / explaining how the man had been in bed for fifty hours, oblivious to food or work. He also recounted what else had happened and said the meal was waiting if he'd had enough sleep. "I'm not surprised I slept so long without stirring," the barbarian replied, / "since ever-vigilant Lautaro, in order to make us more eager for your approach, kept us in battalions under such strict discipline we were forbidden to sit down from the time Apollo completed his course until sunbeams assured us of his return. / If someone moved from his post he impaled him without waiting for an excuse, and anyone who fell asleep from fatigue he hung between two poles. If a man took a single kernel of grain beyond his ration he died on the spot. With strict orders and rules like these he oppressed us, / and for fourteen nights we waited like that, propping ourselves up with our sturdy pikes and longing for your tardy arrival. Hampered by drowsiness and fatigue we endured that hardship until we knew you were coming, at which point our weariness instantly left us." / Noticing how quiet the surrounding valley was, he then asked if the army had departed. "They left yesterday before dawn with a great commotion," the servant answered. "I couldn't tell you why, although I've heard there are signs that the Spanish have abandoned the high-walled city of Concepción." /

[7.44] The truth was that the victorious Araucan battalions had marched on the city abandoned by its imprudent citizens, their passion for pillage spurring them to reach it in only half a day even though it was seven leagues away. / As the houses came into view, the troops split up so the looting would spread evenly through the settlement, now emptied of residents but still filled with their belongings, and the signal to start had scarcely been heard when the enemy fell on the town like a band of black starlings on a mound of golden wheat. / Plunged in profound silence, the deserted buildings await the fierce assault of the barbarians, who descend with great uproar at a run, the least greedy aspiring to the most lavishly furnished homes. Rushing for the doors, all of which stand open, / they quickly dash through the rooms, scrutinizing every corner. Not to be deceived in their search, many break into chests and force open drawers, ransacking tapestries, linens, and ornaments, silk beds with rich hangings, and anything else they see, for there is no one to impede or resist them. / Greeks did not ravage Trojan homes as cruelly, scattering Phrygian blood and ravenous fire as they plundered everything down to the last stone, as did the barbarians, whose vengeance and blind fury is so great that, not content with pillage, they destroy, demolish, and devour and still cannot quench their hatred.[46] / One climbs a staircase as others descend; one hurries to clothing, another to a coffer. This one pries open a lid, that one forces a hinge. Some refuse to abandon not only great bundles but small trinkets, arguing and brawling while others dispute and divide. Indians with spoils are seen on every tower, turret, and roof. / Even dense swarms of bees, with all the care and speed with which they use their secret skill to make honey in hives, coming and going as they diligently draw nectar from delicate flowers, cannot be compared to or provide a picture of the rushing men. / Some are not content to sack a house where the reward is assured, their insatiable avarice making another seem an even greater prize. In a greedy and foolish calculation they abandon

---

46 Troy was located in the kingdom of Phrygia.

the certain to seek the unknown, and when sunset comes and they turn toward home, having attempted too much they are left with nothing. / Unless it is safely secured, they also steal from each other what has already been stolen, for there is little friendship or trust among thieves, the greatest of whom always wants more. One drags away his spoils, another bears them on his back, not trusting his own brother. No one concedes to anyone else what he cannot carry himself. / Like thrifty ants prudently preparing for winter, busy with their cargo as they come and go from a well-filled silo, neither hindering nor stopping each other as those without burdens make way for those that have them, just so the greedy Araucans enter, leave, and hastily return. / Whoever secures a good portion does not wait, but quickly sets the room alight, not caring whether others still remain in the building, for whom they have no regard. Ravenous blazes spread with such fury that the entire wretched town begins to burn, fire running from house to house. / From high and low the flames pour forth, their horrendous sound threatening the skies, and the unhappy city is soon enveloped in the thick, black smoke of a ferocious inferno. The surrounding earth trembles, the fire howls, aspiring to its natural sphere, and ornately carved woodwork collapses, reduced to ash and cinders.[47] /

[7.56] The richest gold-producing city in all the world, famed for the wealth and great treasure within its walls, was thus lost. How many will now live with bitter tears! Far better had they stayed and fought, for poverty is a special misery among those who have known abundance and prosperity. / Some were earning ten, twenty, or even thirty thousand ducats a year. The poorest

---

47 The ancient world envisioned the earth as ringed by a series of spheres, including that of fire.

was earning a thousand, and no one less than that. Valdivia's portion would have been incalculable had the city remained at peace, for the mines surrounding it were filled with gold and easy to work. / A hundred thousand households served the abandoned city, able to extract such quantities of gold that amassing it seemed almost effortless. All this, together with their reputations, its citizens lost by slackening their sword arms, their herds, inheritances, and rich homes all turned to glowing coals. / The barbarians' shouts ring out. Unable to contain the joy in their hearts, they watch as the horrible inferno spares neither beautiful salons nor carved ceilings, not one of the multitude pained by seeing the destruction. Instead they sigh and groan, indignant that the buildings resist the flames for so long. / It takes so much time for everything to burn that the fire seems slow and listless, and they curse tempestuous Thrascias for failing to fan the weak flames.[48] Whenever a house collapses a terrifying yell rings out, rising up with the smoke and cinders to threaten the stars, / and the fierce conflagration grows so great that the clouds are singed. Thrascias suddenly arrives, violently shaking the trees, and drawn by the uproar Vulcan also appears with his bellows, covered with soot. Each does his part abetting the eager flames, and soon all is overwhelmed. / Nero's joy was not as great as he watched the fire take hold of Rome, so vast and powerful, a spectacle delightful only to such a man, nor did it give him the great satisfaction felt by the ferocious barbarians upon seeing the blaze spread and the miserable city consumed. / The explosions and furnace-like roar are terrifying to hear. Dense clouds of insufferable black smoke obscure the air. The horrible fire spares nothing, everything is consumed as lofty, ornate buildings collapse into courtyards. /

---

48   Thrascias is the north-northwest wind.

Yet even in their utmost joy the evil intentions of that vengeful people did not cease, for they left not a single plant standing nor anything else alive. As the fire reached its peak a messenger arrived in great haste from Leocán's son. His mission will be described in the following canto. /

CANTO 8

The caciques and principal warriors gather in the valley of Arauco for a general council, during which Tucapel kills the cacique Puchecalco. Caupolicán approaches La Imperial in the Cautén valley with a powerful army.

Someone of pristine honor, once offended, can never forget the affront, but afterwards remains withdrawn, their silence saying all there is to say. Even amidst great contentment the odious insult comes to mind, along with the fear that everyone is talking about it. / Had our people considered this and bravely fought back their terror, they would still have their wealth and homes or at least have perished in a worthy cause. A thousand vexations would not have troubled them, nor would they have become objects of ridicule among the common throng, who never mention merits but have no limits when speaking of faults. / Yet considering the unequal numbers of soldiers, the defenseless city with its dilapidated walls, and an infinity of other difficulties, in addition to visions of so many innocents being put to the sword, women, children, and virtuous maidens, all this may be sufficient excuse for having fled. / If not, perhaps what happened can be attributed to the just punishment of the Lord, who seeing the great excess of Spanish pride allowed their barbarous enemies, those they had previously subdued and oppressed, to deprive them of their land and possessions, placing their honor in doubt. / There were plentiful soldiers in Concepción at the time, but most of them had white beards and wrinkled brows and were useless for the cruel work of war. Few were of an age better suited to resist the great rigors of Mars, as well as the bias of Fortune, which now revealed itself opposed to them on every front. / Who could stand up to Lautaro's men, seeing how great their reputation had grown, with auspicious Fortune clearing a way forward to their advantage and our injury? They had no intention of stopping until they reached heaven's vault and brought down its monarchy, for such were the outrageous blusters, boasts, and threats of the intrepid Araucans. /

[8.7] I spoke earlier of how a distinguished messenger sent by Caupolicán had arrived at the desolated city of Penco, consumed by the ferocious fire, where he extolled the memorable battle and conveyed the general's thanks for such a great victory. / I also noted, without saying why, that Caupolicán had ordered Lautaro and his swift battalions to head to the valley of Arauco. This was because the senate and warriors were to assemble there to consider the best course of action, the fertile valley having everything necessary for a general council. / Lautaro set out with the army as soon as he received the command. Marching nonstop, he soon put a great distance behind him and was nearing Andalicán mountain when he turned toward the coast, eager to play a joke on those already assembled by approaching from that direction, looking and sounding like the enemy. / He proceeded so quickly that at daybreak he suddenly came upon the general's troops with such commotion and shouting that the startled warriors rushed for their weapons. Once the jest was recognized their alarm turned to joy and both sides put down their arms and ran to embrace each other. /

[8.11] Pleased and amiable, Caupolicán gravely received them and welcomed the good Lautaro with gifts and flattering words, extending to him every sign and honor of a cherished brother. The soldiers, who could hardly contain their joy, scattered in clusters along the banks of a limpid stream, celebrating, as was their custom, with festive drinking. / This continued for a while before the great senate convened to consider every detail of their plans and objectives, from first to last, but at the agreed upon time and place, once everyone had arrived, the land's principal men entered into the customary council of war. / The general was dressed in the uniform Valdivia had worn when brought before him: cloth woven of green and purple and richly embroidered with gold and silver thread; a battle-tested breastplate, well-tempered and embossed; and a helmet of bright, glistening steel with a profusion of emeralds along its crest. / All the important captains wore Spanish clothing. The common folk and soldiers dressed in whatever they had pillaged. Breeches, doublets, and tattered corselets were highly prized, and anyone not wearing

Spanish spoils was considered base and unworthy. / Thus attired, their arrival at the assembly was organized like a triumph. The council was attended by a hundred and thirty chosen caciques, seated by ancient custom according to the fame of their swords. Once the proud company had fallen completely silent, the voice of Caupolicán rang out: /

[8.16] "I'm well aware, gentlemen, that furthering our fame requires no lengthy speech, but only a brief acknowledgment that considering your sturdy hearts, I believe the invasion of Spain and subjugation to Araucan supremacy of the great Emperor, the invincible Charles, should be easy. / We see that the Spanish now know the weight of our iron-plated clubs, since neither in the field nor upon their walls do they await us. We know how weakly their swords cut and how poorly mail protects them against the strokes of our sharpened axes, and while their pikes may be long and sturdy, they've been matched by our own. / It's your intentions I now want to address, being well satisfied with your valor after seeing you level thick walls of tempered steel with nothing more than your chests, and I'll be the first to support your right to conquer mighty Spain and take the field against the whole world! / We'll study this people's god, and should he descend from crystalline heaven on high, as they say, we'll still open a broad swath among them by sheer steel, exterminating their species and progeny, for neither a divine army nor divine power or art will stand against us if we join together as one! / In closing, brave warriors, my determination could not be clearer: now is the time for those who would be my friends to declare themselves, for from this moment on any who side with peace should consider me their enemy!" Here he stopped, and having presented his plans, serenely awaited a reply. /

[8.21] Not an eyebrow had moved, and breath itself scarcely found its way to his listeners during Caupolicán's proud speech, which was followed by the usual flattery and ceremonial courtesy. It was now Lautaro's turn to speak, but he excused himself and Lincoya rose, answering thus: / "Lord, since first arriving in this sad world I've never felt such joy as I feel now, seeing manifest before us the noble spirit of your proud, invincible breast! Moved by such glorious thoughts, I declare myself your slave and captive and wouldn't be the king of heaven and earth itself if it meant ending the war! / In testimony to this I swear to follow and accompany you anywhere, and to never let any obstacle or adversity make me turn my back on the fatherland. Of this you can rest assured, my lord, for everything else will fail and come to ruin before the steadfast word of a man like me, given in pledge!" / Thus he spoke, and after him, ceding to their requests, the good Peteguelén arose, a venerable *curaca*, terrible when angered but affable and tolerant in peace.[49] Withered with age, he was still quite vigorous and lord of the beautiful, fertile plain that lay around them. With measured tones and grave countenance he began to speak as follows: / "Valiant warrior and perfect captain, I'll not yield in being first to test the excellence of this breastplate and see if my axe still shatters fine steel! But, as someone with experience, I assure you much remains to be done before the Spanish leave this land, and even more before we take the war to Spain. / It would be best, lord, to content ourselves with what past ages have bequeathed us and turn to driving out our enemies, who yet control the largest part of it. Afterwards, success will teach us how best to dispose our destiny. This is my opinion. Let anyone with a better idea propose it." /

---

49 A *curaca* is a chief or cacique.

[8.27] This cacique falling silent, Tucapel came forward burning with anger, and showing no respect whatever he arrogantly raised his voice and said in a challenging tone, "I'm not afraid of Spain, and I've no desire to be thought a man if all by myself I don't ravage these Christians, be they human or divine! / Throwing them out of Chile and decimating them in war will never be enough for me, and if they'll only await me I'll confound them in the deepest center of the earth! Wherever they flee, my club will follow, for this is what will hound them from this world! Therefore let no one try to scare us, for in accomplishing this I still won't have done all I can! / I swear to you by this right arm, if my cudgel sustains me for two more years, that in spite of heaven and by steel alone I'll fulfill every part of my vow, leaving no wall in Spain upright. And still my courage inspires me to more, for having leveled their vast land, I'll take the war to heaven on high! / There's no such thing as fate, which is nothing but a weakness that obstructs and holds us back, and believing in Fortune is simpleminded, for fortune lies in the strength of our arms! Heaven's citadel and its machinery will come tumbling down in pieces before Tucapel neglects a single point of his promise in this or any other endeavor!" / Peteguelén's blood, long cooled by age, now burned with wrath, and rising to his feet he begins, "Oh, arrogant man! Temerity without prudence was never courageous—" But Caupolicán, quickly recognizing the old man's rashness, discreetly interrupts him, encouraging others to speak. / First Purén and then Angol express themselves with no less bravado and recklessness. In such circumstances Ongolmo does not hesitate to express his own arrogant thoughts, and so from one to another the number of those with similar opinions continues to grow. Colocolo, who has been attentive to everything, now raises his voice, speaking as follows: / "Unripe youth provokes your fury, my sons, while the world has no more use for us elders than to give sound advice! The vaporous fumes of juvenile ardor and impulsive years no longer blind us, and thus more free we see what as youth we could not. / You, brave captains, priding yourselves on a single victory, have become so full of yourselves that other men now count as nothing. Calm your agitated spirits and curb such vain, ill-governed boldness! Don't be too scornful of the Spanish, for they don't sell their lives so cheaply. / You've been fortunate to defeat them twice, but recall that when they first arrived you couldn't withstand their forces and were routed more than five times, and you've seen what fourteen alone did on the field at Elicura![50] It will be no small feat or easy matter to recover the land and reputation we've lost. / We should strive with skill and good sense to redeem the fatherland and liberate ourselves, and lend less importance to your boasting, which is more likely to harm than help us. Oh, son of Leocán! If you wish to govern us wisely, I must advise you to temper this fury and consider the future with mature good sense! / The soundest counsel would be to divide the army into thirds and attack the hated town of Cautén from three sides at once. There are good soldiers defending it, but they are few, and once this stronghold is destroyed it will be easy to overthrow Valdivia since it has no harquebuses or cannons.[51] / Santiago alone worries me, but in time we'll find a way to penetrate it, and afterwards we'll easily destroy La Serena. Although we're always subject to what fate ordains, this is our

---

50 See 3.10 ff.
51 Valdivia here refers to the town of Del Lago; see n. 17, above.

best approach." With this the prudent elder concluded, and many found his counsel wise. /

[8.39] After him another *curaca* rose, a sorcerer named Puchecalco, considered an expert in divining the future. Burdened by decrepit old age, he drew a profound sigh from deep within and mournfully began to speak: "I offer ill-omened Eponamón as my witness for all I've said before and am about to say now. / Liberty was granted you for a brief period, most of which you've already enjoyed. This judgment, ordained by the stars, cannot be altered, for Fortune's wheel has now turned against you. Behold how inflexible fate now beckons with cruel servitude and terrible trials, and beware the many deaths! / The air is full of portents, and nocturnal birds disturb day's bright serenity with silent flights, auguring a hundred funereal prodigies. Surfeited with earthly humors, plants wither and produce no fruit, the sun, the stars, and moon all attest it, and a thousand sad omens provide confirmation. / Contemplating it all I don't know where to hope for consolation, for armed with his sword, Orion is threatening the land with terrible ruin while Jupiter has retired to the west. Bloody Mars alone now takes possession of heaven, signaling the approach of war as he fans bellicose flames here on earth. / Furious, unstoppable Death is already upon us with his wrathful hand, and Fortune, who once granted us her favors, now shows us a different countenance. Terrifying Eponamón, bathed in our steaming blood, stretches forth a hooked claw to carry us off stiff-spined to an unknown shore." /

[8.44] Tucapel, who was bursting with rage as he listened to the old man, could contain himself no longer. "Let's see if his prophesying protects this fool from my club," he cries, and raising his cudgel he brings it down and lays him out, never again to measure the course of the planets nor divine or foretell the future. / His act pleased him so much he was tempted to go after the revered senate, and I'm not sure why he didn't. Caupolicán, stunned and enraged, was completely beside himself for a moment, then regained his senses and fiercely cried out in a terrible voice, "Kill him, captains! Kill him!" / The men to whom he spoke took less pleasure in these words than did the hot-tempered hero, who realized the opportunity they offered. The tribunal was high above the ground, but his audacity had them leaping so urgently that of the hundred and thirty, a hundred had already jumped with him right on their heels. / Those who remained on the lofty dais, our history's most notable figures, never moved from their seats, but stayed there calmly watching, determined to reveal no concern over anything as insignificant as one man alone. Those who plunged from such a height soon thought less of their feat. / Covered in fine mail, Tucapel landed in the midst of this fearful throng like a lithe, agile leopard, and having made room for himself a mismatched fight began. Whistling and shouting, the crowd attacked the valiant warrior with sticks, stones, arrows, lances, and darts, as though he were a bull or savage beast. / Like a fencing master expertly wielding a two-handed sword as he wounds with singular dexterity in front, behind, to the left, and to the right, ever more confident in the swift delivery of powerful, accurate blows, just so fierce Tucapel spins about in the melee with his massive club. / Not satisfied with crippling and maiming, which are not enough to make him happy, the only figures that count for him are those unfortunate ones his cudgel turns to paste or dough as he smashes, bruises, grinds, and tortures, dislocating and dismembering, ravaging and exterminating. Blows rain down on him like a furious hailstorm, /

but the bloodthirsty barbarian makes his way through the swarm of weapons with no sign of fear. That day alone he crushed countless arms, heads, and proud spirits, splattering blood and fresh brains like fine rain before the wind, making no distinction between kin and stranger as he injured both equally. / With nothing more than his weapons he defended himself from that mob of Araucans, whose fear enfeebled their efforts to wound him. It was astonishing to see him leap and attack with such insane fury, dismembering those who could not defend themselves against the speed of his club. /

[8.53] Caupolicán was burning with such fury at this unexpected turn of events that he was determined to go down among the men, even though his gravity forbade it. But Lautaro was full of joy and admiration at seeing one man alone contend against so many, scarcely knowing whether or not to believe it. / With proper respect and eyes lowered, he therefore said to the general, "A favor, my Lord, I ask, if my valor and zeal merit it, and that is that you forgive Tucapel the enormous disrespect he has shown, since he's demonstrated his worth on the field to be more than all those men combined." / The general was dubious, but finally, considering who made the request, he changed his mind and answered with a cheerful expression, "In you he has found an adequate defender, and thus I pardon him." He then told his lieutenant to go down and order the fighting to stop at once. / Lautaro quickly did so, sounding retreat on his resonant horn. At this signal the warriors all withdrew, their retreat grieving no one except the intrepid Tucapel, who alone was regretful and unsatisfied with his work. Turning a fierce glare upon Lautaro, he said in a loud voice, / "How is it, good captain, that you prevent my punishing this vile rabble and avenging myself upon such peasants so that they acknowledge my valor?" Lautaro replied, "No one dare test himself against your arm after seeing the proof of it you've offered here! / Come with me now, and I assure you no harm or injury will befall you." "I swear such a fear wouldn't slow me a single step!" was Tucapel's retort. "It's my club that guarantees my safety, so let others come and go as they please. Fear is for women and children! But enough said, let's go where you like." /

[8.59] They returned to the tribunal together and ascended its steps, Lautaro first, with Tucapel showing no sign of what had just occurred. The wise general dissembled, treating him graciously, and Lautaro, speaking as follows, resumed the thread of the interrupted speeches: / "Invincible captain, having heard what the chiefs have proposed, I can't tell you the great joy it gives me to see such a show of determination! As to whether my own service will prove worthy, my efforts on your behalf will speak for themselves, and should they prove welcome, then offering my life a thousand times will be nothing! / These brave warriors are ready to help you restore our rightful land, for each of them is a part of it and their passion for war is unequalled. You are the source of all counsel, yet I cannot fail to advise you what seems best and most in keeping with the public good. / My vote is that you follow wise Colocolo's advice, presented in such prudent terms and so perfect in every detail. Therefore, great lord, let it be put into effect without delay, before the Christians learn of it, so that they're less ready to resist us. / And since Mapochó alone is feared, once everything else has been overrun, I beseech you in the name of Eponamón the powerful that the responsibility for ravaging it be granted to me.[52] I have measured that region step

---

52   Mapochó, as noted earlier, is another name for Santiago.

by step, and having fought alongside the Spanish I know their ruses and strategies, their methods and art, their favored times and places. / I ask no more than five hundred Araucans chosen from our army for the enterprise. Not a single soldier more need accompany me, and here I declare, before you and all these wise caciques, that I will duly deliver the city into your hands, along with the heads of a hundred Christian nobles!" / The vaunting barbarian closed with this, and after discussing the plan for some time and finding it worthy, they all endorsed it. Afterwards, they descended to where the people were waiting, eager for news, and a general proclamation was made regarding what had been decided and decreed. / Fourteen days longer they remained in that place in great celebration and festivity, busy with games and amusements and with wagering over who could drink the most. Afterwards, with the jubilant men in orderly ranks, Caupolicán marched with the vanguard against the Christian towns while Lemolemo commanded the rear. / The furious army approached La Imperial, which in spite of its strong site the victorious enemy intended to quickly deliver to death. The all-powerful, eternal Father disposed otherwise, however, ordaining a deferral of the merited lash, as you will learn by lending me an attentive ear. /

CANTO 9

The Araucans come within three leagues of La Imperial with a sizable army, but lacking divine sanction their plans have no effect and they return to their homes. Learning that the Spanish are rebuilding the Penco fort and city of Concepción, they move to attack them, engaging in a bitter battle.

If men now see fewer miracles than in times past, it's because there are fewer saints these days and Christian law is so well established. Anything beyond what's natural therefore frightens them, and they not only doubt those who speak of such things but question their credibility. / Should God want to cure the ill, they gradually recover in the usual way; if he uplifts the lowly and wretched, they rise by ordinary means; if he brings down pompous arrogance, it happens in a familiar fashion, everything in life following its natural course and measure. / In this we see God's wish to naturally work his will, nature being an instrument over which he alone has power. Those who believe through faith alone thus merit more than were they to see firsthand what they would never understand. / No friend of dubious tales, I now hesitate to recount a strange, miraculous event witnessed by an entire army. Yet while I have scruples about reporting it, for the reasons just mentioned, I cannot avoid doing so since the Indians will always affirm it. / In this we see, even today, God's sanction for miracles and for exceeding the natural order to further his sacred law, using wonders to convert a blind and barbarous people to the faith. /

[9.6] I spoke earlier of how the Araucan army set up camp on a suitable, spacious plain three leagues from La Imperial, and how Caupolicán decided to enter the town by force. I also described how God, displaying his clemency with a light rein, deferred the punishment of his stubborn and ungrateful people. / La Imperial lacked weapons, munitions, and food, and even though its soldiers were a select group, they were too few to put up a fight. Any force at all would have sufficed to ravage the town to its foundations, and once the barbarians had come within sight of it no one inside would have escaped. / Their army had decided to advance and the trumpet to march already sounded when the air suddenly began to roil and grow thick with melancholy omens. Clouds mounded on clouds, a turbulent rumbling arose, and the four winds unleashed their furious anger in violent gusts. / Torrents of rain, sleet, and enormous hailstones fell from the entangled clouds. Dazzling flashes, thunder, and

CANTO 9

bolts of lightning repeatedly rent the skies and cleft the earth. The relentless winds exploded, challenging each other to the utmost violence, and whatever the whirling gales touched they seized and carried upward in furious spirals. / Fear tormented everyone equally. No heart or spirit, though made of steel, was so unflinching it did not tremble amidst the intensity and confusion of such a storm. At this point Eponamón appeared to the Araucans in the shape of a hideous dragon, its coiling tail enwrapped in fire. In a vile, hoarse voice he began to speak, / telling them to immediately attack the terrified Spanish town and declaring that from whatever side they approached they would easily take it, delivering it to sword and fire and leaving no wall upright nor anyone inside alive. This being said and heard by all, he dissolved in smoke and disappeared. / The chaotic elements instantly curbed their turmoil, and the four unfettered winds retreated to their caverns. The clouds withdrew to their homes, no longer obscuring the sky and shining sun. Fear alone refused to give way even in the boldest breast. /

[9.13] The storm had ceased and a clear sky was cheering the soggy fields when the figure of a woman wrapped in a beautiful, shining veil was seen rapidly approaching on a luminous cloud. Her splendor was such that the brilliant midday sun was like a star beside the sun itself, / and the sight of her sacred countenance dispelled their terror and comforted them all. A venerable, white-haired figure accompanied her, from all appearances someone of grave and saintly life. Speaking in a delicate voice she gently said, "Where are you going, lost people? Turn back, turn back to your own land and don't go to La Imperial to wage war. / God has resolved to help his Christians, granting them power and authority over you, for you have been rebellious, ungrateful, and inhuman, denying him your obedience. Take heed and go no farther, for God has placed the sword of judgment in their hands!" Saying this she left the lowly earth and ascended to heaven through the great expanse of air. / The Araucans followed that glorious vision in its shining white veil with eager eyes, open-mouthed and scarcely breathing. It had scarcely disappeared when strangely, as when someone suddenly wakes, they looked at each other not saying a word, / and all of one heart and mind, awaiting no command or other sign and as if this were their sole intent, they immediately took the road for Arauco. They left in disorder and as light as the wind, for they seemed to feel painful flames singeing their backs, and thus they ran even faster. / I have inquired of many, my Lord, in an effort to recount with more authority this miraculous event, which took place in the presence of an entire army four years ago, on April 23, 1554.[53] / This is the truth in brief, presented as the barbarians witnessed it and unembellished by fiction, which has no place in such a matter. They regard it as a verified fact (which is not insignificant in attesting to it) and for two years afterwards experienced great hunger, illness, death, and other calamities. / The sea withheld its vapors, water was scarce, with no streams from the mountains, and the sun, abetted by the flames of war, destroyed the budding flowers. As the heat and drought spread, the arid land lay barren, deprived of moisture, and thus fallow it failed to produce its usual bounty. / This resulted in the appearance of an enormous, inhuman evil in the Araucan region, the eating of human flesh, the sin of parricide turning brother into food for brother and

---

53   Ercilla presents himself as writing these lines in April of 1558, four years after the events he describes. The date coincides with his arrival in Chile, on April 23, 1557.

mothers returning beloved children to the bowels from which they once emerged. /

[9.22] Having given way before the tempestuous heavens as I described, the barbarians returned to their homeland in the Purén valley and laid aside their weapons. In this region freezing winter overwhelms everything with ice, putting an end to the waging of war. / The soldiers disperse, leaving battlefields to seek their villages, and their fierce communal exercises cease as wet clouds cover the earth. When the burning sun ignites the quadrant of Scorpio, however, and the hills shake the frigid snow from their lofty crests, now crowned with new grass, / belligerent Mars brings forth his chariot and with a horrifying roar goes racing through ready Arauco, burning with bellicose rage. Urging on his iron-shod horses, he makes all the earth tremble as he pounds the mighty shield in his left hand with the bloody, sharp sword in his right. / Soon the warriors are stirred to fury and, leaving leisure behind, take up their arms. Drawn by the prospect of war, others join them from afar as all begin to sharpen their blades, tighten strings on their powerful bows, add weight to clubs, and test the hard ash of their lances. / Thus the people were engaged in the clamor of weapons, avidly awaiting the bellicose exercise they craved, when their most prominent men gathered to plan their campaign with the usual bouts of drinking, their ancient and deplorable vice. /

[9.27] As the council was discussing the State's well-being and growth, four soldiers with melancholy expressions arrived, informing them that a number of Spaniards were working at the ruined site of Penco to raise a massive, solid rampart. / "Oh, warriors," they said, "we come on behalf of the neighboring villages, authorized to promise that if you expel the Christians once again, we'll pay you a sum of money for the labor of your arms, and should you not achieve the desired result you'll still receive a third of the agreed amount. / Realizing how little resistance the rest of us can offer without your help, we've pledged our obedience to the Christians as we used to during unhappy times, not from violence or oppression, but because wretched as we are we know how brief is the dying breath that brings man's lot in life to an end. / With Arauco so close and Fortune's ever-turning wheel now fixed in your favor, docility seemed the best response to our situation. If cruel destiny spoils everything we'll still have time to die, for our arms won't be so weary that they can't pierce our own sides! / Now that our embassy and its great urgency is clear, we await your answer. We ask for promptness, since this is what will enable us to overwhelm the Spaniards' arrogance with least risk, before delay lends them strength." /

[9.32] One cannot describe the great contentment the embassy gave the caciques. Before it was finished they had all decided to accept it, but they patiently restrained themselves since speaking first was the right of Caupolicán, who having consulted them answered as follows in the name of the senate: / "We're rightly amazed by what we've just heard! Can it be true that there are still Christians so rash as to want to fight us? Forward, then! These brave chieftains accept your proposal and promise, and should they not bring the enterprise to a successful conclusion, they'll ask nothing for their efforts. / You can return with this response, which we'll not fail to fulfill, and as soon as we're organized we'll attack the Christians, making clear the contempt in which we hold them. Until that time, remain alert and prudently warn us of anything that happens." / The four messengers left, delighted to bear such a reply, and soon returned to their leaders, who were awaiting them moment by moment. The favorable response made known, the people hid their contentment and treachery, discreetly enduring their vexations while concealing their true intentions. / Behaving submissively, none took up or defended their cause, knowing the least costly course lay with the Araucan army, and thus with deceptive compliance they hoped for vengeance beneath a show of humility, relying on great secrecy to bring their plan to pass. /

[9.37] I've shown great negligence in not speaking of our people and the ravaged town, but since it's customary in this world to abandon the defeated, I've followed those favored by fortune, and had the present situation not alerted me I might never have remembered the others. / I spoke of Concepción's evacuation and the flight of its citizens, and having brought them to the end of their journey I had to leave them. I now return to that earlier account and the progress of their cruel destiny. During the time I ignored them they were in Santiago, / where having retreated they assembled the necessary materials and by a majority vote resolved to rebuild Penco's walls. They also raised a small number of soldiers, but at great effort and expense, whether due to meager pay or inordinate fear, I can't say. / Arriving at the deserted site, now covered with grass, they fortified a compact square in its center with a great earthen embankment protected by two double-sided bastions, each with a heavy cannon and stout cannonballs to guard the approach. / The surrounding population kept up their pretense of peace as they waited for the assistance promised by the Araucans, who were stealthily advancing. The approaching troops were no secret, however, for it was reported among the Christians that valiant Lautaro had already crossed the foothills with an organized force. / Purén was said to be among their ranks, along with Tomé, Pillolco, Angol, and Cayeguano, as well as Tucapel, who had no equal in arrogance or audacity among the barbarians; also Ongolmo, Lemolemo, and Lebopía, Caniomangue, Elicura, Lepomande, Chilcán, Leucotón, and Mareande. / All these well-known leaders were ready for war, along with two thousand tested soldiers chosen from the enormous army. All were outfitted with sturdy breastplates, solid pikes with hardened points, and iron-plated cudgels, as well as with steely axes and long-handled javelins. /

[9.44] Thus equipped, the warriors were making their way through the silent night's deep shadows under the command of vigilant Lautaro, who planned to arrive as the morning star brought cheer to the gloomy fields, before any warning or betrayal could expose their approach. / The Spanish had learned from a friendly Indian of the cruel purpose with which the enemy army was drawing near, however, and alerted to this as well as to the secret arrangements I described earlier, had prepared for battle, readying their trenches and ramparts. / The captain leading the Spanish was the noble Juan de Alvarado, from the mountains of Burgos, an intelligent, vigilant, and resourceful man endowed with great courage and prudence. Advised of imminent danger, he had wasted no time nor opportunity to hasten the preparations with singular speed and efficiency. / Once the soldiers were ready and everyone in position, he ordered nine of the most experienced fighters to quickly scout the countryside. Trusting in the overcast night, they approached the barbarian camp but were detected by the silent battalion, which raised a terrible yell. / The surprised shouting and sudden din of war, with blasting horns and drums, made the earth tremble and groan. The skilled scouts quickly returned by a shorter route across a low mountain to warn their companions. / Expertly reinforcing the weak parts of the fort, Juan de Alvarado positioned soldiers with harquebuses and pikes where most needed, and having seen to everything else and not wanting to appear afraid of the Araucans by waiting, he spurred forward with a squadron of light cavalry to intercept them. /

[9.50] The new day's light had appeared on the horizon and the sun, fresh from the gilded east, was reddening the clouds when Alvarado and his men left the fort to seek out Lautaro's rapidly approaching battalion. / Our soldiers had not yet advanced half a league from the walls and were descending a hill when they caught sight of the orderly Araucan army, their polished armor more brilliant than sun-struck crystal. The Indians' helmets were topped with tall plumes of feathers—red, green, blue, and white. / Who can describe their joy upon seeing the Spanish, at which they raised their right arms and sent a great shout to the heavens? Hundreds of barbarous instruments rang out as they quickened their pace, advancing with fierce pride as the countryside echoed all around. / The Spanish replied with the terrible sound of their weapons, descending the slope to attack more effectively on the plain with lowered lances, intending to force a breach. The bold display was in vain, however, since the disciplined barbarians kept close together, / and facing forward with their legs well-braced, they leveled a wall of pikes that not only withstood the Spanish assault but repelled it. Our men made an orderly retreat, and the Araucans, glorying in their fury, pressed their advantage in swift pursuit, / hounding them closely as they fought and resisted until reaching a narrow bridge. Here, about as far from the fort as a cannonball flies, Lautaro blew his horn, and at its familiar sound the obedient Araucans came to a halt. / He stopped his troops to await the midday heat, since a cool morning breeze invigorates men and horses, and having reordered their lines positioned them within sight of our troops, who had decided it best to return within the walls. /

[9.57] As the sun reached the exact midpoint of the heavens, inclining no more to one side than the other, and the air was filled with the shrill counterpoint of cicadas, the astute Lautaro formed his men into a tight-knit battalion, which let out a tremendous roar as it headed in orderly march toward the Spanish fort. / Lautaro preceded them with scornful audacity, gracefully trailing a massive lance, long and knotty, which little by little he adroitly began to balance and then to brandish so vigorously its two ends appeared to meet. / Not content to await the enemy within the walls, the small company of Spaniards proceeded outside, a row of harquebuses followed by a line of pikes, with cavalry on either side. They approached the barbarians with fierce expressions, and coming within range of each other the two sides rushed forward. / Deep-seated hatred spurs on the eager armies. Harquebuses are aimed and fired, covering everything in smoke, flames, and dust. Arched bows, tautly drawn, release multitudes of arrows, and clouds of darts are sent flying by strong arms. / Like opposing rivers that rush to meet in raucous torrents and for a time resist merging, although the more violent finally forces the weaker back against itself, just so our soldiers are caught up in the great flood of barbarians, / and unable to withstand the savage onslaught of so many, are swept away like straw before the wind. Now mingled in utter confusion, they enter the fort and a fierce hand-to-hand fight begins within the square of its thick walls. / Some of the Spanish, chastened by experience, recoil at being so narrowly confined, and preferring open ground move to the sides of the turbulent mass. The most valiant, confident in their arms, strive to protect the invaded stronghold, / for this is where they want to defend themselves or die. A few, determined to save themselves, set off on the long road leading away, or unable to endure another moment, rush down to the nearby shore. Giving into fear and base instinct, they quickly board a boat and raise the curved anchor, unfurling its sails to the wind. / Seeing it move away, those slow to arrive do not hesitate to throw themselves into the furious sea, deeming such a death less terrifying. If they could not swim before, they now learn how as they break through the waves, terror making frightened men bold. /

[9.66] The soldiers inside the fort defend themselves like worthy warriors, determined to die rather than be defeated and striving only for an honorable end. Emboldened by their resolve and not expecting to live, they go on the attack, creating such carnage among their enemies that the square becomes a lake of blood. / Lautaro, battling through men and weapons, had entered the stronghold first, killing two soldiers whom fate led his way that day. Lincoya was also wounding and trampling, but who can describe the audacity of Tucapel, who would have attacked heaven itself had a road or ladder led there? / He did not breach the fort by its gate or bridge, but rather with an audacious leap lightly cleared the open ditch and was instantly at the rampart's highest point. No one could match such a move, so all alone he attacked from that side, hurling himself into the middle of the walled enclosure as if guarded by a thousand companions. / Scarcely was he safely on the ground when the infuriated barbarian, wielding his massive, well-worn club, began to scatter his enemies. Neither fine mail nor breastplates were any help at all, and sturdy helmets, unable to withstand the rain of fierce blows, were dented, crushing the brains within. /

Some men he leaves maimed and disabled, others sorry for the rest of their lives. Sinking one man's head upon his chest, he smashes another's ribs and hips as if made of soft wax, pounding, crushing, and breaking backs as he throws himself brazenly into ever greater danger, fearing neither men nor weapons. / With an angry glare he turns on Ortiz, who had just killed a brave young man named Torquín. Fixing him with his gaze, he forces his way through the furious confusion of weapons, his club held high. Whose strong, dexterous arm and exceptional sword now sliced through the Araucan's cudgel, together with two fingers of his hand, I don't know. / At first he is so consumed with rage he doesn't notice the injury, but then as he brings down his arm he feels the absence of his fingers and club. A wounded Hyrcanian tiger is not as ferocious, nor a pursued lion as indignant as the Indian, who filled with resentment blasphemes heaven, hell, earth, and sea.[54] / Rising as high as he can on the tips of his toes, he draws back his arm as far as possible and violently brings down the remaining stump of wood, battering the helmet and head of Ortiz, who was coming toward him with sword raised high, but who dizzied by grave pain now falls senseless to the ground on his hands. / The barbarian, not yet avenged, sets upon him with terrible fury, and angrily seizing Ortiz's sharp sword with his still-strong right hand, lifts the edge of the Spaniard's corselet and runs him through from side to side as his soul makes the difficult departure from its bodily home. / Feeling his right hand crippled, he switches the sword to his left, and with his first blow

---

54 The fierce Hyrcanian tiger (from a region around the Caspian Sea) is a well-known figure from Virgil's *Aeneid*, where lovesick Dido, upon being abandoned by Aeneas, accuses him of having been suckled by Hyrcanian tigresses (*Aeneid* 4.365-77).

strikes another man down, for this hand was equally adept at wounding. And now like a skilled harvester reaping ripe grain, Tucapel, wild with fury, cuts through arms, legs, and necks. / Following wherever his anger takes him, he rushes furiously about, wounding and maltreating some and forcing others to retreat, routing a dense forest of lances. One of his blows strikes Father Lobo, who was fighting off four opponents at once, but who not seeing that dispute to the end, now renders his body to the earth and his soul to God. /

[9.77] Grave Leucotón, no less formidable, uses his heaven-sent valor to injure, stun, crush, and kill, for no one exceeds him in strength and courage. I don't know how to write it all down, for already amidst so much confusion my weary hand cannot sustain my pen, and thus much must be reduced to a brief summary. / Arrogant Angol, brandishing his great curved blade all about, wounds young Diego Oro. The heavy blow knocks him to the ground, but just as Angol raises his raging sword again, Juan de Alvarado checks its furor, piercing him beneath the arm. / The hostile saber meets no resistance, but thrust through an unprotected spot passes straight to his heart, opening a broad, bloody portal. The Indian's youthful, ruddy face is overcome with gloomy pallor, and a mortal chill unhinges his arm as his body strikes the ground. / Stalwart young Mareguano, who was angrily rushing about in all directions, arrived just as Angol, his first cousin and dear friend, surrendered to the cruel steel so skillfully delivered. "As our fortunes were always equal in life, let them be so in death!" he declares, / and turning toward the killer with sudden rage inflaming his heart and veins, he rears a massive beam of a club and brings it down on him with all his force. Alvarado, fearing his demise from that blow and having a sharp eye, quickly pulls his nimble horse to the side and the bludgeon strikes the ground. / Chilcán, Ongolmo, and Cayeguano, joined by Lepomande and Purén, are pressing our men so closely along one side that they gain great renown that day. Tomé, Cayocupil, and brave Pillolco, Caniomangue and Lebopía, Mareande, Elicura, and Lemolemo, all display the utmost valor. /

[9.83] At this point a rumor suddenly sounds through heaven's vault that victory has declared itself for the infidels, and the battered Spanish head for Itata, abandoning the ill-favored ground now covered with blood and enemies. / From all sides they flee, urged on by sharp spurs of fear, as the emboldened barbarian mob takes up the chase, harassing them in a thick cloud of dust and killing whomever weakness makes lag behind. / Spirited Alvarado keeps encouraging and inciting the men who stay to fight, but to no avail, for amidst such havoc they, too, flee death and enclosure. Some soldiers climb the mountain; some attempt the most direct route to Mapochó. Here and there a few brave ones still struggle valiantly with Atropos,[55] / for wanting only to die with honor they disdain a dishonorable life, delaying the inevitable moment with valiant swords and rare courage. Soon there will be no one left inside the fort, now emptied of souls but filled with bodies, as the few who remain commend themselves to their weapons and death. / Some fall with their sides ripped open, others completely run through. Others, covered in their own blood, collapse when none remains, and in the end everyone there is dead, torn apart by brutal steel. Let us now set out after those who are spurring their horses, for it won't be easy to overtake them. / Some give their mounts free rein

---

55 In Greek mythology, Atropos is the fate or *moira* who cuts the thread of mortal life.

on unfamiliar paths, others whip them along steep, treacherous trails that are no longer used, for fear is great and the journey long. With horrifying yells the barbarians breathe down their necks across mountains, forests, plains, and valleys, wounding, crushing, and killing. / Armed men from the surrounding area, who had watched impartially from the sides until they saw their rights assured, now raise a sudden yell and proudly join the victors. Wielding previously neutral weapons against the imperial standards, / they greedily pursue the Spanish, who ride faster and more furiously than the wind, not bothering to keep each other company. The great confusion created by fear carries them far from the road, scattering them across hillsides, meadows, woods, and pastures. / How fiercely those with the swiftest horses are envied, and how little it counts to have been their companion or longtime friend! Promises of money or goods are useless, for terror fills them so fully no room is left for greed. / Disdaining profit and showing little interest in avarice, they fling aside rich helmets and burdensome breastplates of fine silver, and ignoring all promises ply speedy spurs, wishing only for Icarus's wings, even if in crossing the sea they were to melt.[56] /

[9.93] Juan and Hernando Alvarado, swiftly retreating with valiant Ybarra, encouraged the disheartened, but not enough to slow their own pace. Borne on agile horses they forced their way through the obstructed road, yet however hard they spurred there was always one figure they could never elude. / Far ahead of the others, a broad-shouldered, intrepid barbarian named Rengo, a

---

56 In Greek mythology, Daedalus constructs wings for himself and his son, Icarus, enabling them to escape imprisonment in a tower. Ignoring his father's cautions, Icarus flies too close to the sun, the wax securing the feathers melts, and he falls into the sea.

young man of great repute, was chasing and harassing the three all alone as he boldly kept up the pursuit, accompanied by loud abuse. Even running through open country the Spaniards could not get a single step ahead. / "Whoa, whoa!" he cried. "Wait! Wait!" This was the extent of his Spanish, but impudent insults continued in his own tongue. For three leagues he ran like this, right on the tails of their horses, however hard they drove them, calling them infamous and despicable names. / High in the air he held a weapon the likes of which no one had ever seen, a massive, ill-trimmed beech branch the size and weight of a rafter, its head tipped with iron. The youth wielded this with less effort than an expert fencer a slender foil, / and whenever he overtook the horses with this mighty truncheon the blow was so brutal it almost broke their backs. Thus chastened each mount sped forward with no need of spurs, nor was a racing crop ever dreaded as much. / Although the scoundrel had ventured far from the safety of his friends and the other troops, this did not make him relent in his difficult endeavor. Instead he pursued them even harder, continuing to taunt and harass them with his swift feet and massive club while slandering the Spanish nation in Araucan, understood by the three, who fled even faster. / Twenty times the Christians abruptly turned and attacked him, only to be violently scourged by his diabolical dexterity. Meanwhile, the rest of the insolent Indians, no laggards in the pursuit, were getting closer, and the three would again take up the race, with the barbarian and his cudgel close behind. / Neither the rugged mountain nor rocky slope impede the young man's speed and zeal. Instead, like the Puelche, accustomed to running after wild beasts on a wager, he chases, harries, and afflicts them.[57] After ten miles of pursuit,

---

57 The Puelche are an Indian group who live in the region's mountains.

he was finally forced to stop on the damp bank of a river that crossed the road on its way to the sea. / The barbarian battalion had halted earlier; stubborn Rengo alone persisted, not wanting to give up even though no one from his side was left in sight. The three weary Christians were crossing the broad ford when Rengo loaded his slingshot with a weighty stone, / and having fixed his truncheon in the moist earth, twice circled his arm and let fly with the great, rough rock. The mountains resound with a deafening roar as the river nymphs stir in the tranquil depths of the crystalline waters, raising their golden tresses to stop and stare. / The relentless barbarian neither pauses nor slackens in his efforts, but now in water above his waist abuses the Spanish with whistles, shouts, and heavy stones, hounding them so closely he prevents their horses from drinking. "Enough now, come out of there!" he shouts. "Come! I'm waiting for you here on the bank!" / Alvarado, seeing Rengo so arrogant and impatient with such proud obstinacy, says to his two companions, "Oh, what shame, when a single Indian can chase and get the best of the three of us! It isn't right that such be said of Spaniards, so let's turn back and never leave unless we kill him!" / Thus he spoke, and pulling their reins about they cross the ford a second time, determined to die or slay him as they goad their weary horses. Seeing the furious anger with which they turn, the Araucan, forgetting his weapon and resolve, quickly stirs his flying feet, / and the three chase him at full speed for a great distance along the sand. They go to the trouble in vain, however, since the Indian moves faster than they, and finally, lacking not determination but strength, they wearily draw up their horses at a perilously steep slope where the brave barbarian confronts them. / With his back to a great ravine he now boldly turns, and in the absence of his customary club repeatedly deploys his slingshot, assaulting them with mockery, whistles, and flying stones without their being able to attack him in return, for the place is precipitous and he more agile. / Alvarado, realizing that what he longs for so ardently is not to be, turns away from the intrepid barbarian, who remains unwillingly behind. Once again the three Spaniards cross the calm ford and head for the road, saddened to see Fortune so adverse in everything. /

[9.109] It had been a long while since Lautaro's soldiers had given up the pursuit, and the Spanish were proceeding in no particular direction, like sheep separated from their flock. I must leave them, as well, as I have before, but will return to them later. / Now I want to accompany the Araucan warriors, lucky and cheerful for the moment, and as is customary, turn away from the unlucky and defeated. What so many have done before I also intend to do, following their well-worn track, for time and custom have convinced me and all the world exclaims, "Long live the victors!" / How typical it is to flee the downtrodden and follow the high and mighty, those favored by fickle Fortune, only afterwards to be laid low! In the end, reduced to their true value, all such favors are borrowed and must be repaid sevenfold, as the next canto will clearly show. /

CANTO 10

Proud of the victories they've won, the Araucans organize public festivities attended by people from near and far, who compete in great contests.

How bold the fainthearted become when fickle Fortune is favorable and shares her largesse, turning an abject woman into a Mars, while elsewhere she confounds manly courage, making level ground seem a mountain! / One moment the Spanish are praised to the skies and exalted by their famous deeds, with no sign of any change; the next they're brought to ruin, their good fortune turned to misery as they're pursued not by bloodthirsty Mars but by the timid sex! / Behold their luck so altered that men unafraid of heaven itself are chased with virile valor by women adept at the spindle, whose hands accustomed to homely tasks now brandish brazen lances and inflict cruel wounds, driven on by a happy fate! / I'm speaking of the women who had hidden on the mountain for the end of the battle, who once they see the Spanish rout, come down to the plain, wounding the sky with their shouts. Arming themselves with alien courage, they shrug off feminine fear to seize the swords of the dead, / and in the midst of the melee, intoxicated with victory, their gentle reticence turns homicidal. Their breasts neither hinder nor weigh them down as they run, any more than their eighth-month bellies, rather the more pregnant they are the faster they fly. / The last to arrive, unable to move more quickly in such condition, considers herself unlucky and calls on heaven for help. And if the women are rushing like this, just imagine the barbarian mob! Such is the origin of the land's women also going to war: / they accompany their husbands, but do nothing as long as the outcome is uncertain. If their enemies are defeated, however, they bravely set off in pursuit, testing the feeble strength of their swords on the exhausted and making them die a thousand different deaths, for the cruelty of a woman is truly cruel. / They followed our soldiers until the chase ended, then returned to the town, which had already been sacked. Unable to do further harm, they now climbed on abandoned horses that wandered about the meadow and made a game of mimicking their owners. / Some pretended they were fighting, some fleeing, and some went running after those in flight. Others fell down as if dead, or tried to run and pretended they could not. Thus the happy people entertained themselves, putting aside troublesome toil until the next day's sun rose on the hills, when the general arrived with the rest of the army. /

The two groups hastened to embrace each other, but envy creased the brows of some in spite of their efforts. The victors proceeded to generously share their spoils, for such can prosperous fortune accomplish even in vile, unnatural hearts. /

[10.11] Caupolicán decreed that a solemn festival be held in that place for the Araucan warriors, no commoners mixing among them, and with every sign of contentment the men spent several days in games, contests, dances, and other diversions. / Once the amusements ended, they set out for the valley of Arauco, where the entire province's soldiers were gathering for their customary celebrations, set to begin in two weeks. A number of arenas had been laid out here and valuable prizes announced for those victorious in them, prizes worthy of competition. / The celebration's fame outran diligent messengers, and before long the nearby inhabitants, their neighbors, and even outsiders had learned of them. A great multitude gathered, the number of warriors growing so large that the tents of those arriving covered the mountains, valleys, plains, and riverbanks. / At last the dawn of the fourteenth day, so eagerly awaited, began chasing away the somber shadows, restoring color to the countryside, and a boisterous company of valiant youth, full of juvenile ardor and impetuous blood, appeared on the field for the competitions. / The order of the prizes was announced with solemn pomp. The first was a lustrous saber garnished by a skilled silversmith, designated for the man whose arm was mightiest and exceeded all others in hurling an enormous, heavy lance. / A helmet of fine silver covered with enamel designs, rimmed with pure gold and topped with tall colored feathers, would reward the wrestler left standing and lord of the field after a strenuous contest. / An eager, spotted wolfhound, its collar set with sharp iron spikes and closed by a medallion, awaited the runner who armed with both speed and weapons was first to reach a trembling banner that marked the end of the course a good mile away. / A skillfully-crafted, sinewy bow, together with a golden quiver that hung by two damascened clasps from a beautiful, broad strap, was the rich prize reserved for the archer whose well-aimed arrow could pierce the curved beak of a soaring parrot.[58] / A glossy black stallion with a white-streaked tail, haltered and champing at the bit, was destined for him whose quick and agile arm most skillfully wielded a club. Caupolicán was designated the judge and master of the games, and now a fresh blast of the trumpet called the contenders to compete. /

[10.20] The cheerful horn had scarcely sounded when young Orompello, already in position, gracefully throws off his cloak to reveal a beautiful, well-proportioned body, a formidable lance in his strong right hand. Lepomande, Crino, Pillolco, Guambo, and Mareande quickly take their places beside him, / and their lances having been certified as equal by the judges, these six, running in an even line, draw back their right arms as one and hurl them with six groans. Borne by impetuous force the shafts fly forth with a resounding roar, breaking through the air and rising heavenward before falling with the same fury to the ground. / The first to lose strength and fall back to earth is Pillolco's. After this comes Guambo's, Lepomande's is third, Crino's fourth, and Mareande's fifth. The last, its great momentum propelling it farthest, is

---

58 The funeral games described in Virgil's *Aeneid* culminate with an archery contest in which a target bird is tethered to the top of a ship's mast: the first contestant misses the bird but hits the mast; the second severs the cord attached to its leg, allowing it to fly free; a third pierces it mid-flight (*Aeneid* 5. 485 ff.).

powerful Orompello's, which continues five arm-lengths ahead. / Now another six men among those considered strongest take up their lances, and although they make a tremendous effort to surpass the leading cast, they cannot. Six more after these and still another six try, but all to their chagrin are left behind. To spend no more time counting them all, I can vouch that more than a hundred made the attempt. / No one could come within six arm-lengths of Orompello's throw until Leucotón, a great burly man, seeing the competition slacken, proclaims in a loud voice, "There's no doubt that I'll lose, but since you're all watching, I might as well see what this arm of mine can do and find out how far my star will take me." / Having said this and asked for a lance, he quickly assumes position, and giving an agile thrust, offers an impressive display of his strength. Impelled through the air, the lance flies off like a heavy ball fired from a cannon or like furious, breaking thunder rolling through heavy clouds, / its precipitate flight passing four arm-lengths beyond the farthest mark. Once its iron tip pierces the ground, the lance stays trembling there a long time, and a shout rises up from the crowd. Many immediately rush to study the cast, praising the thrower and his strength. / Some measure the great distance by foot and examine the lance's weight; some exalt as miraculous the strength of such a mighty arm. Others head for the prize, while others are already singing the victor's praises, extolling Leucotón by name and celebrating him in loud voices. / Orompello leaps up and angrily cuts through the commotion. "I've not lost yet," he cries, "nor is the first shot alone what determines the winner!" At this Caupolicán extends his baton and quickly quenches a smoldering fire, for Tucapel had joined the youth, who was his cousin, and others had gathered around Leucotón. / Caupolicán shows his impartiality as judge, quickly and discreetly placating Orompello's fury with gentle, flattering words. Arguing no more about it, and in accordance with the rules, the curved saber is justly cinched to the side of the winner, Leucotón. / The dispute having ended with Leucotón victorious, Orompello moved to the side, ashamed and embarrassed, but he prudently pretended otherwise, hoping for an opportunity to enter a new and more decisive contest with his opponent. / Orompello had been athletic and high-spirited since childhood. He was easygoing and even-tempered, but when circumstances called for it, full of valor. Many of the onlookers preferred him for his courage and noble lineage, for he was also the son of the venerable Mauropande, as well as cousin and great friend of Tucapel. /

[10.32] With silence reestablished and the field cleared of competitors, dexterous Cayeguano, another impressive youth, comes forward to prove himself in wrestling, and a moment later Torquín, gifted with both strength and agility, eagerly emerges from the other side. Both are wrestlers of great skill. / The signal being given, the gallant barbarians methodically begin to move. Now you see them draw together, now move apart, now stretch forward, now lean back. Carefully probing this way and that, they twist about seeking a hold or pull away, feinting, turning, coming back, or standing firm, until finally they violently seize hold of each other. / Grips fixed and tightly held, each tries to gauge the other's strength, and inflamed by angry ardor they begin to circle the field. Feet together and interlocked they veer this way and that, neither able to gain the slightest advantage in spite of how hard they try. / Thus the matter stands when the shrewd Cayeguano extends his right leg, and eager to cinch it, Torquín shifts forcefully to that side. His skillful opponent pulls the leg away just in time, however, and with nothing but empty air for support Torquín's own momentum lays him out at his enemy's feet. /

[10.36] After this robust Rengo presents himself, throwing off his clothes to reveal his enormous stature, powerful arms, and bulging muscles. The startled crowd watches attentively, since of the four most famous warriors he's the only one never surpassed by anyone else. / Giving his shoulders a great shake he readies himself for the challenge, and seeing the current champion goes out to meet him with spirited determination. Cayeguano eagerly advances to the middle of the field from the other side, and the two brave adversaries come together, striving for the best hold. / For a while the people are perplexed and the uncertain victory in doubt. But then Rengo gives clear proof of his power, for grasping the wretched Cayeguano tightly in his unyielding arms he turns him this way and that, his mouth gaping open but unable to get a breath. / Lifting him off the ground as he squeezes, Rengo keeps him suspended in the air for some time, until finally, lacking color and breath, Cayeguano's arms and legs go limp. Seeing him beaten, intrepid Rengo, expecting nothing less than victory, with little effort brings him crashing down, imprinting him in the dirt. / Cayeguano was taken senseless from the field and carried on men's shoulders to his tent. Everyone was extolling Rengo's great strength and victory with loud cries, but the noise died out and they quickly returned to their seats when they saw Talco in position and ready for a bout. / This Talco was a great master of competitions, with sturdy limbs and a ferocious countenance. He was agile in wrestling, skilled with weapons, and although arrogant, both swift and brave. Yet with all these gifts, Rengo was stronger, more nimble, and more accustomed to such robust exertions, as his appearance revealed. / Talco advanced first, coming out quickly. Rengo stirred, but slowly. One trusted mainly in his skill, the other solely in his strength. At a moment when Talco was less alert, Rengo, with remarkable lightness, suddenly gave a great leap, catching his enemy unaware. / Like a watchful tiger that sees a swift, muscular leopard approach and indolently begins to move with measured steps, making hoarse sounds, its neck lowered, and then in an instant leaps on the leopard with impetuous fury, seizing him in his claws as he overwhelms and subdues him, / just so Rengo seized Talco, who before he could defend himself was pinned on the ground so violently his hip was injured and his back almost broken. Seeing him thus, the winner let him go and returned to his place to await the next man to come forward, satisfied with leaving the field after such a display of exceptional strength. / No one had the audacity to face the barbarian, however, and since night had come the competition was deferred until the following day, when dawn's chariot would gladden the fields with new light.[59] The sounds of instruments rang out, and the seats at the banquet tables were soon filled. /

[10.46] The next morning raucous music accompanied Caupolicán from his tent to the site of the contests. Rengo took a turn outside the arena to enhance his fame, then made a fine entrance and assumed his seat for the bout. / For a good two hours he remained in position without anyone stepping forward, for not a soldier could be found who seeing him sitting there was willing to occupy the empty place across from him. But having watched all this, Leucotón, who had been waiting to see who was strongest so that his own valor might be enhanced, now gravely entered

---

59   Apollo or Helios drove the sun chariot across the sky each day.

the ring. / Immediately there was confused murmuring and soon a great clamor arose among the chattering crowd, seeing these two facing each other and knowing the great strength of each. Assuming a crouch, Leucotón advances to receive Rengo, who confidently steps forward with bold determination. / Unrivalled in daring and fortitude, the two spirited warriors begin the contest, sometimes pressing each other closely, at other times restraining themselves and holding back. Warily watching and prepared for every trick they circle about, but it's not long before they attack, clasping each other in a compact knot. / Joined chest to chest they exert their utmost efforts, and gripping one another tightly they now stand firm, now hurl themselves all around, entangling and locking first their left legs, then their right. Whatever strength, concentration, or art they employ is not enough to gain either any advantage, however, / and turning furiously this way and that they resist each other's efforts, struggling, groaning, and wheezing so much their limbs grow sluggish. Their weary knees, made only of human flesh and bone, tremble and buckle from fatigue, unable to endure such continuous fury. / Completely bathed in sweat and gasping for air, the two press on, chests resonating hoarsely from their sudden, violent movements. Striving to summon new strength, they struggle with ever growing ardor to bring the bout to an end and win both honor and the silver helmet, / but no clear advantage or weakness could be found in either, since both were in the flower of youth and equal in strength and skill. Then, much to his disgust, Rengo's fate and flagging fortune, favorable until then, caused him to lose all right to the prize and its honor. / At one side of the arena was a hole left by a rock dislodged by the constant tread of the crowd. Weary Rengo, not seeing this, stepped in it, and as a pine falls wounded by an axe, with no less of a crash he came tumbling to the ground. / A ball does not bounce back from hard-packed dirt with as lively a leap, nor does an eagle falling from high above on its prey rise back into the air with such swift flight as the enraged Rengo, who threatening the heavens and beside himself with shame, had hardly got back on his feet when he furiously closed on Leucotón. / Like fearsome Antaeus, who being thrown by mighty Alcides in their terrifying wrestling match gains new strength and redoubled courage from his mother, the earth, thus furious Rengo, having briefly touched the ground, advances upon his opponent in an ultimate display of his well-known power.[60] / Feeling such indignation at the gravity of the situation, in such a public setting, he is inflamed by ardent fury, his strength increases, and he becomes so enraged and impatient that Leucotón retreats, scarcely able to resist him, a development whose conclusion you will hear in the following canto. /

---

60   Antaeus was the son of Poseidon, the god of the sea, and Gaia, goddess of the earth. In wrestling with Alcides, or Hercules, his mother would renew his strength whenever he was thrown to the ground, and he was only defeated by being held suspended in the air.

CANTO 11

In this eleventh canto the festivities and disagreements come to an end, and Lautaro marches against the city of Santiago. Before arriving there he builds a stronghold where the Spanish attack him, leading to a bitter battle.

Hearts that have never shown weakness reveal their true grandeur if publicly disgraced, rallying weary limbs and dismissing exhaustion to easily accomplish that which earlier, my Lord, they found arduous. / Thus it happened with Rengo, whose shame at falling imbued him with such strength that, filled with fury and burning anger, his vigor and courage redoubled, and the powerful adversary against whom he had been unable to advance a single step he now lifted and carried a hundred feet without letting him touch the ground. / His wrath would have grown even greater and the arena been in an uproar had not Lautaro, fearing this, quickly come down from the tribunal carrying Caupolicán's baton. He separated the two fighters, and considering their anger it was not insignificant that they showed him such respect. / The festering dispute quelled with no further disturbance, Rengo's honor was restored, although he remained without any right to the helmet. Every aspect of what happened had still not been settled nor the crowd dispersed, when young Orompello suddenly bellowed, "Now it's my turn and the next bout belongs to me!" / Still remembering the lance throw and impatiently awaiting just such a moment with Leucotón, he now leapt lightly over the barricade and entered the arena with great self-assurance, confronting his enemy face to face. / The noise and murmurings instantly increase, for everyone knows how unhappy Orompello is with the mighty Leucotón. Some fear the two may come to blows, but no one dares intervene; instead they empty the ring and fill any seats still left open. / The crowd, eager for the contest, inclines for the most part to Orompello, observing his lithe body and well-formed limbs, uncovered just at that moment, along with his grace, curly hair, and handsome, youthful face, for he had not yet reached his twentieth year when he challenged Leucotón. / Based on appearances, the spectators judge the strength of the two unequal, comparing the stature, musculature, and maturity of the one with the entirely different physique, tender age, and appealing adolescence of the other, even though Orompello's bold attitude belies such an opinion. / Taking position, he proudly awaits the sound of the trumpet, like a spirited horse awaiting the signal for a race, or like a falcon on the bank of a river, which seeing the distant white of a heron is gladdened and vigorously preens itself, ready to launch from its hunter's hand. / Thus valiant Orompello, eager to satisfy his longing, awaits the happy signal to begin. Noticing a delay and worrying that some difficulty has arisen, considering how long it is taking, he suddenly heads straight for Leucotón, who is not slow to receive him. / Idle murmurings change to utter silence and no one dares make a sound as the two champions proceed to the middle of the ring to test themselves one on one. Just as when a wolfhound and ferocious mastiff bare their teeth, advancing with low growls and rigid spines, their eyes on fire, to tear each other apart, / thus infuriated and waiting neither for the trumpet nor their sponsors, driven by courage and rancor, the two men meet halfway. Momentarily equal, they instantly seize hold of each other with all their might and skill, clinching their powerful arms and interlacing their legs in tight knots. / Dissimilar but balanced strength carries them forward, hurling and turning them about in all directions. At times they appear not to move at all but seem nailed to the ground, and wherever they plant their feet they leave tracks. Digging into the hard earth and gripping each other tightly, knee to knee, their bones and ribs are heard to crack. / Seeing the tenacity and singular strength of his tough opponent, each man deploys all the valor and dexterity he can at such a moment. Neither gains any advantage as they circle around the arena, but at one point, shifting back and forth so much, they both fall to the ground. / The fall is so quick and their instantly getting up so swift that the most attentive viewer, moving an eyelash, would not have seen it. To judge it an advantage or sign of defeat for either is thus not possible, since Leucotón only touched the ground with his knee and Orompello with his hand. /

[11.16] At this point their sponsors intervene, and leading each man back to his side, they resume the match through dispute, arguing their points and reasons as others from both factions gather behind them, adding to the contention and tumult. Some give the prize, honor, and glory to one, some sing the victory of the other. / Seeing what is happening, Tucapel, seated next to Lautaro, leaps into the ring, ironclad club in hand, and with his usual audacity cries, "My cousin won the prize, and if anyone wants to dispute this, I'll soon make him see how little he understands! / The award is Orompello's! Whoever thinks himself able to nullify my vote, let him step forward, for here we are in the arena and I defy and challenge him!" Leucotón arrogantly retorts, "I'll tame your crazy bravado and vain vaunting along with your foolish raving, which I've been wanting to do for a long time!" / "It's me you have to deal with," Orompello tells him, "for we've already begun the match!" "I'll take on both you and your cousin!" the enraged Leucotón replies. Caupolicán steps forward at this point, for after watching everything from his lofty seat he came down amidst the commotion to interpose his authority. / Seeing the great Caupolicán approach, Leucotón and Orompello both lower their rancorous voices, and each goes back to his side. Tucapel still brandishes his club, however, and having no interest in any arrangement and filled with diabolical fury, he does not grow quiet, but defies all the world to battle. / Pleas and terms, whether from the son of Leocán or anyone else, mean nothing to him. He demands they give the helmet to Orompello as the victor and more courageous of the two. He then insists that he himself be left in the ring with Leucotón to decide their dispute, with one or the other of them losing his life. /

[11.22] Placed in this predicament, Caupolicán, driven into a furious rage, tells him, "I'll see to it you maintain the respect due my person and authority!" Tucapel answers, "And I swear I'll not back down from fear, so anyone who disagrees with me is free to do what he can! / I'll respect you if you respect the right of what I justly claim and as long as you calmly consider the case with a fair and open mind. But if you brashly decide it contrary to reason and twisting justice, not for you nor your position nor all the world will I cede a single point of my rights!" / Caupolicán, having lost all patience, moves resolutely toward Tucapel, but Colocolo, the experienced and always somewhat fearful elder at his side, respectfully restrains him, saying, "My lord, have you so forgotten yourself and all our well-being that you would reduce your authority to the strength of your arm? / Think of what's at risk, my lord, and how much contention there already is. You know Tucapel's foolishness and the power of his kinsmen. Don't remedy with innocent blood what prudence can solve, but give Orompello the disputed prize and another of equal value to his rival. / Should you decide instead to hazard the future on bloody measures, even though inflexible Fortune may turn her wheel to your liking and let you punish this rash juvenile fury, in the end your strength will be diminished and your authority less feared. / You'll lose two soldiers and two swords that have expanded the boundaries of Arauco and helped make your name so feared among distant, savage nations. They've been disrespectful here, but remember they've also served in dangerous crises, spilling their own blood as well as that of the enemy." /

[11.28] The old man's fervent arguments impressed themselves on Caupolicán, who restrained his fury, saying, "I leave it in your hands and accept your advice." This being resolved and the wise old counselor having seen the way to a resolution, he spoke with Leucotón, who agreed to everything, and then likewise with the two cousins. / Thus the skilled elder persuaded them, for amidst such discord and divisiveness his discretion and good advice succeeded where nothing else could, and having been led to this point, everyone accepted what he proposed on the condition that the helmet be awarded to Orompello. / The rich helmet was then brought and set on Orompello's proud head, and at the same time a coat of mail bordered in fine gold, of equal value, was brought and placed on Leucotón. Everyone now in accord, they sat down at plentiful tables in joyful celebration, friendship binding them even closer. / When the banquet was finished and the tables taken away, they passed what remained of the day in pleasant amusements, weaving together in circles of their customary dances. A great number of young men and gaily attired young women took part, and in order to avoid new disputes the contests did not resume. /

[11.32] Once night had sealed the horizon, enveloping the world in black shadows, the land's principal chiefs assembled at an age-old site to discuss matters of war and draw up a plan, for everyone was saying the impositions they suffered had to be redeemed with blood. / The prized authority for this they entrusted to the son of Pillán, along with the size of the company he would need, for such was the great renown and respect in which they held him that had he promised to scourge heaven itself his vow would have been believed.[61] / From among the most impressive troops he chose five hundred brave and contentious young men known more for enthusiasm than experience. From those who remained there came so many

---

61 As noted earlier, the son of Pillán is Lautaro.

protests, petitions, and appeals to join the enterprise that neither refusals nor restrictions could prevent the number growing by another hundred. / The soldiers Lautaro selected were inveterate fighters and scoundrels. Fond of trouble, they were perverse, dissolute, and seditious, open to every wickedness and greedy for spoils, reckless, blood-thirsty, and homicidal, thieving bandits and marauders. / With fine men like these he marched in peace to the banks of the Maule, but thereafter the lands they traversed were subjected to blood and fire. Everyone they encountered surrendered without resisting, placing themselves at his command, the caciques generously offering him their services and soldiers along with weapons, food, and clothing. / Thus the barbarians destroyed the region's towns and settlements, devastating homes, crops, and property as Indians fled in fear to Santiago. Their wickedness knew no bounds as they raped and assaulted irrespective of age, condition, or locale, for the war they waged was total and unrelenting. /

[11.38] The Araucans' desire to engage us was so great they never stopped to rest. Those escaping their advance brought the sad news to Santiago, and rumors and agitation growing, the commotion of war revived. Some who considered the situation did not believe the reports / and said it was foolish to think such a disorganized and paltry band would dare undertake such an enterprise, especially against such an eminent city so far from their homeland. Those who had been forced to flee Penco took the danger more seriously than such rumors. / Voices were raised among the young and valiant, who wanted to go out and meet the enemy. Others claimed this would be madness, given the difficult and dangerous locale. Everyone rushed to ready themselves, fortifying the town with strong, well-planned defenses, and they hastily dispatched scouts / under the command of a diligent captain, in order to have an accurate report of the number of warriors and their intentions. The scouts were also instructed that if a favorable occasion arose for the defense of their honor they should attack, sending back two men as quickly as possible to warn the others. / With nothing else of importance, I summarize by noting that on the morning of the fourth day the courageous soldiers set out and soon came upon the enemy army. The game was then begun but not played for long, for the barbarians immediately routed them, and every soldier quickly reverted to being a swift and diligent messenger. / Exhausted, harassed, and out of breath, their return offered ample evidence of how they had been overwhelmed and routed by the powerful adversary. Wounded, belabored, and covered with blood, they had also lost one of their men, who getting ahead of the others and becoming separated from them was killed by Lautaro. / They told how the Araucan leader had constructed a stronghold and how he was choosing the bravest and strongest from the vast numbers of warriors assembling there. They also reported that he was daily amassing more supplies and munitions and affirmed he would undoubtedly soon fall upon the city. / Whoever was incredulous before and had considered his arrival to be nonsense now believed it, given such clear signs, and cold fear froze their blood. Some were sweating from worry alone, already familiar with Lautaro's audacity; others, with ardent and steadfast hearts, were clamoring to advance the encounter more quickly. /

[11.46] Villagrán happened to be ill at this time and unable to pursue the war. Using appeals and favors, however, he had incited the land's most valiant men, and to replace him as their commander he had named a dear cousin of his, Pedro de Villagrán, who embodied everything good and fitting in a soldier.⁶² / Not waiting a moment, this leader set out in search of the barbaric Lautaro, intent on showing him what a foolish miscalculation it had been to come there and how dearly it was going to cost him. He and his troops proceeded so quickly they soon reached the winding banks of the Claro river, which circles back in a great arc before running to the sea. / Here he stopped to spend the night, and after choosing a secure position no more than half a league from where the barbarians were located, surrounded it with sentries alert to any movement or sound. Sometime later, without knowing exactly what was happening, they suddenly shouted, "To arms! To arms! Alert! Alert!" / Having learned of our soldiers' arrival, Lautaro himself had reconnoitered their number and returned without being detected. Then, to show in what little regard he held them, he had the most spirited of his horses released, / loudly proclaiming, "Unless I'm mistaken they must not realize that I'm Lautaro from whom they've already suffered so much abuse—abuse from which they'll never recover! To prevent their confusing me with someone else and ensure they know whom they're about to encounter, I'll send this stallion to bear the news." / In the confusion of our last skirmish he had captured ten horses, my Lord, and it was the best saddled and bridled of these he now set free so that it might provide an unmistakable warning. Driven away, the fiery horse headed straight for the Spanish camp following the tracks and scent of the other horses, and this was how it came to surprise everyone, / arriving with such furious commotion it gave their rush to arms added urgency, the vigilant soldiers leaping up in great shock and

---

62   The first of the two Villagráns mentioned here is Francisco, introduced earlier at 4.85.2.

alarm. Yet their consternation was not as great as the taunting, laughter, and jesting once they realized it was an animal that had sent them scurrying for their weapons like that. / Thus the Spanish passed the night without sleeping and at the new day's dawn, firmly determined to win or die, they eagerly set out from their camp toward the barbarous Araucans, who were no less avid to resort to their swords. /

[11.54] Lautaro had imposed one basic rule, which was that anyone taking a single step beyond the wall of the stronghold would be guilty of the great crime of rebellion and would immediately be put to death, no questions asked. With fear thus restraining their boldness, his soldiers did not break the reins of obedience in spite of their excitement, nor did their temerity exceed what was allowed. / By remaining concealed behind the rampart and not allowing a single warrior outside, the barbarian intended to ensure his advantage, preventing our soldiers from using their fleet-footed horses on open ground while forcing them to rely instead on courage, determination, and the virtue and vigor of their arms. / His plan was that when they were attacked and the fight about to begin, the Araucans would turn their backs and flee so that our men were drawn inside the stronghold. Other warriors would then circle back, and having secured the gates before the Christians realized what was happening, the battle would be fought within that walled enclosure. / With such a ruse they awaited the approaching Spanish, whom as soon as they came into view the barbarians greeted with a terrible clamor, threatening them with great arrogance and disdain, some wielding long pikes, some raising ironclad clubs. / Just as when bulls are about to come out fighting and eager spectators harass them with whistles and calls from the stands, fearlessly threatening them from safety with their keen-edged knives, even so the barbarous Araucans now threaten the Christians from the rampart. / The Spanish, never holding such prey in much regard, move forward step by step, intending to bring its walls to the ground. "Neither bulwark, pike, nor club are enough to stop the death your insolence deserves!" they shout at the top of their lungs. / Coming closer to the fort they examine every side, then facing it directly move straight ahead, assaulting the ditch and wall. Since most of the barbarians turn to flee, the soldiers assume their task is accomplished, and easily gaining the gates, with great glorying they loudly sing their victory. /

[11.61] There would be no report of the Spaniards' contentment had the Indians in the lead only waited another moment for the warriors making their way back to secure the gates. But seeing their enemies enter they could not restrain themselves nor endure it any longer and immediately halted, giving the signal they should not have, which caused the rest who were pretending to flee to also turn around. / The way a stallion reacts, catching scent of the mares it has left behind, desire and instinct calling it back as it snorts and neighs in begrudged separation, slowing its pace and flattening its ears, alert for its master's permission to turn around, and then suddenly, waiting no longer, it circles back on its hooves, / just so the fleeing barbarians, with feigned looks of fear, slow their rushing retreat upon seeing the happy signal and brandish their pitiless swords, those who before appeared defeated now turning on our men with such terrible fury the earth trembles with a horrifying din. / As on a tranquil sea, where stately waves are following the course of a gentle breeze when hostile Caurus suddenly explodes in fury, sucking the sand from its distant bed into a surging whirlpool, and the waves, now swollen, are turned back by the stormy blast,[63] / just so the abrupt change suddenly upset the happy victory our soldiers were pursuing, who now, unable to stop, were violently thrust back the way they had come, even as they resisted the enemy's superior numbers with brave determination. / But like some mighty river that bursts its floodgates and goes spreading through woods, tearing out deep-rooted trees as its roaring, rampant flood carries off everything it meets, even solid, sunken boulders borne away on its furious waters, / with just such violence the Indians uprooted our soldiers, and with nothing ahead to stop them, carried them along in a raging torrent until hurling them with furious force beyond the walls, the path to escape made even clearer by their fear of losing their lives. /

[11.68] With greater haste and lighter step than when they first entered, the speedy Spanish now leave the palisade's narrow confines behind, enwrapped in a cloud of dust. The barbarians are mixed in among them as the two groups crowd atop each other, and no one loses a moment to injure another however they can with hands and feet. / Neither the raised parapet and holes they had dug around the enclosure nor the brushwood barriers, tightly bundled with strong vines, slow the course of the swift horses, harried by sharp steel, which rush to the safety of open ground as if flying before the wind. / The Spanish ride without stopping, leaving the fort freely to their adversaries, who pursue their favorable fortune, afflicting them with ready hands and feet. Fearing death, our soldiers keep increasing their pace and get farther ahead, even though at times the enemy's great fury and force slow them down. / The Indians had already run a good league at full speed across dry sand. Lautaro alone

---

63 Caurus is the northeast wind.

did not pursue them, but filled with wrath and furious regret at the ill-controlled troops' lack of discipline, he blew his strident horn so vigorously that even those farthest ahead heard it, and running no more at that sound they immediately turned back. / He was so impatient and enraged that no one dared look him in the eye, and after retiring alone to his tent he ordered a new edict published, which was that no warrior dare take a single step beyond the trench, even if the Spanish were to return and attack the fort a thousand times. / Later, calling the warriors to assembly, although burning with fury he calmly told them, "Friends, we deceive ourselves if we expect to raze the lofty walls of such an eminent city with such a small number of men. Cleverness is now more important than Mars's fierce temerity, / for this is what curbs fierce spirits and empowers the weak, subduing and forcibly taming unbowed heads. Cleverness is what redeems honor and defeat, and our situation demands we take advantage of it if we expect our fortune and diligent efforts to work together as one. / Now let us leave this place, showing signs we're retreating from fear and thus reassuring the Spanish, who'll think we're abandoning our honor and the field. Afterwards we'll return at the right time and easily accomplish what now would be difficult since they hold the plain and have the nearby fortified city for protection." /

[11.76] The son of Pillán was still speaking when the Spanish suddenly reappeared on the plain, filled with new courage for another attempt. The joy and uproar among the barbarians was so great they immediately clapped their hands and began to shout. / Drawing closer, the Christians gradually approach for battle, and the moment of attack arriving, they rush the barbarous rabble now exposed on the rampart, some with raised clubs, others with lowered lances, all displaying their spirited valor and inciting each other to warlike fury. / Reaching the broad gates the Spanish begin cruel combat, some approaching the defended wall with heads well covered by their shields, others seeking a safer way up where it's less well defended. The deep ditch is crowded with Spaniards and the top of the rampart ringed with Araucans. / Protected by tough shields, the audacious Spanish resist the rain of shots and blows from sharpened lances, and such is the cacophony of shouts and the incessant battering of cruel blows that the nearby Maule checks its torrent, astonished by the tumult echoing on all sides. / The stronghold is attacked and defended at the gate, in front, and along both sides, groups running quickly wherever the danger is greatest. Each man assails his enemy with rapid, powerful blows, their cruel force and fury so terrible that shields and armor serve little purpose. / Three times our soldiers withdraw, driven back by shots and blows, and just as often they return, driven forward by angry shame. For a long time they manage to resist their fortune, but all are badly wounded, weak, and exhausted, their swords dyed red with blood which they themselves are sorely lacking. / Valor and wrath grow so great that cruel injuries increase. The Spanish find the fort ever more invincible and their enemies' blows more terrible. Although they attack with no fear of death, their bravery avails them little, for the least weak and wounded among them has blood streaming from at least six places. / The barbarians themselves are astonished to see how much our men have suffered from the incessant blows, arrows, and rocks raining down on them without pause, and how determined they are and with what fury they have thrice attacked. Growing impatient, the Araucans clench their fists and grit their teeth, / and like a storm that rather than slacken keeps growing in fury, its thick, icy hail battering roofs as its winds increase, thus driven by shame and chagrin they hasten forward with lances, darts, and flying stones to batter bucklers, shields, and helmets. / The weary Christians, unable to withstand the insufferable onslaught, are forced to retreat from the impregnable fort and their futile plans, and in light of their misfortune and wretched fate they withdraw their shattered troops, returning by the same road along which they had come, although now with less fervor. / That night they made their camp at the base of a mountain. The surrounding countryside was secure from enemies, none of whom had come in pursuit. I promise to speak later of Lautaro's remarkable cunning, but now I feel weak and weary myself and my voice is hoarse, requiring new strength for a new canto. /

CANTO 12

Safe in his fort, Lautaro decides against trying to defeat the Spanish in battle. He and Marcos Veaz have a conversation from which Pedro de Villagrán realizes the danger the Spanish are in and retreats. The Marquis of Cañete arrives at the City of Kings in Peru.[64]

Guarding a dangerous secret is a difficult test and virtue, its difficulty proving how sensible and beneficial it is, as well as what little good and great harm attend the dangerous vice of careless talk. The killers of Ibycus offer an example, as do others whose talking cost them their lives.[65] / We see with our

---

64 The City of Kings is Lima.
65 Ibycus, a 6th century BCE Greek poet killed by bandits, whose indiscreet talk led to their capture and execution.

own eyes, as well as in writings past and present, the cruelties, disasters, and misfortunes, the infamy, crimes, and great errors committed at great junctures, the loss of people and entire states, all from the inability of the indiscreet to sustain the perilous burden of secrecy. / The least helpful and frequently most damaging of failures, a frivolous breast's not guarding a secret until the right time undoes every accomplishment, diminishing diligence and fomenting furor, discord, and the flames of war, selling out its own master and friend. / This was why Pillán's prudent son, following the day's victory, concealed from his soldiers the reason for not allowing them to pursue the retreating Spanish, whose fury broken, hastened back to the safety of the city along the usual route. / Lautaro took the precaution to ensure an ingenious scheme, which could have had great significance. Leaving this for another time, however, I return to our soldiers, who after leaving the stronghold halted three leagues away the next day to make camp. /

[12.6] For two days the Spanish remained here in a show of bravery, but the barbarians never approached, nor did any of them make an appearance. Two of our men finally dared reconnoiter their stronghold, and as they neared it they heard a loud voice calling them from the rampart, saying, "Come closer, I guarantee your safety!" / One of the men was hailed by name, and more assurances being given, he left his companion and went forward to find out who this bold person was. Reaching the ditch he recognized the speaker, for it was the valiant son of Pillán, someone he had once treated like a brother. / Lautaro, armed in a shining breastplate embellished with gold overlay, was leaning against an enormous pike he held by its iron tip, the great blade crimson and half its shaft stained with blood.

The Araucana

On his head was a gleaming helmet of filigreed steel. / When the Spaniard had come close enough to hear and speak to him clearly, the brazen Lautaro said, "Marcos, I'm very surprised by you and your naive companions, who blindly believe without the slightest justification that you can make me change my mind and are enough to provoke me. / What purpose or insane fury drives you to try and tyrannize our land? Don't you realize that everything now rests in my hands—your own good and ill, peace and war? Haven't you seen the name and reputation of Arauco humble haughty spirits and the sound of our approach alone terrify the world, shattering its strength and bravery? / You weren't strong enough to defend your households in the towns, even though timid birds will confront a lion to protect their nests, and yet you plan to pitch your tents in this deserted, rocky terrain when you're so frightened and your enemy so eager? / In my opinion it's foolish temerity to try to protect yourselves against us, for neither by skill nor ruse nor in any other way can you get the better of us. If you're counting on valor, your recent rout should be enough to chasten you, for fresh blood still flows from your wounds, staining the grass I see hereabout. / I'll never stop pursuing you, and as I have vowed, so will it be done. I'll even chase you back to Spain, for thus have I promised the great senate! If you surrender in time and meet my requirements, however, I'll renounce my sworn oath and you'll escape destruction. / Our pact will require that you provide us every year with thirty beautiful, fine virgins, fair-skinned, blond-haired, and well-figured, all between the ages of fifteen and twenty, with no deceptions, and all of them Spanish. In addition to this, thirty capes of fine green cloth and another thirty woven of purple, trimmed with fine gold thread. / Furthermore, twelve powerful young horses, richly caparisoned and trained, swift and full of fury, yet submissive to the rein, and six spirited, agile wolfhounds, bred for the chase. This tribute alone will prevent what the rest of the world cannot." /

[12.16] The Castilian listened attentively, enjoying the speech. When it came to these conditions, however, he couldn't stay silent any longer and impatiently interrupted the barbarian, telling him, "Don't be so arrogant, Lautaro, for the tributes you demand will soon cost you dearly should you await them! / In payment for such foolish daring the Spanish will offer you the tribute of a cruel death with terrible torture, covering Arauco in eternal mourning." Lautaro replied, "This is to speak into the wind, Marcos, and I'll say no more about it. Arms, not tongues, are what will settle the matter, and strength and valor determine the outcome. / Say what you want since you've been granted safety, and afterwards you'll do what you can while I do what I've promised. Let's leave this aside and turn to more agreeable matters, for having the opportunity I'd like to show you a fine squadron of cavalry. / To prevent your roaming about in such security, I've resolved that I, too, will have horses, and I'm teaching my soldiers how to handle and control them." Having said this, from the rampart Lautaro now ordered six robust youths, his vassals, to mount six horses and cross in front of the Spaniard. / By two bridges, lowered at the same time, six Chilcános emerged, outfitted with broad, painted bucklers and balancing stout lances in their hands. They wore tough coats of mail and their heads were covered like Arabs, cloaks thrown off the shoulder and sleeves pushed above the elbow.[66] / Twice

---

66   Chilcános are residents of the area governed by the cacique Chilcán; see 9.42.8 and 9.82.1; cloaks thrown off the shoulder and raised sleeves are preparations for battle.

they passed in proud display before the watchful Spaniard, who showed not the slightest reaction, but in a voice loud enough for all to hear, the rampart now being covered with men, said boldly to Lautaro, / "Oh captain, anyone who tries to frighten me with boasting clearly does so in vain! I don't find this show significant in the least, and parades don't frighten me at all. To prove whether or not I fear any advantage these men may have, I'm willing to match myself alone against all six, and you'll soon see if six thousand would be enough! Let them advance right now for the test!" / "Marcos," Lautaro replied, "if you're dying to show us your strength and courage, the least of these, chosen by you, will come forward on foot to accept your challenge in whatever mode and manner you prefer. Choose the weapons and arena of your liking, armed or unarmed, using fists, feet, fingernails, and teeth." / "I assure you my honor will not allow me to punish them one by one," the Spaniard answered, "for people will never say a barbarian dared enter the arena alone with me for one-to-one combat. You may not want to grant my conditions, but I'm unwilling to accept any other arrangement." / Coming to no agreement about this, they went on to speak of other things, and when the time came to depart, the two Spaniards took their leave of the barbarian. They had just reached the road when they heard someone accosting them, and at the sound of the familiar voice they turned back, for it was Lautaro who called out, saying, "I forgot one thing. / My men are destitute and discouraged, for due to confusion and poor planning I don't have enough food for them and need provisions. Since you have more than enough, be generous and share it, providing for us in a way I'm sure will enhance your honor and glory. / In our illustrious State it's an ancient custom between honorable warriors that we nourish the strength of our enemies, only oppressing them by the sword. Hear what I'm saying, Marcos, and imagine what praise there'll be when people report that in order to achieve a greater triumph you fed the force you defeated. / I doubt they'll call it a victory when your adversary's in such extremity, for where valor can accomplish nothing, wretched hunger has the power to weaken and subdue an invincible arm. Thus can scarcity and base means make weakness appear strength." /

[12.29] It was his intention, my Lord, that this feigned need be thought real and our soldiers lured with false hope into remaining nearby, concealing his cunning until the goal of his clever deception could be achieved. / Moved by his words, Marcos told him: "I promise to attend to this for the reasons you've stated and do everything I can to see it done." He and his companion then took their leave, and pulling their horses about proceeded to the Spanish camp. / Informed in detail of all Lautaro had said, Villagrán was surprised and suspicious, and it astonished him to hear that he had asked for provisions. Being astute and prudent, however, after pondering everything in his agile imagination he grasped the hidden plan and realized the danger the Spanish faced. / Determined to act quickly, as soon as the world was plunged into deepest darkness, not blowing a trumpet, they left for the safety of the city, alert to every danger and marveling at the Araucan's clever ploy. I concern myself no further with them at this point, for now I want to recount the extraordinary nature of Lautaro's ingenious scheme and subterfuge. /

[12.33] The next dawn's light had just appeared when the barbarians learned of the Spaniards' sudden departure and retreat. They responded with no small show of regret, realizing that so near their goal, they now would be unable to make such a slaughter among the Christians that none would ever again take up a lance. / The Indian stronghold, ringed by mountains, lay in a narrow stretch of lowland watered by many skillfully constructed irrigation channels and ditches. With these broken open at their sources, the area would have quickly become a vast bog and lake, for when flooded the earth here becomes deceptively soft and deep, hollow, spongy, and unstable. / Had the ditches been breached and the fields flooded, our horses would have been bogged down in the sticky quagmire and unable to move, and thus immobilized, trapped like birds in lime. Lautaro's prompt orders had already put the plan into action. / Bitter at the Spanish departure, he therefore abandoned the stronghold in a rage that very day and marched his battalion of infantry along the most direct route to Arauco. Musing within his anxious breast he considered various ideas, but none offered the consolation or excuse he was seeking, and talking thus to himself he sighed, / saying: "What excuse can now possibly protect me from blame? Did I not boldly claim to undertake an enterprise for which I'm still responsible? Whom other than myself can I reproach, since everything has been directed by my own hand? Wasn't it I who promised within a single year to conquer the world from one pole to the other? / Yet even with these outstanding troops I've not managed to gaze upon Spanish ramparts, while the moon has already illuminated our poorly-disciplined army three times and Phaeton's resplendent chariot has traveled from Scorpio to Aquarius![67] In the end we return ill-treated, with the loss of more than a hundred soldiers. / If I could be sure of dispelling such shame by dying, this lance, grasped by this worthless arm, would

---

67   The sun moves through these two signs of the zodiac between October 24 and January 20.

pierce my feeble heart! But it would give the enemy even greater revenge and glory if he thought I feared his powerful arm more than my own weak, frightened one, cowardly as it is. / I swear to the everlasting infernal power that within one year, if death doesn't lay me low, I'll drive the Spanish from Chile and soak all its ground in their blood! No change of fortune, no heat or cruel winter, will stop the course of the war, and even within the deep kingdom of darkness itself no Spaniard will be safe from me!" / He also made a solemn vow never to return to his own dear home, nor take shelter or protect himself from rain, sun, wind, or the dampness of night, and not to indulge in any pleasure until the whole world knew that Lautaro did not begin a difficult enterprise without bravely bringing it to an honorable end. /

[12.42] With this his sadness, which at times distressed him with such cruel suffering that he almost lost his mind, seemed to abate. Thus the ferocious Lautaro proceeded, and after three days' march set up camp in a fertile lowland by the sea until such a longed-for time might arrive. / The mighty Itata, after cascading down the nearby mountains, crosses this shady locale in stately, tranquil majesty. The surrounding groves induce contentment, and the breezes blow more lovingly here, toying with tender blossoms of red, blue, white, and yellow. / This charming area, spacious and bountiful enough to support many warriors, lies seven leagues from Penco. Not far to the east is the great cordillera and high sierra from which the raucous Itata descends so swiftly, offering its tribute to the salty sea. / For a time this region belonged to the Spanish, but its people renounced the loyalty they had sworn once fortune seemed to declare itself on the side of the Araucan State, which officially encompassed some twenty-two leagues but the reputation of which had now grown so great the entire country feared it. / This was what brought the valiant Spanish so humbly to earth and encouraged the lowly and timorous to revolt against heaven, prompting powerful peoples beyond its borders to live in terror and neighbors as well as distant strangers to surrender and submit to its laws. /

[12.47] Now the flower of the State waited restively on the fertile plain, for hours pass slowly for one who anticipates pleasure, while for him who expects no good they come too soon. Time and opportunity hastening on, Lautaro assembled his spirited warriors, and before setting out said these few words to them: / "My friends, if I thought the will to fight and the fierce ardor I see in your eyes were all that is needed to win, I assure you I believe victory would be within your grasp, and I wouldn't retreat a single step even if the entire world were to attack us! / But a difficult and dangerous enterprise isn't achieved by courage alone, and what good is endless courage if our strength is limited? Yet even limited strength, when governed and guided by ingenuity, makes difficult projects seem simple and the most arduous enterprise easy. / How often do we see wretched exiles, their reputations lost, having done nothing more than endlessly offer brave breasts to the enemy? That isn't valor, but rather madness and reckless, ignorant error! Valor is being obedient to orders, and to be valiant without discipline is folly! / The way we brought ruin upon ourselves in this great campaign, after so much work, was by heeding the blind passion that drove us, and had we not squandered our opportunity through premature fury there wouldn't be a single Spaniard left alive nor anything else for Fortune to decide! / Had you controlled yourselves and been patient as they entered the fort, your efforts would have been celebrated and no enemy would have escaped, for the people in nearby Santiago were unprepared, and with our men surrounding the city we could have achieved a victory that neither time nor death would ever efface! / Therefore I advise you to be governed by reason and resist taking any action until the right moment arrives. Don't disobey me on a single point or get ahead of what I command, for on anyone so reckless and disobedient I'll exact an exemplary and unheard-of punishment! / As we return to the place where our feeble valor, being so ill-governed, was exposed, I hereby vow, raising this right hand, that you'll either be restored to your former glory or our blood will irrigate the battlefield where we'll remain, rendered into food for savage beasts and filthy birds of prey!" /

[12.55] With the speech finished, the trumpet sounded departure and the warriors set out once again, marching with their usual speed. They were approaching a cove and about to enter Mataquito to their right when they met a barbarian on the road, who told them he was coming from Santiago. / He assured them with an oath that their approach was known, either because the wind had brought word of it or because the Spanish had learned of it from diligent spies, and he informed them that the city was prepared with plentiful defenses, entrenchments, munitions, and supplies. / This being confirmed, Lautaro altered his initial plan, realizing it would have been reckless to pursue it with such a small company, and intending to gather more men, quickly began to reinforce a promising site in the valley using all his ingenuity and care. / Given the location's natural defenses and the speed with which he worked, the fortification was swiftly encircled by a ditch and solid rampart. As news of this spread, people gathered, greedy for the spoils of war, but hearing a great outcry coming from our town I must now hasten on. /

[12.59] In Santiago they knew for certain that Pillán's son was coming upon them in all his fury with a battalion of experienced warriors. Sudden fear threw the Spanish into confused vigilance, but soon their blood, first frozen by terror, began to burn with ardent fury. / The stalwart took up arms, while those afflicted by age offered their experience and advice repairing the earthworks and weak parts of the wall. Once this was completed, thirty valiant youths and a skilled captain, accompanied by barbarian allies, prepared to seek out the enemy. / Villagrán was not present in the troubled town at this point, having set out earlier for La Imperial by a route that skirted Arauco. As he was returning with additional troops, however, without realizing it he spent the night near the barbarians' stronghold of great logs and bundled scrub. / Cheerful, refreshing dawn had appeared and he had resumed his march and was descending a hill when he met a local Indian on the road. The young man told him about the nearby camp and described what was happening within it, for he was well informed, having just come from there hoping for spoils. / Villagrán thus learned what Lautaro was planning and how he was continuing to gather men while waiting for the right moment to attack. This did not frighten the Spaniards at Cautén, even less so when they learned that other troops of ours were approaching and less than a day's march away.[68] / Villagrán asked the youth if it would be possible to take the Araucan rampart. He replied with a smile that this was utterly impossible given the site's defenses and location, the rear of which was protected by a steep mountain closing off that side of the stronghold. / Villagrán then told him, "Given what you've said, I'm determined to set out for this lofty

---

68 Cautén is the name of the valley in which La Imperial is located; the "other soldiers" are the thirty mentioned earlier in octave 60.

CANTO 12

mountain whatever the risk. If you can lead me to Lautaro's camp in one night you'll be well rewarded for your effort, but if you're lying you'll be burned alive." / With no trace of fear the barbarian responded, "I swear that in less than a night I'll lead you there by a safe but difficult route. These words you can trust. Afterwards, with regard to Lautaro, I can't promise anything, nor can I keep your soldiers and allies, if you go there, from all being caught and dealt a thousand infamous deaths." / The frightful scenario did not trouble Villagrán, who seeing how fearlessly the youth offered his help deemed him trustworthy. He then dispatched a diligent messenger to the soldiers coming from Santiago, instructing them to join him with all due haste. / Once these men arrived the following day, they all let themselves be led where the barbarian guided them, never ceasing to spur their horses through the dark night. What happened next will be recounted later, for now it is best that I leave them in order to describe the arrival in this land of one who brought fresh forces to the war. /

[12.69] Until this point, my Lord, I myself was not present at the events I've described and being skeptical have not wanted to learn of them from partial observers. Instead I have listened to both parties and only include that which everyone agrees on and where reports differ least. / We see how much blood has already been shed in confirmation of my account. Going forward I vow that this history will proceed with even greater authority, for now I will speak as a witness who was present at every campaign, neither blinded by passion, which I shun, nor depriving anyone of their due. / Not a step has been taken in this land that my own feet have not measured, nor a blow or thrust been delivered without my telling from whom the injury came. As for the few I dealt myself, I must be excused, for my mind was so absorbed in observing that my arm at times forgot my sword. / If one cause above all has driven me to write, in spite of my poor talent and crude pen, it has been that so much valor not perish, nor time unfairly consume it. No one should imagine that I'm moved to display my wisdom, for I know all too well the poverty of my feeble brain. / Of my limited ability there's ample evidence here, where truth is presented so artlessly so that it may proceed on firmer ground. If weakness leads me beyond this, I ask that it be indulged in light of my worthy intention, which is only to be accurate while giving pleasure. / And although my pen has dared to write so much before a beard covers my cheeks, so few years detracting from my credibility, I hope, my Lord, that the zeal and just cause that inspire me, together with my honorable intentions, will be kept in mind and excuse my errors. /

[12.75] I want to leave Arauco for now, since what I have to say about Peru is important to my subject even though it takes place so far away. And in order that what lies ahead be better understood, if Lautaro allow it, I will speak briefly of the men there organizing against him.[69] / The Marquis of Cañete had recently arrived in the illustrious City of Kings, his rare gifts having led to his being made viceroy of Peru by emperor Charles V, who sent him there to restore and maintain its laws following the murder of two of his predecessors by the brazen rebels.[70] / The new viceroy soon became aware of the passions and wickedness that had taken hold, of seditious spirits in the guise of loyal ones, and of great outrages, insults, and treacheries committed with utter shamelessness. Realizing the corpse of the tyrant had not even had time to decompose and was already stirring, / he

---

69   The narrative interrupted here is resumed at 13. 41.
70   Andrés Hurtado de Mendoza, Marquis of Cañete, became the third viceroy of Peru in 1556.

began with prudent caution, not making a show of swords and cruel steel, which would have been dangerous at that point and a serious miscalculation, but rather of amiable benevolence, using flattery until he could halt the evil and devote more attention to justice.[71] / To thoroughly cleanse the wickedness, he dismissed the judges and put hand-chosen magistrates in all the cities, men of integrity and known to fear God and King, men who had proven themselves useful in similar roles. / He then distracted the people with talk of a general division of land and properties, at which, as in the previous regime, the most guilty among them expected the biggest rewards. Meanwhile he was gathering information and planning a different outcome for this false announcement, and in the end he not only punished the guilty but revisited misdeeds that had previously been pardoned, / whose authors had thought that with time's passage their offenses had been forgotten, only to find themselves now publicly condemned and punished. In almost every town that had revolted there came a morning when the rebellion's most fervent supporters were found dead. / I do not condemn those who died, my Lord. They had been pardoned and had returned to your service at a critical time, and their errors were subject to your great clemency. It is yours alone, my Lord, to judge them, as yours alone is the power to save or condemn them. / I offer no opinion on this, for in cases of honor I decline to do so, but only recount the extraordinary terror instilled in those proud people by the Marquis's harsh punishment, which left the realm so stunned and unsettled that even to imagine such audacious measures seemed perilous. / Those of known

---

71 The "tyrant" was Francisco Hernández Girón; the two viceroys killed previously were Blasco Núñez de Vela, the first viceroy of Peru, and Antonio de Mendoza, his successor.

guilt he exiled from Peru as penance, for this is the disgrace they feel most deeply and which most tries their patience. Facing the rigor of angry justice, which had now unsheathed its sword, even exemplars of just and upright lives examined their consciences. / Some captains and soldiers, who had served honorably in the war and were expecting to be rewarded in keeping with the usual practice, he suspected of having offended the realm and banished as prisoners, remitting their pay to the King, all-powerful and supreme. / This was what alarmed the people most, not knowing the cause of their exile or whether it was just or unjust. All they knew was how to keep quiet, and trembling with fear at such severity and not daring to inquire about its rationale, they turned an attentive ear to every rumor, hearing nothing but conflicting reports. / Fear, silence, and confusion grew. The people went about bewildered, not questioning the hidden cause of the punishment, since even to ask about it seemed a crime. They looked at each other trying to discern the answer, and the wisest among them arched their shoulders in anticipation of a rigorous blow that appeared to be driven by chance. / The Viceroy's conduct was so skillful, daring, and impressive that little truly exceeds it, and it was widely celebrated at the time as essential in the face of so many unrestrained spirits. Arrogant Peru, brash and rebellious, was left terrified of him, with justice on a surer footing and with greater hope in the future. / He reined in the country with a bridle from which it will never break free, forcing the ambitious and rebellious to content themselves with what they had. With new control he calmed the tumult and unruly desire, for that which is unsound does not last long, as experience has always shown. / Those who previously could not imagine being content with an income of twenty or thirty thousand pesos now restrained such thoughts, happy to be alive. Afterwards, the Marquis made a distribution among the deserving to encourage the despondent and inflict even greater torment on the villains.[72] /

[12.91] With events and examples like these, how is it so many still go astray, raising lofty edifices on sand and other fragile foundations? How weak such footings prove when we suddenly see them crash to earth, together with the disgraced names and reputations of those whose corruption we flee as best we can. / Oh, vain error! Oh, foolish confusion and ignorance of one who takes a dangerous path, not seeing the tracks of those who came before, who offer such clear examples of how the most loyal friend will spill one's blood to clear himself and his sword of any blame! / Such a man may be falsely sustained for a time on traitorous shoulders, but the noise of every gust excites and upsets him, for no sound is as harsh and terrible as the voice of the King, whose name alone has the power to oppress and break his bones! / Should Fortune grant him some contentment, with what unpleasantness it is mixed, with what suspicion and vexation! What a sad and wary life he leads! Cruel death lurks in every moment, those he used to trust the most he fears, and his earlier freedom and safety are now subject to anyone's sword. / By denying the King his duty and obedience, he places himself at the mercy of the lowliest soldier, someone he must cravenly do his best to please. Meanwhile, those who appear most friendly aim their lances at his side and a thousand ready swords threaten his head! / Every rumor and voice scare him; in every whisper he hears a denunciation. If anyone raises an arm the wretched man thinks it is to kill him: the rope is drawing tight, the knot

---

72 Complaints about Cañete's harsh and sometimes arbitrary response to the unrest in Peru led to his replacement five years later.

is at his neck! What pledges can reassure him, since those who dare deny a king will have little loyalty to a tyrant? / If seeing the guilty eliminated so quickly is not enough to restrain such a man, nor the gallows and neighboring lands filled by those so justly exiled, their factions, houses, and lineages ruined, their names stained and dishonored, then surely the duty we all have from birth to our King and prince will suffice. / Little by little I've turned aside from the subject I was pursuing. Yet even as I blindly make my way without a guide along such a rough trail, Mars's horrifying tumult ensures I'll find my way back, and thus consoled and trusting I dare to rest, for I am weary. /

CANTO 13

Following the Marquis of Cañete's punishment of the Peruvian rebels, envoys arrive from Chile requesting his assistance, and recognizing the importance and justice of their petition, he sends them abundant aid by land and sea. This canto also describes how Francisco de Villagrán, guided by an Indian, comes upon Lautaro.

Fortunate may he be called, and rightly so, who cast amidst perils can emerge without taint and free of reproach. More fortunate still I consider the man who avoids danger altogether, for while it may bring out one's best, the prudent avoid it. / How often one imagines an enterprise to be entirely safe and eagerly undertakes it, only to be confounded by peril when it's too late, imagination overwhelmed by danger and unable to find a way out. / You've seen in Peru how men helped to elevate the tyrant, raising him up only to reveal their treacherous loyalty by casting him down. With malicious intent they first empowered and then came to kill him, their faithless, perfidious swords the source of great evil, traitorous to King and friends alike. / In the guise of feigned loyalty they fomented war and incited dissension, thinking to elevate themselves more quickly by means of this hazardous route, but in the end their wicked designs resulted in the disgraceful outcome of the country's disturbances and civil war. / Once the clouds of conflict had been utterly dispersed by the audacious and prudent Marquis, who treated the rebellions with the rigor of one who well understood the malady, to others similarly inclined he showed clemency, hidden until then by severity, issuing a general pardon that exonerated them in the name of the King. /

[13.6] Neither the most brazen and frightening events that had ever occurred in Peru nor the exemplary punishment that tamed its emboldened people were powerful enough to drown out the barbarous tumult in Arauco, the resounding fame of which reached the northern provinces. / Reports arrived by both land and sea of the injuries and losses our people had sustained in the victorious campaigns of the powerful Araucans, for seeking swift and substantial aid the hard-pressed towns sent accounts of all that was happening and how they were faring. / Gerónimo Alderete, the governor-general to whom military leadership of the southern provinces had been entrusted, was a noteworthy figure in the region, a man of great stature and reputation who had endured dire hardship as a brave and loyal soldier. I do not include his accomplishments in this history since a general one will memorialize him. / Alderete had been absent through many of the difficulties and misfortunes thus far, having accompanied you, mighty Philip, to England, where you planted the faith anew.[73] It was there you granted him responsibility for this land and from there dispatched him with such great favor. Harsh destiny cut his life-thread along the way, however, / and his sad death was keenly felt, its sorrow augmented by seeing the land and its administration gone astray, for each man began to govern for himself, discord was enflamed, and the ambition to command knew no bounds.[74] Yet in the end a headless body cannot survive. /

[13.11] Those who came from Chile to seek assistance, learning the governor-general had died and seeing everything working against them, unanimously petitioned don Hurtado, amidst expressions of grief, for prompt relief.[75] / "Illustrious and excellent lord," they said, "our need is clear, as is the strength of the powerful barbarians who've placed Chile in such extremity. The most effective response would be to levy soldiers, for already you see how dearly their lack has cost us, and thus in the name of your King we beseech you to grant our request. / Your son, don García, is what we ask of you, he in whom such valor and grace are combined, for we're certain that with his leadership our misfortunes and distress will cease.[76] Of his natural gifts we're

---

73 Philip went to England in July of 1554 for marriage with Mary Tudor; the poet, a 21 year-old page, was among the royal household; Alderete was named to his post after the death of Valdivia.
74 Alderete died of a fever in Panama in April of 1556.
75 Andres Hurtado de Mendoza, the Marquis of Cañete; cf. n. 69.
76 García Hurtado de Mendoza went on to become Viceroy of Peru after his father.

well satisfied, lord, knowing it a law of nature and an old saying, even here, that a lamb is never born of a lion. / As for the lack of soldiers, his heading the campaign will inspire commoners and gentlemen alike, who'll be eager to follow such a fine leader. That which great sums of money cannot accomplish, love and camaraderie can, not to mention the shame and fear of offending you and the desire to see you well pleased." / The Marquis of Cañete, gladly acceding to their just demand, graciously granted it, recognizing the matter to be both urgent and essential. His son, pledging his wealth and affiliations, immediately spread among everyone a great desire to cross over to that land and wield their weapons in such a war. / First one man offered himself and then another, and a great crowd of soldiers being moved to do so, anyone who did not appeared to be shirking his duty. Even among weary elders juvenile ardor revived, their languishing spirits and all-but-frozen blood now stirred by the joyous prospect of the campaign. /

[13.17] Oh, valiant Araucan warriors! Make ready your hearts and weapons, as well as your arms' vaunted prowess, so feared throughout the Antarctic region, for a great multitude of brave youth are now unfurling their banners against you and planning to invade your land to wage fierce slaughter and cruel war! / Not with dull, rusty swords that decorate walls do they come, their sword arms listless from idle leisure and only wielded with great sluggishness, nor with spirits made for repose, which the least uncertainty alarms and which disappear at the first strange noise. / Instead they advance with sharp, well-tempered blades honed in the blood of tyrants, and with sturdy arms, robust and muscular, practiced in death-dealing blows! Their bold spirits are devoid of fear and inured to constant danger, and the horrendous sounds that terrify others only serve to gladden and inspire them. / While none of these may dislodge you from your present advantage, there is something else that gives me pause, since none escape it. This is the constant rotation of Fortune, which until now has shown you a cheerful face, but which is erratic, false, and fickle, constant only in evil but ever mutable in good! / As for the Spanish soliciting battle and proudly brandishing their swords, I would ask them, as well, if their blades cut more ably than yours, if the strength of their arms protects them from your powerful, victorious blows, and looking closely at the past, if they see the field still littered with their countrymen's bones. / I don't know their answer, but I see our proud Spaniards consumed by martial fury and the poorest among them outfitted with arms, rich apparel, and ardent desire. Oh, Arauco! If deeds match finery I deem you lost, and unless the road tempers their bravery, woe to your bold presumption! /

[13.23] Men came from distant Quito to take part in this war. They came from Loja, Piura, and Jaén, from Trujillo, and from Huánuco and its territory. A great number assembled from Guamanga and Arequipa, and many well-armed, experienced soldiers also descended from the towns of the high sierra, La Paz, Cuzco, and Charcas.[77] / The earth trembled and the swollen sea roared with all the tumult. The air was agitated by trumpets, fifes, and drums, and powerful cannons were heard all the way to Arauco, threatening the defenses of its bold, rebellious people. / Our brave soldiers busied themselves with equipment, harnesses, and trappings. They brought out visored helmets and the latest, most costly finery. In every street emblems, banners, and

---

77 Loja is in present-day southern Ecuador; the remaining towns are in Peru.

standards trembled in the wind, and tailors and seamstresses were busy with sewing, trimming, and embroidery. / The clamor and commotion grew as the warriors assembled, the rapid hammering of blacksmiths adding a harsh harmony to the clatter of diligent armorers, the deafening noise spreading far and wide as eager horses, snorting with impatience, stamped their hooves. / While the people were busy with the commotion of the new war, a captain, supplied with everything important, had already set out by land, leading the plentiful troops entrusted to him across the high sierra and the uninhabited desert coast of the Atacama, sown with barbarian skeletons. / The principal men and rest of the ready army were only waiting for the right time to embark on the agitated sea, and when the sky finally cleared and the rough waves calmed one afternoon, they set out in rich procession and orderly pomp from the City of Kings. /

[13.29] I, who began and will end my life in your service, my Lord, was among them. I had been with you in England and still not permitted a sword when reports arrived of the wicked disloyalty committed against you by the inhabitants of Arauco and of their shameless disobedience to the Royal Crown. / With your permission I accompanied the new captain and governor-general Alderete from London until the day I left him buried in Taboga, from where, after enduring great hardship and being tossed about by fortune and the winds, I arrived in time to set out with these fine, resplendent soldiers. / I almost forgot another friendly cohort, no less important than ourselves, a mild and gentle squadron of modest monks, vicars, and divines. These were men of honorable and saintly lives, Franciscans, Dominicans, and Mercedarians, ready to remedy the affronts of war, more prevalent in these regions than elsewhere. / Thus

CANTO 13

it was a resplendent company of all kinds left Lima. At the harbor there were tables bedecked with flowers and laden with food and fragrantly flavored wines. Reclining around them on the verdant grass we enjoyed the delicate dishes, / and once our stomachs were satisfied we were gaily led to where skiffs garlanded with green branches were waiting. After saying good-bye to dear friends, we boarded these craft to the lively sounds of varied instruments and their oars plied the waves as one, / pulling away from the land and leaving us with a painful yearning for those left behind on the sandy shore, from whom we never took our eyes. The launches soon drew abreast of ten galleons, and our sailors leapt aboard and lost no time unfurling their sails to the wind. / Adorned with standards, flags, and pennants, with a fresh breeze stirring their foresails, the ten ships slowly began to move to the sounds of cannons, sakers, and falconets, and having circled the intervening islet into the Auster, they spread their port-side sails and set course for the south-southwest.[78] / Our vessels raised white spray on all sides as they broke through the contrary seas, fiercely resisting the southerlies and gaining ground in spite of their fury. Tacking against the Garbino, they drew away from the great cordillera, and with a single further turn Guarco lay to our east-northeast.[79] / Having sighted it from the poop, with Chincha to one side, we made for the high seas, tacking back toward fertile Nazca as we defied mighty Notus, whose fury we fought in addition to the savage waves, overcoming the attack of

---

78   Sakers and falconets are two types of smaller caliber cannon; two small islands lie directly outside Lima's harbor; the Auster is the south wind.
79   Garbino is the southwest wind; Guarco was a location on the coast slightly south of Lima.

both these powerful elements.[80] / What is it about Peru, where within a distance of three leagues there can be such extraordinary variation? When it's summer in the plains, rainy winter envelops the mountains, and when the prairies are blanketed with dense fog, the sun shines brightly on the sierra, making the summer streams run stronger. / Among the winds, it's the Auster that ranges over all that sea, commanding the rain-filled clouds to disperse and banishing them forever. Other winds reign along the Atacama coast, where they blow freely, although none can batter Peru, which is naturally protected. / Thus battling the Auster our ships went cutting through the frothing waves that broke in fury upon them, driven by powerful gusts and lashing their lofty, iron-plated prows. . . But seeing the Spanish draw near Lautaro's stronghold, I must be quickly on my way. /[81]

[13.41] I hurry now to Villagrán, who's also hastening his march across the precipitous mountain, the height of which rivals the clouds. In a moment I'll explain how he fared and which of its faces Fortune showed him. But in order that everything be clearer, I first want to turn to Lautaro, / who had withdrawn with his band of warriors to the location I described, which they quickly fortified with a trench, tree trunks, and bundles of shrub. Inside the stronghold with him were neighboring warriors, drawn by news of the war, along with provisions, munitions, and other supplies befitting the time and place. /

---

80 The Chincha islands lie off the coast of Peru; Nazca is a region along its southern coast; Notus is the south wind.

81 The poem now returns to the account that was interrupted at 12.68; the sea voyage from Peru to Chile resumes at the end of Part 1 of the poem, at 15.56.1, and continues into the opening of Part 2.

Canto 13

The site had only one path leading to it, manned by watchful sentries, nor was there any trace of other trails since the area was largely deserted. That night the barbarian slept with his beautiful, beloved Guacolda, whom he cherished with an ardent passion and who burned no less fervently for him. / It was the first night cruel fate had offered him the opportunity and desire for rest, and after shedding Mars's cumbersome gear a heavy sleep had closed his eyes. Suddenly he awoke, distressed, and the beautiful Guacolda breathlessly asked what was wrong. / "My love," Lautaro replied, "I just now dreamed that an arrogant Spaniard stood before me with a ferocious expression, violently overwhelming my strength and spirit without my being able to do anything at all, at which point the rage and pain awakened me." / At this her troubled voice cried out, "Alas, I, too, have dreamed of that which in my happiness I fear so much—the approach of your end and beginning of my lament! Yet I won't be so unlucky nor Fortune in such control that I can't cut short my fate's cruel course by dying. / Even though it terrifies me and does its worst, casting me from my happy bridal bed, it still isn't powerful enough to part me from you. The blow I await may be unbearable, but with another I'll soon save myself, for before your body falls cold to the earth mine will lie dead on the ground!" /

[13.48] The son of Pillán encircled her neck with his arms in an ardent embrace, burning with new love as he bathed her white breast in his tears. "My lady," he said, "don't take this so seriously nor trouble with such omens the joy and happiness in which I now find myself, holding you here in my arms. / It grieves me to see you so worried, not because I think I'm in mortal danger, but because love's wound is so deep that I fear the impossible.

If you wish me to live, my lady, who is powerful enough to kill me? My life lies not in human hands but yours. / Who was it restored their lost reputation to the Araucans, when their proud, untamed necks lay meekly beneath the yoke? I'm the one who cast Spanish dominion and tyranny from our shoulders, and in this land my name alone is able to wage war without ever raising a sword. / How much less, with you at my side, have I to fear or harm to expect! Don't let a dream, my lady, distress you so much, since reality itself cannot. I'm accustomed to placing my fortune at steeper precipices than this, and from greater dangers I've always emerged with honor!" /

[13.52] Less assured and more distressed, she hung on Lautaro's neck, and with eyes full of pity tearfully beseeched him, her lips against his: "My lord and sweet friend, if that pure devotion I gave you so freely when I was still free, witnessed by heaven on high, is still worth anything, / I entreat you thereby and by the torment I feel whenever we're apart, as well as by the faith you just pledged me with so many tears—if the wind hasn't already carried it away!—that at least you give me this happiness, if you've ever had any from me, of immediately donning your armor and ordering your men to the wall!" / The barbarian replied, "The little esteem in which you hold me is all too clear! Is your opinion of Lautaro so poor and do you regard so lightly this strong right arm, which has given such proof of itself redeeming our dear people? I certainly have a fine reputation with you, since fear makes you weep for me as already dead!" / "Alas is me!" said Guacolda, "I've no doubts about you but am not reassured. What good is the strength of your arm if that of my misfortune is greater? If my fears come true, however, my love for you assures me that the sword that separates us will send me in your wake. / And since inescapable fate and cruel Fortune now threaten me with such a steep fall and force me to face an evil as terrible as seeing you taken from me, let me weep for the little that remains of my life before I die: for whoever feels no misfortune has had little joy from what is good!" / With this she poured forth so many tears it was pitiful to see, and at such a moment the tender Lautaro could not help but join her. But now my troubled pen, finding itself newly amidst matters of love, is confused and fearful, and moving slowly, dares go no further. /

CANTO 14

Villagrán reaches the enemy stronghold during the night without being detected. At dawn he suddenly attacks, Lautaro is killed in the initial skirmish, and a bloody battle is fought.

What insolent tongue will now dare insult women, seeing that prejudice alone is what leads to such vile error, if a young barbarian can give such lofty proof of pure love, expressed in tearful terms from deep within her burning breast? / The confidence and certainty of her friend offered no consolation, nor was the solid fort with its rampart and ditch enough to reassure her misgivings. Her great fear, born of pure love, sees it all tumble down, and the only refuge she finds from fate is in the danger of death itself. / Thus these two hearts, united in love, were divided, their expressions of it feeding the sweet poison even more. Lautaro's soldiers, gathered around half-burned logs and weary of talk, were resting. Sentinels kept watch, while the mountain, as I said earlier, protected their rear. /

[14.4] Villagrán had quickly and silently crossed the rugged mountain with his soldiers, yet not without great exertion, short of which much effort comes to nothing. Reaching a safe position near the stronghold and seeing the sky still filled with stars, he halted to await the bright new day, already dawning in the east. / No one had seen nor heard the troops approach, the night being so dark and the sentinels believing the rear of the fort to be safe. Not a horse whinnied nor was there any other sound, for luck had already taken the side of the Spanish, making beasts alert and people into careless beasts. / As the somber shadows began to disperse in the longed-for light, the guards posted along the rampart greeted the new day from afar, and believing the camp secure they, too, retired to rest, leaving the fort in silence and the soldiers buried in wine and sweet sleep. / The hour had arrived when the world's gloomy darkness retreats to the west, unable to endure the bright sight of Aurora, and when sad Clytie, turning her face to the rosy east, begins to revive, watching the morning star trail after the shadows, followed by blond Delphic Apollo.[82] / Realizing the moment has come, the Spanish approach little by little. Not a single barbarian opposes them, their sad fate having

---

82 Aurora is the goddess of the dawn; Clytie was a nymph who was loved and abandoned by the sun god, Apollo, whose sacred precinct was Delphi; in her grief she was transformed into the heliotrope, a flower whose blossoms follow the course of the sun across the sky; the morning star is Venus.

made them deaf and left them sleeping, entirely unaware of the proximity of inexorable death, a sure sign of its nearness while being thought so far away. / Our men wait no longer, but seeing it time for the assault, raise a sudden, horrifying clamor and in orderly ranks attack the fort, more fortified with sleep than prepared for the present peril. / Like criminals who never enjoy a moment's peace, the natural condition of vice being constant fear of misfortune, so no sooner do they hear some noise than they imagine it to be retribution and run for their weapons, each one doing whatever he can to save himself, / just so the startled Araucans leap up, half-asleep and half-awake, suddenly aware of the danger and thrusting aside the shelters they had raised. Finding themselves without breastplates does not stop them from exposing their brave chests, instead with unshakeable courage they run to the defense of the wall. / Shaking off sluggish slumber and recovering their usual fury, one seizes a bow, another a piece of wood or half-burned log from the fire, another a sword. Here one rushes for someone else's club, there, to be quicker, another emerges with nothing, determined to fight unarmed, if not with fists, with teeth. / At this moment, Lautaro, as we know, was reasoning with the lovely Guacolda, reassuring and scolding her for her lack of trust. She will not listen to reason, however, and is becoming even more upset since such talk only distresses her more, when suddenly the harsh sound of horns and drums interrupts their tender, loving moment. / A miserable miser, doting constantly on his riches, does not leap up with such agility upon hearing the sound of a thief, nor does a mother come running with such haste to the cry of her beloved child, fearing some savage beast, as does Lautaro at the first outcry and tumult. / Having no time to don his armor, the audacious barbarian instantly runs to the gate, his blanket wrapped around his arm and his sword and body both bare. Oh, perfidious, inconstant Fortune! By what cruel means you achieve your ends, snatching away the goodness of so many years with a single blow! / Four hundred Indian allies, having come from nearby to help the Christians, attacked the fort with their painted bows, their ready hands launching great volleys of vigorous shots. As the son of Pillán was leaving his tent an arrow came in search of him— / Oh, cruel fate! —and piercing his left side its pitiless point passed directly through the bravest, most steadfast heart ever held within a human breast. Death gloated over the shot, seeing a single blow achieve such a feat, and usurping the killer's glory took credit for the wound. / The force of the keen-edged arrow was such that it laid the barbarian out on the sand, opening the way for a great rush of black blood from his full-flowing veins. The color left his face, his eyes rolled back, and with raging grief his soul, detached from its mortal body, sank furiously to the infernal abode. /

[14.19] Our men now take the ditch and rampart from twenty directions, and with no one there to stop them most have already reached the stronghold's interior. With courage but no cunning, lacking helmets, shields, and breastplates, the barbarians begin a ferocious, bloody battle. / The Indians who had allied with Lautaro quickly appear at the sound of the tumult, filled with fear and surprise. Hearing the merciless blows, however, their spirits troubled but their ears alert, they seek out wherever the uproar is least. / Like timid deer that cautiously raise their necks and stretch their ears at the sound of a hunter, then hearing the bleating of a doe that the men and dogs are tearing apart, bound away from the danger in a furious rush, / just so this vile, lowly throng, accustomed to yielding to fear, abandon the fort.

Leaving by hidden paths, unseen and unused, they run this way and that, spreading in all directions, for the fear of death is so great the most valiant see a ferocious Spaniard behind every leaf. / Those whom fear could never count among its own, whatever the danger, confirm their ancient renown, using their brave chests as shields. No one sees them deny a bare head to a keen-edged blade, nor does their left hand refuse a sword, assuming the duty of the right. / Young Corpillán, far from daunted when his hand and sword fall to the ground, burns instead with sudden hatred. Standing firm against the enemy, he recovers his sword and with furious scorn throws away his right fist, which was still gripping the handle, offering vengeance to his left. / Nor did Millapol betray any weakness after being run through the side, struck in the head by a back-stroke, and having a lance-thrust pierce his chest. The lance was half-covered with bubbling blood as it exited, but the empty hole it left was filled with new rage and determination. / Firmly gripping his club with both hands, he now wields it with even greater fury, and anyone the ferocious barbarian overtakes can well be called unlucky. In a final, mortal rage he raises the iron-plated cudgel, but just at that moment life fails him, and body and club collapse together. / Death broke his furious advance midstride, but a stalwart Spaniard was still knocked to the ground by his weight and momentum. Once back on his feet, in his delirium this man turns to where his assailant lies, and seeing him dead on the ground attacks him, thinking him still alive. / Throwing himself on the corpse, eager to deal death to the dead, he violently batters the bloody body, wounding it on one side and the other until finally out of breath he cautiously steadies himself and, still suspicious, sees the rolled-back eyes and cold face of the one with whom he has been grappling. / Meanwhile Diego Cano, wielding a sword drenched with blood, draws back his brutal arm as he closes with Picol, penetrating his chest with its point. Confounded by death, the Araucan falls to the earth in agony, his face already ashen, rolling in the mud until his soul leaves all behind. / With two blows Hernando de Alvarado leaves the agile Talco stretched out dead, but is himself badly wounded on his unprotected side by the brave Guacoldo. The Spaniard is stunned for a moment, but then recovering from his stupor runs straight for the powerful barbarian and buries his sword in his chest. / Old Villagrán, attacking the barbarians with a murderous blade, kills, wounds, tramples, and torments, turning in all directions at once. He lands a blow on the head of Nico, whose troubled eyes roll back as he falls dead to the ground, and with another leaves Polo with only his left arm. / Accustomed to meeting steel, when the swords come into contact with soft, naked flesh they need little force to strew arms and legs on all sides. The barbarian who's second in line does not hesitate to be first, rather they all pursue the same goal, and like waves constantly growing stronger they keep coming, bravely offering themselves up to death. / With scarcely enough room to use their swords, men attack each other and no more than fall to earth than their places are taken by someone else. As corpses rise in mounds some men fight atop others, at times packed so tightly they push each other into the swords. / Weapons are wielded with such furious force that most of the blows are fatal, and those that are not leave eternal impressions. Everyone groans when bringing down their arms to strike, but the effects are uneven, for some strike solid steel, others soft, unprotected skin. / Like butchers slicing up meat on chopping blocks with their long, curved knives or like blacksmiths battering solid iron plates on hard anvils, thus do the sounds made by the blows of the fighters differ, some cutting through flesh and bone, others leaving dents in tempered armor. /

[14.36] Juan de Villagrán, firmly in the saddle, sets out full-speed against Guarcondo, the lance he hurls at his breast emerging an arm's length from the other side.[83] The barbarian leans against the rampart in a swoon, his face turning pale, then abruptly collapses, vomiting his soul from the wound. / His brother Rengo, seeing the colorless body fall to the ground, feels his blood curdle and turn to ice as he loses his mind in sudden grief. Once he comes back to himself the arrogant unbeliever turns blaspheming toward heaven, and raising his knotty club, reaches Villagrán in one bound. / Pon had already struck the Spaniard's horse in the middle of the forehead with a swift arrow. The horse rears up, its neck erect, and ignoring bridle and spurs, puts its head between its forelegs, impatiently shaking its haunches and kicking out behind. Surrendering to cruel fate, Villagrán trades his saddle for a seat on the ground / and has scarcely hit the dirt when Rengo's ready club comes down with the force and sound of a thunderbolt or earthquake. The blow puts the Spaniard to sleep as the barbarian spins about with another, bringing it down on his head and driving out brains and eyes and soul. / Not satisfied with this revenge for his ill-fortuned brother, with new rage and even more hatred he strikes Diego Cano so hard that

---

83   There are four Villagráns in the poem: Francisco de Villagrán, who replaces Valdivia and engages Lautaro (5.3.1 ff.), is described as being ill when Lautaro menaces Santiago, at which point he entrusts command to his cousin, Pedro de Villagrán (12.61.1), also referred to as "old Villagrán" in the present passage. Two other Villagráns make appearances: Juan, who succumbs in the present scene, and Gabriel, mentioned a few octaves below (15.36.1).

his chin droops to his chest, the reins fall from his hand, and senseless and almost cold his horse carries him off where it will. / In the midst of the horde, the infuriated Rengo now wields his iron-plated bludgeon on every side. This man he cripples, that one he maims, another is left hugging the neck of his horse; one hangs stunned from its haunches, another is forced from the saddle. Everything in Rengo's path is battered, trampled, and flattened with the same power and insane fury. / He is completely covered with blood, which pours from more than ten wounds, but instead of faltering he bellows, dealing ever more forceful and brutal blows as he nimbly leaps about, running this way and that. Denting helmets and armor, he crushes tall crests and smashes brains, grinding muscles, flesh, and solid bone. /

[14.43] At this point there arose a terrible clamor of swords, lances, shouts, and cries. A crowd of men headed toward it without knowing its cause, which turned out to be a valiant young man wielding an enormous sword and performing amazing feats as he moved among the barbarians' blades. / Driven by diabolical fury and bathed in sweat and blood, the intrepid youth, his ferocious countenance covered with dust, advances like mighty Mars inflamed with bloodcurdling rage and brandishing the sword with which he beats on Vulcan's iron shield. / Maneuvering the weighty weapon with remarkable speed and skill, he slices Cron in two with one blow as if he were a tender reed, then sends agile Pon to hell. After Pon he dispatches Lauco, and no armor proving any defense, he continues to mutilate, mangle, and disfigure. / This soldier, named Andrea, gigantic in size and proportions, was humble in origin, his homeland northeast of Genoa. With a strength and speed to match his brawny limbs, he wields his great sword so well that anyone coming within its reach is killed. / With one slash at the waist he divides Guaticol in two pieces that fall to the sand, then with another cleanly cuts off the right leg of the unfortunate Quilacura. Using similar blows he fills the inner space of the fort with the dead, piling corpse on corpse. / Snatching Colca's head from his shoulders with one slice, he aims his sword at Maulén, lord of Itata, cleaving him from top to bottom with a backstroke. Fending off the lances, axes, and clubs of the attacking barbarians, he leaves a multitude of blows embedded in their chests and backs and sides. / Like a valiant bear harassed by hunters, which feeling itself injured becomes enraged and shatters their knotty javelins, clearing a path through a mountain gorge with furious impatience while pitiful, wounded dogs, chastised, give it wide berth, / just so the fierce Andrea is encircled by barbarians, yet spins about with his sword, opening a broad path. The fervor, shouting, and fighting grow so great that everyone comes running, and just at this moment the blood-stained Rengo arrives as well. / Like two mastiffs surrounded by small yapping dogs that catch sight of each other and come forward growling and arching their spines, thus these two mighty warriors, raising their ruthless weapons, advance to attack. . . But I must defer their combat to the following canto. /

CANTO 15

In this fifteenth and final canto of Part I the battle ends, and none of the Araucans being willing to surrender, all are killed. Also recounted here is the sailing of the ships from Peru to Chile and the great storm they encountered between the Maule river and the port of Concepción.

What good can there be without love? What lyric lacking love can be pleasing? Was there ever a rich vein of verse that love has not inspired? A subject not based on love is not complete, for joys and cares and pleasures, if not of love, are but illusions. / Love shatters the shell of coarse sensibility, engenders wit and true delight, and makes everything finer. Dante and Ariosto, Petrarch and Garcilaso were all inspired to great subtleties by love, and the richest and most copious language, if not of love, is unsatisfying.[84] / How is it then that I, with an uncouth wit, rude style, and subject lacking in both love and ornament, dare subject myself to the sharp tongues of critics? Good intentions and worthy zeal are what have led me to retie the cord I once cut to cure such daring, / having abandoned this account as too long and laborious from always adhering so closely to the truth and to a single theme. No style is so sweet nor pen so fluid it doesn't grow dull in a long harangue, nor is there a taste not cloyed by one food alone. / Were I free to venture farther afield, perhaps a variety of fragrant flowers would revive enjoyment, for then I could, like others, weave a thousand adventures and stories of love into my work. Having come this far, however, I must continue with what I've promised. /

[15.6] I left Andrea and Rengo where their fight was fiercest, coming face to face with sword and club raised high. The Lombardian wore mail, but the armorless Araucan was more nimble and the first to strike a blow. / The great-limbed Italian, seeing the ruthlessness with which the cudgel descended, raised his shield and sheltered beneath it. The solid metal was split down the middle, however, and the blow landed so hard on his head that he ground his teeth and saw a sky full of stars. / Andrea now brought down his arm from on high, expecting with such a tremendous

---

84 Dante Alighieri (1265-1321), whose *Divine Comedy* features his beloved Beatrice; Ludovico Ariosto (1474-1533), author of the chivalric romance *Orlando Furioso*; Francesco Petrarca (1304-1374), important early humanist and author of the *Canzoniere*, a collection of 365 poems, mostly sonnets, dedicated to his beloved Laura; Garcilaso de la Vega (c. 1501-1536), important Spanish poet who introduced the 11-syallable sonnet line from Italian to Spanish poetry.

effort to slice Rengo in half, but the valiant barbarian, not losing a moment, leapt quickly to the side like an agile panther or nimble leopard and the sword fell in vain. / The Araucan circled his mighty club and struck, and had it landed squarely it would have crushed not only Andrea but solid rock. Thus the balanced contest continues, although I fear for Rengo, since the first time the falling blade finds him the fight will end with his life. / With great dexterity and presence of mind, deprived of armor but armed with courage, he lunges, pulls back, and spins like the wind, for in speed and cunning he is exceedingly gifted. He always lands his blow, after which his adversary finds him so far away that even were his sword two arm-lengths long it couldn't reach him. / The furious Italian rends the air with a thousand vain slashes, enraged at seeing a naked Araucan keep him at such a disadvantage, in spite of his armor. Bringing his hands together he grips his sword and lunges, arms aloft, intending to cut Rengo in two. / The barbarian bravely lowers his club and waits, then shifts to the side just as the blade descends, and the arm and blow come down on nothing but empty air. The momentum of the mighty sword was so great that Andrea lost his grip on it and was left standing there with half of his shield. / Seeing him like that, his agile opponent dropped his club and rushed at him, clasping him face to face so tightly that Andrea's mail was imprinted on his chest. This did not worry the Italian, who thinking to get at his adversary more directly, seized him in turn in his unyielding arms, intending to lift him off the ground. / That which valiant Hercules did to Antaeus, our countryman wanted to do to the Araucan, but Fortune did not heed his wish and his effort came to nothing.[85] Instead, the formidable Rengo drove him a good

---

85   See n. 60, above.

distance around the clearing, stumbling over dead bodies while assailing him with ever greater fury. / Andrea, utterly enraged and burning with shame at being so beleaguered by anyone, managed to regain his footing. Drawing strength from his loss of honor, he now hoisted Rengo entirely off the ground, for his oft-proven power was entirely equal to such a burden. / I've seen Andrea, vying with other young valiants in tests of strength, take a rope in his teeth that was tied to four of them, and in spite of their all pulling in different directions, drag them along, his hands bound behind him, using only his teeth. / He could easily pick up the largest barrel of water, one holding some twenty *arrobas*, and lifting it several feet off the ground keep it calmly suspended as he quenched his thirst with long quaffs, not spilling a drop, then lower it to the ground like the lightest pitcher.[86] / Another time, crossing one of the region's raging rivers, the force of the current, surging against rocky outcrops, seized the boat in spite of the swiftly-plied oars. Andrea instantly threw himself into the water, covered with mail as he was, / and with a rope in his teeth, setting his stalwart chest against the furious torrent and pulling with his formidable arms and legs, he forced his way across the channel, towing the boat safely onto the bank and out of danger. A thousand other stories I leave untold. / He got the best of Rengo here, as well, no small proof of his ability, but Rengo, burning with anger at finding himself borne aloft and unable to get control, steadied himself by sheer force and resisted, his shame calling forth new resolve. After some time the two finally let go of each other and resorted once again to their weapons. /

---

86 The *arroba* varies widely depending on locale, signifying three to six gallons when applied to liquids; a gallon of water weighs about eight pounds.

[15.21] As if they had been resting all day, their fierce assaults now began anew, one swiftly and fearlessly attacking the other, now from above, now from below. Unprotected Rengo conducted himself with such skill and agility that he fully sustained his share of the fight, giving up no ground at all. / At one point he landed a quick blow on Andrea's side, the force of it contorting his entire body. He redoubled this with another, and another still, and to my count a fourth, which was coming down even more heavily when the wary Italian managed to step aside, wounding the barbarian in turn with a stab of his sword. / The blade ran through Rengo's powerful arm and opened a wound in his side, but such was his luck that the thrust did not deprive him of his life. Now venomous with fury, the barbarian was instantly at his ruthless enemy, bringing down his club. / The Italian raised what was left of his shield to receive the terrible impact, and while unable to stop it, deflected part of its damage. The brutal blow still hammered his head, and his helmet, as if made of pewter rather than well-tempered steel, was left badly dented. / Dizzied by the stroke, Andrea took two or three wavering steps, his memory and senses awry, and staggered to the point of falling. Blood burst forth in a great gush, first from one ear then the other, as from freely flowing fountains, and it was only with difficulty that he stayed on his feet. / Regaining his senses and finding himself covered in blood and reduced to such a state, he became more furious than ever. Burning with rage at being treated like that by a barbarian, he drew back his right arm and leg to gain more leverage and brought down his weighty sword with a noise that made the mountains resound. / Seeing the force of the massive blade's fall, Rengo bravely crossed his club above himself and got beneath it for protection. In spite of its many steel bars the cudgel was not sufficient defense, however, and a great piece of it ended up on the ground while the furious blade landed on his head. / The blow, from which a crimson geyser instantly erupted, was exceedingly dangerous, and Rengo was on the point of falling, stunned and almost blinded by blood. The Italian did not relent, but seeing it no time to relax again brought down the enormous, sharp sword with all the strength he could muster. / The disconcerted Rengo was struck in the middle of his bare forehead and would have been opened up from top to bottom had the Italian's hand not twisted in delivering the blow, which landed on the flat of the blade. The Araucan fell flat on the ground as though dead, and the sword, shattered by the impact, broke into three or four pieces. /

[15.30] Crino, turning his head at the sound of the mighty blow and the fall and seeing valiant Rengo stretched out like that, thought he had departed this life. Moved by friendship and family ties, he now brandished his murderous weapon in revenge, a sword Tucapel had won from its owner at Penco. / With a stab he pierced the padding of Andrea's breastplate, the cruel point not stopping there, but tearing through the mail at his side to penetrate bone. The Indian was about to follow with a two-handed blow, but astute Andrea, seeing the approaching blade, was so quick to respond that he left it no time to strike. / Instead he quickly closed with Crino and seized him, and in payback for the wound lifted him high above the ground, then hurled him down on his back with a great crash. To bring the fight to a quick conclusion, he then took away the Indian's sword and with it his life. Afterwards the Lombard made his way to where ferocious Mars was spilling the most blood, / cleaving a path through the thickest part of the throng, and woe to any who encounter him!

One he splits open from side to side, another straight down the middle; this one he slices at an angle, those two he threads on the point of his sword. He lays out others, yet still not satisfied, batters and disjoints them with kicks, scattering countless arms and heads through the air. /

[15.34] The good Lasarte erupts in the middle of the tumult with his wrathful right arm, piercing Talcuén in the chest with a stab. He then turns furiously on Titaguán, slicing open his unarmed head, but the raging barbarian wheels about, and before giving up his soul responds with an oblique blow that the pommel of the Spaniard's saddle scarcely stops. / Pacheco opens up Norpa's side and sends Longoval tumbling down dead after him. Nearby, Juan Gómez, covered with fresh barbarian blood, has brought down Colca with a single blow and opened Galvo's unarmed belly. The dying barbarian, now pale, gives up his soul enshrouded in his final breath. / Gabriel de Villagrán has not been idle, and after knocking down Zinga and Pillolco is bravely wheeling about in the midst of the hostile blades. The thunderous clamor of weapons, shouting, and other sounds confound the troubled birds, which stop to watch. / As rage increases and fury burns, the soldiers crowd together to fight, no one seeking more space than is needed to die on one's feet. Some slash, some thrust, others batter and hew, and such is the ferocious jam and crush that the dead, propped up by the living, do not fall down. / I can't fully describe the pride and rage, the courage and disdain, nor can my pen keep up with the rapidity and cruelty of the blows. No one fears death, instead if it turns aside they show their regret, knowing too well that should they live they'll do so defeated. / Even though the Indians despair of survival, with all hope of winning now lost, they delay the moment of death in order to die more fully avenged, nor do they deny their chests to the lances or retreat one step if such a step prevents them from injuring the enemy. / Four here, six there, they fall dead on all sides, some drained of blood by a thousand wounds, others ripped open from head to chest, still others with hearts exposed through backs and sides and still beating within brave breasts, declaring their great courage. / Some, slipping in their own entrails, continue to attack the odious enemy. Others, breathing noisily, reveal their inmost bowels through twenty wounds. One sees life vacillating through which door to make its abrupt departure, then in the end exiting them all, strength, life, blood, and breath all failing in a single moment. /

[15.42] Having died rather than surrender, not an eighth of the barbarians were now left on their feet. Pedro de Villagrán, watching from the side and seeing those who remained so badly injured, sent two Indians on his behalf to say that if they surrendered and accepted the yoke of obedience they would be treated with clemency. / The Spanish checked their swords and remained in place as the two messengers presented the truce with its conditions and assurances. When the Araucans heard that infamous pact, however, their shame was so great, as was their courage, that they made no response at all to the proposed terms, / but turning their eyes skyward roared, "Death! Death!" and nothing else. Thus they called on death, determined to die, shouting, "Life of shame, be gone!" This was their answer and this is what they cried, and with fierce courage they prepared to bring the bloody battle to a close, drawing new strength from adversity. / Shoulder to shoulder they came together, some fighting on their knees since their mutilated legs had failed them and they could no longer stand, yet still brandishing their swords. Others, thrashing about on the ground, rolled against the feet of their enemies to do what harm they could. / Dismembered bodies, collapsed in the mud and pools of blood yet still alive, could be seen struggling with furious death, rabidly writhing like fish in a draining lake, where floundering between two elements they wallow and die. /

[15.47] Had cruel Sulla or murderous Nero, however great their thirst for blood, seen its spilling here, I vow they would have been sated, for here they could have bathed in that vital human fluid with even more savage joy than Sulla the butcher in the Campus Martius or bestial Nero in the Roman Forum. / All those who refused to surrender lay equally prostrate, for having been led to the end of life they inevitably surrendered to death. Exhausted and badly wounded, the Spanish now left the walled enclosure, climbing with great difficulty across the bodies and weapons of the barbarians with which it was filled. / Not a single enemy was left standing inside the fort, nor any arm able to wield a sword. Mallén alone had succumbed to fear and to a base destiny, for being so close to death had given him a violent desire to live, and after his left arm was badly wounded by a ferocious sword thrust he had hidden behind a thick wall. / No longer hearing the turmoil, which had echoed about the entire plain and which, as I said, had now been silenced by death's angry hand, he left the wall, venturing out to see if there might be some Araucan who could bind up his painful wound and save him. / But when he saw the state of the place and such a slaughter among his companions, whom death had disfigured but his envy made known, with shame-filled rage he raised his sword to his heart, speaking thus: "What is this? Do I alone remain as witness to the death and valor of so many friends? / Cowardly heart, clearly unworthy of the blow from a valiant sword, since being denied such a fortunate end stems not from destiny but from my own choice! Your weakness has diverted me from the road to eternal fame, and through your frailty I now come to a shameful death, however much I have tried to avoid it! / Could I but mingle my blood here with that of the State, then seeing my body cast among these others, even if wounded by a feeble blow, I might be numbered among those who defended their fatherland. But woe is me, for my own weak hand would surely be recognized if I wounded myself! / What proof will suffice, what amends or compensation can I make on my behalf to satisfy the injury to my honor, my homeland, and my companions? I tarnish the bright glory and immense fame of so many, since it can be said there was one among them who, vilely and from panic, hardly saw the enemy's face. / Yet why heighten fear, delaying with wordy speeches the journey I must make, and what good does repenting do now when repentance is worthless?" Here he fell silent and with no hesitation brought his murderous sword to his neck, the pitiless blade passing swiftly across it to sever the thread of his young life. /

[15.56] Let Mars's fierce fury now cease for a while and let the swords rest, while I return to the voyage begun by the scattered ships, which after contending with harsh Notus were breaking boldly through Neptune's towering waves against the gales, triumphing over the violent wind and water.[87] / Sailing through the uninhabited Sangallá islands, we passed other unknown ones to the west and nearing Chaule came within view of Arica.[88] Later, with

---

87 This account of the ships resumes from the interruption at 13.40.6; Notus, or Auster, is the south wind.
88 The Sangallá islands noted here may refer to what is known today as Sangayan island, off Peru's southwest coast. Arica is the

Canto 15

some difficulty we made out Copiapó, the first valley in the actual province of Chile, / which is where the winds emerge from their hollow caverns and are truly free to blow. Full of fury they rush violently across that entire vast sea, breaking free of their prisons against the command of Aeolus, their king, who, fearing lest they destroy the earth, has shut them up beneath a great mountain.[89] / This fails to control their fury, for finding themselves constrained to their caverns, with great roaring they seek a way out through closed hollows and clefts. The solid earth trembles at these disturbances, and there are frequent earthquakes in the surrounding mountains and towns that destroy men, herds, and houses. / At this season the rains diminish and the days grow longer, in reverse of Europe, as the sun passes the equinox and moves closer to Capricorn.[90] The ships continued their struggle against Auster and the waves, but assisted by Boreas soon anchored in the port of Coquimbo.[91] /

[15.61] We had scarcely set foot on its longed-for sand, steadying our steps as we left the ships behind, when we forgot about the endless sea and the perils and hardships of the long voyage. Richly harnessed and spirited horses had been readied for our arrival, and once we were settled upon them we were led to the new city of La Serena, two leagues from the port. / Its residents gave us a warm welcome, and gratefully acknowledging our assistance, provided sweet refreshment and nourishing food

---

northernmost city in Chile; Copiapó is the first settled area south of the Atacama desert.
89 In Greek mythology Aeolus is the keeper of the winds; the present passage is inspired by Virgil's *Aeneid* 1:52-53.
90 In the southern hemisphere the September equinox, the point at which the sun enters the constellation of Capricorn, marks the beginning of summer.
91 Boreas is the mythological north wind.

with which the hungry armada, weakened after sailing for so long, was restored. / Everyone now waited for the men making their way so bravely across the harsh desert with the horses. Wearied by hunger and hardship and resisting every turn of fortune, they finally arrived, after which they rested for a month until the horses had recovered. / Afterwards, having recuperated from their rugged journey and not awaiting the fleet, they set out once again, keeping the nearby sea to their right. Crossing through fertile Ligua they bypassed Quillota, for they wanted to reach Mapochó, which is where the refugees who had escaped from Penco were staying. /

[15.65] The sun was now bringing a new season to mortals, leaving the constellation of Gemini and beating down on northern regions from its solstice zenith.[92] Just as its distance from the south was making midday shadows longest, and the winds, given free rein, were blowing so ferociously from their southern caverns, / we returned to our familiar ships. Unafraid of the angry gales that cross the area flaunting their full violence, we hoisted the great anchors with cheerful spirits and unfurled our sails to the northwest. / The sea was calm and the weather good. A cool breeze blew favorably from astern, and the sky was clear and completely serene, with every indication of staying that way. For six days we sailed like this, but on the seventh, Fortune, never fixed in its benevolence, troubled the sky with clouds and shifted the wind, churning up the sea from its bed. / Now Boreas in his fury took the lead with swift, powerful gusts, and suddenly great hills and mountains arose on the level, tranquil sea. The Spanish, anxiously watching the insane furor of water and wind,

---

92 At the June solstice the sun moves from the constellation of Gemini to that of Cancer, marking the beginning of summer in the northern hemisphere and of winter in the southern.

would rather have been on land, even had it meant an end to the war. / I can only speak of the ship I was on, the armada's leader, which tossed about by the terrible storm was proceeding with no control or direction. Yet who, amidst such an assault, would have been self-possessed enough to avoid mistakes? Not even I was spared the fear that took hold. / The wind attacked the vessel with such fury, its violent, unrelenting blows coming so rapidly, that it caught hold of the lofty mainsail and was at the point of breaking the mast. Seeing the weather so agitated, the pilot leapt up and shouted as loud as he could, "Loosen the halyard! Let it out! Loosen it quickly, for the wind is growing worse!" / The furious sea, ferocious wind, and clamor and confusion, the sudden nightfall of dense, gloomy black clouds and the desperate vows, the peals of thunder and countless lightning flashes, the cries of pilots and the rushing about, all made such a din and mournful harmony that it seemed the world was coming to an end. / "Strike the sails!" the seamen shouted, then, "Down with the mainsail! Up with the jib!" The passengers loudly repeated the words, and a great number attacked the halyard. Elsewhere, a confused throng ran quickly to the sheets, braces, and clew lines, but the wind's force was so fierce the rigging could not be controlled.[93] / The skies split asunder, the angry sea bellowed, and the arrogant winds howled in fury. Now a mountain of water rising higher than the clouds attacked one side of the galleon with a great roar, submerging it for a considerable time, and the men's terror was so great they swallowed expectations of death with the brine. / God, however, had decided our ship would emerge from beneath the sea spilling a great river from each side, like a great whale shaking its body as it bursts through impetuous waves with

---

93   Sheets, braces, and clew lines are various ropes in a ship's rigging.

its furious, blunt snout, exposing its immense back and sending water outward in great rings. / Stormy Boreas, grown stronger, was lifting the sea toward the heavens, and even though the mast was a massive mangrove, the topsail arched over the prow. With great effort and loud shouts the men struggled to bring down the sail, since it was bowing the mast so far the parrels couldn't slide.[94] / Aeolus, whether by chance or because he felt sorry for the afflicted Castilians, now began to restrain intrepid Boreas. He meant to lock him up himself, but upon opening the cavern cell he failed to notice Zephyr waiting nearby, who seeing the gate unchained went roaring out to sea.[95] / Snatching up whatever clouds he found in his way, Zephyr hurled himself at the heaving waves in a violent blast, closing in the night with pitch-black funnel-clouds and hampering the mighty swells driven by the sudden fury of the north wind, angering them as he convulsed the churning water even more. / Suddenly a squall and torrent of hail shook the ship from the side, tilting it so far the topsail touched the waves. Its fury was so sudden the men had still not lowered the sails, and seeing the shoreline and wrathful wind the pilots surrendered all hope to cruel fate. / Battered by wind and sea, with its keel exposed, one moment the ship was hoisted on mountains of water and the next completely submerged beneath the waves. At this point a violent blast opened a great breach in the churning waters, the sheet to the topsail broke, and the mainsail tack was all but destroyed. / A cry rose up among the men, thinking that all was lost, and their eyes were fixed on the chief pilot, who was too distraught to command. Some shouted,

---

94 Parrels are rings of wood, metal, or rope encircling the mast, inside of which run rigging for the yards.
95 Zephyr is the west wind.

"Run it aground!" Others, "Pull the rudder to the side!" And some, distracted, looked for the door to a hatch or a plank or beam with which they might face the final test. / Fear grew and the clamor increased. One said, "Out to sea!" Another, "Back to land!" One yelled, "Strike the sails!" Another, "Into the wind, don't strike the sails or we're lost!" And still another: "Grab the axes and cut! Masts and all that's topside overboard!" Beside themselves, everyone rushed here and there in a confused mob. / The cables and rigging were groaning, stretched taut by turbulent Zephyr. The swollen waves roared mightily as they broke on the neighboring cliffs, piercing the darkened gloom and low cover of tangled clouds as they battered the rugged rocks so fiercely the resurge rose whitened toward the sky. / The wind was blowing athwart, and the beaches of the wild coast nearby, filled with reefs, were boiling with a mix of water and sand. The mainsail sheet was severed, the bowline slack, and the foresail loose. The lateen yard was still aloft, and what little remained of our shattered hopes had been snatched away by the furious wind. /

PRAISE BE TO GOD

END OF PART I

1569

Part II of La Araucana

Don Alonso de Ercilla

1578

TO THE READER

Having promised to continue this history, I have with no small difficulty persevered with it, and while this Second Part of the *Araucana* doesn't show the labor it cost me, those who read it can imagine writing two works on such a harsh and monotonous subject. From beginning to end there's only one theme, and it seems to me there's no taste will not tire of following me according to the rigor of a single truth, along a road so dry and desolate. Fearful of this, I've often wanted to introduce some variety, but have decided not to change the style, hoping that what I speak of may counter the book's faults and help ennoble it, as in my description of the lofty beginning the King our lord gave his reign with the attack and capture of Saint Quentin, on the very day we attacked the Araucans in the fort at Concepción, and similarly in my account of the great victory won by don Juan de Austria in the naval battle at Lepanto. Placing two such outstanding events in such humble surroundings is no small daring. Yet the Araucans merit it, having sustained their cause for more than thirty years without ever letting the weapons fall from their hands, and not while defending great cities and wealth, but having willingly burned their homes and belongings in order to leave nothing for the enemy, protecting nothing more than hard-packed earth (however often moistened with our blood) and barren, rocky soil. Such fortitude and steadfast dedication to their purpose offer a vast field to writers. I leave much of it aside, perhaps what's most important, for those prepared to take on the work of it, considering my own well spent if received with the same good will with which I offer it.

CANTO 16

In this canto the storm subsides, and the Spanish arrive at the island of Talcahuano in the bay of Concepción. The council held by the Indians in the valley of Ongolmo is described here as well, along with the argument that arose between Peteguelén and Tucapel and the agreement they reached.

Come forth, weary voice, and with redoubled effort break through the confusion of sounds and pitiful laments troubling heaven and earth! Lending my labored breath new strength, let Fame's loud trumpet spread the fury of weapons and new war across all the world's globe! / Grant me your favor, oh sacred King, for this is what will help me most, finding myself in peril from which your fortune alone provides protection. See where my worthy intentions have led me and accord my words a hearing, for seeing you attentive the wild waters will instantly calm their fury. / Turn your gaze to your ship and aid it in this great crisis, for if saying so be permitted, I believe everything is subject to your will, even the arrogant sea resisting fate's harsh decree as it wrenches reefs from their beds, mingling waves with sky. / I pray that my broken vessel may reach its longed-for port in spite of the hostile seas and angry winds that strive to obstruct it, delaying the moment at which an ancient and bitterly defended cause must finally be defeated in your favor. /

[16.5] Exceeding their domains and limits, the four powerful elements now conspired against the feeble ship, the violent, untamed anger of their ancient enmity resulting in utter disorder, convulsed and churning, as in the confusion of primal chaos. / Attacked by such adversaries, our crippled craft forged ahead and for a time fought back the powerful waves, one side almost submerged. Overwhelmed at last by the raging wind and sea and unable to resist any longer, it then neared the towering cliffs being battered by the violent surf. / In anguish at the approach of death, men's cries and laments grow louder, and borne on tempestuous Zephyr strike the hollow crags from afar. Pilots, sailors, and soldiers rush madly in all directions. Some shout, "Loosen the ropes!" Others, "Pull them tight!" Some dash to halyards thinking them sheets. / Distraught with fear they get in each other's way and hinder each other's efforts. One loudly confesses, beseeching God to forgive his sins. Another makes a special vow, another a promise. One bids good-bye to an absent mother as terrifying panic continues to swell their prayers and shouts and cries. / The entire sky appeared to be falling to earth

Canto 16

in its fury and the arrogant, tempestuous waters to be scaling the sky. Almighty, Eternal Father, what is happening? Is drowning one small vessel so important that wind, sea, and sky employ their utmost powers? / Amyclas's boat was not attacked by such ruthless wind and waves, and though only built of fragile planks it bore the fate and fortune of the world![96] Nor did Ulysses's ship nor the fleet that escaped on Troy's last day see gales so furious and incensed seas so high. / The firmest faith gave way to pressing fear, and death's terrifying visage was imprinted on every face. Resigned to their fate, with no hope of help, the men abandoned control to chance and were running wildly here and there / when a blow from the insuperable sea, wrapped in a sudden squall, burst a thick rope of the mainsail rigging and the galleon began to sink. Now something remarkable happened. A clew of the loose foresail, whipping about, snagged the tip of the anchor, / and ripping it from its place like a poorly secured stake sent it flailing this way and that in the wind.[97] It was breaking and battering everything when God, who never forgets his own, even though he may delay his favor, caused the anchor's curved fluke to catch on the bowsprit. / The sail instantly steadied, the vessel held a straight course, and in spite of the gales and sea, with the rudder turned into the wind the galleon headed west. Our sudden elation was so great our terrified hearts could scarcely withstand the extremes of joy and fear. /

[16.15] As soon as cheer had driven away despair and our frozen blood returned to the limbs it had left, our contrite,

---

96 In Lucan's *Pharsalia*, Amyclas, a poor fisherman, rows Caesar from Greece to Italy in the midst of a storm that precedes a decisive battle in the civil war (5.505-677).
97 The clew is a ring at the corner of the sail used to attach the rigging.

brave company, faces bathed in tears, turned heavenward and with devout prayers and offerings gave thanks to God for his benevolence. / The enraged sea and savage wind continued their noisy attack, but try as they might, Philip's fortune now had our vessel in tow and was leading it over the towering waves, still striving to drown the heavens. / At this point the dark fog surrounding us was scattered by the wind, and we made out Herradura to the east and to the south the lofty island of Talcahuano.[98] Recognizing the longed-for land of Arauco and our good fortune, we came to port with the wind at our backs, gazing upon the bald promontory of Penco. / The harbor here is protected by a small island that blocks the fury of the north wind and continuous swells that batter it so violently from that direction. Its long, curved tip creates a tranquil inlet, and here in the quiet bay our weary ship finally found refuge and sweet shelter. / Having come to rest, destroyed and innavigable, in the protection of a lofty ridge, we secured it with a heavy cable and sharp-toothed anchor that gripped the seabed. The topsail had scarcely been lowered, however, when the happy clamor of war reached our ears, reviving our benumbed bodies and spirits. / The small island was inhabited by a brave, bellicose people, and seeing the good fortune of a ship arriving alone they began to shout, "To war! To war!" Cheerfully taking up their menacing weapons, they rushed to the shore in a furious, disorderly horde / and at the foot of a sharp rise formed into a battalion. Resolved to face any danger or threat, we hastened to arm ourselves, the perils of the recent storm making all others seem like nothing. /

---

98 Herradura is a port between Concepción and Itata river; as indicated in the canto's introductory synopsis, Talcahuano refers to the island in the Bay of Concepción.

Canto 16

With new strength and eagerness we ran to the skiffs, as though the ship were aground on a sandbar far from land, and from its broad sides let down the two great boats, into which as many of us leapt as could tightly fit. / What happened next is not some fictional poetic ornament, but genuine history and a true account. Whether some prodigious event, strange omen, or sad foreshadowing, or perhaps an unusually abrupt motion of a malign star, or whether, as is more likely, the motion of the earth exceeded all order and understanding, / the wind grew calm, and just as our soldiers were reaching the shore a bolt of lightning singed the veil of clouds with brilliant flames and a comet cleaved the heavens, darting down in the shape of a lizard. The sea roared, and the distraught land groaned as though pained by a great weight. / Paralyzing fear suddenly severed the courage of the troubled natives, who took this unusual sight as a sinister augury of their ruin and of coming evils, seeing in it sad signs of loss, destruction, and perpetual servitude. / So terrified they dared not await us, they tossed aside their weapons and the orderly battalion scattered, scurrying to save their unhappy lives. In the end they left their beloved haunts behind, and taking their women, children, and belongings along secret paths, they escaped the island on wooden rafts. /

[16.27] Waiting no longer, our troops ran quickly through the deserted huts and hovels, coming upon stores of rustic provisions. Promptly blocking every trail and outlet, they then searched the caves and marshes for the absent inhabitants, / encountering some poor Indians who had tried to hide, as well as others surprised in small villages, unaware there was anything to fear. All these they reassured with kind treatment, offering them sandals, headbands, and clothing, along with friendly words, and thus calmed sent them peacefully to their homes. / Our men also informed them that the principal purpose of our enterprise was the salvation of the baptized Indians who had rebelled in defiance of Holy Sacrament and taken up illicit arms, perfidiously breaking both the law they had accepted and their own sworn vows. / Were these people to return to the Christian rule they had previously professed and the loyalty they had offered the great Charles V, we assured them everything would be resolved to their utility and benefit, making them firm pledges of such pacts and agreements. /

[16.31] Afterwards, with no one to impede us, we moved the materials we needed for fighting and building shelters to a fitting location on the island. Everyone was instantly busy, one setting up a tent, another an awning or lean-to, while some lighted fires and used pans to dry our damp, moldy grain. / Black, fearsome night fell earlier than usual, quickly covering the earth and sea and wrapping the world in its gloomy veil. There was not an awning or tent or anything else the wind did not then proceed to knock to the ground, as though trying with new violence to tear the islet from its foundations. / The storm lasted until long-awaited day drove off the clouds, leaving the sky serene as it reclothed the damp earth and somber air in cheerfulness. Realizing the instability of the weather, our beleaguered company set out to defend itself against such harsh winter violence, / some taking thatched roofs from the dwellings of the absent Indians, while others proceeded to a more protected site loaded with planks, boughs, and reeds. Here, atop sturdy tree trunks secured deep in the sand, we began to raise a great number of shelters and soon constructed an entire village. / Just as birds, taught by necessity, are seen weaving their meager nests in rooftops and secluded corners, coming and going with beaks full of straw, feathers, and twigs, even so each man made a lodging for himself in this desolate, exposed place. /

[16.36] Once everyone was settled in the marshy site, my Lord, having used all our skill to prepare against the brutal winter, we readied our weapons and released a terrifying volley from the powerful cannons, setting all the surrounding land and sea atremble. / Remote barbarian nations heard the enormous, unexpected blast. Alpacas and vicuñas, jaguars and pumas ran terrified here and there; dolphins, Nereids, and Tritons hid deep within their caverns, while swift rivers and springs, confused, restrained their flow.[99] / The explosion was heard within the State, where some were so stunned their proud, never-defeated heads drooped to their chests. Thus warned of our arrival, their bellicose instruments began to ring out and bright pennants and banners were unfurled along every river. / The sixteen Araucan caciques gathered in the valley of Ongolmo with neighboring leaders, and having resolved to fight us they entered a council of war over place, time, and the necessary preparations. / Rengo attended, as well, admitted to the council because of his courage. If you recall, we left him stunned among the dead soldiers at Mataquito. Shortly afterwards he returned to his senses, however, and in the end he was fortunate enough to escape, holding fast against the fury of wrathful death even though drained of blood.[100] / Caupolicán, standing in the midst of the silent caciques, looked at each in turn as they attentively awaited his words. With a calm spirit and

---

99 Alpacas and vicuñas are llama-like animals native to South America; Nereids are mythological nymphs who live in rivers and seas; Tritons are mythological deities of the sea, usually portrayed with human heads and trunks, attached to the tail of a fish.
100 Cf. 15.29.

serene expression, he then gravely raised his voice and broke the deep silence, expressing his plan and fury in the following way: /

[16.42] "Valiant warriors, we see from signs and tokens that the happy time promised when we must make ourselves immortal has now arrived! Benevolent Fortune has led this great company of soldiers to us from the farthest reaches of the East so you can defeat them in a single day, / eternalizing your swords at the cost of their lives and blood as you restore our ancient, oppressed laws to their full power. Extending to distant realms, our laws must be kept sacred and inviolable, with as many living in equality beneath their protection as live beneath the stars. / Since these soldiers, banners flying, have been so brazen as to invade your lands and forbidden regions with their foolish designs, it's best their insolent daring be punished with a definitive response, before delay encourages their hopes or lends them strength. / I have thus resolved, gentlemen, if you concur, that we will attack them as fiercely as possible in a surprise assault. No one should think there is any other way forward than the one he clears with his own valiant arm, for the furious weapons we hold in our hands are what will determine whether these men are legitimate lords or simply tyrants." /

[16.46] With this he ended his speech, and the good Peteguelén, a severe old man and the oldest among them, proposed the following as a soldier and wise counselor: "Oh, captains!" he said, "I'll not be first to refuse to shed my blood, which even though age may appear to have frozen, still boils fervently in my breast! / One thing alone makes me hesitate, causing me to question such an attack, and it's the reliable reports we've heard regarding the numbers of Spanish and their good organization. It's clear that a great provocation requires a great response, but underestimating matters leads to painful perils. / Since the site they occupy is naturally strong and protected, encircled by sea and lofty slopes and guarded on all sides, it will be more prudent and advantageous to listen to their proposals without denying or contradicting them, for listening alone obliges us nothing. / This cannot hurt, and meanwhile you can ready yourselves by assembling more men, secretly preparing all that's necessary as you resolve any difficulties and forestall any problems, block open trails, and finally take the matter in hand. . ." /

[16.50] He was unable to say more, for belligerent Tucapel furiously interrupted him, saying, "Someone so cautious will never undertake an honorable campaign! Should the entire State recoil because Caupolicán's plan seems dangerous, I alone will take up arms for our cause and bear the burden all by myself! / Have you lost such confidence in your oft-proven strength that even though your arms can still hurl lances and wield swords you'd reveal some change in your courage, staining your victories with some base truce that insults our fame and honor? / Know that as long as I have strength in my arm and a voice in the senate—let Peteguelén say what he likes—this matter must be settled by arms. Anyone proposing another route will first have to forge it through my side, and this iron-plated club, not speeches, will offer them my reasons and arguments! / If those of you who pride yourselves on being well-spoken have the courage and daring to contest this in the arena, I'll prove to you more clearly what I mean. But if you're determined to call fear prudence in order to avoid risking your lives, you'll end up doing nothing but talk!" /

[16.54] Peteguelén replied, "Since reasoning was never an option with you, I alone and old as I am accept your challenge and will punish your foolish audacity! Armed with cured hides or mail, with lance, sword, or club or whatever else you like, I'll prove that when the time calls for it my hands say more than my words!" / Who could describe the disdainful face Tucapel turned toward the sky! With bright sparks shooting from his eyes, not deigning to look down, he said, "Such arrogance is indeed worthy of Tucapel's wrath, but for the sake of my honor and your age I request that someone assist you." / "Never have I availed myself of anyone's help," the old man answered, "not even when my veins were drained of blood, nor do I feel my arm so feeble right now that I don't intend to show you what's what!" But Rengo, his nephew, arose and interposed himself, saying, "If you want, I'll accept the challenge for my uncle!" / "I want it, request it, and am delighted with it!" shouted Tucapel, "and with ten more besides you!" But leaping up from his seat, Orompello now said, "I'm the one you have to deal with, Rengo!" "I'll amend your brashness as well," proud Rengo replied, "and you'll see how little I credit your threat and challenge, once I've finished with your cousin!" / "I plan to punish you first in such a fashion that little will be left for Orompello," Tucapel declared, "since the least that can happen is that you'll end up my prisoner. Come on then! Enough! I've no desire to delay the inevitable, and since we have the weapons and time and will, let's settle the matter!" Rengo and Peteguelén would both have instantly responded with weapons and words if many noble caciques and warriors hadn't intervened, asking that the warriors defer those threats and disputes until fortune might bring an auspicious end to their common enterprise. / Caupolicán had grown impatient seeing Tucapel always upsetting everyone with his insolence, without any cause or concern whatsoever, both in peace and war. But the time and situation required that he indulge him, and thus with a grave but gentle request he mitigated the fury and extinguished the fire, / its being settled and accepted among them that as soon as the war ended the old man and Tucapel would be free to fight in the arena one on one, after which Tucapel and Rengo would decide their case the same way. The clamor abating, Colocolo began to address them, rising alone to speak. /

[16.62] "Noble caciques," he said, "if those of us who've spent so many years scrutinizing the future be allowed to say what we think, we see that we're only using our strength to destroy ourselves and raise the tyrant's mighty blade to our throats! / The clearest sign of the ruin I fear is that Fortune now wavers and begins to disturb the sky. When a great edifice tilts it isn't far from falling, and a building raised on unsound footings will collapse of its own accord. / Given these signs and developments, unless I'm wrong, I have good reason to be afraid, seeing our ill-founded structures scattered across the ground and our warlike customs converted to servile exercises, destroyed, finally, by your obstinacy, which comes from excessive pride. / We now see Lautaro dead, three of our banners lost with great dishonor, and our battalions torn to pieces and left to the wind and sun as fodder for wild beasts. Our forces and opinions are divided, our countryside filled with foreigners, and yet our furious weapons are turned against ourselves. / Behold how the fatherland dies and liberty perishes through blind negligence, your own power favoring the enemy's cause! Incurable and deadly is an illness that doesn't respond to medicine, and bestial a passion that won't tolerate healthy advice! / Why do we strive with such rage to deplete our own strength and blood, and absorbed in internal disputes cede authority to our enemies? Why with such fervor do we tear apart this invincible union, condemning our own just cause and legitimate weapons while justifying those that are unjust? / What foolish rancor have you conceived against yourselves that you would see the Araucan State destroyed by its own hands, its valor and strength choked off and reduced to an infamous name, subject to foreign laws and governance, to cruel servitude and eternal bondage? / Come to your senses, for without realizing it you're running full speed toward a cliff! Rein in your fury and passion, which are what will harm you most in this situation. In your very midst you tolerate an enemy who wants to dominate you like brute beasts, and yet you're too impatient to tolerate helpful advice? / It's clearly a lack of courage and sign of hidden weakness that with the enemy directly in front of you, you turn your own swords against yourselves rather than await with unswerving courage the cruel blows of angry Fortune, which the steadfast heart resists unto death. / Inspired as you are by natural boldness, whose excesses I sometimes condemn, remember your heroic deeds, which fill not only this land but all the world, and cease this madness and disgraceful contention! For the sake of the common good don't break our fraternal bonds in such shameful ways, for we're all members of one body. / If wearisome old age and lengthy days are due some credit and respect, consider my ancient white hair and zeal for the common good and briefly delay your dispute, deferring it until the Spaniards' furor wanes and our common cause is resolved. / And since I expect your own good sense to set you on the proper path, I've no desire to bring up additional arguments, given how amenable you are to reason. Leaving all this aside, the main thing hampering our zeal and preventing our getting the situation in hand, from what I can see, is lack of preparation. / The stretch of water you see before us cuts us off on all sides, and without a way of crossing it hinders our plans and progress. Since our enemies expect to make a new arrangement and pact, it won't hurt us to listen to them even if we never intend to accept it. / This way we'll gain information about their intentions and motives, which being illegitimate, we'll be able to utterly disrupt. Meanwhile, we'll prepare weapons and munitions, for these are what will in fact, in the end, declare our rights. / But be forewarned, noble warriors, that in order to bring these matters to a successful conclusion, our outward intentions must always be peaceful, displaying enfeebled hearts, shattered strength and hopes, and land rich in gold mines, the tempting bait these people always take. / Perhaps in this way we can draw them away from their island fort, reassuring them with feigned docility, and lead them skillfully to their deaths. Thus with neither sounds nor signs of battle, let us change course so that they come onto terra firma trusting in free entry and safe passage." /

[16.78] When the wise old man finished his speech, there were opposing opinions, some saying the danger was too trivial to justify such fear and inconvenience. But Purén, Lincoya, and Talcaguano, along with Lemolemo and Elicura, being more prudent, agreed with the old man's assessment, and thus the few prevailed upon the many. / They promptly dispatched Millalauco, a well-spoken and experienced young man, circumspect, diligent, and clever, so that feigning some genuine and honorable pretext he might penetrate the plans of the Spanish while taking note of our situation, soldiers, and numbers. / After being instructed by the caciques as to what was most important and timely, he set out without further delay in a long gondola-like boat and propelled by swift oars quickly reached our camp, where without any hindrance he immediately leapt ashore, secure with his escort. / In the meantime, driven by a fresh wind, three more of our ships had arrived in the harbor, filled with reinforcements of arms, men, and provisions. The noise and activity of military preparations were so great that the astute Millalauco was amazed and stood there a moment disconcerted. / Hiding this and dissembling his surprise, however, he crossed through the midst of the commotion, his judicious eyes taking in everything as he noted the weaponry, soldiers, and men's spirits. The goal of the Araucans grew more difficult as he viewed the land and sea now covered with armed men and machines of war. / Arriving at don García's pavilion, where I, among others, was present, he greeted us with modest courtesy and cheerfully raised his voice. . . But my own, now wearied with singing, has no strength left to continue, and thus I must bring this canto to an end. /

CANTO 17

Millalauco conducts his embassy. The Spanish leave the island and build a fort on the hill at Penco, where the Araucans attack them at the same time Phillip II is attacking Saint Quentin in France.

One should never not listen to an enemy or suspect friend, for the more cunning they are the more you'll learn. Whether honest or deceitful you'll be wiser having heard them, since a word or sign will always betray their true intentions. / Just when they think they're misleading you most with a deceitful demeanor and clever dealing, they're alerting and putting you on their trail, and thus concealing their deception they reveal it. You see the target at which they're aiming, its strengths and weaknesses, its benefits and harm. No talk is so duplicitous and cunning that nothing can be inferred from it, / and no breast so artful it doesn't reveal some plan. In the end tongues serve their purpose, even more so when the one who listens knows how to be discreet. Speaking never fails to offer a clue, nor does silence ever divulge a secret: nothing's more difficult than recognizing a fool when he's silent. /

[17.4] It's important for a military commander to know his adversary's abilities and temperament, his intentions and motives, and whether or not he's swift or sluggish, prudent and moderate or reckless, diligent and keen or careless, indecisive or resolute. / Thus we see that in order to learn their enemy's intentions, the barbarian senate had sent the cunning Millalauco to the Spanish camp in the guise of friendship and speaking friendly words. Once there, with deceptive demeanor and using all courtesy, as I noted earlier, he looked about him and raised his vigorous voice, speaking as follows: / "Fortunate captain and company, to whom I've been sent for peaceful purposes by the State and seigniory of Arauco, with the voice and authority of the great senate: don't think that fear or cowardice has ever made us desperate enough to resort to shameful pacts or base means! / You surely know how far the name and reputation of Arauco reaches, defending and sustaining distant territories beneath its mighty hand, just as we recognize how you've come to spread your doctrine, moved by Christian zeal and using great discipline and moderation. / This being the case, as your conduct until now confirms and your reputation and fame so clearly proclaim, I come to give you our assurances and certify that the peace you offer, so long desired by us, will be accepted by the caciques. / The illustrious senate, in wise accord and sound judgment, having heard various reports and motivated by legitimate issues and concerns, wishes to accept your proposal, desiring an agreement based on just and honorable conditions, in order that the common people and children do not suffer. / If the inviolable oath and loyalty affectionately sought by you and the gracious and secure welcome offered freely by us can provide a foundation for these matters, with reasonable conditions and equal honor and without our subjects and states being diminished over time, / then without hesitation we'll accept Charles as our friend and lord, willingly offering him a submission and obedience otherwise undue. But if you intend to obtain these ends by violence, you'll sooner see us eat our own children and our swords bravely pierce our own breasts! / With fair treatment you can raise the banner of your King without concern, for the State, having laid down its weapons, awaits you with open arms, realizing that benevolent heaven calls it to a secure and lasting peace that leaves the past forever buried in perpetual silence." /

[17.13] With this he finished speaking and made a reverence in their customary fashion. His presentation appeased both our desires and his malice, for by minimizing the barbarians' power he encouraged our eagerness and greed, leading us to believe they were weak and possessed an abundance of wealth and riches. / Don García, having listened to the envoy, made him a gracious welcome, responding in short that he was pleased with the proposed friendship and offered terms, and that in the name of the King he would match their good will with treatment that not only would not harm the people but relieve them of many labors. / In confirmation of this he had two servants bring out various gifts: bright, multi-colored clothing, sandals, sashes, and strings of beads, ribbons, and insignia, raiment appropriate for noble captains and lords, all of it received by Millalauco with gracious words and bearing. / Thus in the guise of a grateful and obliging friend, asking permission to leave, he returned to the boat he had left and by the time the sun sank behind the mountains, as diligent as ever, he had arrived in the State where he was joyfully received by all that noble company. / In light of the agreement and their present situation, the caciques dissolved the council, and with signs of dispersing their soldiers they returned peacefully to their homes, where they secretly and silently prepared their perfidious weapons while inciting the common people, always ready for some new endeavor. /

[17.18] Suspicious, and not without cause, we remained in that place for more than two months, resisting the implacable winter's harsh rain and wind. But once this season had passed, wanting to know the barbarians' intentions, we resolved to leave our island encampment and make our base on the mainland. / One hundred and thirty hard-working and courageous young men, the most robust of the troops, were chosen and readied, then quietly and discreetly supplied with weapons and the necessary tools. Never averse to testing my fortune, I, too, joined them / in raising a rampart on a small, bare hill overlooking the nearby sea, where surrounded by a broad, deep ditch, our small contingent would be safe until our horses arrived, which we had heard were on the way. / Once on land our troops would hear of any harmful plans among the barbarians, were they secretly to begin readying their weapons under false appearances and feigned friendship, and should they make a move we could assault them with a sudden cannon volley that would break their resolve and bring them suing for peace from fear alone. /

[17.22] It was a foolish fantasy to think the proud Araucans would desire a path to peace as long as their hands could wield weapons. Yet with no help beyond that of the silent night, the one hundred and thirty brave youths crossed to the mainland with all due speed, / and even though Virgo was quickly lengthening the days, restoring the hours that night had usurped, before dawn scattered the stars the lofty hill's summit was covered with men and materials.[101] / Some of the soldiers dug deep ditches with iron rods, picks, and spades. Others used great curved blades, axes, saws, hatchets, and cleavers to cut thick beams and trunks, which they secured in the ground and covered with wattles of branches and brushwood in order to mound up emplacements and curtain walls.[102] / Not with such fervor did diligent Tyrians, as zealous as they were, hasten to build their famous city, nor was Caesar as quick to raise the miraculous wall encircling the scattered enemy army of his careless son-in-law at Dyrrachium, / as were our men in crowning the hilltop with a sturdy rampart and eight stout pieces of artillery, surrounded by a broad, deep ditch.[103] In full view of Arauco they then hoisted the flag of Philip, King of Spain, and took possession of that State, which joined the others relinquished

---

101 The constellation of Virgo and its brightest star, Spica, disappear from view in the southern hemisphere at the end of winter, near mid-September.
102 Curtain walls connect a fortification's towers or bastions.
103 Dido, whose brother Pygmalion was king of Tyre, fled her homeland with her followers to construct the famous city of Carthage (the story is told in Virgil's *Aeneid* 1.425-40); during Caesar's Civil War, Pompey, his son-in-law, gathered his forces in Dyrrachium, where Caesar besieged them (see Caesar's *Bello Civile* 3.41-74, and Lucan's *Pharsalia*, 6.11-14).

by his father.[104] / Those with long experience had never heard of such audacity and thought it more reckless than brave that amidst these proud, feared people one hundred and thirty men were able to achieve, in less than a day, something as difficult as it was dangerous. / Afterwards the rest of our assembled troops crossed safely to the fortress, whose lofty position and terrifying cannons made the crossing uneventful, and once stationed along the curtain walls we placed ourselves as one in Fortune's care. /

[17.29] Garrulous Fame was already flying from tongue to tongue through the Araucan territory, embellishing the size of the small Christian army and frightening the people with hollow rumors and vain uproar, which often affirm the dubious while exaggerating every ill. / Once these reports reached the ears of our enemies, they thought no further of pacts or treaties, but quickly prepared their soldiers and weapons, and waiting no longer, resolved to attack us with flame and sword. / Gathered in Talcaguano for this purpose, a little more than two miles from our position, the valiant Gracolano, a bold and fine-tempered youth, loudly proclaimed, "Oh, great Caupolicán! Should my contribution prove worthy, I promise that in tomorrow's assault I'll raise my standard at the very top of their fort! / And to satisfy you and everyone else with my efforts, my lord, I vow with this well-worn lance to clear a path through our adversaries' chests, my arm being the first to fend off their weapons and instruments of war, even though they block my ascent and the whole universe oppose me!" / Thus he spoke, and with the stars beginning to appear the barbarian battalion approached the fort in a rapid march, concealed by darkness, and hid in a great ravine at the foot of the mountain to silently await the hour of bright dawn. /

---

104 Charles V abdicated his throne to Philip II on January 16, 1556.

[17.34] That night I was uneasy and unable to relax a single moment, both from the danger and from a need I felt to write. Awake and pensive, with my restless imagination churning, I had resolved to take my pen and unburden my memory of some aspects of this history, / and there in the silent darkness, amidst the resting soldiers, I was about to continue my account when a strange affliction suddenly overcame me: a chill ran down my spine, my vision was abruptly clouded, and trying vainly to get hold of myself the pen fell from my hand. / I wanted to cry out but couldn't, for a sudden infirmity prevented it, and a sharp pain and harrowing sensation deprived me of my strength and senses. Once the terrible moment passed and I returned to myself, the torment left me feeling as though I had emerged from a lengthy illness. / As soon as the anguish abated, with many a sigh my heavy eyelids closed, weighed down by fatigue, and thus relaxed my weary limbs surrendered to welcome rest as sensibility withdrew into the noblest part of being. /

[17.38] I had scarcely yielded my exhausted body to the repose of sweet sleep when I heard a tremendous crash that seemed to shake the earth. Standing before me was a woman of haughty expression and furious demeanor whom I immediately recognized by her great stature to be the brawny and brutal Bellona. / Gowned from foot to waist and from waist to head protected by brilliant, scaly armor, she bore a shield on her arm, a great sword at her side, and in her right hand brandished a cruel lance. Hideous Furies encircled her wrathful countenance, the color of blood. Thus she addressed me, burning with bellicose ardor: / "Oh, timid youth, pluck up your courage and recognize the happy opportunity your fortune and good luck now offer! Flee vile and indolent idleness, expand your hopes and heart, and aspire to great things since heaven is favorable if you'll only heed it! / Seeing your devotion to writing, clearly shown by savage arms and cruel combat not upsetting your pen, duty moves me, in consideration of such loyal labor, to take you to a place where you can more fully express yourself. / There, in a fertile field of countless flowers, you'll find abundant topics of greater and more famous wars with which to feed your inspiration, and should you decide to celebrate the sweet pain of love and ladies in your verses, you'll also find more subjects and greater beauty than in any previous or future age. / Follow me!" she said at last, and I, astounded, seeing her return the way she had come, began to follow with rapid steps and bold heart, leaving to the left and right two mountain ranges that the Atlas and Apennines were far from equaling either in grandeur or dense forests. / We emerged onto a broad plain where nature's artful hand revealed its wealth and beauty in all manner of marvelous works, mingling, amidst leaves and other greenery, white lilies and red roses, jonquils, orange blossoms and sweetbriar, lilac, jasmine, and violets. / Clear murmuring streams crossed the delightful terrain, and gentle breezes gladdened the flowers and verdant meadows. Birds of many colors flew through the luxuriant treetops overhead, their melodious songs blending in sweet harmony. / On all sides I saw great numbers of the loveliest maidens scattered about in groups. Some were absorbed in games, some gathered fragrant bouquets, others softly sang sweet songs of love to the lyres and zithers of skilled satyrs and fauns. / The delightful domain offered every pastime and activity, including the arduous occupation of chaste Diana, which a few figures were pursuing here and there.[105] Now a peccary traversed the meadow, now a deer; there a hare was leaping, and antelope, goats, and fawns frolicked

---

105 Diana is the goddess of the hunt.

Canto 17

through the grass and blossoms. / Someone trailing a wounded stag crossed the plain toward the mountains; someone else, urging on courageous wolfhounds, was chasing a bristling wild boar. Some loosed trained falcons that soar above other birds of prey: here they killed a heron, there a crow; here a timid fallow deer, there a doe. / In the middle of the plain was a perfectly round pyramidal peak dominating everything else. Without knowing how, in the blink of an eye I was caught up by fierce Bellona and set on its towering crest, leaving me stunned and confused. / Finding myself elevated so suddenly, I dared not look down for a few moments, then timidly turned my frightened gaze this way and that. A gentle breeze, suffused with delicate aromas, rose to the mountain's lofty summit, which was crowned with greenery and small flowers. / The height here was beyond the flight of agile eagles, and as I gazed fearfully about, it seemed I was near the heavens and able to view the earth's vast sphere, from the lands of unknown barbarians to regions even more hidden and remote. /

[17.52] Seeing me aloft, Bellona said, "Given the little time left to show you what I've promised, I can't delay another moment. Behold the massive army there on the move and the thick black smoke and dust-cloud above that important stronghold on the border of Flanders and France. / The invincible Charles V, having triumphed over so many enemy nations and trod upon regions both arctic and antarctic, triumphed over fortune's vain pretensions, as well, and with his goals and claims secure, relinquished the imperial crown in auspicious circumstances. / Moved by the pious and saintly zeal he had shown for worldly governance, he then turned his gaze and thoughts toward heaven. Earthly affairs seemed little next to those he conceived in his heart, and thus renouncing all titles, realms, and states, the weight he had borne on his shoulders he placed on those of his son. / Gazing upon the felicitous career from which his victorious father had withdrawn, in order to justify the hope inspired by his own abilities, the son took the earliest opportunity to amass that vast army to humble the pride and arrogance of his enemy, France. / You see before you Saint Quentin, a principal stronghold and crucial citadel worthy of mighty Philip's fury, vainly resisting its destruction. Inside is Admiral Gaspard de Coligny, under whose command many experienced warriors have come to the land's protection and defense. / The enemy's army, as can be seen, is divided in three parts: Alonso de Cáceres with his *tercios* on the right, where Philip's standard is; the able Alonso de Navarrete on the left with Count Meghen; and next to the city, Julian Romero with troops of three nationalities: Spaniards, Germans, and Walloons.[106] / We've arrived in time for you to safely watch the bitter fighting and see Philip's troops entering not by ladders, but by the sheer force of their swords through the broken rampart. You'll see the ferocious assault and perilous extremity, and in the end the breaching of valiant France, for against inflexible fate no defense or stronghold is impregnable. / I must leave at once to take my place among the battalions, inciting hearts on both sides with new ardor. From here you can closely observe the opposing armies and nations, then write of their fortunes, giving due attention to each."[107] /

---

106 *Tercios* (literally, "a third") were a much-feared Spanish infantry formation based on a central block of pikemen surrounded by swordsmen and accompanied by harquebusiers or musketeers.
107 The battle of San Quentin, which was fought on August 10, 1557, is narrated in the poem as occurring in real time, that is, on the same day the narrator has just described the Spanish soldiers in Chile anticipating the Araucan attack.

[17.60] The wrathful goddess and her company immediately slipped through the air and in an instant had descended straight to Saint Quentin like a sudden bolt of lightning. Once there, they fanned the already-burning flames and joined forces with her friend, Discord, making her way among the troops inciting hatred in all their hearts. / At this point the infuriated army, set in motion by a final signal, rushed amidst a dense cloud of dust toward the battered but protected wall. Who has language ample enough to describe what I saw! My own talent is far from adequate, yet in the next canto I'll do the best I can. /

CANTO 18

King Philip attacks Saint Quentin and enters it in triumph. The Araucans attack the Spanish fort.

Who would dare constrain your valor and magnanimity to a simple summary and your grandeur to such a humble style? My pen may pass with agile inspiration through fertile fields, yet the present theme is certain to be diminished by it. / Attempting so much will surely be deemed a folly, and I myself fear I've overstepped prudent limits. Perhaps the desire I've always shown to serve you, leading me ever farther along this path, will refine my rudeness and sluggish, stuttering tongue. / I now beseech your favor, the source of my boldness and that which can enrich my meager mind, and being conceded what none are ever denied, my Lord, I cast my timid voice upon the wind, unworthy to recount such great achievements. /

[18.4] Trusting in your benevolence, sought for such a just cause, my Lord, I hope to be heard, which will be sufficient sign of your grace. I told in the previous canto how the furious Spanish attacked Saint Quentin from three sides, through breaches opened by the artillery. / Defying opposing fire and defenders, they forced their way forward in a rapid charge, overrunning everything with courageous hearts and ready hands, and reaching the battered ramparts the two sides began to fight at the most contested places along the walls, probing each other's strength and valor. / The French resisted the impetuous assault and bloody determination of their enemies with a brave show of weapons and devices. Growing more furious the more resistance they encountered, the Spanish overcame the most difficult opposition with stubborn courage. / The contested breaches saw intense combat, turmoil, and struggle; strange deaths, blows, and wounds delivered by powerful arms; heads cleft down to the neck and farther; and bodies cut to pieces, for neither shields nor helmets could withstand the cruel swords. / The fortress was attacked and defended with valiant determination on all sides. The pounding of weapons and battering of armor was something to see: the terrifying artillery, the cannonballs and other projectiles sent flying by gunpowder, the naphtha, tar, and resin, the oil, lead, sulfur, and turpentine. / There were hailstorms of hurled lances and arrows, of stones, planks, and beams ripped hastily from roofs and walls. The terrible rage and determination did not abate as the soldiers continued to wound and kill and crush, both sides enwrapped in fury, blood, and fire. / Some fearlessly defended the entrances with unbound bravery and confidence. Some fought in fear of their lives, hope giving them strength. Others, no longer hoping to live, strove only for vengeance with their deaths, falling so their bodies blocked the enemy's advance. / Like the indomitable fury of a sudden flood encountering an obstacle, the blocked water surging and swelling until it finally forces its way forward with even greater violence, bursting through the obstruction with a roar as it uproots everything in its path, / just so the French, lacking sufficient strength, were uprooted by the powerful current of Philip's auspicious destiny, and unable to do more against such fury, where Cáceres was in command they allowed the enemy to enter. / Even though the Admiral himself was fighting the crush of men at this point, in the end it was not enough against the advancing forces. He was taken prisoner along with the rest, and the fierce, triumphant company, leaving perpetual sorrow in their wake, went forward in pursuit of fate and victory. / At the same time, where the able Navarrete was fighting, the French could not repel the Spanish advancing by the sheer force of their swords, and in spite of ferocious Mars rallying the arms of their adversaries, our soldiers, waging cruel war and wreaking great havoc, quickly gained ground. / Andalot, entrusted with the defense of this side, was taken prisoner here, which is also where Romero attacked the third breach.[108] Indecisive Fortune having now declared herself, opening the way for obstructed fate, she extended her hand to Philip and he entered as conqueror of all France. /

[18.16] A terrifying chill ran through the spirits of the disheartened townspeople. Laments and cries rose skyward through the heavy air as the French soldiers cast aside their weapons in the name of survival, relinquishing their positions

---

108 Andelot is François de Coligny, brother of the Admiral.

Canto 18

in an abject flight to save their lives. / When the victors saw the great fear and lack of resistance, they stayed their weapons to avoid staining their triumph with carnage, and without delivering another blow rushed forward, their bloody furor changed to greed for the eagerly awaited sack of the city, the common soldier's reward in war. / Some battered on iron-plated doors and broke through hardened locks. Others, clambering up ropes and pikes, forced their way through windows and roofs. Smashing and ransacking on every side, no place however hidden was spared their scouring the houses from top to bottom with growing frenzy. / As when a ferocious fire suddenly flares up in a building or neighborhood, and hearing the alarm people quickly come running to offer their help, entering and exiting on all sides, some climbing and some descending, one pulling a loaded sack, another carrying furnishings saved from the flames, / thus the wild, victorious soldiers, greedy for the tempting spoils, flung open doors and windows, prompt hands and agile feet diligently dragging out chests and tapestries, beds and trunks, anything of the slightest value, leaving nothing behind from which they might profit. / Neither pleas nor cries nor the protests of widows and orphaned maidens, piercing the distant skies, diminished their insatiable greed. Instead, breaking pitilessly through their midst, the men rushed into the best-guarded places, believing that where resistance was greatest their gain would be as well. / Young maidens could be seen running frantically through the streets without a guardian, tearing desperately at their lovely faces as they lamented cruel fate. Disconsolate nuns, breaking their statutes and strict cloistering, wandered here and there, borne on by stupefying terror. /

[18.23] Before entering the city, pious Philip had ordered soldiers of every nationality to safeguard the women and houses of prayer with the utmost care, and in amity and concord to avoid disputes among themselves, since fortune would grant each a generous share of the pillage. / On his order the distraught women, carried away by fear as they ran frantically this way and that, were gathered together and secluded in a safe place. Here they were defended by trustworthy guards and protected from the fury of war, and while their houses were sacked, their honor remained intact. / The ruthless soldiers, obeying these Christian commands, showed continence as they restrained their impulses, but the great tumult of people and wild confusion resulted in growing damage to the city, and soon a fire broke out. / Quickly fed, the flames, fanned by Zephyr's fresh breezes, threw off dense sparks as they strove to reach the stars. The wretched, ill-fortuned people turned their tear-filled eyes to heaven in despair, swelling the anguish even more with their sorrowful cries and laments. / Piteous shouts rang vainly through the air on every side as the wretched, frightened French now threw themselves amidst the enemy troops, forced to their shame to choose a death they had earlier rejected rather than be helplessly trapped and burned alive in the searing flames. / The pious King's great clemency blunted the brutal weapons, and with prompt aid the furious flames were quickly extinguished. In the end, without further resistance Philip occupied Saint Quentin, the key to France in his hand and the road to Paris open before him. /

[18.29] The sun was slowly sinking in the glowing antarctic sky, when joyfully watching all you've heard described here in my verses, I saw a woman approach in garments whiter than snow. Her demeanor was grave and venerable, and from all appearances she was someone worthy of great respect. / "If some of the things I'm about to speak of as true and certain prophecies seem baffling," she said, "believe me they are neither fiction nor fantasy, but that which the Eternal Father wishes and decrees from his sacred throne, he to whom everything most powerful is subject: Destiny, Fortune, Time, and Death. / Out of this war and burning hatred between Spain and France, so deeply rooted, will come treaties and pacts sought by both sides, among them the restoration of his states to the Duke of Savoy, along with many other useful measures for the good of France and the honor of Spain.[109] / In order that peace be settled upon a firm and fraternal foundation, Philip will contract a marriage with Henry's beloved daughter. Her premature, cruel death will undo this union, however, for thus it is ordained by divine order and lofty heaven's fatal decree.[110] / During this period France will become corrupt and violate Catholic law, raising sacrilegious arms and denying the obedience it owes its King. Tempted by a life free of responsibility, this evil will gain strength as an army of disloyal soldiers gathers, sworn against the Church and their own monarch. / Ancient insolence and transgression will almost destroy the realm, and Charles will be reduced to doubtful circumstances by his perfidious soldiers.[111] Sumptuous churches will be contemptuously destroyed and the Sacrament and holy Lord himself insulted, his patience prolonging the wickedness. /

---

109 The reference is to the treaty of Cateau-Cambresis, signed in April of 1559.
110 Elizabeth of Valois, daughter of Henry II and Catherine of Medici, died in 1568.
111 The reign of Charles IX (1550-74) saw the beginning of the wars of religion between Catholics and Protestants, which lasted throughout the century.

Your King, with prompt and prudent foresight, will prevent such harm from entering Spain, eradicating the illness there with the necessary rigor and purifying fire.[112] Once the perverse pestilence is cured, Philip's armies, enemies of idleness, will move in fury against the East, and he'll send his soldiers and armada against Peñon.[113] / Although their objective will not be achieved on the first attempt, on the second rugged Peñon will be taken by storm, and the sea routes secured and the Moorish coastline left in fear, the victorious fleet will retire to port for the winter. /

[18.37] "At this time two princes, sovereign highnesses, will come to Spain from Hungary, sons of Caesar the Great and Maria, daughter of Charles and Philip's sister. Augmenting the joy and delight of the court they'll make the era proud: Rudolf, the elder, and Ernest, soon providing fame with their own accomplishments.[114] / Promising hope of high achievements from an early age, they'll grow in years and virtue most worthy of praise, the valor and training of Baron von Dietrichstein, a man worthy of the instruction of such princes, resplendent for all to see.[115]

---

112 The Spanish Inquisition began targeting Lutheran sympathizers in the late 1550s, leading to the effective eradication of Protestantism on the peninsula.

113 The first Spanish attack in 1563 on the Turkish stronghold of Peñon de Vélez de la Gomera, on Africa's north coast, was repulsed; the second, the following year, was successful.

114 "Caesar the Great" is Maximilian II, son of Charles V's brother, Ferdinand I, and Holy Roman Emperor from 1564 until his death in 1576; a few octaves later he is referred to as "Caesar Augustus"; his wife was Maria of Austria; Rudolf succeeds his father as Rudolf II; his brother is archduke of Austria.

115 Adam von Dietrichstein, the princes' tutor, accompanied them to the royal court in Madrid, where they remained from 1563 to 1571.

Canto 18

/ The following year the formidable fleet of the mighty infidel, threatening all Christianity, will sail against the West with such strength and weaponry that the coasts will tremble. The force will anchor at the island of Malta, twenty leagues in circumference, / where the Grand Master and his knights, together with other foreign captains, will offer their lives as they steadfastly resist the terrible siege for many weeks, accomplishing miraculous feats of defense.[116] / After being battered on all sides, by land and sea, from above and below, on the ninth assault the Saint Elmo fort will finally be breached and entered, greatly endangering the baptized souls within, since the Turkish fleet in the harbor will now have free entry through two openings. / Remarkable deeds will be witnessed, along with the perilous efforts of daring spirits when hope is most in doubt: guard posts, trenches, and ramparts leveled, terrible wounds and pitiful deaths, brave acts, an infinity of events worthy of being inscribed for all eternity. / When human valor can take no more and strength gives way to fatigue, the walls flattened, the moat filled in, and all hope lost, just as the bloodthirsty, inhuman barbarian is brandishing his sword above their heads, this is when the world will see what Philip can do and why he is so feared. / With no more than a small part of his fleet and a few scant soldiers guided by his fortune and renown, he'll beat back Ottoman destiny, and with afflicted Malta restored, his severely chastised enemies, unfurling their wearied sails to the wind, will retreat with unthinkable losses. /

[18.45] "One year later Suleiman himself will advance by land with a powerful army against Caesar Augustus, the illustrious

---

116 Malta, held at this time by the Knights Hospitaller, was attacked by Suleiman I, Sultan of the Ottoman Empire from 1520-1566, who besieged it unsuccessfully for several months in 1565.

emperor of the Romans. Hastening through great Pannonia, leaving Transylvania to the right and the vast province of Dalmatia behind, he'll come upon the frontiers of Croatia.[117] / For four weeks he'll besiege the remote stronghold of Szigeth, which having no possibility of assistance, will finally fall to Suleiman's ferocity. This difficult undertaking will culminate along with his life, however, which having run its course, wrathful death will bring to an end.[118] / Elsewhere, in Flanders, those states that have cut themselves off from God will also disturb the peace during this period. Infected by perverse errors and heresies and conspiring against King Philip, they'll attempt various paths of wickedness, bringing matters to such a state that the outcome remains uncertain for some time. / With the same pretense of freeing themselves, the Moors in the prosperous kingdom of Granada will also revolt, denying their sworn obedience to the King. This uprising, underestimated and not dealt with at its start, will prove damaging and costly both to noble blood and courageous soldiers. / A young man, masked by humble dress and appearance, will go to this war, his brilliant imperial lineage assuring him worthy enterprises. This is the child of Charles, still reaching maturity, whom the fates have promised sudden and splendid good fortune, but who'll remain unknown / until his father, on his deathbed, declares him to be his son, instantly elevating him to great estate.[119] Generous, valiant, and strong,

---

117 Pannonia was a Roman and later Byzantine province located in today's western Hungary and Austria.
118 The fortress of Szigeth is located in the town of Szigetvar, in present-day Hungary; Suleiman died of an unknown illness before the siege was completed.
119 Juan of Austria, Philip's half-brother, was given command of war against Granada in 1570.

he'll justly be loved by all. His name is don Juan, but about this I can neither say nor reveal to you anything else. / Let it suffice that in his youth he'll wage war against the rebellious Moors, and having destroyed and occupied their strongholds, force them to retreat to the mountains, where he'll press them so closely that in the end the mutinous area will be subdued and their wicked roots and seeds scattered to different provinces.[120] /

[18.52] "Once this war is concluded, the princess Anna will come from Germany accompanied by her ladies and a great retinue, and betrothed to King Philip as Queen of Spain, their distinguished wedding will be celebrated with rare pomp and majesty in ancient Segovia, home for a time to the famous kings of Castile.[121] / The two princes will then be summoned home by their father the Emperor, who, establishing a new dispensation in his states, will make Rudolph king of Hungary. Embarking for Genoa, they'll pass through Lombardy and arrive at the pleasant banks of the Danube and the famous city of Vienna. / As the period's revolts and disturbances show signs of abating and bellicose furor subsides, in barbarous regions the ruthless Turks will yet again levy arms against the powerful Venetians. / Amassing a mighty armada drawn from all their provinces, their pent-up fury will be discharged on the famous island of Cyprus, which they'll occupy at the point of cruel swords and where Famagusta, badly battered, will be breached through treacherous betrayal.[122] /

---

120 The Morisco revolt in Granada lasted from 1568 to 1571, resulting in the dispersal of the area's population through different parts of Spain.
121 Philip married Anna of Austria, the eldest daughter of Maximilian II and his fourth wife, in 1570; she became the mother of Philip III.
122 Famagusta, on the east coast of Cyprus, fell to Selim II in 1571.

Their arrogance will now be so great that after replenishing the men in their fleet they'll set sail for Italy with imperious designs, scorning the rest of the world and even the power of heaven itself. Such will be their presumption and bold show, born of your own faults and sins. / The Lord on High, disposing otherwise out of pity for your well-being, however, ordains that where merit is lacking his own blood and passion will settle the debt, and with a single breath he'll instantly reinstate the rightful penalty on such barbarian insolence, crushing their haughtiness in one fell blow. / Distressed by the hardships of a sinful but Christian people, he'll wield his powerful hand against the perfidious enemy, inspiring a League in which the Pope and Venetian senate will join their powerful forces and arms with those of the mighty Catholic King. / To everyone's joy, the robust young man in humble garb who went unrecognized among the people will be made general of this league.[123] I'm not permitted to reveal the future, but rest assured that you'll see it, for destiny assures you a life more long than fortunate. / Should you wish to learn the outcome of this as-yet-unheard-of future enterprise, the greatest and most notable that history will ever record, then as you're passing through the valley where the Rauco river is narrowest you'll see a gentle roe-deer standing on its bank at the foot of a cedar. / Follow it until you come to a clearing, at the far side of which, along one side, you'll see the overgrown entrance to a dark wood. On the trail of this timid deer, deep in the midst of that dense grove, you'll find a tiny, hidden dwelling beneath an enormous, overhanging crag, / and there in that uninhabitable place, devoid of any trace of

---

123 The Holy League between Spain, the Papacy, and Venice, organized against the Turks, lasted from 1571 to 1573; the narrative time frame is 1557, when Juan of Austria was twelve years old.

path or person, lives an ancient and venerable old man who was once a famous warrior. He'll tell you how to find the intractable Fitón, a mighty magician and wizard who'll reveal to you many marvelous things that are yet to come. / About future events I'll say no more, since the present offers you such ample material to advance your project. Great opportunities now favor you, and I'm only allowed to tell what you've heard thus far. / But if Mars's raging violence has unsettled your pen and you wish to mix gentle subjects with his harshness, then turn your gaze and look upon these beautiful ladies of Spain, for considering the wonders they embody I'm amazed Love doesn't inflame the entire earth! / But be on guard against the peril to your impressionable eyes, so that you have time to avoid it, and don't wait until the last moment nor count on your own strength nor on my help, for though I try to intervene, you'll willfully turn away from me." /

[18.66] Oh, human nature! Her warning me not to turn my head was enough to inflame the ready appetite, and not waiting for more advice I immediately shifted my gaze and instantly beheld, if such it might be called, a paradise. / There in a fragrant, fertile setting encircled by delightful plants and trees I saw gathered all the beauty nature could conceive, the sky above surpassingly lovely, the fresh, green meadow below adorned with a thousand different flowers and a clear, sonorous stream. / The women in this garden were the ornaments of fortunate Spain, in comparison with whom the bright sun, moon, and stars all seemed dark. Upon their heads were fragrant garlands entwined in myriad ways among blond tresses, braids, and ribbons. / Scattered here and there were throngs of worthy suitors who walked about absorbed in cares and desires, beguiled by delicate, tender love. Some were sustained by hope, others trusted in wealth, all found contentment in gallant, lofty thoughts. / Suddenly, with singular speed and fury, I was propelled through the empty air, leaving behind the mountain's lofty peak and descending to the lush, delightful plain, where, if memory does not deceive me, I saw my guide on the right, worried at having exposed me to such dangerous risk. / Once my feet touched the ground, my greedy eyes, free of the coarse, crude veil that had covered them until then, began to feast, and as an amorous flame and gentle trembling caressed my veins, my rebellious spirit and hardened heart were overcome and surrendered to love. / Instantly eager to busy myself with amorous stories and songs, changing my style from that of brutal, bloody wars, I fervently strove to learn about that setting and the beautiful women, especially one at whose feet I saw my fortune enthralled. / She was of tender age, but her calm discretion revealed maturity, and when she looked at me it seemed her star, her destiny, and my fortune all met as one. Surrendering to her beauty and wanting to know her name, I saw an inscription at her feet that read: DOÑA MARÍA OF THE HOUSE OF BAZÁN.[124] / I was turning my head to question my prudent guide about her, when the terrible uproar and savage harmony of barbarian weapons suddenly roused me from my sweet dream. "To arms, to arms! Quickly, quickly!" I heard, with a clamor of voices and equipment that seemed to split the high heavens. / In this confusion, half-asleep, I quickly ran to my nearby weapons and in a moment was ready at my post. Just then, with a ferocious yell, a multitude of warriors came into view on the steep slope of the hill as rose-hued Aurora appeared in the east. / Immediately, to both sides of me and with

---

124 Ercilla married María de Bazán, one of the ladies of Queen Isabella, Philip's third wife, in 1570.

no less bravura and shouting, there were so many of my fellow soldiers that their temerity would have frightened ferocious Mars. Now I'm too weary to continue, and thus I intend to describe everything more fully in the following canto. /

CANTO 19

This canto describes the Araucan attack on the Penco fort, Gracolano's rushing of the rampart, and the battle on the seashore between the enemy and those who stayed behind to guard the ships.

Lovely ladies, should my frail song now fail to proclaim your praise and these humble verses not rise to thoughts of love, it's because my haste is great and there's so much left to say that a thousand idle writers would be kept busy night and day. / Unwillingly diverted from this new purpose and theme, the desire to satisfy my debt to you will bring me back this way, and if fitting ornament is lacking for now, let my intention to do all I can compensate for the failings of my art. / Spanish

Canto 19

soldiers, complaining with good reason, urge me on, leaving no time to sing of other things, for having quickly surrounded the fort the barbarian army is threatening them with terrible threats and cries, as you heard in the previous canto. / As soon as their three battalions appeared on the crest of the hill they stopped, surveying the scene, and having noted the trench and wall gave the signal to attack. All then moved forward, brandishing their weapons so fiercely it appeared no one would escape death. /

[19.5] Young Gracolano had not forgotten his arrogant offer and bold vow.[125] Crowned with a mix of tall feathers and wielding an enormous, fire-hardened lance, he advanced a good distance ahead of the others, bursting through the smoke and dense shower of cannonballs fired by the formidable cannons and other projectiles hurled by hand. / Grasping the long lance as he reached the right distance, he planted its butt firmly in the ground and hurled himself forward on it with such fury that he crossed the broad trench in a single bound, then triumphantly scrambled up the wall on its shaft in spite of all the lances, pikes, and swords directed against him. / No bull, wounded and enraged by *banderillas*, ever charged the barricades as furiously or was as fiercely resisted by men and weapons as the intrepid barbarian. Brashly breaking through where it appeared most secure, he scaled the protected wall by force, / and casting aside his weapons, which he couldn't take advantage of and which were getting in his way, he strove to take the fort all alone with punches, kicks, and bites. With great skill and agility he fought off the shots, blows, thrusts, and stabs, his chest and shoulders equal to the furious onslaught of his many opponents. / Surrounded by weapons but with none of his own, he gave no ground and kept his promise,

---

125 Canto 17. 31-32.

always striving with little fear and great determination to die farther ahead, proudly persevering in his vain intention although already wounded in a thousand places, for luck and delirious Fortune had been suspending the mortal blow. / Insistent in his foolhardy effort, he threw himself amidst the steel, attacking like a frothing, mad dog wherever they wounded him most, and scorning life and danger, wherever moving forward was most difficult and least certain he confounded the countless blades directed at his stalwart breast from every side. / Finding himself alone in such a place and treated in keeping with such reckless self-assurance, he did not lose confidence, but with somewhat less hope attacked a soldier with his bare hands and took away his lance, planning to catapult himself back across the ditch to safety. / But inconstant Fortune, now weary of saving his life, cleared the way just then for a rock flung from some sturdy arm, and a large part of the impetuous stone embedded itself in the hollow of his temple, instantly bringing him down mid-air and mid-leap. / Like the Trojan Eurytion, who as the timid dove was winging her way through the sky, swiftly drew back his curved bow and pierced her mid-flight, her body twisting and turning as she fell to earth in a ball, just so the youth was struck in open air and fell dead in the deep ditch.[126] / Thirty-six wounds pierced his wretched corpse, not counting the last one to the head, which completed their number. The lance the valiant barbarian had won in a fair fight was left leaning against the ditch and extending partly above it. /

[19.15] Young Pinol had promised to accompany Gracolano in the assault and had fought alongside him as far as the ditch, although he had not dared attempt such a leap across it. Seeing

---

126 The episode is found in Book 5 of Virgil's *Aeneid*; see n. 58, above.

Canto 19

his courageous friend brought down and catching sight of the top of the lance, he rushed to seize it, trusting that a fleet-footed return would save him. / But even as there is no cunning nor skill against inexorable fate and cruel fortune, and neither swift feet nor agility are enough to escape the hands of death, whose inevitable blow comes even more quickly to one who thinks to flee, just so it came to the speedy barbarian at the moment he turned around, / for he had scarcely taken four steps when he was overtaken by two powerful bullets, which simultaneously traveling from back to chest in two different places stretched him out on the ground. He did not give up his soul so quickly, however, that one of two warriors who rushed to help him was able to seize the costly lance and save it at his own peril. / The Indians immediately hoisted the enormous spear on high, and with a mighty roar rising from their horns they furiously surged forward in an even line, coming with great ferocity to the ditch. Forced to halt here, shots on one side and arrows on the other were discharged in such multitudes they darkened the broad expanse of earth and sky. / At this point Martín de Elvira, the Spaniard who had lost the lance to Gracolano, caught sight of it from a distance. Consumed with rage and noble shame and determined to recover his honor, he went out alone through a small door, without his weapon, to confront / the audacious Indian youth of gigantic proportions who came forward scorning heaven and earth as he brandished the double-edged blade. Gracefully maneuvering the enormous, long shaft this way and that, now from side to side, now straight ahead, longing to test it on his enemy's chest, / the warrior gave a hard thrust that wounded the Spaniard, knocking him back six paces so that the brave man was stunned and saw himself practically at death's door. Being courageous and self-possessed, however, he braced himself and resisted, intending to grasp the weapon with his hand, yet he planned so in vain, / for the Indian skillfully leapt back to give himself space. Shaking the great, solid spear, he intended with one more thrust to bring the fight to an end, but the alert Elvira stepped to the side and seized hold of the shaft, and in spite of the other man's efforts rushed forward to close with him chest to chest, / quickly drawing forth a hidden dagger which found five or six ways through his ribs to his courageous heart. The dying barbarian, bleeding profusely, rendered up his soul through them all, and his massive body, now emptied of blood and breath, fell cold to the ground. / The valiant Spaniard, seeing his enemy laid low and victory certain, retrieved his lost lance and reputation and proudly withdrew to the door, which was instantly opened by his companions as he entered to great cheers from the soldiers. /

[19.25] At this point the Indians stormed the fort from all sides, throwing themselves amidst the slashing and firing, determined to win or die. Climbing atop the mounds of dead, the living discover previously unseen targets and better positions from which to fire at them. / Some swiftly obstruct the deep ditch with branches, logs, and earth. Others, prouder of their agility, attempt perilous leaps, and those coming behind are so eager to reach the fighting and trying so hard to advance that they shove those ahead. / The ditch is quickly leveled by the many being killed and wounded by harquebuses, stones, and other projectiles both hurled and dropped. The courageous enemy, putting aside fear, attack across it, reaching the best-guarded areas to match their weapons with ours. / Pursuing their daring design, they now begin the cruel combat anew, while others with even greater audacity scramble up the wall on their pikes. No height is secure from the barbarians' furious frenzy, and there is no place, however difficult to reach, they do not scale in order to fight. / Massed along the wall, our soldiers beat them back, striking and shoving and knocking them down with lances and shots. Those following them are little chastised, however, and do not delay the difficult ascent, but rather with new ferocity instantly take the places of the fallen. / One after the other they come, avid for honor and devoid of fear, the press of the multitude continuing to increase as the fury of the brutal blows intensifies. Covered by their concave shields, they break through our defenses, placing us in such straits that the impossible seems at risk. /

[19.31] At this point the infuriated Tucapel appeared boldly atop the rampart, covered entirely in shining mail and brandishing his hardened, knotty club. Like a shaggy Libyan lion bursting through a timid mob of closely-packed men, clearing its obstructed path with terrifying fury, / thus the contemptuous barbarian ran enraged along the wall, knocking down whoever got in his way or opposed him, even trampling on his own men and troops. Would that I had adequate words and voice to summarize the singular strength and valor shown by dauntless Tucapel that day! / Rows of pikes and other hostile weapons were not enough to resist him, nor could sturdy arms and solid chests block his way. He battered through throngs of soldiers and weapons unable to withstand him, and still unsatisfied with flattening them underfoot, threw himself boldly into the middle of our troops. / His strength increasing with the danger, he circled his powerful bludgeon, pummeling some, knocking down others, always gaining more ground and glory. In the end, fighting off brutal blows, he made his way through men and arms, steadily wounding to left and right with great risk to himself and terrible injury to the Spanish. / Peteguelén had also attacked, along the western side, where in spite of our men he reached the highest part of the fort. The burning valor in the old man's heart had spread a bellicose ardor to his very core, as though he were yet in verdant, robust youth. / But this did not last long, for an impetuous cannonball soon tore his head from his sturdy shoulders, bringing his illustrious career to an end. Another cannon fired immediately at the same spot carried off Guampicolo, who had been following him, as well as Surco, Longomilla, and Lebopía. /

[19.37] Among the men who had stayed on the ships, as soon as they heard the uproar and saw the sudden attack, some immediately rushed forward unarmed while others grabbed a breastplate or shield. Some threw themselves into skiffs; others thought they could reach the shore more quickly by swimming. Each called to the others, but not waiting for anyone else / began to swim or row through the irksome stretch of sea with great effort, setting foot on the shore at almost the same time. With discipline and good order they quickly formed into a tight-ranked squadron intending to march through the enemy to the aid of their friends, / but they had scarcely emerged from the waves when a troop of Araucans charged them with a furious yell. The first to arrive was agile Fenistón, a daring youth, who in his brash desire to distinguish himself came ahead of all the others. / Our brave, well-disciplined soldiers, pursuing their plan and having no patience for delay, attacked those trying to stop them, and to welcome Fenistón the skilled Julián de Valenzuela advanced with no less speed and audacity, sword in hand, his shield at his chest. / Dexterous Fenistón began the combat, anticipating his

CANTO 19

opponent and giving a nimble, unexpected leap with which he brought down his weighty club. Valenzuela, holding his shield high in both hands, stopped its descent, but it left him as stunned as if a mountain had fallen on him. / The violent blow had such force that the Spaniard's great shield came down on his head, and for a few moments the stupefied young man crawled about on his hands and knees in a daze. He quickly got back to his feet, and regaining his senses, although staggered, was able to jump to the side to avoid the cudgel's second descent, / its momentum and great weight driving it a good distance into the ground. Seeing his opportunity, Valenzuela quickly advanced his leg and arm and stabbed his opponent in the chest with his sword, then withdrew the hot, red blade and raised it in a backstroke to the middle of the jaw. / The Araucan swung his arms wildly about, not knowing where. The young Spaniard, changing tactics, responded by pulling out his dagger and quickly and vigorously burying it three times in his body as the great muscled arms and legs, already turning cold, collapsed. /

[19.45] Now no one was idle for even a moment. Each hastened to where the danger was greatest or help most needed, and the turmoil grew so furious it seemed the constant clash of arms would dislodge the sky from its hinges and bring everything to the ground. / Elsewhere, atop the wall, the bitter fight raged with ever growing fervor. Amidst all the confusion victory remained in doubt, with broken mail flying through the air and so many streams of hot, foaming blood flowing into the trench that the corpses there began to float. / From one side to the other the fort and honor were bravely contested, some men climbing eagerly atop the dead, some collapsing in death atop the living. Surrounded by his soldiers, Don García de Mendoza resolutely stood his ground, successfully repelling the barbarians' great fury and violence. / Across the way, Felipe Hurtado, Francisco de Andía, and Espinosa, Simón Pereyra the Lusitanian, Alonso Pacheco, and Ortigosa all gave proof of miraculous efforts as they resisted the Araucan advance, stopping a multitude of opponents through sheer courage and the force of their swords. / Elsewhere, atop the high bulwark, Vasco Juárez, Carrillo, and Antonio de Cabrera, Arias Pardo, Riberos, Lasarte, Córdoba, and Pedro de Olmos de Aguilera were wounding so many of their adversaries that even though their numbers were infinite the wall around them was well-secured. / Fighting no less fiercely were Juan de Torres, Garnica, and Campofrío, Martín de Guzmán and Hernando Pacho, Gutiérrez, Zuñiga, and Verrío, Ronquillo, Lira, Osorio, Vaca, and Ovando, accomplishing feats that even were my ingenuity unlimited I could not adequately describe. / The carnage grew so great that the ferocious Araucans began to falter, and once their furor was broken they began an orderly retreat, never turning their backs. The rest of them, seeing the inconceivable destruction, abandoned their foolish enterprise as well, leaving Tucapel alone inside the fort, wounding, crushing, and killing. / Far from dismayed, but rather burning with rabid fury and frenzied rage, he ran furiously this way and that, wreaking incredible slaughter wherever he went. Having knocked down Bustamante and Mexía, he then sent Diego Peréz and Saldaña sprawling. But having sung so much, it's best to bring the great devastation of this long canto to a close. /

CANTO 20

The Araucans retreat with the loss of many men; Tucapel, badly wounded, breaks through the enemy and escapes. Tegualda tells Alonso de Ercilla her strange and pitiable story.

No one should give their word without first considering their ability and resolve, for the proverb says that he who is quick to promise will long repent.[127] Our word is a genuine pledge we are bound to fulfill, and it's a universal principle and accepted law that even a promise made to an enemy must be honored. / Far short of such principles is the practice of these wretched times, when promises are made that raise one's hopes but then are never honored. Instead we're sustained by vain

---

127 The adage is a vague echo of Horace's *Ad Pisones* (ll. 38-40).

and foolish confidence, built on nothing but air, which comes crashing to the ground when hope gives way to disappointment. / I can say for myself how troubled I remain remembering the word I gave, still unfulfilled, to finish this work I've begun. The dry, unpleasant subject I've chosen, so desolate and sterile, promises nothing but great effort until the end, and squeezing moisture from a stone is never easy. / Who was it set me amidst these brambles and steep slopes, following raucous horns and drums when I could be strolling through groves and gardens? Where gathering fragrant flowers I could mingle fictions, fables, and tales of love with quests and adventures? Where wandering freely I might take pleasure while giving it? / Must everything be harshness, discord, and fighting? Blood, fire, enmity, hatred, and rancor? Rage and savagery? Madness, fury, rashness, wrath, and acrimony? Vengeance and ferocity? Murder, slaughter, carnage, and cruelties that would nauseate Mars himself and exhaust abilities far greater than mine? / Having willingly constrained myself I have no choice but to be patient, and thus I humbly ask, my Lord, that you not be displeased in listening to me. Meanwhile audacious Tucapel leaves me no time for excuses, approaching with such fury I must hurry my pen. /

[20.7] Like a ferocious, cornered beast the Araucan made his brutal and bloody way forward, turning now this way, now that, sharing the carnage equally on all sides, his arrogance such that he would have attacked fierce Mars on his Fifth-Sphere throne if only he could have found a way to ascend the heavens.[128] / Finding himself alone and badly wounded, however, with the barbarian

---

128 In Ptolemaic astronomy the earth is at the center of nine spheres, the fifth of which is that of Mars (following the moon, Mercury, Venus, and the sun).

army in retreat and all that fearsome steel turned toward his valiant chest, he withdrew to a place where the hill was very steep and had no enclosing wall. The drop here was more than forty yards, / but as if he had wings more dependable than Daedalus's he hurled himself off that height and seemed similarly supported, giving great proof of his strength and suppleness, for the deadly leap meant little to the intrepid warrior, who landed like an agile panther or lithe leopard.[129] / As soon as he jumped his enemies fired an infinity of shots in his wake, and although he flew faster than thought some of these reached him before he hit the ground. The volley was so substantial he was instantly struck in more than ten places, not that this caused him to fall or disrupted his progress in any way. / Finding himself on the ground and wounded so repeatedly, he immediately regretted his decision to jump. Inflamed by searing rage, more terrible and emboldened than ever, he now wanted to return to the game and avenge his injuries, but it was foolish to even imagine such a thing with the incline so sheer and there being no way up. / Five or six times he attempted the difficult ascent, testing Fortune's support, for the furious wrath impelling him made the impossible seem easy, and thus he ran from one side of the slope to the other, here and there, like a ravenous, blood-thirsty wolf circling a pen of sheep. / Finally realizing the futility of the idea, with showers of shots falling thickly around him, he withdrew to the side, where he caught sight of the crowd of men fighting on the beach. And now like a splendid soaring hawk that spies a heron high above, but falls instead on a cowardly kite below, descending from the sky on his prey in a furious dive, / just so did bold Tucapel, putting aside his audacious but futile plan, turn back and make his way to the

---

129 See n. 56, above.

bitter, bloody combat. Here the infidels, having lost confidence as well as a great deal of blood and a good many warriors, were in retreat, following the banners of those already marching along the hill. / Not for this did the fearless barbarian veer a single step from his purpose, but fiercely attacked the Spanish all along one side, knocking down many with his blows and meting out terrible punishment as he roved freely from one end of their squadron to the other, wounding, trampling, and opening up a wide space. / Some were crushed, some crippled, and some lamented, others moaned or complained; some fell here, others, stunned, fell there; some, making room, got out of his way, and through the middle of the dense squadron, bristling with weapons, he left a broad breach, like a furious bolt of lightning breaking through heavy air and thick clouds. / In such a manner did Tucapel, forcing his way through the entire Christian contingent, come to his friends, who continued their retreat with the measured pace and orderly formation of long, black flocks of springtime cranes, where none move ahead nor any get out of line. /

[20.18] Although we were few in number, seeing the Indians turn their backs and march away, we emerged from the fort with a great hue and cry and assumed close formation on the field. Determined to take full advantage of our victory, we began to follow them in regular march but then returned, fearing an ambush. / The hard-fought battle had lasted until the sun reached its zenith, equidistant from east and west. Now that we were safe, while waiting for it to complete its course and make way for the nocturnal hours, assuagers of human toil, / we diligently cleared all around the clogged ditch, not resting a moment, removing the many logs and makeshift bridges placed across it and carefully reinforcing the weakest parts of the wall, fortifying our position to withstand another attack. /

[20.21] As the light retreated and black night advanced to cover the earth, everyone retired to their posts. In such dangerous circumstances no one was excused from guard duty, the first watch of which, on a low incline adjoining the fort, now fell to me. / With all the day's exertions, and not having disarmed for fifteen, a troublesome drowsiness soon beset me. Battered and exhausted, I resisted it with constant activity, walking from one side of the hill to the other without stopping, hardly trusting my feet to hold me up. / It was not the consumption of elaborate meals or well-distilled wines that brought on such somnolence, nor a habit of regular sleep. Twice-baked biscuit, moldy, black, and doled out by a stingy hand, was the sustenance of my life, along with tasteless rainwater. / At times our rations dwindled to two small handfuls of barley a day, cooked with grass in brine, for lack of salt. The dainty bed in which I slept was the damp, swampy earth, and I was always armed and ready, now with my pen in hand, now with my lance. / Pressing on with the annoying sleepiness still bothering me as I paced from one end of the post to the other in the profound silence, I saw that one side of the hill was entirely white from the dead bodies covering it, for our harquebuses had made a great slaughter that day. / Shortly afterwards, keeping an alert eye and attentive ear, I heard a noise from time to time that came from the direction of the corpses, always ending with a long, sad sigh. Then I heard it again, and it seemed to be moving from body to body. / The night was so dark and dismal it was impossible to see anything clearly, and thus to solve the mystery and fulfill my duty, crouching in the undergrowth I made my way to the spot where the noise was coming from and saw a black shape on four legs moving stealthily among the dead. / Far from reassured by that sight and feeling a fear I don't deny even now, I rushed upon it sword in hand and shield at my chest, calling on God. The bulk reared up on its feet, however, and with a fear-filled voice and humble plea cried out, "Mercy, sir, I beg you, for I'm a woman and have done nothing to offend you! / If my grief and great misfortune don't move you to pity and your raging sword exceeds rightful bounds, what glory will you win from such a deed, once heaven makes it known you raised your weapon against a woman and wretched widow, so unfortunate and grieving? / I beseech you, sir, if ever there was a day when either by chance or mischance, as with me, you were tenderly in love, with a love that was genuine and entirely faithful, then allow me to bury a body lying somewhere amidst this dead company. Consider that he who denies what is just sanctions evil and himself becomes unjust. / Don't hinder such a pious task, conceded even amidst barbarous war, for it's a type of tyranny to always exert one's utmost power. Allow this soul of mine to seek its body, and then proceed with cruel fury, for my grief has pushed me to such extremes I now fear life more than death. / There's no evil can hurt me now, nor greater happiness than what I've already had, so let what's left of life be over and done with now that my sweet companion is dead! Even though cruel heaven did not allow us to die together, however harshly it hounds me it cannot stop my stricken soul from following his!" / With this she earnestly begged me to end her pain with a blow of my sword. Still confused and afraid she might be deceiving me, I didn't trust such clear signs, suspecting she might be a spy who had come to scout our preparations. / But although I was suspicious and the night was hiding her face, I began to realize from her lack of fear and great calm that everything she told me was true, and that it was treacherous love, blind and heedless, which drove her to seek her husband, who striving to distinguish himself had given his life in the initial attack. / Moved to compassion at seeing her so steadfast in her chaste and loving purpose, I returned with her to my post, where I entreated her to tell me calmly about her sorrows from beginning to end, and in sharing her suffering to find some solace for it. /

[20.36] "Alas!" she said. "For me there will never be solace 'til death, for my terrible grief has no remedy and exceeds all endurance! Yet even though it be insufferable I'll recount the course of my bitter fate, for perhaps the pain of doing so will finally be enough to finish me off. / My name is Tegualda, and I'm the unlucky daughter of the ill-fortuned cacique Brancol. Loved in vain by many for my beauty, for a time I was free of love and its concerns. Incensed at such cheerful liberty, however, Fortune soon troubled my joy so much that in the end I die of an evil I never even feared! / Many asked for my hand in marriage, yet I scorned them all equally. My good father, unhappy at this, entreated me to accept someone, but with a free spirit I dismissed his annoying request, for to think of changing me was foolish, like beating futilely on cold iron. / Yet not even such frank responses made my stubborn suitors relent. Instead they insisted even more on their vain pursuit, seeking with new pleas and pledges, as well as with dances, games, and other festivities to alter my steadfast determination, but none of their guiles could change my mind. /

[20.40] "All too soon, however, the last day of my freedom and sovereignty arrived. If only it had been the last day of my life! Yet being good for me, that could not be. Near our town was a place where the gentle, clear Gualebo, after watering the delightful fields, joins with the broad Itata. / Here where my self-deception would be punished these young men implored me to attend their festivities, and since this would be to my detriment they easily persuaded me. The way there was promptly embowered with marvelous artistry, for they deemed the good road unfit for my feet and the sun itself unworthy to touch me. / Passing through a series of arches, I was led to a beautifully decorated and elevated throne, built to enhance masterful nature's own ornament. The limpid water murmured nearby, and the sound and swaying of trees in the wind were cheering to ear and eye. / I had scarcely taken my seat when a solemn announcement was heard, clearing the milling crowd from the broad arena. Everyone took their places, and the customary wrestling match began amidst silence more typical of painted figures than living men. / Although there were many fine youths there of varied appearance and fortune, all of them rivals and aspiring to the same illusory goal, I paid no attention to who won or lost, seeking distraction in my free and idle thoughts. / Taking no notice of their activities and only wishing the contests would end, I contemplated nature's handiwork, now gazing up at the tall trees, now down at the meadow and stream, where I counted the many small stones. I was feeling entirely free and safe from love, care, and misfortune, / when suddenly a great hue and cry arose among the crowd, something inevitable at such games, startling me and disturbing my reverie. Wanting to know what had happened, I asked the person closest to me the reason for the shouting, the cause of which it would have been better had I never learned. /

[20.47] "'My lady,' he said, 'haven't you seen how every opponent the brawny, young Mareguano wrestles with ends up on his back on the ground? Yet just when he was confidently expecting the victory wreath to be bestowed by your hand, encircling his pleased, proud brow as the prize for being most valiant, / that gallant young athlete there dressed in red and green easily threw him, depriving him of the honor he had won. And now the capricious crowd, marveling at this development, has raised that confused clamor, exalting the young man's prowess. / Mareguano is trying to have the match repeated, alleging that what happened was an accident and bad luck and that the other youth is far from his equal either in strength or skill. But the established rules don't allow for this, even though the other youth has generously said he's happy to agree to it. / The judges see no reason to entertain either petition, nor do they want nor will they allow any innovation in this matter, ruling the two relinquish such requests unless they appear before you and obtain your gracious permission.' /

[20.51] "With this a great crowd of people came to where I was sitting, and once the shouting and noisy tumult subsided, the youth who had won addressed me with humble courtesy, saying, 'My lady, without my actions meriting one I request a favor of you. / Although I'm a stranger and undeserving that you do for me what's clearly within your power, I offer myself as your slave, to live and die in your service. As a token of this pledge, as long as it meets with your approval and even if I suffer some disadvantage by doing so, I'm willing to face another round with Mareguano, / and yet another and another and even more until he's entirely satisfied, for if he wants it, I want it as well. I'll even agree that the next fall determine the contest and all the rights of victory, for being in your presence gives me great hope of emerging from the encounter with

| 269 |

greater glory! Grant us permission, using your absolute power to suspend the rules.' /

[20.54] "Having said this he awaited my answer, gazing at me with humble respect. Yet after watching him closely as I listened, with no cause for concern nor any caution, I not only granted him permission, but began to hope that he would win. 'If I can help in any way,' I replied, 'I freely and unreservedly concede it.' / The two youths eagerly took their leave of me, and to the great excitement of the crowd assumed their places in the arena. Once their sponsors had seen to it that neither had undue advantage from the sun, which was already setting, they were left alone and quickly went for each other. / Instantly joined, they traveled about a good distance grappling with each other as they circled and lunged, sometimes obliquely, sometimes directly, now stretching to their full height, now crouching low, now locked together chest to chest and gasping, gripping each other so tightly they could scarcely breathe. / After this they noisily recommenced the struggle, and it was amazing to see and hear. But now the young stranger, embarrassed by his lack of strength and skill, lifted his opponent into the air, and giving a groan, threw him down on the ground with such force that poor Mareguano was left with neither his senses nor limbs intact. / Surrounded by the crowd, the judges immediately led the winner before me, and there he knelt at my feet as they bade me award him the prize. I don't know if it was his stars or my destiny, or which causes concurred, but I began to tremble as an ardent flame went coursing through my bones. / I was so confused and agitated by this novel experience that I remained in shock for a moment, amidst such peril and all those people. Gaining more control, with all the dignity I could muster I placed the garland on the head of the victor, still kneeling at my skirt, / and constrained by honest shame instantly lowered my gaze, my attention on the young man's words and gracious compliments. At last he left, taking my contentment and leaving my senses unsettled as I went from the first to the final steps of love and pain. / I sensed something new constraining my independent, rebellious spirit, and my reason, liberty, and free will all surrendered to it. Coming back to myself, I felt my cold breast burning with an intense fire and raised my timid, wounded eyes, which modesty had kept lowered until then. / With sudden, furious force the bridle of shame and continence burst, and I followed him with longing gaze, aggravating the injury and poison even more. Looking at him was the only relief I found for my pain, and thus wherever he went he bore my eyes and soul in his wake. / At that point I saw him preparing to run the customary race, whose finish line was marked by a banner more than a mile away. The winner was promised an enameled ring set with an enormous, beautifully-worked emerald offered by my unlucky hand. / More than forty young men took their places to vie for the prize. Each waited with his foot on the mark, poised and ready, and they had scarcely heard the signal when in one long line they took off with such speed their soles hardly left any trace on the sand. / But Crepino, for this was the young stranger's name, pulled ahead so furiously that he left the rushing wind behind. First to touch the red banner at the end of the long course, his gracious attitude delighted the enthusiastic spectators, / who carried him in solemn triumph around the broad, crowded arena. They then turned back to where I sat and asked that I present him with the ring. With everyone watching I hid my frightened trembling, then overcoming embarrassment and fear I presented him with both the ring and my freedom. / 'My lady,' he said, 'I pray you accept it back from me, for though the gift be small and poor, I swear the devotion with which it is offered is great. Your granting me this favor enriches me, and my strength and confidence now grow so great that henceforward no challenge or enterprise will be difficult!' / Using all courtesy, which is what most perfects a woman, I told him I would accept the ring along with the good will of the one bestowing it, and with this the entire company formed a dense circle around me, and after lowering me from that pleasant position they carried me to the house of my father. /

[20.68] "With no small effort and self-control I hid my malady for three weeks to make a proper impression on everyone, but the pain and ardent fire were always growing. Appearing to obey my father and master, I let it be known that his request was my desire, / saying that since he had urged me to accept a husband, as was only fitting, I had chosen Crepino, who possessed valor, good fortune, and an illustrious lineage, while also being discreet, modest, affable, and praiseworthy in all his dealings. / My father, listening until the end of my speech with a joyous expression, kissed me on the forehead and said, 'In this as in all else I yield to your will, trusting that with your discretion and honorable intentions you've chosen what's best, for Crepino's manners reveal him to be someone of good quality and great promise.' / Having satisfied both duty and will, both honor and desire, and with the youthful suitors' vain contentions now brought to a close, my sad, star-crossed marriage was celebrated in public ceremony. Today marks exactly one month since then—oh, bitter fate!—so quickly does ill-fortune follow good! / Yesterday I was happy with my lot and had no fear or suspicion of any trouble. Today cruel, bloody death has brought everything collapsing to the ground.

What consolation can there be for such a calamity? What redress can heaven make me, now that no remedy is possible and there's no good can match such great evil? / This is my story and the certain end of sweet existence. Here my liberty and brief joy are transformed into eternal bitterness! Since you're the cause of my memory's reopening this grievous wound, I ask in return for my pain that you let me bury my husband, / for it isn't right that birds of prey should rend his wretched body, nor that dogs and brutal beasts sate their insatiable bellies on it. But if you're hardhearted and don't wish to grant something so just and reasonable, then with your sword and rigorous arm make us equals in death and burial!" /

[20.76] With this she finished her story and began a lament that would have moved the mountain itself to pity, expressing such anguish I was obliged to keep her company in her pain. No longer was it enough that I reassure her of my promises; now she implored the ultimate sacrifice of death as the only benefit and solution. / I would have found myself in great distress and confusion had Simón Pereyra, who was standing guard on the other side of the hill, not come to tell me our time was up. Troubled as well by what he had heard, having listened to some of it from a distance, he helped me console her, reinforcing my assurances with new ones of his own. / The rapid rotation of the heavens had already tipped the stars into the sea, and the Southern Cross, marking the hours amidst the silent night, was declining to the south-southwest, when Tegualda, realizing how our offers obliged her, restrained her grief, and we took her back to camp.[130] / There we left her in the company and honorable

---

130 The Southern Cross is one of the most recognizable constellations in the sky of the southern hemisphere.

The Araucana

guard of married women as the longed-for day, already near, drew back the black mantle of night. With everyone sleeping as I sing, it's best to leave my song as it is until tomorrow, since I, too, am in need of repose. /

CANTO 21

Tegualda finds her husband's body and returns home with it, lamenting. Spanish cavalry from Santiago and La Imperial arrive at Penco; Caupolicán reviews his troops.

W͟ho has ever provided such proof of love? Who has ever seen piety like that of this beautiful, ill-fortuned barbarian before us today? May fame exalt her, and elevating my feeble voice spread her renown from voice to voice and from nation to nation for all eternity. / Let the pernicious practice of poisonous tongues, whose sole purpose is to offend virtuous women, now cease, for this example alone is enough to confound their malice, condemning them to eternal restraint and shameful penance. / How many heroines we've seen ascend Fame's difficult peak:

Judith, Camilla, and Phoenician Dido, whom Virgil unjustly defames; Penelope, and Lucretia, whose blood bathed the violated bed of her husband; Hippo, Tuccia, and Virginia, Fulvia and Cloelia, Portia, Sulpicia, Alcestis, and Cornelia![131] / Well may the beautiful Tegualda be included among such figures, worthy as much for her remarkable conduct as her pious love. Elevated by her actions she'll shine among the most famous, and her name, now consecrated to immortality, will be celebrated forever! /

[21.5] As I mentioned earlier, Tegualda remained safely secluded among honorable company, grateful for this modest favor considering what she had expected of her venture. With dawn's arrival, even though delightful sleep had sweetly bound my weary limbs, urgent care awakened me. / Hurrying to where she still persisted in her tearful lament, for her grief and suffering had not abated even for a moment, I consoled her with utmost sympathy, repeatedly promising to entrust her with her husband's body and provide an escort with whom she could freely depart. / Skeptical of this kindness and still weeping, she beseeched me with outstretched arms for guarantees, and so I called my Indian servants and went out with her, searching all about. Finally we came upon his cold, bloody corpse lying among the dead, pierced by a bullet. / Seeing his withered, mutilated face, the miserable Tegualda threw herself on the body in a horrified frenzy, and clasping it close to her own she bathed it in a flood of passionate tears, kissing the mouth and the wound to see if she might infuse

---

131 Ercilla mixes figures from Greek and Roman history (Lucretia, Hippo, Tuccia, Virginia, Fulvia, Cloelia, Portia, Sulpicia, Alcestis, Cornelia) with those from the Bible (Judith) and other literature (Camilla, from Virgil's *Aeneid*, as well as Dido, whose reputation the poet will defend at length in Canto 32).

some life into him. / "Oh, wretched me!" she cried, "What can I do amidst such pain and misfortune? And how is it that even now I've still not satisfied cruel love by ending my bitterness with one more blow, fainthearted as I am? What is this? Or has injustice come to the point that even inevitable death is denied me?" / Thus raging to die she clutched her white throat with cruel hands, but incapable of more, spared no affliction to her face and hair. I tried to stop her, although it was scarcely possible, so great was her anguish and overpowering her frantic desire for death. / Afterwards, when her agony had been soothed somewhat by my constant entreaties and her promises had reassured me regarding her pagan ravings, my ready *yanaconas* lifted the cold, stiff body onto a plank and took it to where her servants were waiting.[132] / To ensure she suffered no harm or outrage, war being so disorderly, I and my men accompanied her to a nearby mountain, and once in secure territory and set on the right road she bid me good-bye, grateful for the help she had received. /

[21.13] Returning to camp, we spent an entire week rebuilding what had been destroyed and repairing the trench and damaged rampart. Once this was completed, with great effort, we awaited the enemy every day in good order and high spirits, hearing repeated reports that they were approaching. / It was also reported that soldiers of ours were coming from Mapochó to join us, supplied with munitions as well as a thousand horses and two thousand archers. The rainy winter had swelled low-lying swamps and rivers, however, and after some of the men, animals, and equipment were swept away they were forced to stop. / Such was the situation when an Indian hurriedly arrived

---

132 *Yanaconas* are Indian youth who work as Spanish servants; Tegualda's heathen intentions are those of taking her own life.

at the fort one morning. "Oh, reckless fools!" he cried. "Flee your impending death, for the indomitable Araucans are coming upon you! Neither walls nor defenses offer any protection, nor is there anywhere you'll be safe!" / The same advice was brought midday by a friendly cacique from the mountains, affirming for certain that all the land's forces were arrogantly advancing with tools of war: bridges, ladders, logs, planks, and other useful implements. / Our soldiers were not dismayed by the news, but rather more eager to begin, the least courageous boldly seeking out the most perilous positions. Everything having been readied with all due speed and thoroughness, we warily awaited the day that would menace so many lives. /

[21.18] Our Indian spies had warned us that the enemy would surely attack from three sides during the silent night's last watch, but just as we were giving up hope, not of divine, but of human help, our reinforcements suddenly appeared in orderly ranks at the crest of the hill. / Who could describe the great joy and excitement among both our groups, the orderly review, the commotion, the resounding tumult of furious Mars! So many flags unfurled to the wind, so many pennants and standards, the horns, trumpets, voices, and cries, the neighing and snorting of horses! / With the greetings and warm welcome completed, we made space for the foot soldiers and animals, then raised such a multitude of tents and pavilions within that narrow field it seemed a city had been born. / The arrival of these troops prompted the nearby barbarian army, after new deliberations and prudent decisions, to change its plans. Astute Colocolo, wisely opposing the advice of many, spoke so skillfully that he persuaded everyone to accept his position. / This was preceded by great dispute and disagreement, as I reported, but in the end they delayed for a time the implementation of their terrible sentence, and the powerful army withdrew until they could gain better intelligence about the Spanish forces that had arrived, whose numbers fame kept exaggerating. /

[21.23] Our men, despising idleness and longing to display the valor in which our nation excels, wanted to invade and ravage the enemy's territory. Eager to hasten battle, they showed great diligence preparing whatever was most important, / and once they had repaired any equipment damaged in the difficult journey, these brave and restless soldiers began to murmur about the disgraceful lack of action. Incited by valor and greedy for honor, they asked that our departure be accelerated, and thus the date everyone longed for was set for five days hence. / The happy hour having finally arrived, just as the first march was set to begin, a great company of cavalry and other armed troops arrived from La Imperial, having crossed through rebel territory in spite of the disturbances, accompanied by a horde of servants and baggage and well supplied with food and weapons. / Once these additional soldiers, arms, and equipment were assembled, provisions were made and locations, quarters, and squadrons assigned so that every man could reach his standard at the first sign of attack. /

[21.27] Elsewhere, Caupolicán was employing no less care and foresight dividing the men of his army among capable captains, those most proficient in the cruel exercise and art of war, and with everything organized, one day he decided to review the troops at his command. / First to appear was the cacique Pillolco, covered in sturdy armor and carrying a great cudgel reinforced with iron in his right hand. The squadron he headed, adept at accurately hurling darts, advanced in fine order and attitude, in a formation thirteen by thirteen. / Close behind them came the mighty Leucotón, accompanied by a dense band of archers firing great volleys of arrows in all directions. Rengo then appeared with measured pace and grave demeanor, arrogant, vain, and dauntless, a lance in his hand the size of a cedar, his men armed with clubs. / Next in line was the robust and ruthless Tulcomara, fierce in expression and wearing the skin of a savage tiger he had killed in place of armor, its terrifying mouth encircling his broad face from forehead to jaw with a double row of sharp, white, glistening teeth. / His tough, rustic soldiers, covered with animal skins and making a great clamor, had him enclosed in a tight-packed circle. Now the Talcamavidans passed by, more impressive in appearance than strength, under the care and command of the boastful youth Caniotaro. / Following them came Millalermo, a young man in the flower of youth wearing painted armor. Descended from the famous Picoldo, he ruled over those who live along the banks of the great Nivequetén, the currents of which absorb the surrounding streams and bear them on to the Biobío. / After this Mareande passed by, a youth of great presumption and pride, tall in stature and proportionately muscled, carrying a scimitar and broad shield. His cousin Lepomande marched alongside him with a great long blade unsheathed and laid across his shoulders. The two shared one banner and were surrounded by armed men, all proven soldiers. / Now Lemolemo appeared at the head of his squadron, dazzling and resplendent among all the others and trailing his formidable pike. A few steps behind came Gualemo, covered with the tough, hairy hide of a seahorse his father had killed defending his mother. / I don't know if it's only a tale, but they say she was bathing in the sea, some distance away, when a seahorse suddenly seized her. Rushing to the cries of his dear wife as she was being taken away, her husband, faced with the pain and sadness of losing her, immediately threw himself into the water in pursuit. / Such is the power of love that the daring young man caught up with the fish as it was escaping, and fixing his grip on it skillfully forced it toward the nearby shore as it swam. At this point the sea monster, which had remained on the surface (for love had blinded it as well), continued abruptly onto dry land through the reflux of retreating waves. / Letting go of its prisoner, it shook its powerful tail, lashing the ground and twisting its enormous body this way and that as it turned upon the courageous youth, who seized the opportunity to rush to his nearby weapons. A battle now began between the two, which the sea grew calm and the sun stopped moving in order to observe. / Combining strength and agility, the brave barbarian wounded the voracious monster in the forehead with his iron-plated club, and in the end he valiantly brought the encounter to a happy conclusion, leaving the great fish, which measured more than thirty feet long, stretched out on the shore. / To memorialize this heroic feat, worthy of being recorded in writing, he used the fish's tough, hairy skin to fashion strong and supple armor. When Guacol died, the valiant Gualemo inherited the armor along with Quilacura, a densely-populated valley whose people are rich in gold and herds. /

[21.40] Talcaguano, whose land is enclosed by sea, came next in the review of warriors, a gallant figure adorned with tall feathers, brandishing a mast-sized spear as though it were a tender reed. His fighting men followed him, their chests banded in slanting stripes of blue, white, and red.[133] / Now Tomé appeared, trailed by the factious Puelches, whose weapons are solid, sharpened clubs

---

[133] Talcaguano, the cacique of Talcahuano island, cf. 16. 17.

the length of an arm, and after them the sword-wielding Trulos, a people of shifting loyalties who live in no fixed place, troublesome men of low quality, great in strength but small in understanding. / Andalicán did not fail to arrive with his outstanding, seasoned soldiers, all in close order. He wore the finest mail and wielded a formidable, thick lance. Orompello was there, as well, still not fully grown but impressive in bearing and filled with great hope, leading another squadron of veterans and accompanied by Ongolmo on his right. / Elicura passed by, richly armored, leading a band of dauntless youth, full of pride and courage. The Llaucos followed, a robust and intrepid people with red-dyed faces, their chief, son of the celebrated Ainavillo, in their midst.[134] / Next came Cayocupil, his imposing stature and great fervor for all to see, proceeding gravely with his beautifully adorned, well-tested men. Then it was Purén's turn, leading with no less grace and composure a noble squadron of soldiers skilled in war's hard work. / The gigantic Lincoya was next, his crest rising above all the others, armed with a solid, shining corselet, his helmet topped with plumes. Filled with disdainful mien he led a gleaming, tight-knit squadron, while the young Peycaví followed with another close-packed company of courageous men. / Also making his appearance in the review was the grave Caniomangue, saddened by the death of his illustrious, elderly father, to whose position he succeeded. His white armor was covered completely in black, and his squadron, clothed in the same color, moved to the slow, irregular beat of raucous drums. / Last to appear in this catalog, but first in everything, was the audacious Tucapel, his gleaming visor checkered in large gold and gray squares. Enormous in stature and terrifying in appearance, he advanced with a brisk but measured

---

134 References to Ainavillo are found at 1. 61 and 2. 38.

step, behind him a throng of soldiers, fearless, presumptuous, and vain. / The great Caupolicán led the rest of the Araucan army, carrying a short baton and more impassioned than wrathful Mars. Beneath his standard were valiant Curgo, Mareguano, and the grave and eloquent Colocolo; Millo, Teguán, Lambecho, and Guampicolo. / Caupolicán's Pilmaiquens followed, along with the Tuncos, Renoguelons, and Penconians, men of the Itata and Maule rivers, and the Cauquenians, with their painted insignia and pennants; also the Nivequetenians, Puelches, and Cauténians, as well as a dense battalion of foot-soldiers and a confused mass of allied warriors from near and far. / As sea waves spread and swell, so swelled the ranks of these ferocious warriors, while all about them the earth, trampled by so many feet, shuddered and quaked. Filled with clamor, the air grew dark as an enormous cloud of dust rose heavenward in a vast whirlwind, like a dense, blinding fog or murky haze. /

[21.51] With our own army similarly well-ordered, don García appeared before the brave company as we prepared to set out, his cheerful countenance promising a successful outcome as he began to stir gallant hearts, speaking as follows: / "Valiant companions, driven by nothing more than your natural courage to discover the southern pole, crossing the sweltering torrid zone and distant tropics that Apollo himself, however close he comes to the vault of heaven, has never passed, since the Sovereign Author will never allow it:[135] / having followed the Catholic standard so zealously all this way, subjecting countless people to Spanish

---

135 A reference to the furthest point south reached by the sun (Apollo) in the southern hemisphere, at summer solstice in December, when it is directly above the Tropic of Capricorn; the poem's main action takes place further south.

dominion, set your courageous hearts and enduring spirits in earnest against these barbarians, for having conquered these few, you'll easily hold all the world in your hands. / As long as we defer this encounter and the completion of what we've begun, we accomplish little or nothing. Not even the honor you've already won is secure, for as long as the issue is undecided, the ferocious enemy, armed and in the field, has an equal right to all your glory and good fortune, which he can win back with a single victory. / All I ask and say to you now is that in these battles and skirmishes, even if the enemy has wounded you, never attack him when his back is turned. Instead, if fleeing from death in battle he surrenders his weapons and hands them over, defend him like a friend, for it is greater to grant a life than take it! / Remember the cause for which you've always carried arms, for when anger exceeds its bounds right is violated and loses legitimacy, just as excessive violence, unrestrained by reason, justifies the enemy's cause. / I've nothing more to say nor additional words with which to counsel you, and I'm already worried at having delayed the fury of your hearts so long. Now onward, onward! Strike the tents and pavilions as quickly as you can, and let us go forth as one to where our fortune calls us!" / Immediately the swift squadrons, dauntless in their ardor, marched to the sandy banks of the broad, majestic Biobío, and in great oared boats they quickly crossed the mighty river, entering forbidden territory in orderly ranks. / Considering the effort that lies ahead, it now seems best to rest a while and gather the strength I need, for my weary voice is failing and I feel its force begin to ebb. Once restored, I will do my best to please you in the following canto./

CANTO 22

The Spanish enter the State of Arauco, meeting the Araucans in a hard-fought battle in which Rengo gives great proof of himself. Courageous Galbarino is sentenced to having his hands cut off.

Perfidious and tyrannical love, what good do you hope to gain from my distress? Isn't my promise enough without your always tormenting me? Alas! Already I feel a lively fire working its way little by little into my anxious heart and tenderly spreading through my veins and bones. / Traitor! All this to divert me from bloody Mars's grim style, tiring me at every step with troubling memories? Let me be, for you don't want it said that having no one to celebrate you, you sought me out at the ends of the earth and forced me to do so. / Can't you see the disgrace of having so many celebrated followers yet coming to beg of my poverty, so lacking in language and conceits, and amidst the countless hazards of brutal weapons, of burdening me with a possibly empty dream? / Let me be, for the terrifying trumpets of the nearby barbarians leave me no time for anything else. I have chosen my path and now hear a battle building that would not give a moment's rest to the most fertile wit embroiled in its tumult. / Finding myself on the field, what can I do but fulfill my vow, even though desire draws me elsewhere? Thus constrained, but taking the shortest route possible and avoiding delays, I intend to pursue the work I've begun, free of artifice and ornament. /

[22.6] Returning to my account, our orderly army marched so quickly it had soon traveled a good distance from Talcahuano, beside the Biobío, and as the sun began to set we made our first camp in a spacious, level site at the foot of a hill beside a lake. / We had no more than settled ourselves along its shore when shouts were heard on all sides: "To arms! To arms! Harness the horses! Be quick!" Scattered here and there, the men immediately came running to their standards, and with good discipline quickly formed into orderly squadrons. / Our scouts had been riding across that broad expanse at the edge of the sierra, near lofty Andalicán mountain, when they saw warriors descending its slopes and cutting them off, calling out as they came, "Wait, wait! Stop! Let's see who's brave today!" / Regrouping beneath the protection of a hill, the greatly outnumbered Spanish awaited them with a show of courage, but the ferocious barbarians, not slowing down a moment, attacked and soon forced them to flee in utter disorder. / From time to time our men would regroup and with a valor unknown to the defeated turn back to attack the arrogant victors face to face. Compelled by such great fury, however, they soon continued as they had begun, one of their many pursuers now and then left dead and trampled underfoot. / The agile Indians, always growing in numbers and fervor, kept up the chase, wrapped in a thick cloud of dust. Our soldiers loosened their reins and rushed on with more fear than judgment, digging their spurs into the flanks of their racing horses, / yet however much they urged them on with their bodies and shouts, with arms and heels, the barbarians on foot kept catching up to the riders and forcing them from their saddles. Finally, having no choice, our men fought like wounded bears or lions that see their lairs and pathways blocked and are constantly harassed by wolfhounds. / Like a sudden, terrible wind that comes sweeping across a dusty plain in a roaring storm, its powerful funnel seizing and scattering everything with unstoppable violence as it furiously uproots trees from the ground, / with just such ease the weary Spanish were caught up by that violent barbarian fury and unable to resist it. Some, ashamed for their honor, would turn about with fierce intentions, but another wave of adversaries would arrive and carry them off with even more speed and injury. / Thus the Araucans continued to batter them, following fate and favorable fortune as they executed their ravenous rage on those who surrendered, showing no mercy whatever. The tumult and constant shouts of the barbarians echoed throughout the long valley, and the news, borne by swift winds, quickly reached our camp. /

[22.16] Juan Remón was the first to hear the reports and quickly rushed to the scene from the west, arriving with no small uproar and a large number of troops who raised a terrifying yell as they bravely attacked the raging enemy, already whetted on blood and victory. / The Spaniards met a solid wall of cruel spears, however, and having made a splendid charge and suffering grievous injuries from one end of their line to the other, they halted. Some had been run through from front to back; others had flown far from their saddles. Some were wounded, some maimed, others trampled underfoot by their horses. / Oh, pen of mine! It's not right to pass so quickly over the memorable deeds of that day and the brutal effects of those valiant swords and lances! And although a greater wit could scarcely describe every feat, it's only proper to celebrate some part of the many you might. / Arrogant Lincoya, fearlessly leading the foremost Araucan contingent, was advancing with steady strides and a ferocious expression when he suddenly lowered his massive pike, fixed its butt on the ground between his feet, and caught the body of bold Hernán Pérez on its cruel iron tip. / The sharp blade made a terrible wound as it entered the Spaniard's side, and having passed through his double-layered corselet and coat of fine mail, the fat, unyielding spearhead, covered with blood, tore open an exit through his shoulders and left his body, now pale, suspended above the pommel. / Audacious Tucapel took on the valiant Osorio, who came rushing forward with more courage than prudence, working his mount with his iron-shod heels. Tucapel was facing him, but at the last moment stepped aside and circled his club, bringing it down with such force that not one of the Spaniard's limbs or bones was left intact. / A second blow knocked down Cáceres, who was coming behind him, but with great effort he got back to his feet and grasped his sword and shield with enough courage to fight the war all by himself. The boldness of his stand struck fear into even the most daring opponent, / but while he managed to stand firm, his strength was not enough against so many, for already a tight-packed, noisy mob was circling him in a confused mass. At this point more than fifty cavalry led by Reynoso charged from the other side, arriving just in time. / Their attack was so fierce that even encountering a wall woven of stout spears they broke through the closely-spaced warriors, more than ten of whom tested the hard ground. Surrounded by enemies and far from secure, they rescued the valiant Cáceres, who was holding his own with ferocious determination, delaying death by dealing it. /

[22.25] Ignoring great danger, Miguel and Pedro de Avendaño, Escobar, Juan Jufré, Cortés, and Aranda bore their share of the battle. Also making their presence felt and causing terrible injury were Losada, Peña, Córdoba, and Miranda; Bernal, Lasarte, and Castañeda; Ulloa, Martín Ruiz, and Juan López de Gamboa. / But soon the Araucan army, now baited on Spanish blood, forced them all to turn back and take up the route they had begun. After this a second squadron of our men attacked with sudden fury, but gaining no ground at all they also had to pull up their reins and turn about, / and even though Juan Remón and the others would stop abruptly from time to time to fight, it wasn't long before they resumed their original course with new losses and even greater haste. Thus they were proceeding, all mixed up together in a thick cloud of dust, when the orderly ranks of our army appeared in battle formation. / The Araucans were advancing so fiercely they almost impaled themselves on our pikes, but coming to their senses they checked their headlong rush, and assembling into ranks, quickly withdrew across the plain to the foot of a hill, next to a lagoon and vast quagmire. / A large number of our infantry attacked them here, firing a dense volley of shots as soon as they came within range, then following them as they retreated into the swamp to fight sword-to-sword, testing our strength and courage with steady hands and hearts. / Germans never fought so stubbornly, face to face and one on one, dealing and receiving unending and ferocious double-handed blows, as the two sides here, who became so firmly stuck in the mud they couldn't take a single step back, and promptly striking, were promptly struck.[136] / One man, up to his waist in the sodden mire, was fighting two or three at a time. Another, wanting to move to gain more mobility, became more entrapped. Still another, testing his strength and luck, assaulted the enemy next to him by biting and blinding him with mud, seeking to win however he could. / The furious battering and wounding went on equally, and since Fortune gave no sign of declaring herself, the outcome remained unclear. Now these men seemed about to prevail, now those appeared to be winning the lagoon, its troubled waters turned red by all the blood they were spilling. /

[22.33] Rengo, whose hatred and burning rage had blindly led him far in front of the others, as soon as he realized our camp was nearby and that he was headed straight for death, also withdrew to the lagoon. Turning his ferocious countenance and fearless chest to face our entire army, he then cried in a threatening voice, / "Come to me, you common peasants! Turn your wrath on me, for I'm the one who persecutes you and desires your death more than life itself! I won't rest until I've seen the Spanish nation destroyed, and I'll sate my hunger and ravenous thirst on your odious flesh and blood!" / Thus standing in the middle of the swamp and brandishing his bloody cudgel he threatened heaven

---

136 The ferocity of German soldiers or *landsknechten*, who often fought as mercenaries, was proverbial in early modern Europe.

and earth, terrifying the weak of spirit. Scarcely had his voice been recognized when some of our soldiers who were nearest, giving little heed to his threats, hastened toward him with their weapons drawn. / But the *yanacona*, Juan, drawing ahead of these other bold men, had his head bashed in by one of the Araucan's blows, and Chilca's body was then pummeled by another. Rengo directed a third blow at the young Zuñiga with such rage that he sank him up to his chest in the bog, as though hammering him into the wet earth. / Now a dense rain of shots was fired at the barbarian from all sides, clouding the clear air as they headed for his valiant chest. Not for this did he desist, but rather redoubled his blows and fury, up to his waist in mud, a fearless bulwark for his men. / Like a bristling wild boar that once it is wounded withdraws into a narrow marsh pursued by eager bloodhounds, and surrounded by skilled hunters it snorts and snarls, then snarls even more as it swivels from side to side, smashing, ramming, and trampling, wounding and killing as it brushes off their many shots, / just so the intrepid barbarian, all alone in the middle of the swamp, consumed by wrath and mad with rage, covered with blood, sweat, and mud, resisted the fury of the innumerable shots coming from all sides, obscuring the sun as they rained down on him like a storm. / The obedient barbarian army, scattered by their stubborn pursuit of us and seeing our soldiers on the plain, began to draw apart and regroup. Rengo alone, ferocious and fearless, equaled unequal odds, for the swamp was deep and surrounded by dense woods. / Realizing the dubious benefit and certain peril, however, and seeing the many attackers closing in on him from both sides in such a rapid, orderly fashion, he finally decided to retreat along a hidden, woodland path protected by the rugged mountain, saving himself and his soldiers. / To these he now said, "Friends, let's not waste our strength and time on a useless fight, but conserve the blood we still have in order to sell it later for a higher price! It's best we withdraw rather than let the enemy corner us in this marsh, losing our reputation and they their respect." / Dutiful to Rengo's words, they immediately restrained their ready arms, retreating along a narrow and densely overgrown trail to the sound of their drums. The ruggedness of the location prevented any pursuit by our soldiers, some of whom were so enmired they had to be rescued. / And so the fierce enemy departed, skirting the slopes of the lofty mountain. Brutish Rengo, bloodied and drenched with mud, herded them along as he brought up the rear, like a jealous bull following a slow herd of cows, slowly turning his thickset neck and lofty forehead this way and that. /

[22.45] With order restored and the enemy withdrawn, some of our soldiers returned with a barbarian they had seized after he strayed too far from his companions. By chance he was brought to my section of the camp, and here they ordered his hands be cut off as a warning to the rebellious villages thereabouts. / In my presence he first placed his right hand on the stripped trunk of a tree, and after a harsh blow had severed it he cheerfully extended his left, which without his moving an eyelash or wrinkling his brow also leapt up as it was cut. With contemptuous disdain he then lowered his head and stretched out his neck, / saying, "Here, slash this throat which has always thirsted for your blood, for I don't fear death and your threats and cruel spectacles don't frighten me! My loss isn't so great that this right hand will be missed, for there remain many others who can skillfully wield a sword! / If you expect to gain some benefit by sparing my life, I'll die to spite you, for if you wish me to live, then I don't! In the end I'll die happy having done so against your will, for if it's the only way to offend you I'll do so with my death!" / Thus he stubbornly sought death by insulting us, and growing ever more enraged threw himself to the gore-soaked ground where he rolled about in his own blood, striving to end his life while gnawing frantically with his teeth at his lifeless stumps. / His obstinacy was such that pity was beginning to temper our anger, when he noticed one of our slaves coming down the hill loaded with barbarian plunder. Like a ferocious wild beast catching sight of some solitary prey, he rushed across to attack the man with just such sudden fury, / and using his feet and arms laid him out on the sodden earth and beat him about the eyes and nose with his tough, pale stumps. In the end, unable to defend himself, the man would have been eaten by mouthfuls right in front of us had he not had help, which even though it was prompt did not prevent his being badly mauled. / Back on his feet, the diabolical barbarian boldly declared, "Since I still have enough strength and blood left to injure Christians, I'm glad to accept my life from you after all! And even though it's conceded to me so shamefully, I still hope to get even with you without my hands, nor will I need them to avenge myself! / Just wait, accursed ones, just wait! For I tell you that in my hatred and rabid passion you'll find an implacable, tormenting foe, even if these are the only way I can harm you. You'll soon see how I'll harass you and how much better it would have been for you had I died!" Saying other things I do not repeat, he set off from there as light as the wind. / It isn't right to leave in oblivion the name of this determined barbarian, who due to his courage and daring was called the audacious Galbarino. But such brutality has exhausted my voice and strength and I must stop, having no more words or breath. /

CANTO 23

Galbarino appears before the Araucan senate and makes a speech that upsets many. The Spanish set out in search of the enemy. The cave and many marvels of the sorcerer Fitón are described.

No enemy should ever be disparaged, my Lord, for a spark can cause a fire that may consume us. It's also wise to be wary when our happiness is greatest, since those in Fortune's favor are most prone to its reversals. / A good death is the only guarantee of a happy fate's brief course, for nothing is safe from change as long as life persists. Those who have never had good fortune are thus the fortunate ones, for lacking prosperity they live contented and fear no disaster. / Knowing for certain that no good lasts for long, a universal law to which even the happiest are subject, to spend more time on it is tiring, and to avoid such tedium I will speak of what came of underestimating young Galbarino. /

[23.4] Even though he was maimed and bleeding, the rage and courage inspiring the barbarian were so great that he made his way to Andalicán, where Caupolicán had positioned the army and where the illustrious senate was meeting in secret council to discuss the war. / Some of the caciques, with justifiable concern, were pointing out the difficulties of imprudent ambition; others, to show their valor, were making every difficulty and inconvenience seem easy. Some were approving a well-thought-out plan; others, dissenting, were attempting to persuade the rest with their arguments and opinions. / Scarcely alive, Galbarino appeared in the midst of this confusion and disagreement, and having asked permission to enter, was readily granted it. Completely covered in the blood he had lost, he rallied his weakened voice and with due reverence began to complain as follows: / "If ever you truly sought vengeance for your injuries, honored lords, your banners striking fear into foreign lands and nations, how is it that within your own territories degenerate foreigners now oppress and defeat you and yet your revenge is so timid? / Behold my broken body, one of your own, which as further insult your enemies send covered with wounds as a message to the senate. Behold their contempt for your courage and the threat the tyrant makes through me, vowing to dismember each and every cacique one by one! / Clearly it was all in vain that your ancestors gained such honor and glory and that the Araucans' reputation once rose heavenward on their virtue, since it now travels from tongue to tongue through the dirt, defamed, degraded, and debased, while your illustrious blood, now chilled, is shed in obscure encounters! / What province was there anywhere in the entire wide world that once did not tremble upon hearing your name? What nation did not surrender its weapons, compelled by force or fear? Did you ascend this peak only to make your fall from it greater, contempt now reaching those heights once held by esteem? / Under the guise and pretext of clemency, these foreign enemies now offer to accept you as friends, desiring your return to obedience. Should you refuse to submit, they vow to chastise and compel your insolence, their swords exempting neither sex, religion, age, nor status. / Come to your senses! Don't listen to their hoaxes, deals, and wiles, all of which are directed toward the same goal of defiling your achievements! That which has brought them here across so many strange lands and seas is the tantalizing gold held in the fertile veins of our home. / Attempting to prove that their purpose is to spread the Christian religion, when its foundation is sheer self-interest, is a pretense and empty affectation! Their presumption flows from greed and all the rest is deception, for we have seen how much more thievish, insolent, and adulterous they are than other people. / If sinister fate and affliction threaten us with ruin in days to come, we can always choose an honorable death, a quick, easy, and reliable remedy! Therefore set your formidable shoulders against fortune and your hardened hearts against cruel adversity, for a courageous heart and invincible spirit can achieve the impossible!" / Swooning from the blood he had lost he was unable to say more, and his weakened, weary neck could no longer support his head. Deathly pale and disfigured, he fell to the blood-soaked ground, leaving even the most indifferent feeling pity for his approaching end. / As his wounds were not severe enough to grant him access to death, however, once his bleeding was stanched he held on to precarious life. With constant care his health returned, and eventually the determined young man recovered his original strength. / His words were so forceful and the hatred they aroused against us so great that the most timid hearts were now consumed with frenzied rage. Different opinions were thus reduced to one proposal and one goal, and anyone counseling moderation or terms was henceforth excluded. / The impatient younger men, boastful and eager to resort to arms, harried the indolent hours with passionate displays. Those who were calmer and more mature, while concurring in the general decision, tempered their imprudence and incendiary anger. /

[23.19] Let us now leave the Araucan warriors for a while, planning not only for one battle but a hundred, with their arrangements, tactics, timing, and locations, with their multiple proposals but one purpose. Little by little I've been neglecting our own busy camp, which with everyone inside was well guarded and prepared. / When the longed-for sun finally rose, the cavalry, leaving the infantry and rest of the army behind, set out in an orderly march, proceeding so swiftly that by midday we had climbed the steep, fearsome slope of Andalicán mountain, still littered with the white bones of Christians, causing us both anguish and concern.[137] / We then descended into the Arauco valley, buffeted by the sea on the west, and as soon as we had set up camp in a level area with adequate food and pasture, we sent some of the local men to the people thereabout with promises of secure peace and Christian law. / When these men did not return as expected, and after several more days during which we

---

137 The Spaniards' earlier losses on Mt. Andalicán are described in Cantos 5 and 6.

were unable to learn anything of the inhabitants' intentions by ruse or by skill, we decided that at the late rising of the waning moon a few of us would set out for the nearby hamlets in search of news or information. / Thus it was, proceeding cautiously one dark and silent night, I came upon some settlements in the midst of dense woods and brush. A wretched, miserable people were living here, their poverty ensuring their peace, for the shock and uproar of the war had not yet uprooted them from their land. / Afterwards, nearing Chayllacano, where our camp was located, I caught sight of a feeble Indian moving along a narrow path on a hillside at the edge of the plain, a man so old and thin that his feet could hardly support him, bent over, fragile, and as withered as a root. / Disturbed by this bleak vision of old age, I rode closer to offer assistance in his infirmity and to see if he knew anything, but a timid deer hearing the sound of greyhounds does not flee with the agility the old man displayed as he bounded up the hill. / Not giving it another thought I clapped my legs to my horse and set out after him as fast as I could, expecting to reach him even though he was flying away. He left the wind in his wake, however, and I was forced against my will to give up the chase, quickly losing sight of him and unable to follow any farther. / I found myself descending a slope near two abandoned trails where the Rauco narrows, constrained by ridges along both sides. Gazing down and almost directly ahead, I saw a gentle deer enjoying the dew-covered grass in a lush grove of trees next to the river, / and I remembered that Reason had told me in my dream that one day I would happen upon an innocent doe along a riverbank.[138] With great joy I began to move down the slope step by step, coming out almost next to the animal, / which was

---

138 The poet's encounter with the deer is foretold at Canto 18.60.8.

easy given how blithely it was cropping the tender grass and how loud the river was in the ravine. Although it had been paying no attention to where it walked or what it heard, once the animal sensed my presence and raised its proud head, it left that grove and pleasant fodder by way of a narrow, rugged path. / I hurried to follow, working the flanks of my horse, but taking a different, intersecting trail it entered an area of rocky hills and finally headed toward dense thickets and closely-set trees, darting along while I came behind as fast as I could. / The trail soon came to an end and I lost track of it. A turbulent wind kicked up, and soon I was ambling blindly here and there, from one patch of brambles to another, by touch alone. Realizing my foolish temerity, I repented my plan and would have turned around and proceeded no farther had I been able to find any trace of the path. / After wandering about like that for some time, unable to find a way out, I heard the murmur of a nearby stream, and following its sound, at the foot of an oak on its bank I saw a tiny, miserable hut, and there beside the doe an ancient man. /

[23.33] "What fate or misfortune has led you so far from the road," he asked, "through such wild woods and thickets, where I've never known anyone to come? If ill-chance or hard luck has separated you from your company, I'll do what I can to help." / Hearing this welcome offer from that strange, amiable elder, I was happier than I had ever been in my life. After explaining how I came to be there, I told him I was looking for the sorcerer Fitón and asked his advice in finding his cave. / The venerable old man and ancient father emerged from his fragile dwelling with a sigh and gentle demeanor, and taking me tenderly by the hand, its being the beginning of summer, we sought the refreshing shade of a nearby rocky spring, where he told me the following: / "Arauco is my home, and I'm known as unlucky old Guaticolo. In my prime I was a soldier and held the post now filled by Colocolo, and seven times I won bouts in the arena, one on one. Hundreds of times laurels wreathed this bald and aging brow, / but since what's good in life never lasts for long and everything is subject to change, my good fortune turned to bad and my honor to perpetual disgrace. Through ill-luck and a strange accident in a bout with Ainavillo I lost the glory I'd won over many years, depriving me of my honor but not my life. / Finding myself alive but dishonored—I'd rather have been dead a thousand times!—and with no hope of my reputation being restored, I came to the wilderness you see here, where I've lived more than twenty years without ever being discovered by anyone but you, which I find no small miracle. / But since fortune has brought you to this melancholy and humble dwelling where I've lived so long in lonely isolation, I'll willingly comply with your request. I know Fitón, who while curt and intractable is my uncle, the brother of my father, Guarcolo. / He makes his home at the foot of a treacherous mountain rarely trod by human feet, where he leads a strange life in a dark and gloomy abode that the cheerful sun never enters. This is well suited to his temperament, since he's irritable, reclusive, and a mortal enemy of human contact. / Fitón's knowledge of and power over animals, plants, and stones is such that his science and art encompass all natural causes, while in the somber realm of fear his rigorous spells compel the mute infernal deities to reveal the past, present, and future. / Amidst the full fury and bright light of day he shrouds the world in nocturnal gloom, and in the absence of wind makes it rain and thunder from untimely, tranquil skies. He restrains the rushing course of rivers and with potent words forces birds to fall drowsily to earth midflight. / He revives dried herbs, knowing the virtues of each, and stirs the sea, countering the force and influence of the moon. The winds obey him, and the solid earth trembles and shakes at the sound of his powerful voice, contracting violently toward its core without any other cause provoking it. / All other elemental powers are also subject to the words of this man, who annuls the force and impact of heaven's movements and intentions. In brief, his knowledge and incantations allow him to penetrate secrets and through astral influences to grasp men's fates and destinies. / I'm not sure how to properly impress you with all the abilities of this divine sorcerer. As his nephew I only want to assist you however I can, and the best chance of doing so is for us to set out now, for it's a time of day he's not as busy and we're more likely to gain entry." /

[23.46] The two of us then rose from that place, and having secured my horse by the reins we hastened along a narrow, winding trail, which we followed for some way before entering a fearsome grove. Here, where the sun's bright light never reached the shady ground, / we came upon an overhanging crag, hidden by dense branches, and saw beneath it the entrance to a little alley, at the end of which was a small, open door surrounded by the heads of wild animals. The robust old man grasped my hand and set off toward it, / and after a hundred paces or so, not without some fear on my part, we passed through the door and came out beneath an enormous vaulted ceiling at the center of which a perpetual light was burning. All about us on every side were orderly stone shelves filled with multitudes of labeled flasks of unguents, herbs, and innumerable liquids: / preparations made from penetrating lynx eyes, acquired at certain times and astral junctions; from poisonous basilisk and the blood of wrathful red-haired men; from the saliva of rabid dogs afraid of water and old, dried skin of spotted Chersydrus.[139] / Elsewhere: ferocious hyena hump and essence of Cenchris, nourished in the burning sands of Libya; a piece of harpy's wing, gall of the two-headed amphisbaena, and coiled tail of asp, which delivers death wrapped in sweet sleep;[140] / moldy skulls severed from unburied bodies; the flesh of a female fetus, unnaturally extracted; disjointed spine of the cerastean serpent, and dried haemorrhois tongue, whose victims die by sweating out all their blood.[141] / The skin of every monstrous prodigy produced by supernumerary nature, the spittle of venomous serpents, the wings of the fearsome Iaculus and poisonous fangs of the seps, whose bite makes men and animals suddenly swell like wineskins, rotting their flesh and bones.[142] / In great transparent jars were the transfixed heart of

---

139 Much of Ercilla's catalog of magical ingredients is derived from Lucan's descriptions of the witch Erictho (*Pharsalia* 6. 670ff. and 9. 701ff.); a belief in the medicinal properties of lynxes extends to antiquity; the basilisk, a legendary reptile, was associated by the early Christian church with the devil; the Chersydrus is an amphibious retile of the Libyan desert, one of several deadly snakes mentioned by Lucan (and Ercilla) that sprung from the blood that dripped from the severed head of the Medusa as Perseus flew with it over the African coast.
140 In addition to Lucan, Pliny the Elder's *Natural History* notes various properties of the hyena (8.105); Lucan's spotted cenchris is another Libyan snake; mythological harpies were monstrous birds with the heads of women, known for snatching and fouling food; the amphisbaena snake is said to have a head at each end of its body; the asp, the first snake to be created from the Medusa's blood, was believed to be the deadliest of these snakes.
141 The cerastes and haemorrhois are also mentioned by Pliny (*N. H.* 8. 85 and 23. 43).
142 Lucan describes the Iaculus as a flying snake.

a griffin, ashes of the oriental phoenix, which sets itself afire when weary of life, oil of the Scytala snake, and Echeneis fish, which intercept ships on churning seas and hold them back despite the wind.[143] / Scorpion heads were also there, along with deadly, festering vipers, Alacrans, dragon tails, and stones from nesting eagles; maws of ravenous sharks, milk and menses from flogged women, swollen glands, plagues, toxins, and every other pestilence produced by nature.[144] /

[23.55] Gazing in rapt attention at this bountiful pharmacopeia, I saw an ancient, emaciated man emerge from a door in the corner, leaning upon a crooked staff and instantly realized it was he who had ascended the hill so swiftly that a crossbow shot could scarcely have kept up with him. / "'Tis no little daring has brought you here today, despite your youth, to my hidden abode," he said, "where no one has ever come against my will. But since I know the motive that drives you to such lengths to find me is an honorable one, I've decided this one time to do something for your benefit I've never considered doing before." / My obliging companion, seeing how favorable the situation was, with the usually intractable old man so sociable and mild, waited a moment, watching me with an encouraging expression to see if I wanted to respond. When I remained silent, he said, / "Oh, great Fitón! Able to penetrate the secrets of the heavens, which drawn from their eternal courses obey no laws but

---

143 The legendary griffin had the body of a lion and the head and wings of an eagle; the mythological phoenix cyclically arose from the ashes of self-immolation; the Echeneis was believed to latch onto ships and arrest their motion.

144 Alacrans are similar to scorpions; various ancient authors refer to *aetites*, or stones found in the nests of eagles, as having beneficial effects on childbirth.

The Araucana

yours! You who at will revoke the decrees of Fortune and cruel fate, upending the natural order to compass things yet to come, / who through occult sciences and infinite learning penetrate solid earth, bringing bright daylight to the profound dark realm and tormenting with stringent spells the infernal throng who tremble there in terror at the effects of your power, formidable enough to suspend their eternal laws! / Know that this young man has been drawn here by the great renown of your awful name, which has spread throughout the Indies to the northern pole. Overcoming a thousand dangers he has pursued his desire, which calls him to celebrate the course of the war and bloody destruction of this land. / One night when he had retired to write about the day's events, he was suddenly swept up in a dream that showed him all that was happening in Europe. It was also revealed to him that in your hidden cave he would learn about extraordinary things worthy of memory with which he could ennoble his history, / and that you would make known to him matters past, present, and future, miraculous feats and conquests, singular adventures, terrifying, audacious enterprises, and exploits never yet seen in writing. These superlatives torment him, and we're both in suspense awaiting your response." /

[23.63] The wizard rejoiced upon hearing how far his fame had spread beyond that region, and turning his timeworn face to mine he eyed me from top to bottom. Finally, in a vigorous voice scarcely in keeping with his white hair, he assumed a grave demeanor and with a somewhat severe expression answered as follows: / "Although it's forbidden to prophesy about things to come and easier to prolong a life against the laws of fate, considering the desolate trails you've followed to reach my abode and my nephew's acting as your interpreter and sponsor, I'm

CANTO 23

willing to gratify your wish." / Speaking thus, he took me by the hand and with measured steps led me through the small vaulted door into another room, and from there into a beautiful chamber whose wondrous workmanship and decoration were so detailed and costly no tongue could ever describe them, nor is there an imagination they would not exceed. / The floor was paved with transparent crystal tiles, their varied colors mingling in changing patterns; the lofty, diaphanous ceiling was starred with countless brilliant stones, whose shimmering reflections cheered the entire hall. / Atop gold columns that lined the walls were a hundred statues, so lifelike in their art that someone deaf might have thought they spoke. Their deeds were pictured behind them on spacious walls, which displayed the finest accomplishments of arms and letters, of virtue and continence. / In the middle of this spacious chamber, some half-mile square, was a great, miraculous orb enclosed within a shimmering glass sphere. Marvelous construction and art held it suspended in mid-air, as though the enormous device and mechanism within it were supported from their own center. / After briefly sating my greedy gaze upon the pictures and looking at the various sculptures and immense richness of the walls, floor, and ceiling, the wizard led me directly to the sphere, where turning to face the many statues he began to point with his crooked staff and instruct me, speaking as follows: / "You should know, my son, that these are men, most of them having left this life, whose renown for great deeds has been and always will be celebrated. Many, of humble name and origin, were elevated by their own lofty accomplishments, having been placed at the pinnacle of glory by propitious fortune. / The orb and artifice you see here are the world's vast dimensions made small, the painstaking construction of which has cost me forty

| 305 |

The Araucana

years of study. There's nothing in the long ages ahead nor any occult ordering of inflexible fate that's not perfectly patent and clear to me here, where it has its vivid image and essence. / But since your noble intention is to write of martial deeds, which the rigorous stars have ensured such plentiful examples of in this land, I'll leave aside some of what the sphere and world contain at present and show you one thing alone that will amaze you with its importance for your undertaking. / The subject you seek is indeed found here in our Arauco, where swords and protective mail are used more often than elsewhere, but what your history truly lacks for authority is a naval battle, with which you can write of war at sea as well as on land. / This you'll now see, and I vow the witnessing of it will leave us incredulous, for neither in the past nor future was there nor will there ever be any as terrifying. The great Mediterranean will be secured by the victors, and the maritime power of the defeated will be broken and destroyed.[145] / Don't be alarmed by my words nor let my horrifying conjuration frighten you, rather pay close attention and you'll soon be shown the future. Everything you'll observe here, point by point, has been disposed by fate, and I assure you you're about to become an eyewitness and genuine chronicler of it." /

[23.76] With even greater eagerness I brought my face to the side of the transparent sphere, where I saw a world as large and distinct as our own, just as when viewing a small picture through a convex lens we perceive an immense palace and vast expanse within a small space. / Inside was the turbulent and storm-tossed Ausonian sea, where the great dispute between

---

145 The Battle of Lepanto, described in the following canto, was fought between the Holy League and Ottoman Empire off the western coast of Greece in October of 1571.

Canto 23

Caesar Augustus and Mark Antony had once been decided, and just as then, the entire area between the coastline of Lepanto and the Curzolari islands to the west was covered with galleons.[146] / Seeing the famous insignia of the Pope, Philip, and the Venetians, I immediately recognized the armadas of the Christians and infidel Turks, drawn up in battle order and prepared for combat, although to me they did not seem to be moving nor be more than figurines. / "You're about to witness an extraordinary naval battle in which the supreme valor of your Spain will be amply shown," Fitón said. Then with a wild and baleful expression he struck the great globe with his staff, once crosswise and once directly, and bringing forth a horribly raucous voice from deep in his chest, / he cried, "Pale Orcus and Cerberus! Mighty Pluto, ruler of the infernal abyss! Weary Charon, ancient oarsman, and you, Stygian marsh and Lake Avernus! Demogorgon, inhabiting the depths of the eternal Tartarean realm, and you boiling waters of the Acheron, Lethe, Cocytus, and Phlegethon![147] / You Furies,

---

146 The final confrontation between Octavian (subsequently Caesar Augustus) and Mark Antony was the naval battle of Actium, which took place in 27 B.C.E., a few miles north of where the battle of Lepanto would be fought; the sea in question is the Ionian rather than *Ausonian*, a term signifying Italian or Roman; the Curzolari islands lie some forty mile west of Lepanto (present-day Nafpaktos).

147 Orcus is a Roman god of the underworld akin to the better-known Greek god, Pluto, who rules over Hades; Cerberus is a three-headed dog that guards the entrance to Hades; Charon is the boatman said to ferry the shades of the dead across the Styx or the Acheron, which together with the Lethe, Cocytus, and Phlegethon comprise the underworld rivers often described as converging in the Stygian marsh; in antiquity lake Avernus, near Naples, was believed to provide an entrance to the underworld;

cruel torturers of damned souls, whose brows of bristling vipers the infernal deities themselves fear to look upon, and you Gorgon potentates! Compelled by my powerful words, make this naval battle, although still in the future, clearly visible here!148 / Oh, smoke-trailing and hideous Hecate, show us what I ask! Hark! I'm speaking to you! What is this delay, that my terrible voice doesn't make you tremble? Beware I don't burst through the intervening earth and wound you with horrid daylight, shattering Erebus's laws with my invincible strength and novel power!"149 /

[23.83] He had scarcely finished speaking when the seawater began to churn and a dry wind blew from the east-northeast, stretching taut the cables and broad sails of the ships. Taking a sudden breath, little by little the figurines began to move, and everything else similarly felt the effects of his words. / Astounded, I carefully watched that multitude of men, seeing the name and position of each inscribed on their brows and marveling at those I presently knew as children yet saw there in all their vigor and vital years, along with others, now flowering youth and there white-haired.150 / At this point the Christians fired a cannon as the

---

    Demogorgon is a powerful underworld demon or pagan deity; in Greek mythology Tartarus is both an underworld deity and a part of the underworld itself.

148 The Furies or Erinyes were underworld goddesses described as having serpents entwined in their hair; the three Gorgons (sisters, one of whom was Medusa) are female monsters with snakes instead of hair who turned those who looked at them to stone.

149 In Greek mythology Hecate was an underworld goddess associated with ghosts, magic, and witchcraft; Erebus was both a deity and another name for the underworld itself, as here.

150 The poet is referring to the difference between narrative time—the end of 1557 or the beginning of 1558—and the date of the battle of Lepanto some fourteen years later, in 1571.

signal for attack and hoisted a crucifix on high, increasing their fervor and excitement. All humbly saluted it with great reverence and devotion, the armies of faithful allies at their sides, / and then with great noise and commotion the vessels got underway, the armadas drawing ever closer to each other. Standards, flags, and pennants fluttered over lofty poop decks; well-ordered troops and squadrons could be seen brandishing their weapons on galleys lined with bronze cannons and netting. / Given how faint my voice has become, it isn't fit that I continue to sing of such an important event, which calls for new strength, a more fluent tongue, and more powerful delivery. Thus reluctant and not daring to proceed further, my Lord, I ask that you grant me your favor and attention in the following canto. /

CANTO 24

This canto is devoted to the great naval battle of Lepanto, the rout and destruction of the Turkish armada, and the flight of Ochalí.[151]

The time has come, mighty Philip, when granted your favor my voice shall sing of the great, world-wide campaign decided upon Ausonian waters, of the proud Ottoman overthrown and his maritime force destroyed, of diverse fates and diverging fortunes, of bloody devastation and cruel death. / Open your founts to me, sacred Muses! Grant me new strength and inspiration, together with a style and language befitting my audacious undertaking, so that I may fully convey the course of this great battle and

---

151 At the time of Lepanto, Ochalí was the Pasha of Algiers; see the following note.

Canto 24

the many men brought together here by fortune's blow. / Who could count the immense number of squadrons and galleys, the mix and multitudes of nations, standards, insignia, and flags, the equipment, munitions, and defenses, the different weapons and their uses, the instruments, devices, and machines, preparations, ornaments, and emblems? / I saw Croats, Dalmatians, and Slavonians, Bulgarians and Albanians, Transylvanians and Tartars, Thracians, Greeks, Macedonians, Turks and Lydians, Armenians and Georgians, Syrians, Arabs, Saracens, Lycians, and Lyconians, Numidians and Africans, captains, janissaries, and sanjaks, chauces, beylerbeys, and pashas.[152] / I also saw the flower of Spanish youth and valor, the nobility of Italy and Germany, a brave and gallant company, all sumptuously attired and displaying their pride and spirit, along with countless pennants, banderoles, and streamers flying from crows' nests, foremasts, and poops. /

[24.6] The two fleets advanced in such close formation that it appeared two dense forests were slowly drawing near one another. Burnished weapons shimmered across the troubled sea, their flashes and sharp reflections dazzling the eye from afar. / Racing

---

152 These descriptions reflect a mix of ancient, medieval, and early modern terminology: Lycia was an ancient region on the southern coast of present-day Turkey; Lyconia lay to its northeast; Saracen refers to inhabitants of the southern Arabian peninsula; the Roman province of Africa lay along the continent's Mediterranean coast, roughly contingent with present-day Tunisia; janissaries were elite Ottoman troops, originally composed of Christian youth drafted from the Balkan provinces and converted to Islam; *sanjaks* were both Ottoman administrative regions and the governors thereof; *chauz* (fr. Turkish *çavuş*, cf. *alguacil*, or sheriff, in Spanish) refers to a justice official; beylerbey is a high-ranking Ottoman official; *pashas* are Turkish generals or governors.

from side to side amidst our fleet was a light frigate, upon it a statuesque young man of gallant appearance, armed with an opulent breastplate and displaying such authority he seemed in his deportment and valor to be the very son of Fortune and Mars. / Beguiled by his stature and poise and avid to know his identity, I was closely observing his elegant demeanor when I saw embossed in raised gold letters on a blood-red background at the crown of his sturdy helmet: "Don Juan, Son of Caesar, Charles V." / The youth moved tirelessly here and there amidst the tumult and clamor, while the frigate next to him carried his secretary, the venerable Juan de Soto, who the sorcerer told me had great aptitude in many matters, being a man of reasoning and experience, of great adroitness and insight. / Don Juan now exhorted the men to the perilous battle with a bold confidence that calmed any doubts and assured them of victory, his noble heart facilitating what fear restrained as he spread a bellicose fury and ardent fire through all those present. /

[24.11] "Oh, valiant company," he said, "impregnable fortress of the Church! The time has come, for this is the day that will assure your names a place in memory! Ready your weapons and agile oars, prove your invincible power and inviolable faith against these perfidious pagans who come to die at your hands! / Whoever wishes to return alive to the fatherland and beloved home, know that your swords must open a way through the midst of our enemies. Remember that you fight for your God, your King, and your life, which can only be saved by dealing death to the enemy. / Today the great weight and very existence of the world hangs on your swords and valor, and the glory and reward you all seek rest in your own hands! Let us hasten success, for delay is detrimental, and the only thing left between you and your goal is this brief stretch of sea. / Onward to victory! Let's not hinder the call of good fortune, but follow the course of our prosperous fate, offering fame a new subject and new feats. Here with one blow we'll destroy barbarian arrogance, for the great clamor of this battle will reach every corner of the earth! / Gaze joyfully at the glory prepared for you upon this sea, for God has assembled this multitude in order to cast them down at our feet, forcing all the Orient to bend its obedient neck to our yoke and allowing us to abolish and dictate laws to its mightiest kings and princes. / Today with their ruin we establish Christianity's credit throughout the world, for it's our God who wants us to crush the Mohammedans' pride and fury. Brave men! What danger can we fear fighting beneath his arm, and who can resist your swords when the divine hand itself is guiding them? / Trusting in Christ, who offered himself up to death for you on the cross, I ask only that each of you fight for him, proving yourselves worthy of being called his soldiers. Determine to win or die with steadfast resolve, for while victory is a glorious prize, to die for such a God is no less a reward! / This is the reason we run the risks and rigors of this campaign and come to the defense of his law against an infidel, renegade race! The justness of our cause confirms our success, and thus promised by heaven, I assure you that victory is ours!" /

[24.19] The coldest hearts were instantly inflamed with noble fury. Shaking shameful fear from their benumbed, leaden limbs, the men raised their right arms and all promised him victory or death, and from that moment on it would have mattered little had all the world's power been ranged against them. / Praising their firm resolve, the intrepid youth quickly crossed through the midst of the fleet, raising a wake of white spume as he sliced through the sea like a shimmering comet bursting boldly through dense air, its trail lingering long afterwards. / Having rapidly organized the men and galleys, he then boarded the royal vessel where he was joyfully saluted, and with everyone in their assigned places and the artillery readied, they headed for the Turkish ships. / Commanding the right wing was the successor to the illustrious Andrea Doria, whose memory the entire Mediterranean will celebrate forever. The Venetian Agostino Barbarigo, supplier of the senatorial fleet, led the left wing, no less impressive in its grandeur.[153] / Between these balanced, well-ordered arrays Charles's worthy son directed the battle, at his sides the galleys of Malta and Pier Battista Lomellini, as well as those of Venice and the Pope. Thus they advanced, the ships' enormous, long-bladed oars plied forcefully in regular strokes.[154] / Six galleasses, loaded with men and cannon, preceded them two by two in the shape of a crescent moon; thirty galleys assigned to assist wherever needed followed behind, bearing the marquis of Santa Cruz and his valiant company.[155] / Thus the Catholic fleet approached the infidels, who had the advantage of the wind at their backs as they entered open sea. But then the wind abruptly died and the high sea's waves were calmed as Fortune remitted its decision to bravery and the excellence of arms. /

---

153 Giovanni Andrea Doria, the great-nephew of Andrea Doria, commanded fifty-three galleys, as did Barbarigo.
154 The central component of the fleet consisted of sixty-two galleys, lighter vessels with both oars and sails and a few cannons mounted in the bow to fire ahead prior to ramming.
155 Galleasses were larger, heavier vessels with fewer oars and more sails; they usually carried some twenty cannons mounted along the sides; Álvaro de Bazán was the 1st marquis of Santa Cruz.

[24.26] Opposite Barbarigo, on the right wing, was the viceroy of Alexandria, Siroco, with the corsair and celebrated commander, Mehmed Bey, at that time governor of Negroponte. The renegade Ochalí was on the left of the fleet accompanied by his son, Cara Bey, while Ali Pasha, the armada's mighty admiral, was well surrounded in the center.[156] / Recognizing cruel fate and the arrival of his final, calamitous hour, the bold and prudent Ali Pasha made the following brief speech from the royal galley's lofty poop, feigning a confident, cheerful demeanor as he belittled Christian strength. / "My soldiers!" he cried, "Seeing such clear signs of your ferocious determination, I find no need to incite or exhort you with words! Unleash the wrath and desire in your fiery hearts as you take up your weapons, to which the fates today entrust our rights, / for never before has Fortune revealed itself so openly benign, coming directly to our door laden with such glory and spoils. Bring all the effort and affliction of this long war to an end, vindicating the great hope and honorable reputation your valor has always inspired! / Don't be alarmed by the noise and show with which the enemy fleet draws near: know that this eager army and all these men, assembled from a thousand diverse realms, have been united by Fortune into a single neck in order to be severed with a single blow, your hands bestowing the monarchy of the entire earth upon our Great Lord in just one day![157] / Inferior in both courage and

---

156 Suluk Mehmed Pasha, known as Mehmed Siroco, commanded sixty galleys; Negroponte, the present-day Greek island of Euboea; Ochalí was an Italian captured by Barbary pirates as an adolescent who converted to Islam and later became the viceroy or Pasha of Algiers; the supreme commander of the Turkish fleet was Muezzenade Ali Pasha.
157 The "great lord" of the Turks is Selim II, Ottoman Sultan from

numbers, these men approaching in such disorder impede and delay our being conquerors of the world. Show them the power of your weapons, seize the western realms and provinces from their unworthy possessors who advance so blindly to attack you! / Their cavalier captain, short of both years and competence, was unworthy of being promoted to his position. Lacking maturity, understanding, and experience, he's vain and reckless, his juvenile ardor and carelessness condemning all those men to the fury of your cruel swords.[158] / Don't think that fate will make our victory today a costly one, for most of that fearsome fleet comes from the Venetian Signoria, whose soldiers are neither skilled nor experienced, but more adept at comforts, courtesies, and their city's tender delicacies than the rigorous exercise of war. / The rest of that mob are an abject, barbarous rabble corralled from sundry nations and devoid of any cohesion, men who have never known the meaning of a sword and who'll be routed by their own disarray before the battle and terrible artillery roar even begin! / But you, invincible warriors, reared amidst cruel arms and tested time and time again by war and insufferable hardship, what perils or enemy army could ever be horrible enough to cause you the least fear or chill your fervor and courage? / Already I seem to see the glorious slaughter at your hands and the intervening sea more swollen, its whitened foam stained red with blood! Break through this horde, send Christian power to the abyss, and in a single blow take possession of everything from the Ganges to Chile, from pole to pole!" / Thus in the little time left the Pasha inspired his valiant soldiers, assuring them of the happy outcome of their heroic enterprise and lofty deeds. But in the hidden

---

1566 to 1574.
158 Don Juan of Austria was twenty-five years old at the time.

Canto 24

depths of his heart the situation appeared more difficult and the adversary's great determination an ill omen. / This was made worse when one of the janissary conscripts, keeping watch from the crow's nest, from which he could clearly identify the galleys, called out, "Unless my eyes deceive me, the center of the fleet and right wing, as well as the reserves that follow behind, are made up of navies and soldiers from the West."[159] / The Pasha heard this Christian's announcement as nothing less than death itself, but hiding his secret anguish he showed unflinching courage as he directed his larger squadron, protected by its extensive wings, toward the center of the fleet and his portion in the battle, which lay directly ahead of him. /

[24.40] The moment of attack appointed by inexorable fate having now arrived, the powerful armadas collided with equal force and ferocity. Loaded cannons were fired from all sides at once, their cacophony so terrible the entire earth seemed to tremble. / The smoke, flames, and terrifying roar of their furiously spewed shots, the horrendous collision of prows and terrible crash of broken masts, the stupefying noise of firearms, the clamor of shouts and screams, all this compounded the confusion, creating a spectacle of horrifying harmony. / Priam's ravaged city did not blaze as fiercely in as many places, nor did the cruel effects of pitiless Greek swords create as much havoc as the Turkish and Christian armadas enveloped in smoke and fire, the sea appearing not only to burn and the earth to collapse, but the lofty sky itself to come tumbling down.[160] / The intrepid don Juan, seeing

---

159 Janissaries were Christian youth conscripted from subject populations, converted to Islam, and trained as elite forces to protect the Sultan; the "western" armada refers specifically to Spain.
160 The destruction of Priam's city of Troy is told in Homer's *Iliad*.

the approach of the enemy flagship, cleaved boldly through the churning waves, bursting through the searing flames. The Turk impetuously drove forward to receive him, and they collided with equal violence in an impact that shattered their ironclad prows. / The royal vessels had scarcely grappled each other when seven well-armed Turkish galleys suddenly appeared and noisily attacked the Christian ship. Driven by no less ferocity, the papal and Venetian flagships came to its aid both left and right, / led by the second-in-command and admiral of the supreme Pius V, Marco Antonio Colonna, accompanied by a company of ardent young men. Spain's *Capitana* and *Patrona* followed, coming through an open passage to assist in breaking up the pagan multitude's assault.[161] / The valiant prince of Parma, aboard the Genoan *Capitana*, swiftly forced his way amidst the vessels, cleaving through the churning, frothy sea. The confusion and frenzied tumult with its dense cloud of black smoke obscured my eager vision and prevented my recognizing many others. / De Leinì's galley quickly attacked and blocked the approach from his side, where the first of those to be seen was the valiant prince of Urbino, withstanding the barbarian fury with exceptional fortitude and singular proof of his courage and determination.[162] /

[24.48] Now the galleys begin to board each other with equal ardor and audacity, drawing so close the men stand where they are to use their swords. Death does not frighten them, nor do any among them flee danger, even when the attackers see

---

161 The *Capitana*, or flagship of Castile, is second in command to the *Real*, or royal flagship; the *Patrona*, or royal squadron flagship, is next in authority.
162 Andrea Provana di Leinì; the duke of Urbino at the time was Francesco Maria II della Rovere.

cannons fired directly at their chests. / Thus the impassioned fighters advance, eager to deliver their blows, their raised arms falling and shots flying with the violence of a raving tempest. The fervor and speed with which they wield their weapons is something to behold. The sea is quickly covered with blood and begins to swell with dead bodies. / From prows and sterns and gunwales they attack without pause: some fall overboard and are drowned, others die by the sword, others by fire. The most hazardous positions never lack for someone to instantly take the place of the dead, and neither the ferocious artillery nor death itself can make a breach in the ranks. / Some, trying to leap to an opposing vessel, are pierced midair. Others, in excess haste to harm an opponent, are carried away by their fury and fall to the sea. Still others, with audacious, brutal forethought, trusting in the strength of their swimming, seize hold of an odious enemy and hurl themselves amidst the churning waves. / Who would not tremble at seeing the end and total destruction of the world, so many men perishing all at once, so many bombards, culverins, and cannons? The sun withdraws its shining rays, hiding its bewildered, blood-red face inside black clouds to shut out the day's destruction.[163] / Ferocious, bloodthirsty Mars, his breast bared and visage raging, speeds here and there upon his swiftly rolling chariot, accompanied by Tisiphone and Alecto. Now he shakes his mighty arm, now he pounds his resplendent shield, infusing the savage fighters with hatred, frenzy, and all-consuming rage.[164] / Some men, lacking ammunition, seize a piece of spar or oar. Some knock down galley slaves and unshackle them in order

---

163 Bombards and culverins are heavy artillery pieces.
164 Tisiphone and Alecto, sisters, were Furies or Erinyes, mythological deities who pursued and punished evildoers with madness.

to wield their fetters and chains. Nothing of metal, wood, or earth was unfit for hurling: broken benches, oarlocks, railings, barrels, hatches, portholes. / Even rebounding off hard steel the flying shots and lances find enemy targets amidst the bloody waves. Burning in rage they fight in freezing water, refusing to surrender to adverse fate until the inexorable last moment when life and strength both fail. / Some, afloat in the waves, die swallowing their own blood. Others, holding on to planks or cables, give up their souls but do not let go. Still others, unable to inflict more harm, seize hold of someone less injured and plunge with him to the abyss, content to die as they kill. / The confounding chaos with its enormous uproar and deafening clamor cannot be described. Burning tow flies through the air, setting fire to resin, pitch, and tar. Fed by pitch, the ready flames go running through dry wood with ferocious, crackling sparks that threaten the stars. / Some, persecuted by flames and cruel steel, leap into the sea to save themselves. Others, about to drown, embrace burning timbers. Thus they die, vainly grasping at anything in their desire to save themselves, burning to death in the water and drowning amidst the flames. / Many, already grappling with death but fighting for their convictions as they die, lay hold of lances and other missiles rebounding off stout armor. Supporting themselves in the fleeing waves, they flail their exhausted arms, inflicting their rage and the little strength they have left on anyone they meet. / The furor increases together with the harsh cacophony of incessant, rapid blows. The sea, confined and battered on all sides, boils up, vomiting cadavers. Bloody and agitated, as though driven by opposing winds, it roils everything together in a dense foam ceaselessly lashing the ironclad galleys. /

[24.61] On the lofty poop deck, next to the royal standard, the illustrious don Juan stands out resplendently amidst a distinguished company. More incensed than ireful Mars, he provides support wherever needed, urging on some and sending help to others, his person assuring them all of a superb triumph and the naval crown. / Commanding the *Capitana* at his side, Luis de Requesens inspires and inflames his men as he dashes, returns, and goes forth again, heading wherever the peril requires him most. Aiding and assisting, he directs, commands, exhorts, hastens, coaxes, and entreats, now on the right, now the left, at the poop and at the prow, winning esteem and eternal praise. / The alert and industrious don Fernando, count of Pliego, diligently goes where support is least and most in doubt. Among both Christians and Turks each man seeks an honorable death, striving, as I have said, to kill and die aboard enemy ships. / The fury and pandemonium grow so great it seems like the end of the world and final day, and a dense rain of terrifying blows obscures the blue sky and crimson sea. Rage increases, the continuous, rapid firing of the batteries does not cease, and clashing swords thunder along distant shores. / The good marquis of Santa Cruz was ready to assist wherever needed. Realizing how close the game was being played and how unequal the sides in some places, he wasted no time hurling himself amidst the fighting and great uproar, impetuously attacking wherever the tumult and danger were at their height. / Seeing the royal galley surrounded by such determined enemies, with another vessel of well-armed reinforcements racing to attack, he drove his rowers forward, speeding to defend it against the assault, his quick action blocking the barbarian's insidious design. / Without waiting he then ranged furiously through the brutal fighting, engaging, moving on, returning to help, fending off three and four assailants at a time. Who could describe, blow by blow, the valiant swords that distinguished themselves amidst the turmoil that day, swelling the sea with Turkish blood? / Impatient and full of wrath, don Juan was hastening sluggish fortune, rousing and inspiring his men, covered in their own and others' blood. Ali Pasha, filled with fervor, rallied his troops with no less diligence, constantly reminding them of the magnificent reward and honor of victory. / But the Christian *Real*, having the advantage of its commander's great valor, forces a wide breach among the opposing ship's defenders through the sheer strength and tenacity of its swords, and a dense throng of soldiers, their opponents unable to resist them, immediately swarm aboard the enemy vessel with a furious roar, shouting, "Attack, attack! Spain, Spain!" / The Turks, roused by the fear and peril of seeing their galley boarded, rally so fiercely the Christians are repelled. Redoubling their fury, the indignant Spaniards overcome their resistance and drive them forcefully back / to the mainmast, where renewed confidence and determination revive the fight with its terrible slaughter and barbaric killing. Men rush this way and that in their effort to help. The delay in arriving at victory or a desperate death exhausts and torments them, hastening their uncertain fates. /

[24.72] The great multitude of wounded gathering on the battered prow at times obstructed the fighters, but once their wounds were bandaged they quickly returned to the battle, seemingly recovered, to repel the enemy. / Amidst the frenzy of this vast commotion, more intense here than elsewhere, don Bernadino, gifted with more courage than foresight, was rushing to help when he was knocked down mid-course by the sudden fury of an esmeril's powerful blast, the brutal blow cutting short his advance and brave intentions.[165] / Neither his sturdy breastplate nor well-tested shield could resist such great weight and momentum, and in the end the young man assuaged a troubled life with an honorable death, while in Spain the countless swords sworn against him were sheathed.[166] /

[24.75] At this point the celebrated Maltese *Capitana* was attacked from three sides at once and furiously battered in a frenzy of ancient enmity. The well-known strength and courage of those audacious Christian knights withstood the pagan multitude, however, and little by little they were overcoming it[167] / when the viceroy of Algiers, an expert corsair who until now had done nothing but observe, saw an open path through the right wing. This part of the fleet was not well attached to the main array, and before the error could be corrected he forced his way to the Maltese accompanied by three additional vessels bearing an infinite number of infidels.[168] / The stalwart knights fought back, resisting the sudden maneuver, but in the end, my Lord, superior numbers overwhelmed strength and the enemy came aboard and slaughtered them with terrible brutality, not taking a single man alive for ransom and spilling a foaming river of baptized blood into the turbulent waters. / Seeing their flagship boarded

---

165 Bernardino de Cárdenas, marquis of Beteta, among the nobility aboard the royal galley; the *esmeril* is one of the smallest early modern artillery pieces, which increase in caliber through the falconet, falcon, and culebrina, among many others.
166 The reference to don Bernardino's personal troubles is unclear.
167 Based in Rhodes since the early fourteenth century, the Knights Hospitaller or Knights of Malta had long resisted Turkish power in the Mediterranean.
168 As noted earlier, the viceroy or Pasha of Algiers was Ochalí; see n. 151, above.

with such ferocity, the Maltese galleys scorned the enemies with whom they had begun to fight, and beating the waves with their oars, they hurled themselves with renewed rage against the pagan multitude, executioners of those Christian martyrs. / So great was their outrage and thirst for vengeance that they attacked the Turks from both sides and having boarded them wrought a savage massacre. Thus avenged and victorious, they recovered their honor and galley, where the only ones they found alive were the commander, the admiral, and four knights. / Nearby, Marco Antonio Colonna, scorning the enemy's brash violence, fought with great determination, his ambition for glory well-matched by his strength. And Sebastiano Venier, checking the Turks' barbaric ferocity and momentum, avenged himself with justified wrath for the injury he received at Famagusta.[169] /

[24.81] Elsewhere, the Sicilian *Capitana* was battling Pertau Pasha, whose vessels had surrounded it from two directions. Christian fortitude was such that not only did they offset the disadvantage and maintain their position, but they managed to gain ground, / for don Juan de Cardona, fulfilling his ancient office, exposed himself to every danger in lasting proof of his valor. The fierce Barcelonans also made a sacrifice of the enemy, sinking their swords to the hilt as they bathed them completely in blood.[170] / The astute Barbarigo fought with no less bravery and vigor, his valor matching the hope promised by such renowned

---

169 Colonna, as noted earlier, was admiral of the papal fleet; see 24.45; Sebastiano Venier was captain-general of the Venetian fleet during the loss of Cyprus to Ottoman forces, which culminated with the taking of Famagusta following an eleven-month siege.
170 Juan de Cardona was the captain of ten Sicilian galleys, which were part of the reserve force; Pertau Pasha was a commander of Turkish infantry.

CANTO 24

courage. Now he boldly assaulted the Turk, now he fought off death itself, forcing it to delay a raging arrow aimed directly at him. / But while he resisted the Saracen onslaught with exceptional valor and tenacity, he could not hold back cruel fate, or more precisely, divine decree, and coming to his final moment the furiously speeding shaft struck him directly in the eye and he fell dead. / Seeing such a captain fall, the Venetians' pain and sorrow was enormous, but not for that was there any slackening in their bold resolve. Instead, provoked to greater rage and a passion for just retribution, they abused his killers so fiercely his death was well avenged. / At this point the battle was closely contested along the right wing, where the resourceful Juan Andrea was proving himself an experienced master. Ettore Spinola was also contending with vessels both left and right, demonstrating Ligurian agility and expertise amidst all the fury.[171] /

[24.87] The bitterly-fought battle had lasted more than two-and-a-half hours, without either side being able to gain an advantage or declare victory, when the intrepid don Juan, consumed with wrath and indignation at fate's suspension, began to prevail and his fortune to become entirely clear. / Now, with great uproar and vehemence the Mohammedans' fury was overwhelmed by valiant Christian swords: the Turkish royal galley was boarded from all sides, the barbarian standard torn down, and the Redeemer's Cross hoisted in solemn triumph and great glory to a loudly-sung victory. / A sudden, icy fear went running through the wretched Turks, benumbing their limbs and leaving them weak and discouraged, and yielding up swords and resolution they resigned themselves to their miserable fate, offering free entry to the enemy's violent advance. / Now on

---

171 Ettore Spinola commanded the Genoan flagship.

both the left wing and the right the victors exploit their bloody advantage, massacring all in their path with inexorable fury. Some men throw themselves into the waves, their chests sliced open; others, fleeing brutal, keen-edged swords, surrender to the flames, finding the inferno more compassionate. / The astute Ochalí, seeing his compatriots annihilated by the Christians and the ruined armada consigned to swords, sea, and conflagration, set a westerly course in abject flight. Remnants of the devastated barbarians followed after him, barely escaping the fire and steel. / Realizing the traitorous renegade's base intent, Charles's son instantly set out after him, bursting through the agitated sea in furious pursuit. Bazán and Doria also headed for the fugitive, their squadron of galleys taking an oblique, downwind course as they tried to cut him off.[172] / The wretched scoundrel, seeing the route before him narrowing and fearing the open sea, turned his prow to the nearby coast and ran violently aground, and like grasshoppers seen jumping about in a confused mass, his men jumped frantically into the pounding surf, fleeing a danger they feared even more. / Some, using arms, shoulders, heads, and chests, cut through the tide's powerful pull. Others, considering neither the depth nor distance and not knowing how to swim, suddenly learned how. Here there was neither family tie nor bond of friendship, nor did a father wait for his own dear son, for fear, the enemy of duty, has no friends in times of peril. / Driven by terror itself they gained a foothold on the sandy beach and fled as fast as they could, escaping through the rocks and dense woods. The wretched barbarians were left utterly devastated and ravaged, the Austrian name prevailing over the Ottoman in

---

172 Álvaro de Bazán, the marquis of Santa Cruz, and Gian Andrea Doria; see 24.22 and 24.24, above.

courage. Now he boldly assaulted the Turk, now he fought off death itself, forcing it to delay a raging arrow aimed directly at him. / But while he resisted the Saracen onslaught with exceptional valor and tenacity, he could not hold back cruel fate, or more precisely, divine decree, and coming to his final moment the furiously speeding shaft struck him directly in the eye and he fell dead. / Seeing such a captain fall, the Venetians' pain and sorrow was enormous, but not for that was there any slackening in their bold resolve. Instead, provoked to greater rage and a passion for just retribution, they abused his killers so fiercely his death was well avenged. / At this point the battle was closely contested along the right wing, where the resourceful Juan Andrea was proving himself an experienced master. Ettore Spinola was also contending with vessels both left and right, demonstrating Ligurian agility and expertise amidst all the fury.[171] /

[24.87] The bitterly-fought battle had lasted more than two-and-a-half hours, without either side being able to gain an advantage or declare victory, when the intrepid don Juan, consumed with wrath and indignation at fate's suspension, began to prevail and his fortune to become entirely clear. / Now, with great uproar and vehemence the Mohammedans' fury was overwhelmed by valiant Christian swords: the Turkish royal galley was boarded from all sides, the barbarian standard torn down, and the Redeemer's Cross hoisted in solemn triumph and great glory to a loudly-sung victory. / A sudden, icy fear went running through the wretched Turks, benumbing their limbs and leaving them weak and discouraged, and yielding up swords and resolution they resigned themselves to their miserable fate, offering free entry to the enemy's violent advance. / Now on

---

171 Ettore Spinola commanded the Genoan flagship.

both the left wing and the right the victors exploit their bloody advantage, massacring all in their path with inexorable fury. Some men throw themselves into the waves, their chests sliced open; others, fleeing brutal, keen-edged swords, surrender to the flames, finding the inferno more compassionate. / The astute Ochalí, seeing his compatriots annihilated by the Christians and the ruined armada consigned to swords, sea, and conflagration, set a westerly course in abject flight. Remnants of the devastated barbarians followed after him, barely escaping the fire and steel. / Realizing the traitorous renegade's base intent, Charles's son instantly set out after him, bursting through the agitated sea in furious pursuit. Bazán and Doria also headed for the fugitive, their squadron of galleys taking an oblique, downwind course as they tried to cut him off.[172] / The wretched scoundrel, seeing the route before him narrowing and fearing the open sea, turned his prow to the nearby coast and ran violently aground, and like grasshoppers seen jumping about in a confused mass, his men jumped frantically into the pounding surf, fleeing a danger they feared even more. / Some, using arms, shoulders, heads, and chests, cut through the tide's powerful pull. Others, considering neither the depth nor distance and not knowing how to swim, suddenly learned how. Here there was neither family tie nor bond of friendship, nor did a father wait for his own dear son, for fear, the enemy of duty, has no friends in times of peril. / Driven by terror itself they gained a foothold on the sandy beach and fled as fast as they could, escaping through the rocks and dense woods. The wretched barbarians were left utterly devastated and ravaged, the Austrian name prevailing over the Ottoman in

---

172 Álvaro de Bazán, the marquis of Santa Cruz, and Gian Andrea Doria; see 24.22 and 24.24, above.

face-to-face, straightforward battle.[173] / I was joyfully watching this promised, felicitous event when Fitón struck the globe with his powerful, crooked staff, and the air within it began to grow dark and turbulent. The great uproar was instantly silenced and the sea grew tranquil and lay in profound calm, now obscured by mist and dark shadows. /

[24.97] The sorcerer then led me about the chamber in beguiling talk, and without neglecting a single item explained everything to me in great detail. Fearing a lengthy account may prove tedious to you, I leave all that aside, for while worthy of memory it neither matters to nor affects our history. / I only add that having said goodbye, greatly contented, to the sorcerer and to Guaticolo, even though it was late I made my way back to our camp, where they feared I was lost. Now, turning my pen to our affairs, from which this long digression has diverted me, I can report that we stayed in that location for two more weeks, with false alarms and vain hopes, / in the end learning nothing of the plans or intentions of our wary enemies. This left us baffled and suspicious, and thus we moved on, tracking them through perilous passes as we searched, penetrating ever farther into their

---

173 In fact, Ochalí managed to escape with some forty ships and make his way to Constantinople. While Lepanto was a terrible loss for the Ottomans, who suffered some thirty thousand casualties, three thousand men taken prisoner, and fifteen thousand galley-slaves freed—in addition to losing more than two hundred vessels either captured or sunk—in contrast to Christian losses of some ten galleys, eight thousand fatalities, and twenty-one thousand wounded (Fernand Braudel, *The Mediterranean and the Mediterranean World in the Age of Philip II*; vol. 2, p. 1102), within six months they had largely rebuilt their fleet and continued to be a significant force in the Mediterranean for a number of years.

territory with the goal of bringing the war to an end. / One evening as the sun was sinking we came to a densely populated valley crossed by a large river and surrounded by cultivated hills. This being a convenient location, the soldiers set up camp on a level hilltop near the valley's entrance, raising their tents and lean-tos by squadrons. / The site was scarcely organized when a bold, well-armed Araucan emerged from among the trees, looking for the tent of don García. Brought into his presence, the barbarian began to speak without any sign or show of politeness. . . But now it will be best to bring this long canto to an end. /

CANTO 25

The Spanish make camp in Millarapué, where Caupolicán sends a messenger to challenge them. A bloody battle follows in which Tucapel, Rengo, and many Spanish distinguish themselves.

W orthy of our attention and not to be taken lightly are an unknown people, who isolated from interaction with others and surrounded by innavigable waters, achieved what the world's most illustrious heroes alone attained through the practice of war. / Let writers cease to praise the inventors of military arts and celebrate no further those who first forged metal and unyielding steel, for here in Arauco the Indies' most remote inhabitants have attained such order and discipline in war that we might learn from them. / Who was it showed them how to organize battalions, present themselves in battle formation, raise fortifications and bulwarks, employ protective ditches, ramparts, trenches, and other novel defenses and strategies, along with everything else found in military practice, all ample evidence of their valor and experience? / Their silence and obedience in such matters is to be praised above all, for no secret of theirs was ever exposed through gifts or threats or violence, as shown by what I've recounted thus far. Neither through cunning nor spies could we gain any news of them for days, / and even the many residents we seized without warning from the neighboring villages resisted the rigors of torture with such constancy that we were left to worry how they might harm us if their cleverness grew and our deception continued. /

[25.6] I noted earlier that our men had just set up camp when a brash young Indian arrived asking where the captain was lodged. Led before him, and in the presence of many others, he freely began to speak in a haughty tone devoid of respect. / "Oh, Christian captain," he said, "if you're ambitious for well-earned honor, good fortune has brought you to an opportune moment! The great Caupolicán, wishing to confirm your vaunted valor and see if such courage and strength are indeed to be found in you, offers to fight you one on one. / Having heard that you're a noble and exceptional young man, and as the captain and leader of these soldiers someone practiced in the military art, he graciously offers you the advantage in choice of arms, to be freely made by you with no conditions whatever, wishing only to test your bravery and his fortune. / And since he understands you're interested in finding the Araucan army, he informs you that tomorrow at daybreak it will appear here on this plain, where with the full assurances of both sides, should you wish to fight man to man between them on these terms, he'll entrust all rights to arms. / Know that if you win he'll submit the land to your rule and you can do with him as you like, without regard for respect or clemency, while if you lose he'll leave you free in your authority, for he desires no prize or glory beyond that of victory. / Consider that as news of this spreads you'll gain fame and renown for valor, and that as long as the sun continues to shine your memory will persist among men, who'll say how courageously you entered the arena, worthy to meet the mighty Caupolicán eye to eye and hand to hand. / This is why I have come, and I ask that you promptly respond as you see fit, whether you wish to accept or decline the challenge and offered terms. The peril is manifestly great, but given your pride and courage I'm confident that in the end you'll satisfy both your own lofty honor and him who has sent me." / "I gladly accept the combat," don García replied, "and I give him my assurance that he can safely come to the specified location at the agreed upon time." The Indian, who was listening attentively, cheerfully told him, "I swear to you this bold response will make you eternally famous among men!" / With no more ado he then turned his back and set off, his arrogance revealing the low opinion in which he held us. Some judged him by his countenance to be a cunning spy, using this pretext to reconnoiter our troops and the camp's arrangement. /

[25.15] Night having fallen, we put our soldiers in battle order, and leaning upon our upright pikes stood counting the stars, wearied by drowsiness and the weight of our weapons. We never truly believed the Indian, who we decided had only come to gain information and see what might be possible. / The languorous night was already declining, stars circling westward as dawn appeared in the east to eclipse their light and bedew the flowers with freshness, restoring the colors that gloomy darkness had reduced to only one. / Suddenly there was a piercing yell, and the well-ordered barbarian army appeared on both sides of us divided into three distinct companies, each packed with soldiers and rapidly advancing in grand display as their even ranks encircled our narrow encampment. / Our cavalry was ready, awaiting the enemy, reins in hand. Before they could reach us our men took the initiative and launched themselves down a rugged slope toward the battalion on the left, charging it so fiercely a solid embankment or bulwark could not have withstood the violent impact. / Caupolicán, coming slightly ahead of the troops, immediately turned around and had the men set their pikes. Steadied with arms and feet, these received the full fury of our ferocious assault on their keen, hard points, causing great injury among the first to arrive. / Some of the attackers, having no wings, were surprised to leave their saddles in airy flight; others, their soles turned skyward, had their ribs imprinted in the dirt, and even those who proved more stalwart, knees clasped tightly enough that they did not test the ground, were left ill-treated by the encounter. / Our soldiers were not hesitant with their own blows, all unerringly aimed. Some of the enemy they pierced from side to side, some they knocked down with their horses. Everyone was instantly mixed together, coming so close and so quickly to swords that the awful uproar sounded like Vulcan's terrifying forge. /

[25.22] The valiant general, Caupolicán, his pike now broken, grips his club, wounding, crushing, and killing both to left and right. Finding himself next to Berzocano, he clenches his teeth and fists and lands such a blow atop him it crushes his skull inside his helmet. / After this he knocks down another and kills a third, who, to his misfortune, was nearby, and forcing his way forward, smashes, maims, and crushes, smoothing out the rough way ahead. Seizing hold of Tambo the *yanacona,* like a falcon does a chicken or dove, he tears him apart, choking him with his bare hands without anyone able to help. / Bernal and Leucotón, wanting to join the dispute, attack each other in a rage, bringing down their arms with equal, furious force, their proud heads both bowing in spite of themselves, as though from good manners, as they simultaneously sink to their knees with a clattering of teeth and bones. / Each quickly gets to his feet, and they begin a brutal fight. Now they aim at the legs, now the head; now helmets are battered, now shields. They persisted like this for some time but could not continue, for a great throng of attacking soldiers forced them apart against their wills. / Miguel and Pedro de Avendaño, Rodrigo de Quiroga, Aguirre, Aranda, Cortés, and Juan Jufré, fighting amidst great peril, defended Spanish honor. Making their presence felt as well while doing great damage were Reynoso, Peña, Córdova, Miranda, Monguía, Lasarte, Castañeda, Ulloa, Martín Ruiz, and Juan López de Gamboa. / Luis de Toledo, together with Carranza, Aguayo, Zúñiga, and Castillo, resisted the Indians' onslaught alongside Diego Cano, Pérez, and Ronquillo. Juan Alvarado and his cousin Hernando, Pedro de Olmos, Paredes, and Carrillo bravely brought down many opponents at the cost of their own blood. / The center battalion, seeing the fierce fight on the right, hastened to help in a horrifying fury. Organized in *tercios,* our soldiers advanced at full speed to intercept them, and with the terrifying crash of the brutal collision the earth contracted toward its core. / There were many noteworthy falls and powerful blows and thrusts from bludgeons and pikes. Lances, darts, and clubs flew heavenward in countless pieces as men resorted to their swords, and some, even more incensed, dealt deadly, piercing wounds with poniards and daggers. /

[25.30] Ferocious Tucapel came face to face with a fine soldier and killed him. Little satisfied by such a masterful blow, he seized the man's keen-edged rapier and used it to drill into Guillermo's chest, then with a violent backhand sent two heads still wearing their helmets flying far from their trunks. / With one stroke he easily took Torbo's life and dealt Juan Yanaruna such a wound that his armored head, split open at the brow, fell in halves upon his shoulders. Aiming a blow at brave Picol, he ripped out his life with his bowels, even though by this point, without realizing it, he had already been wounded by more than ten swords. / Hearing the commotion surrounding such slaughter, others attacked, surrounding him like a wild beast and harassing him in a confused throng, but with great scorn he spun his mighty arm about, punishing and reproving them for their eagerness and daring. / His frenzied wrath burned ever brighter as the perilous work increased. Wherever the danger was greatest and the outcome least certain was where he strove for glory, his great heart and invincible spirit making that which was possible unworthy and that which was not all too easy. /

[25.34] The third and largest battalion, following their plan, now ascended the long slope in a rapid but orderly march. Once they saw the full extent of our troops on the open summit, however, they prudently stopped for a moment to take stock of the situation and our soldiers. / Young Galbarino came at their head and urged them on, his amputated arms in plain sight, their wounds still bloody. Moving swiftly from one side of their ranks to the other, he pictured their common peril, inflaming their hearts to fury with compelling words and gestures. / "Courageous soldiers," he cried, "so worthy of the name! You in whose hands Fortune and the favorable fates have today placed the fame and very existence of Arauco! Be confident of victory, for this vain pomp and tumult you see are all that's left, the dregs of those you've beaten so many times before! / Once this final battle you've yearned for so fervently is over, there'll be nothing left in our way, not one upright lance or opposing sword! Consider the infamous death or wretched life awaiting the defeated, as well as the brutal torture promised those who survive! / If you're beaten in this battle, law will perish and liberty be lost, and subjected to cruel servitude you'll grow inept in the ways of war. Yoked alongside brute beasts, you'll be forced to plow and cultivate the land forever, fulfilling the most servile duties and base, womanly chores. / Always remember, warriors, that dishonor lasts forever, while victory here assures your accomplishments for all eternity! Think of the glory that Fortune has prepared for you, and of the splendid prize and honor you'll attain with so little effort! / He who proves himself a brave soldier holds his future in his hands, for today Fortune requites us with everything we've longed for! Remember as well that those who lose will be condemned as rebels and traitors, for the defeated are never right or undeserving of punishment when the enemy is their judge!" / The valiant barbarian awoke their rage and hope to such an extent that the battalion could scarcely endure further delay, and hearing the final signal, with great resolution they lowered their pikes in close formation and let themselves be swept away by their fury. /

[25.42] Our men immediately spring forward as one to meet them on the open, rocky ground, which stretched more than a bowshot in length, and here the enraged troops attack each other with inhuman fury and determination, each man's ardor driving him forward as bodies fall in mounds. / Pikes do not remain intact for long but soon are flying through the air in splinters; long battle lines and ranks of soldiers break apart with the impact. Death now assumes a thousand faces, for many perish without being wounded, choking on dust and the smoke of firearms, while others are crushed in the terrible collision. / A horrific battle develops with feverish intensity and frenzied hatred, everyone exerting themselves with the same resolve and utmost effort and skill. A deafening roar rises up to the heavens, resounding through the countryside, and a deluge of dead bodies soon covers every open space. / Wrath increases and the never-ending battering grows ever fiercer. Neither fine mail nor tempered steel can block the entry and transit of furious death, which with unstoppable rage transforms everything into its own image, the ferocious, fatal carnage spawning a vast lake of thick, black blood. /

[25.46] Arrogant Rengo was steadily driving forward the fighting on the left. Goaded by the festering insult he had received from Andrea in Mataquito, he now ranged across the entire field, circling here and there and from side to side, his arm hoisted to strike as he raised a hoarse cry, vainly calling out the name of his enemy.[174] / Andrea, equally eager to settle the dispute, was looking for Rengo as well. But that which the one and the other both sought was frustrated by their fortunes, for the Italian youth was some distance away and fighting with another contingent, achieving great exploits with his singular strength, which despite their legitimacy were pitiful to see. / Killing Trulo

---

174 Rengo was left for dead by Andrea in a previous battle (15.5-30).

with one blow, he aimed his cruel blade at Pinol, transfixing him, then sent Teguán tumbling a good distance across the ground missing an arm. He took off Changle's head with a single swing and cut Pon in half through the waist. Norpo he cleaved straight down through the chest; Brancolo he left standing on one leg like a crane. / Now Orompello, waging murderous war as he headed this direction, came upon the tremendous uproar and shouting to find a large area covered by the dead. Recognizing the valiant Genoan, he attacked him like a ravenous tiger, balanced on the tips of his feet with his club held high and his face burning with rage. / The cudgel caught Andrea on the lofty crest of his helmet, which it utterly crushed, leaving it sunk in the quilted cotton padding. Stunned, the Italian turned pale and vomited blood, and falling to his hands on the ground saw sparks and flashes. / The other bold youth immediately struck again with even more fury and less control, and had the blow not been glancing, the fierce game between them would have ended once for all. The Genoan, stupefied and blinded, struggled backwards a little, but then recovering, got to his feet with unexpected speed and raised his broad sword in both hands. / With singular fury and exceptional force he then brought it down on Orompello in such a way that had the Indian's ironclad club not blocked it he would have divided him in two from top to bottom. The blade sliced through the club as though it were a cane or tender reed, and if the sword edge had not twisted, the wound would have penetrated so deeply it would have deprived him of his life. / The Araucan now found himself without a club, but not for that did he trim the sails of his rage. Instead with great agility he snatched a piece of shield from the ground, and like one who cares nothing about injury, and with nothing more than the stump of his shortened cudgel, he confidently assailed his enemy, / striking him on the head and leaping lightly to the side with such agility the Italian was robbed of his enemy's body, slashing at nothing but empty air. Orompello intended to repeat the move, but only in vain, for the Genoan was so prompt in advancing as he swerved that his opponent could do nothing but cover himself with the broken shield. / The furious sword sent a large piece of this to the ground and landed forcefully on his helmet, which was unable to protect his head, but allowed the blade to penetrate to his skull. The Araucan was stunned for a moment, but coming back to himself and seeing his opponent so close, he immediately grasped him in his powerful arms. / The headstrong Genoan, who thought himself capable of dismembering savage Mars, gripped him roughly in turn but was deceived, for in this art no one surpassed agile Orompello. They began to circle about from side to side, attacking each other's feet and intertwining their knees and legs with cunning feints. /

[25.57] Meanwhile, don García de Mendoza was not resting, but being brave and diligent at times fought fiercely and at times went among the men encouraging them. Nor was Juan Remón idle, fulfilling his duties as a soldier and prudent captain with the same discipline and energy wherever he went. / Santillán and Pedro de Navarra, Ávalos, Viezma, and Cáceres, Bastida, and Galdámez, Francisco Ponce and Ibarra, all dealt out death while skillfully defending themselves. Vega the steward and Segarra the bursar were reckoning their own accounts, followed by Velázquez and Cabrera, Verdugo, Ruiz, Riberos, and Ribera. / Elsewhere, given the number of enemy rushing in, it would have gone badly if don Felipe, don Simon, and Prado, don Francisco Arias, Pardo, and Alegría, Barrios, Diego de Lira, Coronado, and Juan de

Pineda, had not driven back their adversaries, fighting together with brave determination. / Adding to the carnage were Florencio Esquivel and Altamirano, Villarroel, Dorán, and Vergara, Lago and Godoy, Gonzalo Hernández and Andicano. If I fail to mention anyone, the fault is not of intention but of my hand, which cannot describe what so many were doing as they fought there all at once. /

[25.61] At this point, near midday, a great commotion arose among other troops, where the wildly infuriated Rengo, carried away by his strength and audacity, had gotten himself so embroiled in the fighting that he could not get back to his companions, but surrounded by common soldiers was being sorely wounded and harassed. / The blows he was delivering on one side and the other were forcing them to keep their distance in a circle, many of them chastened by the mistakes of their neighbors, but still the agile throng was driving him this way and that, afflicting him on all sides with shots, cudgels, and spears thrown from a distance, as at a wild beast. / Here he left one crippled, there another one dead, no defense or armor offering them any protection at all. Those hit squarely were completely crushed and deformed by his blows, the most feeble and least effective of which broke arms, legs, and joints, so that all one could see were shattered armor and battered helmets still atop crushed heads. / Although his fighting displayed the invincible strength and courage I'm describing, they were still pressing him so tightly that escape was impossible, and however fiercely he resisted, when all is said and done he was made of flesh and could feel, and the fury of the incessant assault was draining his strength and spirit. / He already had one knee on the ground and even so could hardly sustain himself, bands of tenacious fighters fatiguing him and not letting him catch his breath, when Tucapel arrived from another part of the high hillside, clearing the usual broad swath with his mighty truncheon wherever he went. / Like an infuriated, hamstrung bull, bellowing with its tongue out and surrounded by a mob of men, each trying to take a stab at it, when suddenly from the other side of the ring another of Jarama's illustrious offspring appears with its sturdy neck and lofty brow to break up and scatter the crowd,[175] / just so the famous Rengo was half kneeling as he fought in the midst of the relentless throng closing in on him little by little, when bloodthirsty Tucapel, hearing the shouts and seeing him treated like that, without thinking twice broke through the horde to help him. / The width of the passage they offered him was so narrow he left four or six of them stretched out on the ground. The others circling weary Rengo now broke apart, furiously directing their weapons and shouts at Tucapel, but he acquitted himself so well they were forced to keep a good distance away. / Arriving at Rengo's side, he told him, "Even though we are enemies, Rengo, have courage, have courage! Stay strong today, for with the incomparable Tucapel beside you your fortune cannot be bad! Favorable heaven and the friendly fates have reserved a better death for you, one entrusted to my arm, if, when the time comes, you accept my challenge!"[176] / "Were it not considered ungrateful at such a moment, I would instantly acquit myself both of you and my duty, for I'm not as weary as you think!" Rengo replied, and with this he got to his feet more quickly than if he had been resting in bed for ten hours

---

175 Bulls raised along the banks of the Jarama river, east of Madrid, were known for their ferocity.
176 Tucapel is referring to their previous confrontation, at Canto 16.61.

and went on the attack, his muscled body unwavering and his cudgel held high. / "It would be base and condemned among men were I to attack you now, given your weakness and the advantageous circumstances of my strength," Tucapel responded. "Regain your vigor and recover your fortitude, for the time will come when this iron-plated club will deliver the punishment and death you deserve, just as it has clearly granted you your life here today!" / The two Araucan rivals spoke no more, but acting as friends and companions made their way forward as if they were brothers, guarding and defending each other, and with brave, ready hands soon opened a way through our troops and rejoined their companions. /

[25.73] At this point the battle was raging bitterly and bloodily on all sides, its terrible savagery such that no arm was idle nor any man without a wound. The ground was littered with broken mail, the brutal clamor resounding as on the impetuous winds of distant, cavernous Scythia. / The uproar of the two armies and the furious pace of the fighting were like a black, wind-swept cloud, which lashed by Zephyr or Vulturnus unlooses a sudden hail, leaving branches without their leaves and walls, roofs, and housetops battered by its relentless, terrifying blasts.[177] / Just so and with even greater fury the soldiers deployed their murderous weapons, and terrible, deep wounds drained bodies of their blood. The enormous tumult and fearsome cries echoed off the nearby mountains, and hearing the appalling sound the startled sea retracted its swollen waves. / But now on the left-hand side where the battle had first begun and where Caupolicán was valiantly resisting the fury of cruel fate, the Christian troops, overwhelmed by their enemies' tenacity, began to lose ground and

---

177 Vulturnus is the east or southeast wind.

little by little to retreat toward the wooded slope of the mountain. / Here the press of barbarians was so great and their momentum so overwhelming that the Araucans loudly began to sing their victory. Mocking Fortune gave an abrupt turn to her wheel against the party she had been favoring, however, confounding the apparent outcome, / for our final squadron, on whom our last hope of relief depended, now attacked the adversary with such savagery and great slaughter that neither the bravery of Ongolmo nor the might of formidable Lincoya could withstand it. I also cannot recount so much at one time, but must defer what remains to the following canto. /

CANTO 26

This canto describes the end of the battle and Araucan retreat, together with the obstinacy and death of Galbarino. Described here as well are the garden and residence of Fitón.

No one can call themselves lucky before reaching life's unknown end, nor is anyone on stormy seas safe until anchored within a harbor. One good following another is unlikely, whereas evil upon evil is always certain, for good times never last, nor do wretched ones ever cease. / We have an example of this here at hand, for history shows us quite clearly how briefly the Araucans' new joy and illusory glory were to last. Having routed the Christians and sung their triumph, they were beaten back by contrary fates and the vanquished ended up the victors. /

[26.3] I've already described how our last squadron, which I belonged to and whose actions I witnessed, kept gaining ground against the retreating enemy, for even though the mighty Lincoya was at their head and defying adverse fortune, they were ultimately unable to resist the violent fury of our soldiers. / Once the barbarous horde's audacity was broken and vile fear prevailed, they turned their broad backs and escaped through a rugged, overgrown ravine between two hills, fleeing the enraged face death had so clearly shown them. / Not interested in coming to terms, our men quickly followed up on their victory, probing the hidden depths of the tangled undergrowth and dense woods, and thus the terrible carnage continued, the gruesome din of destruction resounding from blows and thrusts struck blindly amidst thickets and impenetrable groves. / Never were wild beasts so fiercely chased by a great ring of hunters burning with impatience, who slowly close in on their prey until all escape is cut off and they can hurl their darts and javelins, / as when our soldiers, Christians until then, but now exceeding just limits, began to tarnish our great victory with their cruel weapons and inhuman acts, for neither surrendering and holding up their hands nor vowing obedience and service were enough to restrain the enraged swords of those heartless men. / Inured to war's destruction, my mind and pen still recoil before the enormous slaughter that day among the land's defenders, the blood that coursed through the mountain crevasses, and the shouts, laments, and moans of the wretched, defeated barbarians. / The Araucans fighting on the left, seeing their largest battalion destroyed, lost all courage and abandoned the ground and honor they had won. Sounding the horn to retreat, they began to descend the slope in a quick although orderly march, their shining banners held high. /

[26.10] It wouldn't be right to pass in silence over the boundless bravery of the indomitable Rengo, who although his men had been routed and driven away in wretched flight, was holding the ground they had won all by himself and, as impatient and arrogant as ever, still wielded his ironclad club with even greater fury as he ignored the threat to his life. / For a long time he stayed there fighting alone, valiant and invincible. But seeing his fruitless efforts and none of his companions, with a grave and measured pace he took a trail to the right, turning around from time to time until he entered an overgrown wood / where some of the frightened men had hidden. At Rengo's arrival they instantly recovered their spirits, and with new courage and a show of confidence formed into a squadron, setting their faces and sturdy chests against the current of inflexible fate. / I was also in the area, following some noises I had heard, when new shouts and commotion arose from a nearby grove. Hastening toward the sound, I saw some Spaniards I knew halted at its entrance, / with Juan Remón at their side. "Forward, gentlemen! This is nothing!" he shouted, but they were weighing the danger and hesitating at the hazard. Catching sight of me as I approached the wary men, Juan Remón decided to oblige me publicly. / "Don Alonso!" he said; "For anyone striving to win fame and advancement, now is the time and here is the place to distinguish himself! Don't let this thicket where the Indians are trying to hide obstruct good fortune, for he who leads us forward will have the glory of our victory!" / Hearing myself acknowledged by name, with everyone turning to look at me, honor and shame prevented my avoiding the challenge, and I resolved to try my luck, forcing my way into the densest, most fearsome part of the bramble. Arias Pardo, Maldonado, Manrique, Simòn, and

Coronado then followed, / all prepared to die as they attacked the stubborn Indians, awaiting our weapons in a tightly-packed circle. By this time many other Spaniards had arrived at the tumult from all sides, their ardent fury inciting a bloody and perilous fight. / The carnage began anew, and victory was once more uncertain, with the least courageous attacking the most daunting obstacles. Who could describe the furious motion of men's arms, the many wounds, and who it was took whose life? / Some cleaved their opponents in half, some bore through angry chests from front to back; others sliced through thighs and torsos, and others collapsed, cut to pieces limb by limb. Cruel blows echoed through the grove, and both sides grew so desperate that some among them, impatient with their weapons, resorted to fists and teeth. / Death was driving that cruel, relentless fight, and assisting the winners it soon brought the bitter battle to an end. The Araucans inside that narrow space were overwhelmed, preferring to surrender their lives to the sword than submit to the hated Spanish. / The indomitable barbarians were left in mounds upon the ground, while the rest, as I said, made an orderly retreat. Our soldiers collected what spoils they found and taking a large number of prisoners returned to camp. /

[26.22] Twelve of the most imposing and valiant prisoners, whose dress and insignia revealed them to be eminent leaders, were chosen to be hung from the trees in an exemplary punishment meant to terrify their countrymen. / Arriving as the selection was being made and deploring its cruelty, I attempted to save one of them, who I pointed out had once approached our troops. But at that moment he raised his arms, hidden until then behind his breastplate, and displayed to full view the absence of hands on his severed and still unhealed stumps. / I'm speaking

Canto 26

of Galbarino, whom I told you about in a previous canto, where it was decided that as an example his hands be cut off.[178] Giving vent to his stifled hatred with his usual audacity and with no fear of death, he looked around at us and then spoke as follows: / "Detested and perfidious people, unworthy of today's victory! Glut your insatiable throats on my abhorrent blood, for even though cruel, inconstant fate overthrow the Araucan monarchy and we be killed, we can't be defeated nor can our free spirits ever be suppressed! / Don't think we flee from death, for in death now rests our hope, and if we prolong a life we loathe it's only to magnify our revenge! We may not achieve a just resolution, but we're confident that our swords, turned against ourselves, will deprive you of the glory of granting us our lives. / Come then! What are you waiting for and what delays your granting me my just reward and compensation? Death, not life, is what befits me most, for with my death I satisfy my duty! If this end I've sought so long holds any bitterness or pain, it's in not seeing you first torn to pieces with these teeth and amputated arms!" / Thus the brave barbarian loudly solicited death, weary now of an ill-starred life that had lasted too long against his will. Stubborn in his heathen intent, he continued to insult us, hoping to earn an honorable end by having a sword bring his wretched life to a close. / Standing beside him and moved by his bravery and unwavering resolve, I argued with some of the men, trying to save the life of one who now abhorred it. In the end the officials insisted it was for everyone's good and forced me to step aside, and he was taken with the caciques to be executed. /

[26.30] At the foot of a mountain near the camp, on a slope crossed by a wide road leading to the valley of Lincoya,

---

178 See 22.45 ff.

the indignity and unjust punishment was inflicted upon them with great solemnity and pomp, and a debt many considered undue was paid for with their lives. / In the absence of an executioner, whose duty it would have been but none of whom were present that day, an unheard-of method of killing was used. Each Indian in the group was given the necessary length of rope and told to choose whatever tree he liked from which to hang himself. / Experienced fighters, hearing the signal for attack, do not scale a rampart as quickly with their ladders and pikes as those caciques, who scrambling up the largest trees and quickly reaching their tops, hung themselves from the highest branches. / One of them, repenting his prompt resolution and resigned to obedience, turned back and asked for permission to speak. This being granted, with a troubled expression and faltering voice he spoke contritely as follows, moving Christian hearts as he did: / "Valiant nation and invincible people, embodying the utmost virtue, know that I am a cacique and descended from this land's most ancient stock. I have no father, brothers, or relatives left, all of them already killed in the war, and since our lineage ends with me, I beg you to treat me with clemency." / He would have continued had Galbarino, who was watching in outraged indignation, not suddenly come forward, interrupting his servile speech and saying, "Pusillanimous wretch, defiler of illustrious progeny! How can the shameful fear of a quick death drive you to such degradation? / Tell me, infamous traitor and man of shifting loyalties, do you think it a boon and better luck to live in a state of misery than to die as a strong man should? Follow your destiny, adverse but tolerable, for death is the end of hardship, and it's craven to let such disgraceful pleading take this remedy from your hands!" / His speech had scarcely concluded when the penitent cacique, the knotted rope around his neck, was hanging from a lofty limb. The audacious and obstinate barbarian, not even defeated by death itself, soon followed him, those mighty oaks bearing early fruit that year from this ordeal. /

[26.38] Victory won, as I have described, and the routed enemy having retreated, we departed our sad encampment, strewn with barbarian bodies, and proceeded without further mishap to that unhappy location where Valdivia had built the fort and afterwards been so infamously killed.[179] / We quickly raised a wall encircling the site, where the baggage, servants, and remaining men would be better protected, and from which we could confront the unruly area with greater safety, always doing our best to elicit obedience without bloodshed. / One morning at daybreak we set out to scout an area where we had confirmed reports of barbarian fighters. Falling some way behind my companions, I was near a dense wood, high on a mountainside, when I heard an aged voice nearby, saying, "Where are you going? There's no exit that way." / Turning my gaze and reins toward the place from which the strange voice had come, I saw the sorcerer Fitón bent over his ironclad cane and leaning against an enormous, worm-eaten oak. On recognizing him I quickly leapt down from my horse and cheerfully and courteously greeted him. / "No doubt I could take legitimate revenge on you and the men proceeding here," he told me, "for you've made a great slaughter among our warriors. But even were there greater justification, it wouldn't be right after you confided in me as you did, nor have I any desire to harm you, but only want to assist you in any legitimate way. / It's in the heavenly order of things that our untamed people suffer their punishment, and that before their arrogance can be turned against God it be

---

179 I.e., the Tucapel fort, as recounted in Canto 3.

humbled by the enemy. While your own good fortune is now ascendant, it won't last for long, for I assure you that, as with all others, cruel fate has readied your fall. / If Fortune now opens a path to prosperity, giving you what you want, in the end you'll derive great trouble and little profit from your enterprise here. It's not up to me to say more, so I'll return to my home, which also has an entrance on this side of the mountain, although it's well hidden from everyone." / Astonished to see him and even more to hear his sinister prophecy, I tied my horse to a cedar and offered to keep him company for a while. After much entreaty he acquiesced, and with the debilitated old man as a guide we made our way through the thickets and tangled undergrowth until we came to the base of a slope. / Here, in a secret, hidden spot with no cleft or opening, he gently tapped the hard rock with his powerful staff, and with a horrifying noise a narrow passage and dark cavity instantly opened. I followed him through, my hair on end, feeling my way along the rocky walls / until we emerged into a beautiful green meadow, refreshing to both eyes and spirit, in which there was a great square enclosure. Its walls, of heretofore unseen beauty, were checkered in jasper and porphyry, with amethysts at each corner, and its iron-plated cedar doors were carved with a thousand delightful scenes. / Just as the sorcerer arrived they opened, and we entered a spacious garden that one could say conjoined all nature and art. No lovely leaf, whether round or square, differed at all from any other; in the middle was a limpid pool where murmuring fountains sent forth their waters. / Even the most luxuriant spring does not produce as many flowers in such varied colors as appeared in that delightful locale, where the freshest, most dulcet aromas and birds with their melodious accompaniment filled my senses with an intoxicating lightheartedness. / For a great while I was so captivated I would have forgotten where I was going and why, had not ancient Fitón called me, motioning to me with his head. Taking my hand he led me into a vaulted room of shining alabaster, which I recognized as the one with the miraculous globe where I had been before. / I would have liked to see the sphere, but dared not approach it without the wizard's permission. Penetrating my thoughts, however, and wanting to gratify me, he clasped my hand, drew me near it, and began to point out things to me, showing me the world as if in its real and actual state. / To describe in an orderly way all that I saw within that great lucid orb, I must now collect my memories and begin a new canto. I beg you to forgive me, my Lord, if I leave the account at this point to revive my weary voice, for I cannot recount so much all at once. /

CANTO 27

This canto describes the many cities, provinces, and natural features within Fitón's sphere, famous either for their beauty or for events associated with them. It recounts as well how the Spanish raised a fort in the Tucapel valley and how Don Alonso de Ercilla came upon the beautiful Glaura.

Brevity is justly praised by all, for speech is more enjoyable the more concise and less affected it is. Thoroughness may be useful, but it also irritates and tires us, just as the most delectable food in excess leaves us cloyed. / Such is the danger in which I find myself repenting the long road ahead, for how can I take such a lengthy detour yet still satisfy listeners and good taste?

CANTO 27

While my aim is to please, one cannot travel far in a single step nor fit a great subject in a tiny vessel, / and if it appears to some, my Lord, that I linger along the way, let them keep in mind the novelty of my journey with its many stages. Being as brief as I can, I return to my account, where I told you how the ancient Indian wizard was pointing at the crystal globe. /

[27.4] The enormity of the shining sphere was such that twenty men could not have encircled it, while everything it held was clearly visible in its actual form: fields and cities, the traffic and commotion of people, birds, animals, and lizards, even the tiniest insects. / "As there's no one to disturb or interrupt us," the sorcerer said, "you'll now see the vast plan of the universe here without the least part of it remaining hidden, all there is from north to south and from east to west, as well as whatever the sea embraces and the air surrounds: rivers, mountains, and lakes, lands and seas, places made famous by nature and by wars. / Behold Chalcedon there at the opening to Asia, next to the Bosporus and across from Thrace; see Lydia, Caria, Lycia, and Lycaonia, Pamphylia and Bithynia, Galatia and Paphlagonia, next to the Pontus Euxinus; the plains of Cappadocia and Pharnacea; the famous Euphrates, swift and deep, entering the Persian Gulf.[180] / See Syria and the unworthy promised land, forsaken by God, and fortunate Nazareth in Palestine where

---

[180] The canto cites a number of ancient locations in and around present-day Turkey: Chalcedon was a city on the eastern side of the Bosporus; Thrace was the region directly across the Bosporus to the west; Lydia, Caria, and Lycia were regions running from north to south along the western coast; Lycaonia, Pamphylia, Bithynia, and Galatia were neighboring regions to the east of these; Paphlagonia was a region to the north, on the coast of the Black Sea, or *Pontus Euxinus*; Cappadocia is

THE ARAUCANA

Gabriel made his embassy to Mary. Behold the sacred ruins and relics of the city razed by Titus, where the Author of all life was mocked and led to a shameful death.[181] / Consider the vast Mediterranean, which separates Europe from Africa, and the Red Sea below it to one side, where Moses parted the waters with his staff. Note the Hormuz and Persian Gulfs, and although the land is somewhat obscured in places, you can see in that open area there the two Arabias, Felix and Desert.[182] / Look at Persia and at Carmania, which borders it on the west along with Susiana, where steel of such fine temper is forged. See Drangiana and Gedrosia, which extend to the Indian Ocean and the bazaars of the East, and farther in that direction sweltering Arachosia.[183] / Behold all the land of India, stretching toward the east on both sides of the Ganges. There you see Cathay and its main city, Canta, built alongside the Indian Ocean, China and the Moluccas and all that sea extending eastward, and there by itself famous Ceylon, which in antiquity was the end and farthest point of the Orient.[184] /

---

  a region just to the southeast of this; Pharnacea was a city further east on the shore of the Black Sea.
181 Jerusalem was razed by the Roman emperor Titus in 70 C.E.
182 Cf. Exodus 14.21 ff., Quran 26.61 ff.; the Straits of Hormuz; *Arabia Felix* refers to the southern part of the Arabian peninsula (present-day Yemen and Oman); *Arabia Deserta* to its interior (present-day Saudi Arabia).
183 The octave refers to regions of ancient Persia (present-day Iran): Carmania and Susiana lay to the southwest, near the Persian Gulf; Drangiana was an inland region further east, Gedrosia lay to its south, on the Indian Ocean, and Arachosia was inland and northeast of these.
184 In antiquity Cathay denoted an extensive area including present-day Mongolia and parts of China; Canta may or may not indicate Canton; Ceylon denotes present-day Sri Lanka.

Behold Hyrcania, Tartary, and Albania, which extends to Trebizond, and the other small neighboring realms, tributaries and allies of Persia: the Iberians known as Georgians and the poor, scattered Circassians, whose narrow, crescent-shaped country embraces the Black Sea coast.[185] / Observe the deep, turbulent Kura encircling Iberia and Albania, and the lofty Caucasus mountains, whose peaks lord over such an immense area. Look there at the realm of Colchis, so famous for the island named by Medea, where weary Jason came in search of the golden fleece.[186] / Behold mighty, memorable Armenia, noteworthy for the city of Tauris, and southward the venerable and religious Sultania, insolently overrun by the terrible Tartar fury of mighty Tamerlane, who as he passed razed everything to the ground like heaven's wrath or a sudden thunderbolt.[187] / Gaze upon the Tigris and Euphrates, marking the limits of

---

185 Hyrcania and Albania were ancient regions bordering the Caspian Sea, the former to the south, the latter to the west; Tartary denotes a vast area extending eastward from the Caspian; Trebizond, or Trapesus in antiquity, was both a city and region southeast of the Black Sea; Iberia refers to an area between the Black Sea and the Caspian in present-day Georgia; Circassia denotes a region of the Caucasus bordering the Black Sea on the northeast.

186 The Kura river originates in present-day Georgia and runs through Azerbaijan to the Caspian; for Iberia and Albania see the previous note; Colchis refers to a region on the eastern side of the Black Sea, home to the sorcerer Medea, where Jason and the Argonauts went in search of the golden fleece (the story is told by Apollonius Rhodes in the *Argonautica*).

187 Tauris probably refers to present-day Tabriz in northern Iran; Sultania is present-day Soltanieh, midway between Tehran and Tabriz; Tamerlane, or Timur, was a medieval ruler who conquered much of Asia, the northern and central region of which was home to the Tartars or Tatars.

Mesopotamia as they run beside each other to the Persian Gulf, leaving Egypt and Syria to one side. See Parthia and Media, arching their curving coasts to embrace the southern Caspian Sea, also called the Hyrcanian Sea, with its oval extending southeast.[188] / Look at Assyria and its celebrated city where the confusion of tongues arose and whose marvelous walls were built by Semiramis, mother to Ninyas. This was where swift, sudden death assailed Alexander, severing the thread of his life and fate in the middle of such an auspicious career.[189] /

[27.16] To the south observe Africa and the extensive realms of Prester John, among the most illustrious and refined of these Sceva with its resplendent buildings. At 22° beneath the antarctic pole, it has three harvests spread across the year and three times its crops are gathered and renewed.[190] / Look at Gojjam with its lofty mountains, their grandeur exceeding all others and their peaks eternally white with snow, beneath them a rugged wilderness of dense undergrowth creating an enormous refuge for bears, boars, lions, and tigers, panthers, griffins, and dragons.[191] / From these craggy slopes, now known as the Mountains of the Moon, the

---

188 Parthia and Media were Persian regions abutting the southern edge of the Caspian Sea, also known in antiquity as the *Hyrcanum Mare*.

189 The celebrated city of Assyria was Babylon; its legendary queen, Semiramis, credited with restoring the city's ancient walls, ruled after the death of her husband, Ninus; Alexander the Great died in Babylon at age 32.

190 Prester John was a legendary Christian patriarch thought to rule over what was often identified as Ethiopia; according to ancient geographers Sceva or Sabae was on the African coast of the Red Sea near the 22nd parallel.

191 Gojjam was an ancient province in northwestern Ethiopia; the griffin is a legendary animal with body of a lion and the head and wings of an eagle.

headwaters of the famous Nile arise, as well as other rivers having neither name nor fame, their waters meandering and separating, then coming together in a lake so vast its coves and inlets lap the edges of three provinces:[192] / Gojjam and Begmender to the east and Dembiya to the west. Along its shores are islands inhabited by many tribes, and its entire great circumference is populated. From here the gentle Nile gradually increases in size and strength to divide Gojjam and Amhara, their banks offering little resistance to its growing breadth[193]/ until, constrained by rocky narrows, it emerges with a furious roar in great waterfalls. Wider thereafter, it arrives slowly and solemnly at the shores of Meroe, an enormous island containing three eminent kingdoms, each with its own laws and customs.[194] / Now behold Cairo with its three cities and royal palace of Tulbiya, as well as all the towers, gardens, and estates within its immense area. Gaze upon the vanities of the ancient pagans with their pyramids, proof of wealth, but even more of the folly that led to their construction.[195] / Observe the Libyan desert's sandy wastes, parched and burning, and Garamantes with its sweltering towns, home of the brutish

---

192 The Mountains of the Moon are a legendary range in East Africa near the headwaters of the Nile, the source of which is identified here as Lake Tana, in present-day Ethiopia.

193 Begmender and Dembiya are additional historical regions of ancient Ethiopia.

194 Meroe was an ancient kingdom on the Nile, often described as an island, possibly due to its peninsula-like location between the Nile and Atbara rivers, in present-day Sudan; Meroe's three kingdoms may refer to Halfa, Wadi, and Chendy.

195 Cairo's three cities may refer to the Babylon fort, an ancient structure near Fustat or Old Cairo, and the new or Grand Cairo which was built to Fustat's north; Tulbiya was the wife of Al-Nasir Muhammad, a medieval sultan of Cairo.

black race. Look at the warlike Troglodytes and others bathed by the waters of the Gambia: the Mandinka, Manikongos, and horrid Zapes, the Biafrans, Wolofs, and Guineans.[196] / There you see the great stretch of Africa's coast, its noteworthy places and seaports from the mouth of the Nile to the straits where the two seas meet: Apollonia, the Syrtes, and straight ahead, Tripoli and Tunis; search nearby and you can still see vestiges of the famous city of Carthage.[197] /

[27.24] Behold fertile and abundant Sicily, Sardinia with Corsica across from it, and along the coast of Italy all that delightful land running westward. See illustrious and famous Naples, and Rome, which saw itself lord of the world for so long, only to have all nations later tread it underfoot. / Look at Siena and Florence in Tuscany, and leaving this southern coast, at Bologna, Ferrara, and the eminent island city and Signoria; at Padua, Mantua, Cremona, and Piacenza; at Milan; and at the grounds and park of Pavia, where Francis, king of France, was taken prisoner by Charles in a decisive defeat.[198] / There you see Alexandria, and entering Liguria, magnificent Genoa and Savona; crossing the Piedmont and Savoy you find Lyon, Toulouse, and Bayonne. Now facing into the Caurus: Bordeaux, Poitiers, Orleans, Paris, Peronne, Flanders, Brabant, Guelders, Frisia, Holland, England, Scotland,

---

196 Garamantes denotes an area in the south of present-day Libya; troglodyte was an ancient term designating the inhabitants of a region from Libya to the Arabian Gulf; the Mandinka, Manikongo, Zapes, Biafrans, and Wolofs are all West African ethnic groups.
197 The straits are those of Gibraltar; Apollonia was an ancient city on the Libyan coast; the Sirtes refers to two gulfs, those of Sidra in Libya and Gabes in Tunisia; Carthage, near present-day Tunis, was an ancient city destroyed by Rome in the Third Punic war, in 146 B.C.E.
198 Francis I; the Battle of Pavia was fought in 1525.

and Hibernia or Ireland;[199] / Denmark, Dacia, and Norway toward the Baltic and its icy coast; Sweden, with Gothia along its border, fortified on all sides by the sea, from where one sails to Iceland. See Greenland there, beyond solar and zodiacal routes, with six months of night and six of day.[200] / Then look north to Muscovy, considered the world's furthest inhabitable region, bounded on one side by the Riphean mountains and stretching from the headwaters of the Don to the Hyperborean peaks and frozen sea, bordering Sarmatia and Tartary and thence in the direction of the Auster to Russia.[201] / Regard Livonia, Prussia, Lithuania, Samogitia, Podolia, and Russia itself; Poland, Silesia, and Germany; Moravia, Bohemia, Austria, and Hungary; Corvatia, Moldavia, Transylvania, Wallachia, Bulgaria, Slavonia; Macedonia, Greece, and the Morea; Candia, Cyprus, Rhodes, and Judea.[202] /

---

199 Alexandria refers to Alexandria della Paglia, north of Milan; Caurus is the northwest wind; Hibernia, the Latin name for Ireland, was also considered a part of it during the early modern period.

200 Dacia, an ancient region extending northwest from the Danube, here indicates part of Scandinavia; Gothia refers either to an ancient region of southern Sweden or to the island of Gotland off Sweden's coast.

201 Muscovy denotes the duchy of that name; the Riphean mountains are variously located in northern Europe or Asia by ancient authors, some of whom identify them with a Hyperborean range and cite them as the source of the Don river (south of Moscow); alternatively, Hyperborean may here refer to the North Pole; the "frozen sea" is the Arctic ocean; in ancient sources, Sarmatia denotes the western part of ancient Scythia, corresponding to a large area of present-day Poland and Russia; Tartary designates a great area of northern and central Asia to the east of this; as noted previously, Auster is the south wind.

202 Livonia denotes a region east of the Baltic that corresponds roughly to present-day Estonia; Lithuania designates an area east of Poland

[27.30] To the west see Spain and the ruggedness of ancient Biscay, where nobility undoubtedly arose and spread through all that region. Gaze upon Bermeo, crown of Biscay, surrounded by dense forests, and rising above its port the mighty walls of the Ercilla ancestral home, whose stones were laid before the town was founded.[203] / There you see Burgos, Logroño, and Pamplona, and descending eastward Zaragoza, Valencia, and to the left Barcelona, with León and Galicia to the right. See the famous city of Lisbon, Coimbra, and Salamanca, which has shown itself so felicitous in all the sciences and where necromancy once was taught. / Observe Valladolid coming back to life, like the Phoenix wrapped in burning flames, and next to it Medina del Campo with its ennobling fairs. See Segovia with its famous aqueduct, and crossing through the forests and valley of Fuenfría, see Pardo and Aranjuez, which nature has adorned with such a bounty of greenery and flowers.[204] / Look closely at that wild, mountainous site at the foot of a high, isolated pass, for although it appears nothing more than a rocky wilderness it will soon be well peopled,

---

much larger than today's country of that name; Samogitia refers to an area in the northwest of present-day Lithuania; Podolia is a historic region in the southwest of present-day Ukraine; Corvacia corresponds roughly to Croatia, and Moldavia to Hungary; Wallachia was a region north of present day Bulgaria; Slavonia lay east of Croatia, in present-day Hungary; Morea corresponds approximately to the Peloponnese; Candia may designate the island of Crete or the city there known today as Heraklion.

203 The *Torre Ercilla*, a fifteenth-century structure built by the poet's ancestors, is still standing in Berceo.

204 Valladolid declined in importance after the royal court was moved to Madrid in 1561; early-modern Medina del Campo was renowned for its trade fairs; the Roman aqueduct at Segovia brings water from springs at Fuenfria, to the city's south.

since that is where victorious King Philip, having defeated the French at Saint Quentin, will raise a Catholic trophy in testimony to his noble purpose.[205] / This will be an incomparable temple of sumptuous size and construction, an establishment distinguished by its religious zeal and immense wealth, standing for all eternity as an edifice of great majesty and enormous beauty, the work, in short, of such a great Christian and benevolent, powerful king. / Now observe Madrid, for which the lofty heavens have readied such propitious fortune, and Toledo, founded on an impregnable site above the golden Tagus. Look further to Córdoba and to the death that angrily threatens Granada, wielding its sword above so many important heads and throats.[206] / Look at Seville and at the majesty of its churches, buildings, and dwellings, its multitudes of people and the grandeur of its trade with the distant Indies, from where two fleets arrive each year loaded with riches, gold, silver, and pearls, and to which another two set out with merchandise and soldiers, munitions and artillery.[207] / See Cadiz, where famous Hercules, pursuing his auspicious fate, triumphantly raised the two pillars, inscribing their marble with *Nihil ultra*.[208] This is where glorious Ferdinand the Catholic, pushing beyond

---

205 The reference is to monastery and palace complex of San Lorenzo del Escorial, built between 1563 and 1584.
206 The description of the Tagus as golden, due to the presence of gold in its waters, originated in antiquity; an uprising by Moors in Granada in 1568 led to the War of Las Alpujarras, which lasted until the rebels' defeat in 1571.
207 Convoys heading for the Indies usually left Spain in May and August; those returning departed the Indies in April.
208 For much of antiquity the pillars of Hercules, near present day Gibraltar, marked the end of the known world, beyond which there was nothing: *nihil ultra*.

prescribed boundaries, opened the way to the vast New World, because one world alone could not contain him. /

[27.38] Moving down across the ocean, between the humid Notus and west winds, behold the Canary Islands, particularly waterless Hierro, where animals, birds, and humans drink the distillations of a tree from a broad and beautifully decorated basin.[209] / To the right see the Azores, occupied by the Portuguese, and moving southwest and populated by people stranger than any ever seen before, the first islands discovered by Columbus, among the most notable the Lucayas, San Juan, Dominica, Santo Domingo, Cuba, and Jamaica.[210] / See the narrow Bahaman channel, and further west, Florida and the infertile land along the shining coast all the way to New Spain, where Cortés, at no small cost and great risk to his life, expanded the boundaries and crown of Spain so enormously. / Behold Jalisco and Michoacán, famous for its medicinal root, and Mexico, enormous, populous city, which still today retains its ancient Indian name. To the south see the mountainous, populated region tapering to a point, along whose sides two vast seas compress the distance between their coasts.[211] / Look at Panama and Nombre de Dios, defending

---

209 Notus is the south wind; according to ancient legend, El Hierro, the smallest and westernmost island of the Canaries, was supplied by water from the moisture of passing clouds that condensed on the leaves of a laurel tree, filling basins beneath it.
210 Columbus's initial contact with the New World was reported to be with the *islas Lucayas* (part of the Bahamas), originally inhabited by the Lucayan people.
211 A medicinal "root of Michoacán," sometimes referred to as "rhubarb of the Indies," was first imported to Europe during the colonial period.

their constricted borders against these two opposing seas, which angrily strive to break into the land and drown it. Behold the rugged mountain range of Capira at Cartagena, and the lands extending from Santa Marta and Cabo de la Vela to the lake and city of Venezuela.[212] / See Bogotá and Cartama bordering a long stretch of land with Arma and Cali, and Popayan, Pasto, and Quito near the temperate equinoctial line. See Puerto Viejo, where the rich emerald mine was discovered, and the other lands that Eurus caresses: Vulturnus and Mediodía.[213] / See Guayaquil, whose dense, dark forests abound in wood; Tumbez, Paita and its harbor, the first port-of-call for anchoring ships; Piura, Loja, Zarza, and the Cordillera, where so many rivers are born and descend to irrigate more than two thousand miles of earth untouched by heaven's rains.[214] / Behold the massive mountains and high sierras beneath the snowy torrid zone; Mojos, Bracamoros, and the lands inhabited by the

---

212 The Spanish may have called the bay connected to Maracaibo Lake "little Venice" or Venezuela because of native dwellings they found there on stilts.
213 Cartama was a Colombian province east of Caramanta; Arma most likely refers to Santiago de Arma, founded by Sebastián de Belalcázar in 1542; the "long stretch of land" probably refers to two parallel valleys between the three branches of the Colombian Andes; the "equinoctial line" is the equator; Puerto Viejo is Portoviejo, in present-day Ecuador, near which early explorers discovered large number of emeralds; Eurus is the east wind, Vulturnus the east or southeast, and Mediodia the Auster or south.
214 Guayaquil, Tumbez, and Zarza, the old name of Loja, capital of the province of the same name, are in present-day Ecuador; Paita and Piura in present-day Peru; vessels traversing this coast frequently anchored at Piura for supplies; *Cordillera* often designated the Andes, specifically.

savage Chachapoyas; Cajamarca and Trujillo, ever famous and noteworthy in the wars; and the illustrious City of Kings, home of tribunals and viceroys.[215] / Also Huánuco, Huamanga, and the temperate terrain of Arequipa, as well as the territory of Cuzco, ancient city and renowned haven of the Incas and their *Orejones*. Looking beyond the Tropic of Capricorn and solstice line, see the southern regions with their many strange, barbarian peoples, rivers, lakes, valleys, and mountains.[216] / Look at Chuquiabo, the ridges running south there to one side, and straight ahead the magnificent, immensely rich mountain of Potosí, which swells the earth around it with fine metal of the highest quality, for every *quintal* of its soil yields two *arrobas* of pure silver.[217] / See the town of Plata, the last on the left, toward the east, and crossing the high cordillera, Calchaqui, Pilcomayo, and Tucumán; the Juries, Diaguitas, and shoreline of Comechigone; and then the vast plain and remote, fertile territory until the fortress of Gaboto.[218] / Turning toward the

---

215 Mojos and Bracamoros are regions in the north of what is today Peru; Lima was founded as *La ciudad de los reyes* or the City of Kings.

216 Huánuco, Huamanga, and Arequipa denote regions in colonial Peru; *Orejones*, as noted at 1.48, were Incan nobility; the Tropic of Capricorn marks the southernmost trajectory of the sun; see n. 135, above.

217 Chuquiabo was the Indian name of the site where La Paz was founded; Potosí, in colonial Peru, was the site of the New World's largest silver mine; a *quintal* is approximately 200 pounds; an *arroba* is approximately 25.

218 Plata refers to present-day Sucre, Bolivia; Calchaqui and Tucumán designate regions in the northwest of present-day Argentina; Pilcomayo indicates an area around the river of that name, which flows from near Sucre to Asunción, Paraguay; the Iuries, Diaguitas, and Comechigones refer to indigenous groups in the province of

coast, note the hills that run alongside the Atacama, and to the right the coastal desert bereft of birds, animals, plants, and trees. Gaze upon the brawny Copiapó Indians, famed as great bowmen, then upon the Coquimbo, Mapochó, and Cauquén rivers, as well as the Maule, Itata, and Biobío.[219] / Behold the city of Penco and mighty Arauco, strong and free; Cañete, La Imperial, and eastward, Villarrica and its fiery volcano; Valdivia, Osorno and its lake; and further ahead the famous islands and archipelago. Following the coast due south, Chiloé, Coronados, and the straits[220] / through which Magellan and his men entered into the South Sea and, turning westward, steered northwest to the Moluccas. See the islands of Acaca and Sebu ahead, and then Matán, where, in the end, he died fighting; and then Bruney, Bohol, Gilolo, Ternate, Machan, Motir, Banda, Tidore, and Mate.[221] / Look at those traces of earth, so hidden they can scarcely be discerned: those have yet to be discovered or trod underfoot by outsiders, and they'll remain under cover and veiled by those clouds until God permits them to appear, magnifying the grandeur of his secrets. / Just as you now see the earth's true form and great circumference, if there were

---

Tucumán, in what was then the southeast of colonial Peru; the fort established by Sebastián Gaboto, at the confluence of the Carcaraña and Paraná rivers, was the first European settlement in present-day Argentina.

219 Copiapó, Coquimbo, Mapochó, and Cauquén refer to regions of colonial Chile from north to south, a movement mirrored in the naming of the Maule, Itata, and Biobío rivers.

220 Coronados may refer to an early Spanish settlement of San Jose de Coronados near the Gulf of Corcovado.

221 The South Sea refers to the Pacific Ocean; the names that follow are islands in the Moluccas.

more time you could also study the excellence of the celestial bodies, the mechanism and harmony of their spheres, and the virtue and influence of the stars with their varying revolutions, movements, and courses, both natural and anomalous. / I would gladly leave you happier and more satisfied, but it's been a while since the day began to decline, and you have a long way to go to your camp." Having thus spoken, the sorcerer accompanied me until he had set me on the right road, where I found my worried companions searching for me. /

[27.55] We arrived at our camp just as our friends were posting the guard and went on to spend some days there trying to bring our enemies to peace, sometimes treating them well and caring for them, at other times using threats and punishment, all the while making incursions into the surrounding towns and villages. / Such diligence did not achieve our goal, however, any more than did promises, terms, or pacts, for the people became ever more adamant in their stubborn plans and purposes. Given the site's importance, situated as it was in the heart of the region, after careful consideration we decided to maintain a stronghold here. / Although the year promised to be a bountiful one, the crops had only just sprouted, and in order to acquire the provisions we needed, in anticipation of hostilities, Miguel de Velasco, Avendaño, and I, along with some other ready companions, set out for Cautén. / We passed through that dangerous territory without interference, in spite of the risk, arriving safely and within the time we had foreseen at the city of La Imperial, where our affectionate appeals to each and every inhabitant induced them to liberally offer us not only their food, but their possessions and lives as well. / Thus cheered and hearing no rumor of war, we quickly returned with bread, fruit, grain, and livestock through areas where the Indians were sometimes peaceful and at other times agitated. On reaching the Purén sierra we encountered an escort of soldiers, our own compatriots, who had come to protect us on the dangerous road. / The sun, setting in the west, plunged its rays in the sea, while the night brought relief to the labor and fatigue of our men. At dawn the baggage train and livestock promptly set out once again with great commotion, surrounded by our troops. / I was in the vanguard, scouting a densely overgrown ravine, when I saw a seemingly agitated woman crossing ahead of us. Digging in my heels in pursuit, my horse quickly overcame her, but whoever wishes to learn the end of this story, let them carefully read the next canto. /

CANTO 28

Glaura recounts her misfortunes and explains how she came to be here. The Araucans attack the Spanish at the Purén ravine, and a pitched fight follows in which the enemy is routed but left content at having sacked the baggage train.

Those whose lives are free of care should be on guard, for anyone careless of danger is in danger of a fall. How often we see good fortune turn to misery, liberty become cruel servitude, and prosperity followed by distress! / Fortune is so fickle that even when befriending us, good has scarcely knocked at the door when evil troubles us within. Knowing that good is never not followed by ill, let us pray that good never comes, and that areas where the Indians were sometimes peaceful and at other times agitated. On reaching the Purén sierra we encountered an escort of soldiers, our own compatriots, who had come to protect us on the dangerous road. / The sun, setting in the west, plunged its rays in the sea, while the night brought relief to the labor and fatigue of our men. At dawn the baggage train and livestock promptly set out once again with great commotion, surrounded by our troops. / I was in the vanguard, scouting a densely overgrown ravine, when I saw a seemingly agitated woman crossing ahead of us. Digging in my heels in pursuit, my horse quickly overcame her, but whoever wishes to learn the end of this story, let them carefully read the next canto. /

CANTO 28

Glaura recounts her misfortunes and explains how she came to be here. The Araucans attack the Spanish at the Purén ravine, and a pitched fight follows in which the enemy is routed but left content at having sacked the baggage train.

Those whose lives are free of care should be on guard, for anyone careless of danger is in danger of a fall. How often we see good fortune turn to misery, liberty become cruel servitude, and prosperity followed by distress! / Fortune is so fickle that even when befriending us, good has scarcely knocked at the door when evil troubles us within. Knowing that good is never not followed by ill, let us pray that good never comes, and that when it does the following ill be small. / Well-versed in this, I feel good fortune is to be feared, for happy times pass in an instant while sad ones last until death. And since it fits so well with my theme, listen to the barbarian I overtook in the undergrowth, a woman whose clothing revealed her to be of good family. / She was young, tall, and well-proportioned, with a noble brow and fine eyes, a perfect nose, crimson lips, and teeth that seemed set in fine coral. She had a large, firm bust and beautiful hands, well-turned arms, and a natural grace and elegance that enhanced her beauty even more. / Wanting to know why she was making her way alone through those desolate woods with more self-assurance than her beauty and gentility would have promised, I first calmed her fears, after which, breathing a sigh that would have moved the most hardened heart to tenderness, she began to speak as follows: /

[28.6] "I'm so unhappy I don't know whether to complain of fate and fortune or be grateful for their opening a door that may lead to my death! But if you wish to hear of my ill-starred history and my pain, made worse by the frailty of my grief, I implore you to listen carefully. / My name is Glaura, born at a fateful hour the daughter of the good cacique Quilacura, of illustrious Friso blood. Rich in possessions but poor in luck, I was respected and served by many for my lineage and vain beauty, but woe is me! How much better had I been a poor, simple shepherdess! / As his only heir I lived happily in my father's house, his only pleasure that of giving me joy. My wishes and commands were obeyed as inviolable laws, and when it came to my happiness, nothing was ever too difficult. / But jealous, tyrannical love, deliberate disturber of the peace, soon brought Fresolano, a young man of great strength and courage, to my land and my home. He was my unfortunate father's cousin, but much more a friend than kinsman, for there was nothing my father wouldn't do for him and nothing the two didn't share. / As his devoted companion my father expected me to entertain him, and in order to please him I cautiously made every effort to do so. Yet Fresolano soon abused the situation and with lax loyalty debased their friendship, violating propriety and charting an improper course. / Whether it was his familiarity with me or, more likely, my misfortune, which certainly was more significant than my ill-prized beauty, he fell in love with me and began seeking a way to relieve his distress, heedless of hospitality and little concerned with obligation. / I had often seen indirect signs of his anguish and knew his evil intentions and desires went beyond honorable bounds. But alas, I realize what I'm suffering now the wretch suffered then, and even here at death's door I can't condemn him! / A thousand times I found him sighing, his beguiling eyes fixed on mine; at other moments he would timidly try to achieve his rash designs. I avoided these dangerous encounters, gravely rejecting his wayward fantasies with virtuous words suited to restrain such daring. / One day I was alone in my room, fearing some incident, when he entered and kneeled before me in great agitation. 'Oh, my Glaura!' he said to me, trembling. 'Neither reason nor patience will suffice any longer, nor have I any strength left with which to resist the power of love! / My lady, know that from the first day of my happy arrival here, love has led me to the last stage of this painful and ill-starred life! But as I die for you and your love, I want to know if it's something you welcome, for if so then there's nothing will give me more pleasure!' / Seeing him set on some violence or disrespect, I managed to get away and boldly told him, 'You wicked, incestuous, and ungrateful man!

Canto 28

Corruptor of sworn friendship and the bounds of family ties!' / I was saying this and other things prompted by my impetuous anger, when suddenly there was a great outcry and Christian troops surrounded our lofty home, then attacked us in tightly-packed ranks. In my presence Fresolano sprang to a proper and worthy resistance, / saying to me as he did, 'Oh, fierce, hard-hearted tiger, so cruel and inhuman to men! Come back and finish your work as my killer, leaving nothing for the Christians to do! Come back and watch me end my life at their hands since I cannot at yours, for while such a death is less noble at least it's more compassionate!' / Thus enraged he hurled himself without another thought amidst the armed men, where a speeding bullet immediately pierced his naked, ardent breast. He fell, and turning pale cried in an anguished voice, 'Glaura, Glaura! Now at last accept my dying spirit, weary of lending life to this unfortunate body!' / At that moment my father arrived at the fray, armed only with courage and determination, but was instantly wounded in the side by a furious lance, and his mortal body fell colorless to the ground. Seeing my calamity, I left by a hidden door, more dead in my own mind than they. /

[28.21] "Running frantically here and there, I finally hid in the woods on the side of a mountain, letting myself be guided by my fortune, which never fails to lead me to a precipice! Thus distraught and not on any trail, I tried to get away, miserable as I was, my great fright making it seem that no matter how fast I ran I wasn't moving at all. / As often happens when we flee some present evil only to encounter a greater one that overwhelms us, thus it was with me, who to save my tiresome life went from evil to evil and from crisis to crisis, always coming to greater danger and a worse disaster. / Despairing, I kept running through thickets and thorns, turning this way and that, my eyes alert at every step, when I suddenly saw two blacks loaded with spoils emerging from some trees, and the moment they caught sight of me they attacked their wretched prey. / They quickly stripped me of everything I wore, and although I was so frightened that I took the loss of my clothing and my life as nothing, I was at the point of losing my honor and precious chastity, and my cries and laments were such that the woods themselves were moved to pity. / Heaven showed me its clemency then, guiding Cariolán to my shouts, for he had seen the heinous insolence of those enemy felons and came running with timely assistance. 'You dogs, barbarians, and traitors!' he cried, 'Unhand the maiden! Unhand her this instant or forfeit your lives!' / The two made for him at once, but drawing the bow he carried, he quickly buried an arrow up to its feathers in the swifter one in front, then deftly took two steps back and sent a second toward the other with such sure aim that it found its way to his brutal heart. / The man fell dead, and the first, badly wounded and enraged, furiously attacked him. But brave and agile Cariolán was an experienced wrestler, and even though the black man was enormous and muscular, using his strength and agility Cariolán raised him skyward in his arms and hurled him to the ground on his back. / Pulling out a polished dagger with which to bring the story to a close, he then plunged it into his naked belly and side three times, three times withdrawing it covered in blood. The man's soul fled swiftly away, and Cariolán, now free of that menace, approached me with great civility, begging my pardon for having arrived so late. /

[28.29] His words were so adept (for this is how love worked its way with me), that fearful of putting my honor at risk and wanting to avoid any rumors—while showing I wasn't ungrateful

Canto 28

for his help in such a crisis—I took him for my guardian and husband. / Afraid that soldiers would come for us, we set off into the deep woods. With no trace of a trail we wandered about lost for some time, but as the day was ending we came out onto the banks of the Lauquén. Here a squad of Christian soldiers was approaching with ten Indians whose hands were bound behind their backs. / Catching sight of us as we appeared, for Fortune was always dogging our heels, a group of them came running, shouting loudly, 'Halt! Halt! Stay where you are!' My new husband, fearing for my dishonor much more than his death, begged me to hide in the woods while he died delaying them. / At that point terror, so capable of confounding a feeble, imprudent woman, got the best of me, placing before my eyes a horrible death or precious life. Frightened, cowardly, and inconstant, giving in to my first impulse upon seeing the soldiers so near, I pushed into the thickest part of the undergrowth as fast as I could, / and there I hid myself, panting and senseless, in the hollow of a tree trunk surrounded by a tangle of brambles, scarcely able to breathe in my fear. I soon heard a great tumult of swords, lances, and men, as in a fierce fight, resounding far and wide through the woods. / Little by little the noise and shouting came to a stop, and as a sense of duty began to warm the blood that my fear had frozen, I came to my senses pondering the wickedness and treachery I had committed by not facing as one with my husband the same fortune and danger and death. / Emerging from that place—would it have pleased God I remained there buried alive!—I quickly ran to the riverbank where I had left him so rashly. Seeing no sign of him nor having any way to find him, you can imagine how I felt, alone and anxious, since it was clear he couldn't have escaped being taken prisoner or killed. / In vain

I fearlessly raised my voice, calling on deaf heaven, unjust and cruel, asking, 'Where is my Cariolán?' In response all was silent. Now I forced my way through the underbrush, now ran through clearings, for the sharp pain in my entrails grew ever fiercer, not giving me a moment's rest. / I've no desire to tire you or grieve myself describing the agonies I felt. Not knowing what to do nor how to proceed, I ran furiously about in a frenzy. Many times I resolved to kill myself, and it's a depravity and great wickedness that my pain alone was not enough to end my life! / Consumed by such distress and battling conflicting thoughts and doubts, I finally resolved to go in search of him, since my anguish was not going to finish me off, and that night I turned back toward the Spanish camp. Once there I hid myself some way apart for the sake of my honor, my youth and misfortunes offering me little assurance. / Learning that the soldiers had been heading for Cautén when we met them and that they had to return through this very pass, I decided to come here in different garb, thinking that disguised among so many I'd discover some news or trace of the one from whom fortune had separated me. / But now taken prisoner and subject to another's will and command, what remedy is left me, when in order to torment me further, death, being welcome, still doesn't come? Cruel heaven may wish me to live, but so much pain must surely be the end of me, although no one chooses their time to die, even in distress such as mine!" /

[28.41] Thus the beautiful, disconsolate young woman was recounting her misadventures, when a dense mass of barbarians, waiting in ambush alongside the road, raised a sudden yell. They quickly surrounded us and blocked the trails, their number increasing so rapidly it seemed that Indians were springing from the ground. / At that moment a *yanacona* of mine approached, a man I had won in a fair fight less than a month before. "Head for the river, sir, and I'll protect you," he said, "for I know the area, and to think of resisting these men coming down from the sierra is folly. You can trust me, sir, for here you'll see me die to ensure your escape!" / I was turning to thank the youth for such good will when I saw Glaura rush wildly toward him, crying, "Oh, just God! What is this I see? Are you my sweet husband? Oh, life of mine! Here I am holding you in my arms, yet I don't believe it! What's happening? Am I dreaming or awake? Alas, something so good is never certain!" / Stunned by this development, I watched with as much joy as amazement as Glaura's pitiable lament came to a felicitous end. But with no place for ceremony in such pandemonium and not a moment to lose, I said to them, "Farewell, my friends! The only thing I can do for you, which is give you your freedom, I hereby grant you!" /

[28.45] With no further offer or promises I set spurs to my horse, which rushed forward. But however hard the Indians press me, my Lord, I first want to tell you how Cariolán came to be my prisoner at the edge of the dense forest, when Glaura, fearful of losing her life, was still hiding in the trunk of the tree. / Know then, Lord, that having spent the day searching for enemy rebels I was proceeding with some fellow soldiers, and just as we were nearing our camp with ten bound barbarian prisoners we caught sight of Cariolán, near a wooded mountain at the edge of the plain. / Everyone immediately ran to attack him, expecting that fear would grant him wings, but with great disdain and head held high he stayed where he was, readying his bow. As our men came within range he skillfully wounded Francisco Osorio and Acebedo, and taking out his knife, he removed his long blanket and wrapped it about his arm. / Such was the art and agility of the fearless Araucan that the great throng of soldiers could not force him to give up a single step of ground, and their blows all fell in vain as he leapt from side to side, dodging some with his body and deflecting others with his blanket and knife. / Admiring the young man's courage and having no desire to watch such a fight, I thrust myself between them all, saying, "Back, gentlemen, back! Move aside! It isn't right that the brave youth die, but rather he deserves a reward, and to kill him like this would show neither strength nor courage, but villainy." / They all stopped, recognizing the wickedness of such shameful behavior. The Indian alone persisted, as though the prolongation of his life annoyed him, but he finally lowered his knife and stepped aside, then courteously turned to me and said, "What does it matter to you whether my life be long or short? / I nonetheless acknowledge your benevolence and the piety of your deed: pious in intention, although one might say impious and in fact inhumane, since for one who must live a miserable life an early death can't be bad! I'd thus say that by not killing me you treat me with cruel compassion. / But to prevent anyone's claiming that I deny receiving my life from you, I hereby place myself in your power and surrender, defeated, to wretched fortune." Saying this he immediately threw down his knife, and from that moment on, as docile as he had been indomitable, he was always with me, more as a friend than a servant. /

[28.53] Now the bellicose clamor of shouts and weapons rang out. Some of our men stayed together and ran, others called for help. The road was narrow, and the baggage train, livestock, and servants, unable to move either forward or back, blocked it completely. / The route to Purén runs straight until it comes to this pass through which one enters the Araucan State. Afterwards it proceeds obliquely a good distance, constrained by two steep hills that eventually squeeze it so tightly two men can scarcely travel side by side, the way made even narrower by a stream. / Our soldiers were crowded together here and there and calling to each other, everyone moving in a whirlwind of confusion as they shielded themselves from a tempest of missiles. Finely tempered alloys were not its equal, and greaves, breastplates, and helmets were battered on every side by furiously whistling boulders, lances, javelins, and arrows, along with stones from slingshots. / Some men, struck in the head, could not keep their saddles and fell to the ground. Others were stunned and like toads that try to move but cannot. Some crawled on their hands and knees; others, with a crushed hip or back, dragged themselves along trying to find refuge in some shelter or cavity where they could defend themselves from the storm. / The enemy, with their men and ammunition above the road, had the advantage of the incline and their stones, and I can affirm as a witness that the shower of rocks was so thick and fast it seemed the entire hillside was coming down in pieces. / Just as when one sees the angry heavens engulfed in dense, dark clouds and looking as though they intend to deluge the earth and destroy it, with lightning, hail, and fierce winds, and birds are knocked down mid-flight while men, wild beasts, and livestock run frantically this way and that seeking some shelter or safety, / just so the Spanish soldiers, badly battered, were forced by that furious hailstorm to seek anywhere they could for some tree or rocky hollow. Finally, somewhat protected, they called on their ancient valor, and having recovered their courage and aspiring to victorious revenge, / with their customary dispatch and sharp aim they fired a barrage of shots that instantly brought down many of the enemy. Rocks and bodies came hurtling down the rugged incline with such terrible, strange fury that even the dead wrought great havoc. /

[28.61] While this was taking place among those fighting in that narrow space, there was no less uproar at the rear, where great shouting could be heard. Here the Indians were so undisciplined that they began to plunder the baggage and supplies, creating great destruction and slaughter among the guards and servants. / Some climbed lightly to the top of the neighboring slope carrying meat, bread, fruit, or fish; others ran easily even though burdened by bundles and hampers. From high and low and from one side to the other a great crowd now hastened to the pillage, like a flock of summer doves hurrying to spilled grain. / Seeing ourselves hopelessly overwhelmed by the multitude rushing in, I resolved to make a final effort for our lives and abruptly forced my horse through the tumult on the crowded road. Coming to where ten soldiers were huddled in a hollow of the hillside, / I explained that given how fierce the fight was on both sides, if we could reach the top of the ridge victory would be ours, for those below were absorbed in the pillage and the surprise of seeing the high ground taken would be enough by itself to defeat our enemies. / Immediately resolved to die courageously, we eleven formed a squadron and launched our horses up the slope, each man high in the saddle. The incline was sheer and rocky, but following a long, knife-edged ridge we reached the crest, which was covered by dense scrub and trees. / Everyone instantly leapt to the ground, for the horses were of no more use at that point, covered with sweat and wheezing and unable to move. Quickly positioning ourselves on the side most crowded with Indians, above them at the top of an enormous, sheer drop, / we delivered

Canto 28

such a sudden barrage of bullets and stones that I promise you while many were hit, the sudden terror of it had greater effect. Rushing about in confusion, with the threat of attack from above and below, it seemed both heaven and earth had turned against them. / At this point additional soldiers arrived on the road, and filled with courage and eager for harsh revenge, they spread such fear and injury among the enemy that some of them lost hope and others began to retreat, setting their swift feet in flight since it was the only way to save their lives and goods. / Loaded down with boxes and bundles, they fled in every direction. Some, dragging their booty, made their way through dense growth on the hillside. Others, driven by base gluttony and greed, stopped to take more, their boundless avarice costing more than ten of them their lives. /

[28.70] Thus the festivities came to an end, and partially pillaged but triumphant we celebrated our honorable victory with trumpets, bugles, and drums. These sounds continued as we marched away well-guarded, and with skilled scouts in advance we arrived at our camp, all of us injured, where we were welcomed with cheers. / The barbarians quickly retreated through the dense woods and among rocky crags, consoling themselves for the outcome with their gratifying spoils. But when they came to where their general was waiting and he learned of the disorder and excess that had given victory to the enemy, he exacted an exemplary punishment on a number of them. / Once the remnants of his routed troops had gathered at Talcamávida, he convoked the principal caciques to consult on affairs of the State, and after dealing with the most pressing matters he freely told them what those who read the next canto will learn. /

CANTO 29

The Araucans enter a new council at which they propose burning their homes. Tucapel asks that his dispute with Rengo be allowed to resume, and the two have a spirited fight in the arena.

What power love of fatherland has to incite and inspire us, justly demanding we set all else aside! Seeing our country in peril, we face any danger and even death, abandoning parents, wife, and children for the sake of a closer bond. / Clear testimony to this can be seen in the remarkable deeds of the ancients, those who turned their own swords against themselves for a dear homeland and whose glorious fame the pens of celebrated writers have spread far and wide: Marius, Cassius, Philo, and Codrus of Athens;

Canto 29

Regulus, Agesilius, and the Utican.[222] / The Araucans should be counted among their number, baring their throats to the blade in service to their fatherland with such courage and constancy that it seemed neither the rigors of fate nor the blows of fortune, however harsh, had any effect on their spirits. / After losing four large, important battles in only three months, they gathered in a council of war, as you heard earlier, and not with downcast or sad demeanors but rather with the greatest confidence, determined to attack us again. Caupolicán came before them, speaking as follows: / "Oh, great and sacred senate! To win or die is what we must resolve, trusting only in our valiant arms, which are our ultimate salvation. As for our homes with their useless furnishings and comforts, beckoning us with repose, let us burn them, for if we must die everything else is superfluous, while if we win we'll recover it all afterwards. / It's essential that the great benefit of this be understood, for it's not good to be secure in our possessions when honor itself has no place among us! It's also not right for a

---

[222] Gaius Marius the Younger was the commander of a defeated Roman army who committed suicide rather than be taken captive by the enemy; Gaius Cassius Longinus similarly took his own life after leading his troops in a military loss; Philo may refer to Quintus Publilius Philo; Codrus was a legendary early king of Athens who sacrificed himself when the Delphic oracle revealed this was the only way to save the city; Marcus Atilius Regulus was a Roman general who defeated Carthage in the First Punic War, but was subsequently captured and sent to Rome to negotiate peace, where instead he urged the opposite; honoring his word to his captors, he returned to them and was put to death; Agesilaus II was a king of Sparta who hired himself out as a general at an advanced age in order to raise badly-needed funds for his country; the Utican is Cato, who took his own life after the death of Pompey, whom he supported against Caesar in the Civil War.

soldier to attend to anything other than that which furthers victory, nor for love of home and patrimony to undermine our ardent wills. / To those who long for respite from this bitter war, realize, as I've said, that there's no honor, property, or life beyond that to be seized from the enemy. The well-known valor of your arms will be your ransom and true friend, for henceforth there'll be neither truce nor treaty, but only kill or be killed!" / Many of the caciques were surprised when they heard this, but said nothing; others looked at each other with troubled expressions and raised eyebrows. Breaking their silence they then disputed the issue for a time and found so many arguments in its favor that all were convinced. / Valiant Ongolmo, not waiting for anyone to precede him on such an occasion, approved the motion amidst shouts, urging that it be put into action immediately. Purén followed with the same opinion, vowing not even to enter a village until he saw his fatherland restored to freedom and lasting peace, not by treaty or pact but through sheer force. / Lincoya and Caniomangue were not slow to swear to the edict, and being gallant and brave, promised even more than was possible. Rengo and Gualemo and the rest of the proud caciques stepped forward as well: Talcaguán, Lemolemo, and Orompello. Even the good Colocolo agreed with it. /

[29.11] Everyone being resolved, a decree was issued in keeping with what has been described. Once the difficult business was concluded and the excitement had died down, Tucapel, who had remained silent through it all, listening attentively with complete composure, rose to his feet, and in an ardent voice never known for its gentleness / spoke as follows: "Captains! Finding it just, I'm the first to agree with what the general proposes, and therefore I'm resolved that everything I own be burned and destroyed! As for what comes next, I trust in this arm, for if I can sustain its strength for one more month, I expect thereafter to choose the largest and finest portion as my due. / If there's any wretch who won't concede what's so rightly asked of him, let him be an enemy of the fatherland and excluded from this band of warriors! In our position we can come to no pact or arrangement without losing, for the struggle is over our liberty and our lands! / Yet while I'm committed to carrying out your votes and decisions, and although it may appear I'm creating new problems at a difficult time, I can by no means abandon an important matter that's still unresolved, urged on as I am by my natural honor and other legitimate reasons. / You recall the dispute that Rengo and I put aside, the one he was maintaining with his uncle, who, in desperation, chose to die.[223] Seeing the great dishonor and aggravation done me, and how long the affair has been deferred against my will, I want to comply with duty and desire with no further delay. / Rengo has won enough glory and honor among the people, yet now that he must enter the arena with me, he vaingloriously puts off doing so. I've grown weary of such procrastination, and since every situation disrupts the matter further, I demand our contest be concluded, for it's not right that my reputation suffer! / After our earlier confrontation, Peteguelén, that imprudent old man, thrust himself into the thick of battle to die under the guise of courage, finding such a death more compassionate than one facing me, and thus he craftily escaped. This was sheer terror on his part and nothing else, for if ambition had moved him he would have sought death at my hand.[224] / Rengo as well, clever and prudent, made his way deep within the enemy's ranks, seeking some obstacle or honorable way out of complying with what he'd

---

223 Rengo comes to his uncle's defense at 16.55 ff.
224 Peteguelén dies heroically in battle in Canto 19 (19.35-36).

promised, and under the pretense of courage he did his best to be maimed or crippled and left unfit to fight, glorying in having defied me." / Thus the arrogant barbarian was speaking when the enraged Rengo, breathing fire, stepped forward without waiting to be acknowledged and said, "Let's fight right now, for neither your bluster nor bragging troubles me in the least! Arms are what will speak, not words, which belong to pompous babblers!" / Tucapel would have attacked him had not Caupolicán prevented it, swiftly placing himself between them and cutting off his retort and way forward. Rebuking such mad audacity with a sharp look and grave demeanor, he nonetheless acceded to Tucapel's request in order to put an end to their rivalry. /

[29.21] The time and place for the encounter having been set for four days hence, many wagers were made among the excited crowd over the uncertain outcome. One man bet his belongings, another some cattle, another a field or a crop; some, not wanting to win, wagered old wives. / In an open, level clearing they encircled a space with wooden staves where the two indomitable champions, fully armed, would fight one on one, and in keeping with Araucan custom, the rules were publicly announced so they would be clear to all and no one could claim ignorance of them. / When it was time and the day awaited by so many finally began to dawn, an exuberant crowd quickly surrounded the ring. The crush was so great there wasn't a tree, window, wall, or roof to be seen not filled with people. / The sun had scarcely emerged from the east, languidly and only partly afire, when bold Tucapel appeared on one side amidst a great uproar. At the same time and no less proudly the valiant, presumptuous Rengo stepped out from the other, both men with measured steps and fierce expressions. / Their robust bodies, outfitted with sturdy, double-layered breastplates worked in relief, along with helmets, cuisses, and pauldrons, were armored all the way to their feet.[225] They carried short clubs reinforced with iron, heavy shields bound in metal, and hanging on the left each had a long, curved cutlass garnished with jewels. / The arena, my Lord, had gates at both ends as in a jousting field. Entering through these each Mars now made a broad, circular promenade, and having completed this courtly walk remained balefully on his side of the great walled arena. / Once their sponsors carried out the offices required at such events, scrupulously resolving any sign of advantage or ruse, the tumult and commotion among the attentive spectators instantly ceased and the blast of the trumpet was heard, depriving more than one countenance of its color. / The two famous champions, who were only awaiting the dilatory signal, immediately advanced to the fray with dauntless, scowling expressions, and simultaneously bringing down their powerful arms they battered each other with such blows that for a few moments each remained with his head on his chest. / They then redoubled their assault, and while the first had been onerous, had the second not been met with such defenses and parries the combat would never have progressed to a third. Who could describe in fitting style the fury of these barbarian champions, combining all the world's valor and with their burning rage at its height? / Tucapel was struck such a blow above his shield, in the middle of his forehead, that he was momentarily stunned, out of his senses and his mind. Rengo swiftly followed up with another, but this blow had a different effect, its noise and fierce pain rousing his opponent from the dream into which the first

---

225 The cuisse is a piece of armor that protects the thighs; the pauldron covers the shoulder and upper arm.

had plunged him. / One never saw a serpent so venomously defend its offspring as the furious barbarian, who felt the loss of his honor even more than the pain. Beside himself with wrath and driven by diabolical pride, he instantly turned on valiant Rengo, discharging his hatred and bludgeon both at once. / Such fury and impetuous brio was in Rengo's favor, however, for the heavy end of Tucapel's unstoppable, ironclad club missed its mark, and the blow, while vigorous, was tolerable. The frenzy with which it was delivered deprived it of its power, for had it landed squarely I believe the fight would have been finished. / Even though it landed obliquely, Rengo, dizzied, moved back a few steps, and unable to resist such great force, ended up resting his hand on the ground. Realizing his not insignificant peril, he boldly returned to his formidable adversary with his cudgel at the ready and gave him an even weightier reply. /

[29.34] The ferocity of these two, unique throughout the world for their valor, was something to admire. Their vigilance, art, and skill, their lunges, strokes, and defenses, were such that I fear ineptitude will prevent my properly describing the most singular and bitterly-fought fight ever to occur among barbarians. / The savage combat proceeded in balance, the blows from both sides falling so heavily that the lightest did not fail to pummel flesh or break bones. The air resounded near and far with clamor and labored breathing, the din growing so great it could have been that of an entire army. / Mighty Rengo dealt Tucapel a blow, hitting him on the helmet with such force his senses were dazed and he saw the ground littered with stars. Coming back to himself and cursing heaven, Tucapel used his greater strength to strike him in return, doing this so quickly as Rengo was stepping back that he had no time to defend himself. / The ponderous stroke

CANTO 29

landed squarely, hitting him so hard on the head that everyone took him for dead. For some time it seemed he slumbered, but awakened by the peril and pain Rengo straightened his battered helmet and assaulted Tucapel so fiercely he broke the handle of his club. / Seeing his adversary deprived of his cudgel, which went flying off broken in two, Tucapel scornfully threw his own to the ground and grasped his formidable sword. Now he attacked anew, raising the blade on high, but Rengo dodged to the side, forcing the stroke to fall in vain. / Even though the ground was hard the blade penetrated a good way and became stuck, and while dealing with this impediment Tucapel was wounded in the side, where his brassard and the flesh beneath it were sliced open at an angle. Rengo intended to repeat the move but was unable to do so before his opponent's enormous, keen-edged blade descended again. / Drawing beneath his shield, he awaited the prodigious blow, which split the shield in two and continued through the steel crest of his helmet to the crown of his head. Rengo was stunned, the impact lacking but little of laying him out on the ground. His singular courage overcame the grievous pain and disorientation, however, / and rather than fearfully retreat he was even more determined to exact cruel revenge. Thus filled with wrath and burning with indignation, made worse by this new insult, Rengo delivered a backstroke of such extraordinary power and colossal force that had it not encountered such impregnable armor it would have split Tucapel in half to his belt. /

[29.42] So far forward he couldn't evade his opponent, Rengo threw down his broken shield and resorted to the use of his arms. Tucapel, stalwart and muscular, attacked him at the same moment, clasping him so tightly it would have crushed a fat, solid oak. / But it was Rengo he confronted here, whom no one surpassed in bravery, for whether against ten or six or two, he was always the one with the greatest agility and fortitude. Gripping one another with great force and equal skill, each man struggled, seeking this way and that to overcome the other's dexterity and power. / Contending chest to chest they moved furiously about, their hard arms knotted so tightly that both could scarcely breathe. Both strove to win, adding new effort to art and seeking through sheer strength to bring their enemy to the ground. / It was terrifying to see them so tightly and unrelentingly locked together, sweating profusely and covered with blood, their faces and eyes on fire, their breathing belabored, grappling, groaning, and snorting, not resting a single moment the entire day and neither of them gaining any mastery or advantage. / Inflamed by searing rage and considering himself weak and humiliated, Tucapel worked and reworked the entire arena, charging impetuously up one side and down the other. Rengo, with great skill and prudent cunning, his strength contained and deliberate, sustained his part in the fight along with his hopes. / Seeing his adversary somewhat exposed, he wanted to attack his right foot, but Tucapel, withdrawing it just in time, lifted him off the ground and clenched him tightly to his chest in his rock-hard muscles, jerking and shaking and squeezing him so vigorously he neither let him touch the ground nor take a breath. / He thought he would easily terminate the matter like this and bring the fight to a close, but Rengo, who was exceedingly agile and determined, managed to get a foot on the ground, and furiously enraged and impatient, with a violent twist now freed himself and grasped his opponent as tightly as he'd been held before. / Tucapel was disconcerted a few moments, staggering this way and that, and Rengo sank to his knees from his effort. Both men then ran quickly to their weapons and proceeded to batter their shields into splinters with a tempest of rapid blows that were even more forceful and fury-filled than when they began. / The crowd marveled at such stubborn determination and valor, seeing the two wounded in a thousand places and all the blood that soaked the earth, their armor and shields destroyed and with no arrangement for or means of stopping until one of them ended up dead, although it was more likely that both would die. / Rengo now dealt Tucapel a wound, catching his buckler obliquely and cutting through it like soft leather even though it was embossed in thick rings. The sword did not stop there, but made a large hole in his cuisse and double-pleated, thickly-woven breeches, penetrating flesh down to the bone.[226] / No heart was so steady it did not leap in its chest upon seeing the horrible expression and hate-filled face of the impatient, wounded Tucapel, who throwing aside the ruined buckler and possessed by infernal fury, hoisted his sword so high that I swear no one there felt safe. / On guard, Rengo! On guard, on guard! Down comes a blow of furious violence and irresistible force, delivered by the mightiest arm ever to wield a barbarian sword! May those expecting the conclusion of this fight forgive me if I leave the story cut short at this point, since by doing so I believe they'll await my return with greater desire.

END OF PART II

---

226 The buckler is a small, round shield, in contrast to the large shields the fighters employ at the beginning; the cuisse, as noted earlier, protects the thigh.

Part III of La Araucana

Don Alonso de Ercilla

1598

CANTO 30

This canto recounts the end of the fight between Tucapel and Rengo, as well as what transpired between Pran, an Araucan, and Andresillo, a *yanacona* of the Spanish.

Duels are condemned by divine and natural law unless for the common good, conducted not for private ends but under public authority, which is what justifies the use of prohibited weapons in fights and bouts. / Many say that dueling is a common, legitimate practice, since anger originated with man's free will and very being. But anger must be controlled by the bridle of reason in order to remain contained and not pass beyond just limits. / The Prophet himself teaches us that there are occasions on which we may grow angry, yet not without the restraint that prevents our crossing the line. Letting ourselves be carried away by passion we lose our rationality and humanity, revealing how little distinguishes a man who's angry from one who's mad.[227] / It's rightly said that the impulse inciting us to anger is a natural one, which also stimulates our will to fight, but the act of fighting itself is rebuked when the passion impelling it is not subject to reason's yoke. / Anger, being natural, is an appropriate part of man as long as it is rationally restrained, and thus in matters of public concern one champion can inflict his wrath on another as long as his opponent is legitimate. / But if the fight is frivolous, or due to vain boasting or bragging, or is only meant to demonstrate strength or fortitude, or arises from anger, hatred, or a desire for vengeance, or from a challenge being issued and remitted to arms, then such combat is prohibited and unlawful, even though approved by tradition. / We have proof of this here before us with Rengo and Tucapel, who fought solely over presumption and vain pride, tearing each other apart like wild beasts as they sought with inhuman obstinacy to arrive at death, to which they both were as close as their quarrel was distant from any justification. / I repeat that such commonplace fights, introduced through the corruption of the ages, are condemned by all laws and prohibited by military discipline, except in a few cases important to soldiers, as we will learn. /

[30.9] I leave the matter unresolved for now, for seeing Tucapel's uplifted arm I reproach myself at having left him like that for so long.[228] Returning to my narrative, you heard me shout at angry Rengo that his adversary's furious sword was descending upon him. / Finding himself too close to avoid the tremendous

---

227 Cf. Isaiah (63.3-6).
228 Part III of the poem was published eleven years after Part II.

Canto 30

blow, he raised his buckler in both hands and sheltered beneath it. The keen-edged blade did not stop there, nor was his helmet, as sturdy as it was, enough to halt it, for it sliced through both of these down to his forehead, where it opened a copious red fountain. / Rengo was stunned for a moment and only stayed on his feet with difficulty, dizzied by the terrible pain and staggering about in a swoon. Coming back to himself and realizing his extreme predicament, he hurled himself at Tucapel, who was just about to strike him to the ground. / Given how near he was to his surprised opponent, it wouldn't have taken much for Rengo to knock him over, and the force of his momentum caused Tucapel to lose his balance. Quickly recovering to find himself so pressed by his adversary, Tucapel threw his strong, knotty arms around him, intending to break him into a thousand pieces. / Using his measureless strength he then lifted him up and held him suspended, shaking and turning him all about, but Rengo kept his wits and soon managed to employ his own strength and skill. Neither the blood they had lost nor the long, stubborn fight lessened either man's energy or ardor, but instead their fury kept growing. / Suddenly shifting his feet, Rengo managed to encircle Tucapel's sturdy right leg with his, and holding him tightly in his powerful arms gave him a violent shove with his brawny chest. The force of the move was such that unable to do otherwise and much to their dismay, both men fell to the ground on their sides, like the collapse of a great rampart or tower. / Now with new ferocity and even greater intensity they began to roll about the arena, both of them striving so hard to blind each other with fistfuls of dirt that in the end both were left sightless, and unable to use their swords they impatiently bit and tore at each other with sharp fingernails and teeth. / Savage, bloodied, and enraged, each man now on top and now on the bottom, they tumbled about, hoarse, belabored gasps resounding from their tightly constricted chests. Not for this were they the least bit lax nor did they slacken in their violent frenzy, displaying instead new energy and new strength in their relentless struggle. /

[30.17] It had been more than three hours by the time the two equally valiant champions, their fury failing, gave any sign of being mortal, and now having exerted the last of their strength without either being able to win, they were left completely immobilized and by all appearances more dead than alive. / Both were dazed. Drained of blood, breath, and vigor, their robust chests were heaving and they were covered with dust and bloody sweat, their arms and legs entwined. Neither displayed the slightest sensibility, although Tucapel may have made more of an effort to rise. / He had his right arm and leg thrown over his opponent, something his friends considered a decisive lead and advantage, although to this day many still dispute the point. Neither of the two men was moving, the only sign of life from either being their beating hearts and harsh breathing. / The great Caupolicán, acting as referee and deploring the grave situation and possible loss, quickly entered the arena, and seeing they still had some blood and life left wasted no time having them lifted onto two great planks by twelve of the most celebrated warriors. / Followed by the rest of the nobles and important men, each fighter was then taken with solemn pomp and honor to his own fine tent. Here remedies were promptly brought, the loss of blood stanched, and with good care life was soon restored to both. / A critical period having passed, both men continued to improve, although Tucapel, aggravated by the outcome, could not be cured of his threats. The patient and prudent general, however, gently mollifying his anger, gradually restored him to the rule of reason. / Peace was established between the two, and it was solemnly sworn that for the rest of their lives they would have nothing more to do with the past, nor for any reason in the future, whether public or private, would they fight or get into quarrels or cross each other with words or insults, / but instead from this point forward would always conduct themselves as the best of friends, coming quickly to each other's aid in any danger or predicament. Thus reconciled, in order that their concord be more firmly established the two famous warriors ate and drank together amidst great public accolades and celebration. /

[30.25] I leave them here in their concord and comity, for now it's important that I return to the banks of the river of many names. Dealing with matters so far from our troubled camp has left me with much to relate in the wake of our earlier perils and final battle.[229] / Once we attained that victory, one with more loss and injury than gain, we quickly returned to the distant fort at Tucapel, where we soon had a number of other significant encounters that were not without cost in blood and great effort, although in order not to tire you, my Lord, I leave them aside. / I pass quietly over another bloody battle, as well, bitterly-fought on both sides, but while I do so to avoid tedium, another author will celebrate it.[230] Having provided the fort with two months' supply of food and munitions, we decided to leave it under the command of Captain Reynoso, / since other towns, weakened by earlier battles, were asking for our help, their unenforced laws crying out from afar. With everything so unsettled, everyone was

---

229 The reference is to the many tributaries of the Biobío; the previous battle was that of Millarapué, described in Cantos 25 and 26.
230 The reference may be to Calvete de Estrella; see n. 35, above.

governing without governing themselves, and the realm, being surfeited with governance, was at the point of collapsing from a lack of it. / Considering how populous, fertile, and abundant the surrounding region was, and thus well-suited for settlement, in addition to its location being so important at that time, before we departed we laid out plans for a town. We'll speak of this below, for although it had a solid beginning, it later changed its name and location.[231] / Leaving the most experienced soldiers to guard the area, we then assumed battle order and set off into forbidden territory with a warlike clamor, and after crossing the Purén sierra, exhausted by hunger and the weight of our armor, we came safely at last to La Imperial. / Here don García quickly reinstated the rule of law, reestablishing justice and reforming practices corrupted by the turbulent times. He also eliminated the excesses arising from a new avarice, and having arranged everything in the town in a fitting manner, set it on a proper course. /

[30.32] We had scarcely restored our bodies from lack of sleep and wretched hunger when we learned that the surrounding areas, growing rebellious, had broken our agreements, and seeing our forces divided were collecting theirs, determined to leave no Spaniard alive nor stronghold standing. / Thirty of the most experienced among us immediately began the return to Tucapel, and having crossed the densely wooded, ravine-filled country around Tirú, full of confusing trails where we had no few engagements but stopped neither night nor day, we made it back to the fort and our companions. / The men there had already heard reports of the rebellious land's activities and due to unusual circumstances had also been warned about the plans

---

231 The reference is to the founding of Cañete.

of the gathering enemy. Thanking us joyfully for our unexpected support, they then told us what they had learned, which occurred, my Lord, in the following fashion. /

[30.35] The Araucan army, realizing its good fortune was on the decline and that Caupolicán was losing the formidable stature he had enjoyed in the beginning, was talking in secret meetings, murmuring about the now-despised captain and saying that the war was being prolonged to preserve his dignity. / This was not said openly or brashly, for the freest and boldest among them would have been afraid to do so, nor would they exceed his most minor edict in any way. His punishments were so severe that no one dared ignore his orders, so greatly was he feared and respected. / Being prudent and seeing the wretched state of his men, however, Caupolicán began to dread the unstoppable rotation of fate and lack of obedience among the troops, for while good fortune easily carries inconstant loyalty in its wake, one disaster after another, day after day, chills even the most ardent devotion. / In order to leave no measure untried in pursuit of his duty, he therefore decided to devise a new test of fortune in which it might clearly declare itself, finally settling on one plan from among many. Before making it known he quickly amassed the required arms and provisions, / and not allowing any delay in which fear might focus on danger, or where some incident or sudden change might dampen enthusiasm, with great self-assurance he ordered as many soldiers as possible to be ready at the hour of deepest silence. / He then made a long speech to the senate in which he announced they would attack the Spanish fort at Ongolmo at midday, for a certain spy had informed him that the soldiers defending it, in addition to being overly-confident and careless, were few, inexperienced, and poorly armed. / Furthermore, their captain was absent with the most battle-hardened men and not due to return until the surrounding area had been pacified. Busy with these new conquests he would be unable to help them, and the fort could quickly and easily be overrun and its men slaughtered. / The gravity of his reasoning and authority of his presence was such that he carried every opinion and vote in complete unanimity, and thus with high spirits and firm resolution the caciques swore anew to obey him and faithfully follow his banners until death, in good fortune and bad. /

[30.43] The plan being set, Caupolicán then summoned an able fighter named Pran, who appeared crude and simple but who was not only subtle, keen, and resourceful, but also cunning, deceitful, and malicious. A glib talker and speaker of Spanish, he was also experienced, secretive, diligent, and discrete. / Once privately instructed in everything the delicate situation required, he set out poorly dressed for the Spanish fort, where he pretended to be lost and entered the Christian camp among the other Indian workers, by all appearances being one of them. / Under this guise he carefully observed everything taking place without drawing attention to himself, and with clandestine vigilance studied the most hidden activities. He entered the stronghold several times as this rustic figure, taking note of the men, weapons, and organization, of the site and its layout, and of the strongest and weakest parts of its defenses. / Meanwhile, he was also listening to and questioning the least wary around him, skillfully scrutinizing their secrets and private affairs. Disguising his reasons, he went about here and there testing their attitudes, always seeking the right receptacle in which he could unburden his brimming heart. / Carefully considering how the affair might best be concealed, he made his way from probe to probe and from case to case, entering at last into a dangerous port, for he was himself deceived by another Spanish-speaking barbarian named Andresillo, with whom he had agreed to go in search of food, something permitted the *yanaconas*. / Hearing the duplicitous language Pran brought to his task, the other man began to speak of the vexations suffered by the Araucan people, the insults and aggravations, the injustices, killings, thefts, violence, and tyranny, pitifully recalling the loss of their previous freedom and of so much that was good. / Credulous Pran, hearing his false friend express himself so forcefully and finding at last a willing listener as well as the ideal time and place, was persuaded by this deceitful display and dropped his own mask, opening his heart and revealing his secret plan as follows. /

[30.50] "Oh, Soldier!" he cried, "If you're grieved by Arauco's lamentable losses and the wretched oppression of our fatherland, then Fortune and all-powerful fate are smiling on us today, placing in your hands alone the life and salvation of an entire people! / Mighty Caupolicán, unequalled throughout this land in which he enjoys such obedience and supremacy, both in idle peace and bloody war, has seen your great valor, industry, and self-sufficiency, and on this auspicious occasion has decided to entrust the State to your fortune. / The beginning and end of this magnificent enterprise will be attributed to you and yours will be all the honor, authority, and reward. One thing only he wishes for himself and with which he'll be proud and satisfied, and that is having chosen you from among his subjects for such an immensely important task! / Entrusting this to you ensures its propitious outcome, for that which is attached to your happy fortune will surely turn out well! I've come as you see me here, disguised as a humble figure no one will suspect, in order to inform you of this plan and to make you its anchor. / Know that excepting some hidden obstacle, Caupolicán has decided to launch a terrifying attack on the fort at midday with an enormous number of men. A certain informer has advised him that at that time of day the soldiers, wearied by vexing night, are quietly resting on their beds, / while the ironclad gate, barring no one, is always carelessly left open as the heedless troops sleep within. It will thus be easy to kill them in a surprise attack, and once the fort is destroyed there'll be no one left in these southern regions to resist our power. / Trusting in your help, which is what will assure and facilitate everything, Caupolicán has come within three leagues of our location under the cover of night's somber shadows, and there, away from the army, he wishes to speak with you alone about the things I've summarized, giving you his word and guarantee of safety. / Therefore expand your hopes, for if you decide to embrace the good fortune being promised you, beyond the great honor you'll receive by saving the country, you'll owe your glory to no one but yourself, while everyone else will owe their lives to you, something we'll acknowledge forever after! / Just think what this means for you, recognize how auspicious the time and occasion are, and don't be ungrateful for what heaven is offering if only you'll accept such an important endeavor. Extend your hand to your fatherland, which is perishing from cruel and shameful servitude, and ask in recompense for anything it's possible to ask, for going forward everything will be granted you!" /

[30.59] With this he ended his speech, attentive to the Indian's tranquil expression, which remained unchanged until the talk was finished. Hiding what was in his heart and not hesitating a

Canto 30

moment, Andresillo contentedly replied to the proposal: / "Who could describe my deep joy and delight at finding the good of my dear, beloved fatherland placed in my hands? Neither riches, honor, position, nor office, nor even command and sovereignty over the entire world could count as much with me in this affair as our common and general good. / The insolence and unrestrained ambition of these people cannot be tolerated, nor the despotic empire and violence usurping our liberty. Divine providence has already announced its judgment, entrusting the deserved and exemplary punishment to strong Araucan arms. / Return to Caupolicán, assure him for me of my ready will, for whatever you wish to affirm on my part I'll make good on. Tomorrow, without fail, I'll meet him on a deserted stretch of the barren coast where we can speak at greater length of the responsibility I now assume. / To avoid any suspicion, it's best that you and I go our separate ways as we return where we're expected. Tomorrow at midday we can talk more freely, and then you'll be better satisfied with me. It's already late, so good-bye! The way back is long, good-bye!" / They quickly parted, taking separate paths, for one returned to the Araucan camp and the other to where our soldiers were waiting. There, with joy in his malicious heart, the latter spoke in secret with the captain, telling him point by point everything those who listen will hear in the following canto. /

CANTO 31

Andresillo tells Reynoso what was agreed upon with Pran. He then deceives Caupolicán, who attacks the Tucapel fort expecting to find the Spanish asleep.

The wickedness most condemned and abhorrent to divine goodness is the betrayal of friendship, which outrages heaven, earth, and hell. He who benefits from such treachery, while pleased, will always detest the betrayer, for the crime is so nefarious it even disgusts the one it helps! / Loved by no one and hated by all, a traitor is rarely safe for long and even those who share his cause abhor him. His friendship is always suspect, appearing otherwise even when genuine, and in the end he cannot escape certain punishment. / If the law of war deems it perfidious to harm an enemy who has surrendered, what would it say of someone who sells the blood and freedom of his friends? Someone who feigning loyalty betrays his fatherland, as happened here, setting a keen-edged knife at its throat with so much raging hatred? / Those who are vigilant can protect themselves against a known enemy or criminal, but not against a traitor who has not yet acted and hides a naked dagger beneath a show of camaraderie, for no door is secure against disloyalty nor any enemy as dangerous as one who's hidden. /

[31.5] Proof of this can be seen in Andresillo, who left his friend Pran deceived and satisfied, and with a swiftness that made short work of the distance returned to the Spanish camp. Here he appeared before Reynoso, who suspected nothing of what had happened, and priding himself on his malice revealed his treachery. / "Know that fate has dealt with you favorably today," he said, "shaping events so that Andresillo can be a useful friend, for it has placed your enemy's death or salvation at my disposal and entrusted to my hands alone the final judgment and executioner's blade! / Renouncing the duty and loyalty owed my fatherland out of respect for you, my lord, I'm ready to sacrifice my life to save yours from the present peril, turning weapons and fate's harsh decree against my detestable country while deflecting the multitude of swords now aimed at your chest!" / He then told him everything involving Pran that you heard in the previous canto. Reynoso was surprised and troubled, but with expressions of gratitude he affectionately embraced Andresillo and earnestly thanked him, / praising the cunning with which he had accomplished the double-dealing. The captain went on to exalt the splendid service being rendered the entire realm and Christianity, assuring him that such a magnificent benefit would remain forever in our memory and be richly remunerated with an honorable reward. / The two agreed that on the following day, unbeknownst to anyone else, Andresillo would meet the Araucan commander at the agreed upon time and place, and using his eyes and ears to learn the key elements of his plan, would lead him through clever misdirection toward the desired goal. /

[31.11] Thus it was arranged. Prior to this, Andresillo found Pran waiting at the entrance to a deep valley to lead him to where the Araucan general, joyously advancing ahead of his troops, welcomed him with courtesy and affection. / "Oh, captain," Caupolicán said, "a distinction in which heaven today confirms you, having been so justly entrusted with redeeming the land of our fathers! I know full well that driven by nothing but the honorable zeal of your own virtue and valor you aspire to a place where no man's name will ever surpass your own! / Having penetrated your heart's bold design and pursuing the happy outcome your good fortune promises, I've resolved to attack the Spanish fort with an overwhelming number of men in the middle of the day, you alone being our guide. / Thus it is that I come so stealthily to this place to assure you of a just reward—in whatever terms you like—and to see if you're willing to take charge of this enterprise and of all of us, acting as our supreme leader and issuing all the orders, instructions, and necessary measures. / In addition to these honors, on behalf of the senate I also promise you your own domain, which I swear by all-powerful Eponamón you can choose of your own free will. I now place myself in your hands, subordinating my judgment to yours so that you may take command and the desired outcome not be delayed. / Your help and my firm hope thus promising a successful attack, I've already concealed my soldiers nearby, and it's important we hasten the plan's execution before they're discovered and the fort alerted, which is our only danger. / Promptly confirm our expectations of you, mighty warrior, for on the seashore behind this mountain is an enormous, obedient army! You can go there now to see for yourself their discipline and courage, their weapons and great numbers. I'll await you here filled with confidence and high hopes." /

[31.18] Having listened attentively to all the general promised him, the determined traitor was dissuaded neither by the offers nor rewards from the ugly evil he was planning, although he felt some trepidation upon seeing the man's valor, audacity, and ferocious demeanor, his gigantic size and proportions. / Caupolicán's broad torso was protected by a sturdy metal breastplate, and adorning his lofty helmet was a scaly dragon worked in relief. He carried an ironclad cudgel in his right hand, and a sharpened machete was cinched at his side: in size and bearing he was the very figure of furious Mars. / Andresillo, having advanced his treachery so far so quickly and seeing how easily he would be able to accomplish his heinous deed, fell to his knees with a joyful, gratified expression. Although his duplicitous heart was filled with deceit, he replied to Caupolicán, / "Oh, mighty Apó! Don't think that honor, riches, or rank have brought me so obediently to your feet, determined to die in your service, for everything you've offered me and all that's most desirable doesn't inspire me as much as the obligation of the great cause itself![232] / I give thanks to heaven, for I feel my hopes, relying on your wisdom and great valor, are now headed to harbor on calm and prosperous seas! To avoid the danger of delay, it's best that you hasten the attack and follow Fortune, which has now declared itself in our favor. / When the sun reaches mid-

---

232 *Apó* is an Araucan term for *lord* or *captain*.

heaven, our enemies, used to nighttime alarms, go untroubled and unarmed to their tents, where shedding their garments and stretching out on their beds they pass the sultry siesta in utter repose until the torrid sun begins its decline, buried in wine and sweet sleep. / If you're ready, as you say, with your men nearby in battle formation, then I beseech you to take advantage of the occasion and not let such an opportunity pass. Time, once lost, is difficult to regain and hindered by delay, and since there's nothing to detain you, don't obstruct your own fate and fortune! / I'm committed to delivering victory to you, not because of the reward that awaits me, but because virtue entails its own compensation and is itself the true prize! It's enough that I can serve you, and thus I vow, at little cost, to place the tyrant's naked throat in your hands. / Tomorrow, as the sun reaches the midpoint of its journey, Pran will come disguised to my dwelling, where I'll be eagerly awaiting him. Entering the garrison and open fort, he'll see the men abandoned to their usual carefree sleep, with no precautions or commander. / Tonight, in utter silence and secrecy, gather your men in battalions to the right of the road, no more than a mile away. As the sun appears in the east await my signal and command, keeping them tightly together with their weapons lowered to avoid the first rays of light. / Now, to complete my joy and satisfaction, I want to see that fortunate army under your command and assembled for such a noble endeavor, for once it has thrown off Spanish tyranny, Arauco will not only be restored to its original rights and power, but its supremacy and renown will grow even greater!" /

[31.29] Caupolicán, convinced by the man's attitude that the plan was assured, responded with words that would have moved not only a sensitive soul but a wall of stone, and in token of such genuine resolve he gave Andresillo a shimmering headband of pure gold and a thick strand of fine beads, something the Indians hold in great esteem. / Accompanied by cheerful Pran, the traitor then proceeded to view the Araucan army with its enormous number of brave warriors, lying in ambush at the base of a high, wooded hill. Seeing this he was somewhat troubled and his false faith shaken, for in an inconstant spirit fear sometimes accomplishes what virtue cannot. / Invigorated by his wickedness, however, which spurred him on and gave him the courage he needed, he suppressed his doubts and proceeded with his evil plan. Disguising his deadly purpose with lying looks, he earnestly praised the site and the orderly soldiers with their weapons, / and having inquired about and made note of everything significant, observing the great preparations and calculating the strength and quantity of armed men, he returned well-informed to the fort as the day was ending. Reynoso was waiting for him, suspicious about his long absence, / but the Indian gave him a full and detailed account of his mission. The captain's confidence and courage were bolstered even more by our arrival at such a propitious moment, for if you've been attentive to my verses, you'll recall that I and the thirty men I mentioned returned to the Tucapel fort that very day, crossing through the mountains and forested coastland.[233] / All of us then spent the night readying our weapons and equipment, and after examining the ditch, rampart, and fortifications, assigned the men their places as dawn's troubled light began to unveil the deep valleys, sending a sad signal of the day denoted for so much blood and death. /

[31.35] Never in austral regions had the sun been seen to leave so late upon its daily journey, refusing to provide its usual light

---

233 Cf. 30.33.1

and clarity to mortals. At last it emerged, ringed with portents and preceded by a waning moon that turned its pale, mutable face toward heaven rather than gaze upon the land of the Araucans. / Both forces confidently and secretly readied themselves, their hopes and plans the same, their fates and fortunes opposed. Here you see Pran, coming alone like one of the diligent Indian workers, bearing a bundle of white wheat and looking for his treacherous friend, / who was watching the roadway from the door of his hut and thinking the time for their meeting had already passed although it had not yet arrived. Thus fiercely was evil pressing him, spurred on by malignant fury, for when something is desired so intently even promptness seems a delay. / Pran arrived and assured him that the troops, divided into two battalions, had come within sight of the stronghold without being seen or heard, and that moving silently and uniformly in well-ordered ranks, crouched over and trailing their weapons, they were now headed straight for the fort. / Andresillo, with his different plan in mind, expressed his pleasure, saying our soldiers were undoubtedly already asleep as usual. Without waiting any longer the two impostors then quietly entered the readied fort together, the false deceiver and the deceived, / where they found the officers and soldiers upon their beds, sleeping without being asleep, discreetly and carelessly careful. Here their armor lay strewn about, there horses were unsaddled, everything deliberately disordered in appearance and enveloped in sleep and utter silence. / Seeing them at rest and noting the fort's serenity and lack of vigilance, Pran, as happy as he was blind in not realizing how suspicious this was, did not wait another moment, but set off by way of a shortcut he knew, testing both speed and stamina to bring the Araucan army the expected news. /

[31.42] The barbarian had scarcely disappeared when Andresillo cried out, "Brave soldiers! You to whom is entrusted the longed-for end to the war! Take up your victorious weapons, and breaking this now useless silence, hasten forth with all speed, for I tell you the enemy is at your gates!" / Sailors never leapt as lightly from their blankets, hearing the pilot's shouts in the throes of a sudden storm, as did our men, who hearing Andresillo's outcries, burst impetuously from their tents and rushed to their nearby arms. / Some seized a well-worn breastplate, others put on their gorgets and helmets; these men saddled their horses, those emerged with an harquebus, lance, or sword. The cannons were immediately aimed at the open gates. Flanks and embrasures and curtain walls were supplied with hundreds of missiles of all kinds.[234] / Once the fort was ready and each man had assumed his post, utter silence was imposed, binding tongues and stilling the clamor. The ramparts were so quiet that the servants who worked outside the walls, seeing such peace and calm, assumed that all within were lost in sleep. /

[31.46] Pran lost no time as he ran. We had scarcely armed ourselves when our enemies suddenly appeared on both sides of us, leaning forward with their weapons lowered and approaching with such stealth that were the eye not faster and more agile than the ear they would have made it inside. / Just as an experienced hunter, having scouted his prey and terrain, little by little draws closer, crouched down and hidden amidst the brush and scrub, now hurrying forward, now holding back, taking a step and then stopping, not making a sound, until he comes close enough,

---

[234] The gorget is a piece of armor protecting the neck; flanks and curtain walls refer to parts of fortifications; embrasures are narrow openings from which weapons are fired.

still concealed, to be sure of his shot, / with no less silence and even greater vigilance the hidden Indians appeared and in a moment were less than thirty feet from the fort, at which point not sounding a single horn or instrument they attacked in a silent mass, more than two thousand men now rushing the gates left open not by negligence but design. / I know not with what words or sense of pleasure to describe the cruel and bloody assault, nor the just pity and justifiable hatred I feel conjoined. My spirit, now heartless, now humane, leaves me wavering and unsure, for if I respond with compassion I condemn what I did and consider it evil, / while if I were to distance myself from the attack and abandon it at this point, I would comply only poorly with what I have promised, since I was present within the fort and a part of it. Thus with a perplexed and hesitant heart, fighting these conflicting thoughts and in need of counsel, I leave them for the next canto. /

CANTO 32

The Araucans attack the fort and are repelled in a terrible slaughter. Caupolicán disbands the army and retreats to the sierra. Soldiers ask Don Alonso de Ercilla to tell them the life and true history of Dido.

How excellent and praiseworthy a virtue is noble clemency, rightly celebrated by all and never at home in a servile heart. It was through clemency that Rome became so powerful and conquered more people than by the sword, bending the proud necks of mighty kings beneath its laws. / Glory is gained not solely by winning, which is not where greatness and excellence lie, but by knowing how victory should be used and by further ennobling it with mercy. A victor worthy of memory restrains his own anger, and the greatest triumph is that of the merciful who simultaneously conquers his own passions. / The victory of a cruel, implacable captain is less glorious than one less bloody, which is thus more laudable, for while wielding a pitiless sword in the midst of wrath can be excused, once fury has passed and the blood has cooled it is vengeance, cruelty, and tyranny. / It was the spilling of so much blood that utterly destroyed the hoped-for benefits of this land (unless I misjudge), for here the laws and limits of war were exceeded to an inhuman degree, and our invasions and conquests caused enormous and heretofore unseen cruelties. / Although what follows was part of this, in my opinion, common sentiment has convinced me that in the end, according to fortune and human law, everything is permitted those who win. But putting aside such troubling talk, the time has come for the terrible slaughter and excess to begin, partly justified but entirely regrettable. /

[32.6] I left the barbarian army in the midst of their furious attack on the fort, where silent, hidden death was awaiting them with a thousand ready weapons. Having been led there in a fast and deadly race by fate and cruel fortune, the enormous mass of tight-packed troops now burst through the misleadingly open gates. / Everlasting God! What utter havoc, carnage, and devastation there was, what a battering among those wretched men, blindly rushing forward in their deception, expecting to deceive! Who could describe the grievous injuries, the tremendous, terrifying artillery, the sudden, turbulent storm of shots all fired at once? / Some were pierced clean through, others had their heads and arms taken off or were pounded into shapelessness, and many were punctured by pikes: limbs without bodies, bodies dismembered, with chunks of flesh raining down far and wide, livers and intestines, broken bones, palpating entrails, heaving lungs. / Like a narrow, well-charged mine that explodes with a deafening roar, its tower and tools sent flying through the air in a sudden, furious blast, with even greater thunder and more destruction the violent explosion of our gunpowder instantly cut to pieces and sent flying all the barbarian battalion within its reach. / Cruel Fortune, chaotic and capricious, tore the Araucan army apart, not a single shot missing its mark nor any stroke falling in vain. Never have so many been seen to die all at once, and however I hurry my pen I cannot advance, slowed by so many blows and wounds and so much death. / The volley had scarcely been fired when the cavalry, spurring their horses as one to reach open ground, broke through the crowded entryway into the second group of Indians, massed together in shock, where they wreaked greater havoc and carnage than the artillery could have. / Some use their lances to stab one after another, opening a broad, bloody way forward. Others, their swords slashing left and right, first take lives on this side, then on that. No spirit or arm is too timid to open and deepen a wound, no blade too dull to distill a steady stream of blood. / If only I could adequately depict the dead: some trampled by horses, some with their heads and chests torn open, some, a great pity to see, with brains and entrails exposed. Some bodies are torn to shreds, others are left whole but have no heads. / The shouts, laments, and moans, the pitiful, wretched wails and clash of weapons rise through the air, filling the vault of heaven. The fallen, wrestling with death, twist and turn in the dirt as countless lives depart all at once through countless kinds of wounds. /

[32.15] His sudden panic had hardly subsided when the deluded Pran, seeing the manifest disaster and dishonesty with which the traitorous Andresillo had dealt with him, felt such pain and sorrow that even though he was outside the fighting and could have escaped, he desperately threw himself amidst the weapons, unarmed, to die. / The Indians in the rear, hearing the tumult, were more fortunate, quickly turning their backs and showing the soles of their feet as they fled. Eager in their pursuit, our soldiers raced after them, striking down and wounding the least agile and diligent among the stragglers. / Some of the more valiant, caring more for their honor than their lives, turned back to fight, restraining the panicked flight of many others. But even though they fought with tremendous effort the battle was soon decided, for furious death had sharpened both edges of its sword. / Just as when countless clouds begin to take shape in a turbulent sky, some growing larger and some smaller as others continue to appear, and frigid northeast gales start driving them forward, mounding them up until they seek refuge in the south, leaving behind empty sky and clear air, / even so the stunned and frantic Indians broke up and scattered, then sometimes came together, bravely resisting, to attack. Overwhelmed at last by the violence, the battered squadrons abandoned the field and their banners that day, leaving behind an enormous number of dead and prisoners. / With the barbarians utterly devastated and the pursuit concluded, we divided up the prisoners and spoils and returned to our camp. Thirteen caciques were then chosen as an example and warning, and after having been tied to the mouth of a cannon, its fuse was lit and they were executed. /

[32.21] Many will be eager to ask if any of the bravest chiefs were killed in that confused mass of men, for in every significant encounter Rengo, Orompello, and brave Tucapel had always come in front of the troops, leading the way forward. / The answer, my Lord, is that since the general had resorted to a fraudulent tactic they all condemned, no noteworthy captain or cacique was present, believing it vile and cowardly to attack an unprepared enemy and saying a victory achieved by such ignoble means deserved neither glory nor praise. / Thus their arrogant dignity spared them this catastrophe and cruel death, for none of them, either through entreaty or any other means, could be persuaded to take part in or assist the attack. They considered it shameful to defeat unarmed, unclothed men, the peril of war being that which makes it honorable, and dishonorable those who win without it. / The venture left Caupolicán broken, ruined, and powerless, for a great deal of blood had been shed for very little vengeance. Seeing the frightened throngs of men with their cooling ardor and expectations, he decided to disband the army and release the weary soldiers. / He also resolved to wait until his own contrary fates had run their course, realizing he was fighting with the help of an old, exhausted fortune. The soldiers went their separate ways with the command that they be ready for his alerts and orders at any sign of trouble. / Withdrawing with only ten trustworthy warriors, Caupolicán then concealed his whereabouts, at one point being sighted in a mountain wilderness, at another in a village, always staying in hidden locations and never for long in any one, relying on his barbarous arrogance to keep the people fearful and obedient. / We made countless forays blindly following his uncertain trail, nor was there any area thereabouts we did not either attack or surveil by night. Even far from the road we found hovels filled with people displaced from their lands and fleeing the fighting. / Many said they would gladly return to their abandoned properties were it not that the general was compelling them otherwise with his inhuman cruelties, and that if a remedy were found for this the soldiers would be willing to put down their weapons, exhausted as they were by the never-ending war. / And although this was a pretense, we took great care in searching throughout the land, leaving behind no village or valley, no sierra, mountain, plain, or shore where the barbarian leader might be found. Yet neither through kindness nor cruelty, peace nor war, even with all of us doing our utmost, did we ever encounter any sign or mention of him. / No threat or punishment or torture could extract any news or clue whatsoever, nor were flattery, favors, or bribes ever able to corrupt anyone. Amazed by this we cautiously moved on, guided by instinct, wandering day and night, here and there, fatigued by our armor and lack of sleep. /

[32.31] Setting out one day with a squad of experienced soldiers to explore the area's less-used roads and trails, we happened upon the secluded dwellings of some local Indians. The inhabitants, who must have thought their settlement safe given the immensity of the woods and its great distance from everything, were absent, / but lying there on a mound of bundled grass was a young woman with a wound to her head. A girl no more than fifteen years old, noble in both dress and appearance, she was pale from loss of blood, which having spread across her delicate white garment enhanced her beauty and our compassion. / I asked what had brought her to such a wild and isolated place, and how and why someone had wounded her with such inhuman cruelty. With a forlorn expression and weary spirit, her voice barely audible, she replied, "The only thing certain after a happy life is a sad death! / To grasp the cruel folly of human happiness, know that it's not yet a month since my father, showing me his special love, granted me a husband chosen of my own free will, a husband and dear friend of such fine qualities that I found in him the satisfaction of all desire. / But the rare strength and courage with which he was supremely gifted led to his early death on the day our army was torn apart. I was nearby and following him when a bullet pierced his side, one that would have been less cruel and more just had it opened a pathway through my heart! / He fell dead, and I remained alive in a life that's worse than death. Seeing me thus afflicted, a soldier, sympathizing with my misfortune, dealt me this wound to finish me off, using an arm that while compassionate was not strong enough to free my spirit to follow my husband, so that something good succeed so much bad! / He easily knocked me to the ground, although this didn't deprive me of my senses, and the furious crush of the army swept by in a terrible roar. Then a cacique who's related to me, who had been hiding in a hollow, carried me away from the tumult in his arms and brought me to this hidden grove. / Now every moment I hope to die, but like a longed-for good my death delays, since it's the habit of happiness not to come to those who wait. And while I feel myself to be near life's end, heaven hasn't yet set a term for me, nor does the moment of death I call upon arrive, since my desire impedes and detains it. / Tiresome life thus fatigues me, and having seen the death of my husband and sweet friend, each hour I'm alive I commit a great evil by not following him. Now that chance offers me this opportunity, have pity on me, sir, finish here today what the soldier's weak arm began!" /

[32.40] Thus the sad young woman demanded an immediate death in a way that some simple person, pitying her plea, might have been moved to grant out of barbarous compassion. But realizing her wound was less cruel than her love, whose ravenous fire had once been at work in my own guileless heart, I hastened to save her life, / and having consoled her somewhat led her to understand that dying was not only forbidden but would not bring back her dead husband. I then applied the juice of some herbs these people use in their medicine to her pitiful wound, which looked worse than it was, / and having left an experienced Indian servant there who could take her back to her home and protect her from the dangers along the way, I resumed my duties. Before she left I learned that her name was Lauca and that she was the daughter and heiress of Millalauco. /

[32.43] With nothing pressing us as we returned to the fort, I was talking with the soldiers about the loyalty and devotion of Indian women, many of whom, even though barbarians, had demonstrated such steadfast love and praiseworthy perseverance. Not even chaste Elissa Dido, I told them, had guarded her loyalty to her husband with greater care. / A young soldier listening to our conversation interrupted me to say he didn't consider Dido to be so chaste, since in Virgil's *Aeneid* one sees that consumed by sensual love and pursuing ignoble desire, she had broken her faith with and promise to Sychaeus.[235] / Given the gravity of this insult and the malice of the soldier's objection against the unblemished Phoenician, based on such noteworthy but unreliable testimony, I thought it reasonable to show that he was mistaken, as were any others who shared his opinion.[236] / I explained that the Mantuan poet decided to embellish his hero, Aeneas, because Octavian, Caesar Augustus, prided himself on being his descendant, and that this was why he had used cruel language with regard to Dido, defaming her falsely and unjustly, as we know from the fact

---

235 Sychaeus was Dido's husband.
236 Dido came from Tyre, in Phoenicia, near present-day Lebanon.

that Aeneas preceded Dido by a hundred years.[237] / Surprised to hear me say that Virgil had slandered her, they all insisted I tell them about her life, and thinking thereby to distract myself and lighten our efforts, I was happy to comply. But first I want to give you a more personal reason for doing so, / for here I will speak of a chaste life and of true loyalty offended by public opinion, offering it at this juncture as a remarkable lesson and example. A reputation tarnished for so long is not easily altered, nor such deeply rooted error uprooted from among uncouth, misinformed people. / And since there's nothing amusing between here and the fort and I cannot refuse to tell a story that's so enjoyable as well as historical, as long as it does not annoy you, I would like to use it to fill this idle time, spurring my horse all the while and not losing a single moment. / My harsh, unpleasant subject, so bleak and sterile, together with the narrow road I've been pursuing with such effort, have left me longing for some expanse or open space where I might freely and without fatigue amuse us both. / The disquieting clamor of arms, always the same with no variation, has surely confounded and deafened you, and thus to refresh your weary spirit I will use this tranquil interlude for the following digression, made to measure for the road ahead. / If an insolent and honor-destroying fiction is worth listening to, one that unjustly defames the queen of Tyre's faultless life, should it not also be good to hear the truth, that universal law restoring her honor, wherever it is proclaimed? / What moves me most, beyond the requests I mentioned, is faithful Dido's honor, so carelessly condemned. Whoever is interested in hearing the truth, therefore, lend me your attention and willing ear, for speaking ill

---

237 The Mantuan poet is Virgil, his hero Aeneas, of the *Aeneid*.

of someone, even in passing, is harmful, while the time is always right for telling the truth. /

[32.54] Carthage, as commonly calculated, was founded seventy years before Rome by Dido, an illustrious queen once venerated as a goddess among the people of Tyre, where her father, King Belus, had married her to the high priest and guardian of the great temple of Alcides.[238] Second in dignity only to the king himself, / this was Sychaeus, mentioned earlier, for whom Dido preserved her inviolable loyalty, someone both learned in ritual and endowed with inestimable wealth. That which he amassed for his comfort was the cause of his deplorable death, however, for whatever is coveted by many can never safely be possessed. / Belus left two children as heirs, one, Pygmalion, the other Dido. In his final hours he enjoined them to concord and filial love, and while this lasted during the early days, the brother was soon driven by greed to possess the riches of his brother-in-law, whom he killed by poisoning his food. / Dido felt Sychaeus's death so keenly she could not bear the pain and sent forth great floods of tears in grief-stricken lament. Enveloping her fair face and comely figure in a somber black veil, she bequeathed his body to burial with all the pomp and ceremony of a sumptuous funeral, / and while the magnificent sepulcher was a fitting manifestation of her chaste love, its grandeur did not match the pain and suffering of the queen, who continued to keep her husband's cold ashes company with devout sacrifices and never-ending sighs and mourning, calling upon his unhearing spirit. / "Oh, gods," she would say, "is it right that I'm left behind in such lonely isolation? Alas, the only thing that keeps sorrow from killing me is my own tepid love and loyalty. An evil that's endurable cannot be so great, nor

---

238 Alcides is another name for Hercules.

one beyond endurance last so long! But heaven must want to delay my death in order to prolong my grief, which is stronger." /

[32.60] Although she hid the hatred she felt for her powerful, treacherous brother, with mute fury and frenzied groans she cried out unceasingly to heaven for vengeance. Finding herself alone at times she gave vent to her terrible agony, voicing her repressed rage with a low moan. / "Traitor!" she would say: "Tell me what desperate thought drove you in the guise of brotherhood and feigned loyalty to commit such detestable wickedness against your own blood? If it was an insatiable thirst for riches, you could have taken his treasure but left him his life, tempering your insane fury and impiety with love and respect for your sister. / If you didn't value him as a brother-in-law, you ingrate, you might still have thought of the nefarious sacrifice you were making of your own mother's brother.[239] Having nursed such a horrible crime in your breast for so long, you can't claim it was spontaneous, for no one suddenly becomes evil. / Had I seen any sign of your folly and perverse plans, you wouldn't have had to resort to such cruel, brutal means to acquire the treasure you craved. But an evil ordained by destiny cannot be stopped and, alas, what good does grieving do me now? By the time one weeps it's already too late. / Savage enemy, how could you let yourself be carried away by your passion, so blinded by greed you couldn't see that in killing Sychaeus you also killed Dido? With such an appalling deed you offer the world an epitome of evil, and the story of your abominable treachery will be remembered throughout the ages. / Is it lawful or even conceivable that being a traitor and tyrant, nefarious, perverse, sacrilegious, and homicidal, you also enjoy

---

239 King Belus's wife was the sister of Sychaeus, who thus married his niece.

the name of brother? Seeing me together with you, people will talk and my honor will suffer a grave injustice, for fame rarely speaks the truth. / If I flee, ferocious enemy, I'll provoke you to follow, while if I follow my husband's fate everything you pretend to will be yours. If I stay with you now that you've killed him, however, I tarnish my honor and ruin my reputation, for anyone who forgives so quickly appears to condone the crime. / What remedy must I seek against such grievous evil, since heaven and earth offer none and the inevitable and ultimate one is withheld by fortune to make me suffer even more? Alas! If it's wrong to long for death, it's worse to fear it when it's fitting, and dying isn't agony for the wretched but rather the end of their agony and pain! / Now that being king and on your guard denies me open vengeance, I'll strive to foil your wicked designs through double-dealing and feigned filial affection. And just when you expect to find everything in your power, my sudden departure will leave you deprived of a sister, the treasure, and any legitimacy, the only thing left the infamy of your odious act!" /

[32.69] Thus the grieving queen lamented over the rich sepulcher, leading a sad and solitary life while longing for the right moment for vengeance. Wary of some violence, she wrote to her brother, who was elsewhere, and using all her discretion along with loving, tender language, / she let him know she was weary of grieving and of the solitude she suffered in those palaces where she had previously enjoyed such happy companionship, the memory of which was now so painful. She told him that in order to bring some relief to her sorrow, she had decided to put an end to her mourning and to join him, bringing all her riches and treasure, / and that toward this end he should swiftly and secretly send her a sizable fleet in which she could embark all her people and wealth. With fitting security she could then cross the sea that separated them, which was the only impediment she feared to her ultimate happiness. / Once the ambitious king received the news he had awaited so ardently, he was happier and more greedy than ever, and seeing that fortune was guiding his affairs to an auspicious port, he immediately dispatched a formidable armada of ships well-stocked with men, provisions, and gifts. / The fleet arrived with unexpected speed, and the king's men disembarked and immediately went to pledge their obedience to Dido, who after expressing her pleasure at their arrival took every consideration in lodging them in great sumptuousness and splendor. / When the time was right, vigilant Dido then ordered her own men to load her crated possessions with great fanfare and public show, while hidden by night she had her treasure taken aboard the ship in greatest secrecy, so that no one saw any trace of it whatever. / Sixty chests of heavy sand had been prepared, furnished with sturdy locks and reinforced with double metal plates. These were later brought forth publicly and loaded in full sight of everyone, making it appear they contained the gold, silver, and jewels. / Elissa now boarded the ship amidst the tender expressions of her sorrowing subjects, and having quickly unfurled the sail to a gentle breeze blowing favorably from astern, the vessel cut calmly through the tranquil sea with the rest of the fleet following the lofty flagship's course. / That night and the following day the armada sailed with a propitious wind. When Dido saw that land had finally sunk beneath the horizon and they were on the high sea, she assembled her noble and obedient company on the deck of her ship and directed the rest of the vessels to come alongside so they might also hear. / She then boldly told them that her intention was not to join her malicious, unjust brother, who was now her sworn enemy after being driven by sacrilegious desire to so treacherously kill her Sychaeus in the guise of fraternity. / Instead, wary of his secret perfidy, she had decided to leave her dear, beloved fatherland, kingdom, home, and possessions, and entrusting herself to uncertain seas and winds, to seek a new land and country where far from his tyranny she might live in safety. / Since her wealth had been the cause of her suffering and loss, her husband being murdered for this reason, and since it might also lead to her being pursued, she had furthermore ordered everything brought aboard with the firm intention of casting it all into the sea where it would perish and never come into his power. / She immediately had the reinforced chests filled with sand brought forth and in view of everyone cast into the depths of the sea. The king's ministers, looking on with rueful expressions, were stunned and confused by the audacious queen's extraordinary act. / The gravity of the situation left them speechless and terrified, for they knew the rage of their youthful master, which the loss would only intensify, and in their fear and confusion they could think of no reason or excuse that could shield them from blame or keep him from exercising his fury upon them. / The astute queen had foreseen a ready route by which she might lead her brother's frightened people to her own devotion, and before any delay could occasion a new plan, she quieted them all and addressed them as follows: / "My friends, now that you've seen proof of my steadfast intention with your own eyes and realize how fortune, at its whim, leads me wandering across the vast sea, you can return home, if doing so isn't folly, and bring the king the unpleasant news of the sunken treasure and of my flight to unknown lands and regions. / You've already experienced his violent, ungovernable fury, however, and when he sees you before him without the wealth and treasure he was expecting he'll lower his wrathful arm upon your heads with brutal impatience, and without bothering to listen to excuses or explanations he'll add to his crimes with further guilt and wickedness. / Since the violence and tyranny of a young, wrath-filled king are something to be feared, these being the very things that have wrested me from my dear home and kingdom to seek new lands, any of you who wish to join me will not find yourselves abandoned, but instead will be my companions and share in all the good I'm expecting. / The place and time are auspicious, and my earnest counsel is that each of you, as wise as you are, should choose the lesser of these two evils. If you return to the king none of you will escape, and my sorrow and pity at this prospect urge me to sincerely entreat you to come with me, so that I not be the cause of your punishment. / Imagine the deaths and cruelties sure to befall you and don't dwell on your homes and belongings, for giving up everything in order to live is the right thing to do. Amidst great storms of adversity one thinks only of saving oneself, realizing that possessions are subject to perils and fluctuations." / The anxious ministers listened intently to the queen's arguments, their minds troubled by a thousand thoughts. In the end, while their motivations differed, they all reached the same decision, which was to accompany Dido to the end of her voyage, offering her their vassalage and obedience. / Their loyalty confirmed with vows, which none refused, Dido ordered the sails of the halted fleet be unfurled and a course set for Cyprus. Here, after being graciously received and making known her plans, eighty young virgins from among these Cyprian friends were brought aboard, / so that in times to come they might be married to the devoted men she led in her service. Thus

The Araucana

seeking some suitable land where she might found a city, with a favorable wind the company continued westward on a route to Africa. But given my fatigue, it's necessary to divide this story in two. /

CANTO 33

Don Alonso continues with Dido's voyage and arrival at Bizerte, telling how she founded Carthage and explaining the reason she took her own life. Caupolicán's capture is also described.[240]

Many embark impulsively on the rigorous road to virtue, only to end up afterwards on the busier one to vice, from which it's difficult to return. The path is level and the exit easy from a well-ordered life to one of license, while the route from vice to virtue is more difficult and demanding. / Pygmalion showed signs of good character in childhood, and his fine beginnings promised high hopes of justice and liberality. Perverted by greed, however,

---
240 Bizerte was a coastal city in present-day Tunisia.

he soon changed so completely that he became not only covetous of wealth, but also inhuman, perfidious, and bloodthirsty. / We see this clearly in the treacherous murder of his brother-in-law, who lived contentedly, trusting in fraternal loyalty. Making it worse was the king's apparent devotion to virtue, for no wickedness is as insidious as that which presents a virtuous front. / Matters did not turn out the way he planned, however, but differently and utterly to the contrary, for not only did he not achieve what he sought, but he also lost his men and ships. The queen was sailing westward, as I said, with a wind from astern, touching down from time to time with her ships on the shores of neighboring lands. / Not trusting the shallow Syrtes as she tacked back and forth, she kept her course to the right, passing within view of Licudia on Africa's sandy coast. Navigating from headland to headland, she passed between Djerba and Lampedusa and led by fate's decree came safely with her fleet to Tunis.[241] / Seeing this spacious, fertile region, adorned with fruit-bearing trees, clean air, and a serene sky, the climate apparently quite gentle and mild, and far enough away from her brother that she no longer feared him, she decided to lay the foundations for a city that would become her home and haven. / To this end she quickly came to an agreement with the local inhabitants, according to which they would sell her as much land as could be encompassed by the skin of an ox. Thinking of the profit they would gain from the arrangement, the people settled with the queen on a price and drew up their contracts and conditions. / Payment being made and a site selected, Dido

---

241 The Greater and Lesser Syrtes, two gulfs off the coast of Tunisia and Libya, were known in antiquity for their dangerous sandbanks; Licudia refers to an ancient settlement on this coast; Djerba and Lampedusa are islands off the north African coast.

ordered an enormous, fat ox be found, and after it was skinned she had the hide stretched in her presence. Once this had been cut into the thinnest of strips, it encompassed such a great area that some were inclined to call the queen's prudence and rare acumen deception, / but she compensated them with a premium and left them well-paid and contented. She then revealed to her followers that the rescued treasure was safe, having used the ruse of the chests of sand cast into the sea so that when her brother learned of it he would have no reason to follow her. /

[33.10] Having first addressed problems prejudicial to orderly life, the prudent queen chose magistrates and officials, and bringing in master architects and the necessary materials, she began building the famous metropolis. / The city was constructed on an orderly plan, the fates proving so favorable that it was soon embellished and ennobled with sumptuous, lofty structures. Once the new republic was organized and its laws established, institutions were created enabling the citizens to manage their affairs and live in peace and civil harmony. / Given the great resolve and intelligence with which Dido governed her obedient subjects, the population grew and the limited area of the town expanded. Its trade and pleasant location also appealed to peoples' tastes, and many came from different lands to live there. / In those years paper was not yet in use, being invented only later, and people wrote on animal skins. A skin was called a *carta*, the same word we use today, and so it was that Dido came to name the city Carthage, because it was built on a site measured by the skin of an ox.[242] / Within a short time Carthage grew so

---

242 This invented etymology is based on the Latin *charta*, from Greek *charteis*, which denotes Egyptian papyrus or paper; the actual name is from the Phoenician language.

famous, with such grandeur and magnificence, that the crowds and concourse of its citizens were marvelous to see. The intrepid queen displayed such prudence in governing the population that many other kings and princes adopted the new city's laws. / Her bearing and wisdom were such that the people considered her a goddess, and there was no one of the era to rival her beauty. She thus came to be thought of as something heretofore unknown and as a miracle of nature, and I know of no woman idolized here on earth to whom heaven ever granted greater gifts. / There have been great matrons who were eager for fame and sacrificed their lives, and others who liberated oppressed lands through miraculous feats. Yet never were so many perfect qualities united as in Dido, who was wealthy, beautiful, utterly chaste, wise, clever, trustworthy, and supremely prudent. /

[33.17] Word of this soon reached the ear of high-spirited Iarbas, the king of Mauritania, a bold and courageous young man feared throughout the great expanse of Africa. Driven by the juvenile ardor of a new and unrelenting infatuation, he dispatched the most important men of his council and kingdom as ambassadors to the queen, / asking, in compensation for the torment he suffered every hour on her behalf, that she agree to their felicitous marriage and become the mistress of his person and realm. If not, with justified resentment against anyone who would scorn such a mighty ruler, he would march against her with his army, devastating both her city and her people. / In the senate, where the queen did not wish to be present when the embassy was received, the senators learned simultaneously of the petition and threat. Knowing the faithful queen's vow of chastity and the continent life she led, so counter to Iarbas's proposal, there was great consternation, and / as soon as the elders had heard the arrogant demand they decided to approach the difficult issue through artifice. Appearing before the queen with doleful demeanors, their faces flushed and their eyes downcast as a sign of their displeasure with the embassy, / they told her, "Know that having heard of your fine leadership and governance, amplified by garrulous fame, as well as of the growth of your city, Iarbas, driven by laudable aspirations, is requesting that twenty of your most knowledgeable councilors be sent at once to reform his statutes. / But since it's unfitting that anyone of our age and status should suffer such a troublesome undertaking, leaving behind our dear fatherland and pleasant tranquility to travel to uncouth regions to amend the ancient customs of a seditious people, all of your counselors are refusing to go, excusing themselves with legitimate reasons. / By rejecting this cruel request, knowing we would be giving up our final, cherished serenity with no hope of returning, we have placed the city in grave danger, for very soon we'll have the indignant young king upon us with his formidably powerful army, come to lay waste with fire and steel to your noble metropolis and celebrated renown. / This, in short, is what Iarbas has demanded through petitions accompanied by threats, but our weary senectitude forbids it, and as veterans we're legally exempt. There's no reason, if reason be the measure, that we should leave our homes during the last part of our lives to be exhausted by such strenuous service. / When young we hurl ourselves into danger to win honor, but in our final feebleness it's only proper that we enjoy the rest we've earned and have, at death's uncertain hour, someone beside our lonely beds to tenderly close our eyes and bury our ashes. / And just as it was our duty to bring this menacing demand to your attention, yours is to use all your skill and prudence in readying a response to the Mauritanian king, your prescience forestalling the evil he threatens so that peace is maintained and we are shielded from novel endeavors." /

[33.27] Queen Elissa listened attentively to the artful speech, and while she felt otherwise within her heart, with a regal smile and cheerful countenance she dealt with everyone so affectionately that had their story been true she would have coaxed them from their hearths and homes. / "Cherished friends," she said, "whom I've never once seen so overwhelmed by the fates, for even amidst grave dangers you've always resolutely faced your fortune: how is it that on such an occasion as this, forgetting so many pledges, you'd see your homeland brought to ruin only for the brief inconvenience of a journey? / Everyone recognizes and agrees that as members of a larger union citizens owe the city not only their leisure but their lives, and that obligated both by reason and by a just and natural duty they forego private tranquility for public. / If offering my life were enough to please all-powerful Jupiter on high, an appreciative world would soon see how willingly I offered it! And since you yourselves have spent your long careers on such a narrow and difficult road, it wouldn't be right as these come to a close to erase and undo all you've accomplished." /

[33.31] The senators saw how Dido, borne along reason's road and ensnared by her own speech, had fallen into their ready trap, and exchanging their afflicted expressions for happy ones, they raised their arms and voices, saying, "All of us here approve such timely words! / Your ruling, mistress, is not only just, but extricates us from doubt and a great dilemma, for no argument can withstand the authority of such a decree. Wasting no more time, we'll now reveal what we concealed, since you cannot contravene your own judgment. / Know then, queen, that Iarbas hasn't sent here asking for your ancient, enfeebled elders, for in all matters he maintains his own kingdom and subjects through wise governance and administration. The only thing he desires is you and your gracious companionship, offering in return a thousand advantages, with practical and honorable conditions, in addition to an infinite number of gifts. / Beware that were you to reject this sacred, conjugal union and in misguided judgment scorn his generous offer and affection, Carthage will be razed to its foundations by the swords and fires of his armies, and thus the choice of war or peace is entirely up to you. / If good citizens should cheerfully offer themselves to their beloved country, with what greater rationale and urgency does the law oblige you as our leader to do so, for there's no reason you should refuse to redeem us from our anguish, providing us, additionally, after a happy interval, with the welcome benefit of a successor. / If you're determined to persist in your chaste and sterile plan, consider the prostrate citizens at your feet and the rope now placed around their innocent necks, these very people who renounced their beloved homeland for you based on your promises and commitments, you who pledged to put public tranquility before your own peace and quiet." /

[33.37] The queen felt the enormity of the unexpected demand and proposed solution so sharply that no matter how much she tried to hide her dismay, her face revealed clear signs of it. But with her usual reserve and great prudence, waiting a moment before responding, she spoke to them in a serene and steady voice disguising her great agitation. / "Friends," she said, "to avoid any sign of scandal I would prefer to answer you immediately, before Iarbas makes other demands. But the issue is one in which my dignity and grandeur do not allow such a rapid reply, however honorable you may consider the matter. / It would show frivolity and, even more, a failure of duty and loyalty were I to be dissuaded from my chaste intentions and explicit vows at the first appeal, effacing the inviolable seal of my first love beneath another, newer one. Beset by conflicting thoughts I thus require more time and counsel. / I ask only three months, my friends, in which to determine what should be done to satisfy my people and not make too hasty a decision. The slanderous rabble malign even that which is honorable, and as instigators of laws monarchs have all eyes upon them. / Iarbas will not declare himself our enemy before three months have passed, and by then I'll give a gracious reply to his request. Less time would impugn my modesty and respectability, and it would not be proper for Dido to give some excuse, since that's a sign of error and guilt." / With this the queen fell silent, and a new arrangement had to be made with Iarbas's ambassadors so they would wait the designated time for a decision. Meanwhile, at the senate's request, they remained in Carthage where they were graciously feted with grand receptions and entertainments. /

[33.43] The senate continued to emphasize the benefit and tranquility of the people, but the queen delayed her response while lending them a gracious ear. In secret, meanwhile, she prepared what she'd been intent on from the beginning, which was to end her unhappy life before altering her inalterable loyalty. / When the final, doleful day arrived and the people had gathered in the city's broad plaza, the richly attired queen ascended a lofty dais, at the foot of which a pyre had been built for the customary sacrifices. Addressing the attentive crowd, she said, / "Oh, loyal companions, you who have repeatedly proved yourselves such in all our hardships, renouncing your homes and fatherland to follow my course and fate! Today, in the crowning

Canto 33

conclusion to their adversity, fortune and cruel destiny force me, against my will, to forsake your dear, beloved company. / Leaving behind such loyal friends makes my departure a grievous one, but the celestial gods I've consulted are neither inclined to nor capable of anything else, and having placed in my power a way to divert the great disaster that has frightened all Carthage, I'm determined to pursue it. / Since heaven's cruel decree prevents my being happy, and seeing my city in crisis would require my breaking my faith, I've decided to deprive Iarbas of the object of his misguided love and bring my life to an end, for lacking the cause, everything it entails will cease. / Taking my own life will accomplish this, and while the solution may seem extreme, it's easier, swifter, and requires less courage, and in the end it's private and will cause little harm. With no risk to you the deluded Iarbas will emerge from his error, while I preserve with even more purity the spotless chastity of my widow's bed. / Today, for the price of one brief life, I redeem Carthage from danger and leave behind a precedent obliging you to act as I have acted, for by spilling my pure blood I satisfy both heaven and earth, dying for my city while remaining loyal to my first, inviolable love. / Do not mourn my early death, for heaven approves and applauds it, and brief anguish and an honorable death ensure a life that lasts forever. The Parcae's angry knife may terrify those who want to live, but Dido's dying shouldn't grieve you, since one who kills himself lives as long as he wants.[243] / Good-bye, my friends, good-bye! Now you are free and my husband satisfied . . ." She said no more, intent on completing the terrible deed, but calling the

---

243 The *Parcae* are three mythological female figures associated with destiny: one who spins the thread of life, another who measures it, and a third who severs it, causing death.

name of Sychaeus pierced her chaste breast with a dagger and fell into the flames of the ardent fire. /

[33.52] Dido's death was felt so keenly in Carthage that they mourned her there for many years. In memory of the extraordinary event they raised a sumptuous temple, and for as long as her illustrious city continued to prosper they worshipped her as the country's goddess with cults and sacrifices. / Following the memorable queen's death they renounced the title of ruler, and henceforward the city was governed by a hundred wise and venerable senators. Its throngs of citizens continued to grow, and it finally became so strong and fearsome that at the pinnacle of its power it threatened Rome itself with dire peril. / This is the true story of the famous but defamed Dido, whose history and precious chastity were so thoughtlessly falsified by Virgil in order to embellish his fictions, for we see that the troubled queen, who could have married and not burned, preferred to burn than marry. /

[33.55] Everyone was listening attentively to these strange and remarkable events as we came to the fort, and the narrative and our march ended together. We rested that night, but once morning arrived we had resumed our diligent efforts to gain intelligence about the enemy, / when an Indian whom one of our scouts had taken prisoner, a man by all appearances of bold spirit and prompt hands and feet, swayed by gifts and promises, began to speak. "I've decided to deliver the great Caupolicán securely into your hands this very day," he said. / "Nine miles from Ongolmo, in the middle of dense woods and underbrush, there's a site that's naturally strong and surrounded by marshes and ravines, a place so secure he's only accompanied by ten men as he waits for the rising flood of your good fortune to

Canto 33

run its course. / Using a narrow, abandoned trail where we won't be seen, I'll safely guide your men there through the dark of night, and before day dawns I'll bring you to this hidden dwelling. At the risk of my head I vow that all I've said will be so." / The young man's speech was well received, and given the firmness of his promise a squad of experienced soldiers was immediately assembled, one large enough for any contingency. As soon as it was dark, with the friendly Indian at their head, the soldiers departed in great secrecy, and setting a silent, rapid pace / they swiftly made their way along an overgrown trail, climbing and descending precipitous slopes where the barbarian led them. Once gloomy darkness began to disperse at dawn's approach, the Indian stopped beside a brook flowing from a rocky spring, and turning back to our soldiers told them, / "I'll go no farther, nor can I possibly continue along this path. It's overwhelming, and a terrible fear slows my steps as I imagine the great Caupolicán's enraged countenance upon discovering that I alone am the traitorous soldier who has sold him. / Straight ahead along this arroyo, which you follow although there's no trace of a trail, you'll soon come to his camp in the middle of a dense stand of trees. Hasten to get there before day dawns so the sentinel on the mountain doesn't detect your stealthy approach and my great offense. / Having met my obligation I'll go back, leaving you where I've safely brought you at such risk to myself. Now that you're where you wanted to be you must hurry on, for time, once lost, is gone forever and always a risk. / The site is rocky and obstructed, and if they hear you coming it will be easy for them to escape along a steep cliff, so remember delay is dangerous and pursue prosperous fate, for your enemy is less than a mile away!" /

[33.65] No bribe or promise could make the barbarian take a single step forward, nor was the threat of death or a life imprisoned enough to shake his resolve. Realizing time was short and speed essential, the soldiers left him tied to a sturdy pine and went ahead as he had described. / After a mile, at the entrance to a dark, forbidding wood that rose above a rugged ravine, they came upon a large thatched hut. Its location was fortified by a sheer drop to a river, and nearby were hovels and lean-tos roofed with reeds. / At this point, catching sight of our men from the crest of a hill, the sentinel gave a warning shout to alert the unsuspecting general, but our soldiers, approaching at a run, quickly surrounded the hut just as the fierce Caupolicán sprang to the open door. / Seeing his escape blocked on all sides and the imminent danger to his life, he resolved to force his way forward with his formidable, iron-plated club, as he was accustomed to doing. Grasping it with both hands, he rose on his toes to bring it down more forcefully, but its point pierced a rafter overhead and couldn't be dislodged. / A soldier then stepped forward, and nearing the door dealt a blow to his arm, penetrating the unprotected flesh to the muscle. With this the general stepped back, and realizing the futility of further defiance, admonished his men to give themselves up and not resist in any way. / Stepping outside without his weapon, he assured the Spanish they could safely enter the dwelling, since all of them there were just poor, frightened soldiers fleeing the war, and it was their fear of being attacked by outlaws that had made him rush to the door with his club. / Our men burst in and found eight or nine sizable warriors who surrendered their arms, giving themselves up with every appearance of innocence. After tying their hands behind their backs, our troops divided the spoils they found, guarding the dissembling captain with double shackles and special care. / He assured them with a serene expression that he was a lowly soldier, but his stature and powerful body suggested otherwise. It took some time to get information from the others, all of whom affirmed he was someone of common status and unimportant family. /

[33.73] Our men were eagerly engaged in the permitted pillage, with the usual shouting and no hut not sacked and torn apart, when a woman came running from a dwelling near the top of the ravine and quickly fled through the most impenetrable part of the undergrowth. / One of our black servants darted up the slope and soon caught her, however, for the trail was narrow and overgrown and she was not familiar with it. At her breast she carried a poorly wrapped, perhaps fifteen-month-old infant, a token of his ill-fortuned, captive father, fiercely loved by both his parents. / Unaware she was such an important prize, the servant was nonchalantly leading her back as the soldiers and prisoners began to leave, guided by the sound of the stream, when the grim lady suddenly saw her husband ahead of her, stripped of his insignia and weapons and manacled amidst that common rabble. / Her great pain did not erupt with weeping, nor did she give any sign of feminine weakness, but rather bursting with fury and fierce indignation, holding her child in front of her, she cried out, "The foreign power that bound your effeminate arms would have shown more pity had it pierced your cowardly heart! / Are you that mighty man who only a few days ago was boasting of his deeds, whose voice alone could set the most distant, unknown nations atremble? Are you the captain who promised to quickly conquer Spain and subject the entire arctic hemisphere to the yoke and rule of Arauco's empire? / Alas is me! How deceived

I was in my pride and haughty thoughts, seeing that I alone in all the world was called Fresia, wife of mighty Caupolicán! And now in a single moment I'm wretched and ill-fortuned, for everything has proved in vain, seeing you taken prisoner in this wilderness where you might have had an honorable death! / What of the perilous exploits that cost so much in blood and lives, those arduous, risk-filled campaigns you led with so much courage? What of the glorious victories achieved by those now bound arms? Does it all end with your leaving amidst this lowly mob? / Tell me, did you lack the strength or have no sword with which to triumph over fickle fate? Don't you know that a quick, honorable death ensures a glorious, immortal life? Behold this ill-fated babe, the only thing that will remain of you, since word of your death will no sooner reach me than I'll follow, happy to die! / Here, take your child, the knot with which our love has kept me bound, for this bitter blow and grievous pain have withered these fertile breasts! Take and nurse him yourself since your powerful body has become that of a woman, for I've no desire to mother the infamous son of such an infamous father!" / Saying this and mad with rage, she hurled the tender infant to the ground and turned away in frenzied, furious wrath. In the end, to be brief, nothing, neither pleas nor threats, could make this now cruel mother take back her innocent son. /

[33.82] The soldiers found the child another mother and quickly started back down the trail. Along the way they released the faithful guide left tied to the tree because of his fear, and as the day was ending the long column entered the fort to a joyful welcome and great applause. / Our men made every effort among the Indians to learn with greater certainty if their prisoner was Caupolicán, whose appearance gave every indication of his being.

But neither in nor out of his presence would anyone say he was other than a lowly, unknown soldier. / Later, pressed individually and assured of his impending death, some were more animated, confirming the suspected deception, but when brought before him they recanted with frightened trembling, denying the truth confessed and corroborated in his absence. / Finding himself enchained, imperiled, and unable to hide, he finally dropped this fruitless ploy and determined to try a further, final one. Thus calling on Captain Reynoso, who quickly came to see what he wanted, with a serene and dignified demeanor he told him what the following verses convey. /

CANTO 34

Caupolicán speaks to Reynoso, and learning he is to be executed, converts to Christianity before bravely dying a miserable death. The Araucans gather for the election of a new general; King Philip raises an army to enter Portugal.

Sad, arduous life, subject to such misfortune, and frail prosperity, which never lasts for long! Is there nothing sweet and enjoyable that doesn't turn bitter and unpleasant in the end? No delicacy or delight comes without its cost, and the aftermath of joy is always pain. / How many famous men there've been over the centuries whom long life has dishonored, and whom the world would have thought more highly of had death come sooner. Hannibal is a good example, as is the consul defeated at Pharsalia, who lost not second but first place in all the world by living so long.[244] / Caupolicán confirms this, as well, a famous captain and mighty warrior who achieved military preeminence among the American Indians, only to have fortune prolong his final hour, chastening him so harshly that his sudden, wretched fall was much greater than his rise. /

[34.4] Realizing the loyalty of his people was beginning to waver and seeing his fortune's auspicious ascent in rapid decline, Caupolicán decided to speak frankly with Reynoso. When the captain came to see what he wanted, the barbarian, with everyone gathered around, spoke gravely as follows: / "Had cruel destiny reduced me to such a shameful state before some unworthy captain, this arm of mine, using my own sword, would not have been too weak to open a door for death in my chest and bring life's wretched race to an end! / But deeming you dignified enough to grant me life without disgrace, once that's done I'll concede whatever you want. Don't think I'm afraid of death, for that's something feared by the happy, while I know from experience how difficult life is for the unfortunate! / I am Caupolicán, my rule upended by destiny, yet still with absolute control over the Araucan empire. Peace rests within my power, as does the making and affirming of any agreement, for my authority and jurisdiction encompass the obedience of the entire land! / I'm the one who killed Valdivia at Tucapel and left Purén in ruins, who razed Penco to the ground and won all those battles! But ringed as I am by such triumphs and victories, the opposition of a hostile heaven now places me at your feet to plead for what little remains

---

244 The "consul" is Pompey, who was defeated by Caesar in a naval battle near Pharsalus, Thessaly.

of my life. / While my cause may not be just, remember that he who most forgives is most humane, and even though your passion prompts you to vengeance, my asking you for my life should be enough. Calm your wrathful spirit, for anger in the powerful is unbecoming, but if you're set on killing me, doing so quickly will be humane. / Don't think that if I die here at your hands the State will lack a leader, for there will instantly be a thousand other Caupolicáns, none as unlucky as I! Knowing the Araucans as you do, of whom I am the least of warriors, it would be a mistake to test your fortune anew because mine has fallen so far. / Realize that in mastering yourself you master many and thus restrain your violence and ruinous rage. Anger tests the hero, and forgiveness is the vengeance of the generous. With my death you'll destroy communal peace, so keep your rigorous sword in check, which threatens not only my throat but your own good fortune. / Aspire to greater glory, don't sink in shallow waters, for the only thing fortune requires of you now is that you take advantage of it. Recognize the occasion and grasp your good luck, for now I'm in your power and control, whereas dead you'll have nothing to show for what you've done but a useless corpse. / If this unfortunate head of mine were enough to satisfy you, Captain, I'd extend my neck so that your sword could put an end to my sad fate! But he who hastens his death will find his life eternally damned, especially as mine would disturb universal peace. / You've clearly seen that whether I'm free or in chains, hidden or in public, my soldiers still fear and respect me and everything is still subject to my will. Once I establish Christ's law and we've laid down our weapons, I promise the entire land will come to pledge its obedience to king Philip in my presence. / Keep me securely imprisoned until this vow is fulfilled, for I know that the army and senate will approve of all I do. And should the time and place pass, I can just as well die then, so choose whichever you like, for I'm ready for either." /

[34.16] The Indian said no more, but calmly watching the captain awaited his reply, holding his peace with a steady expression as he asked for precious life or a speedy death. However much hostile fortune tried to humiliate him it could not, for even though defeated and a prisoner, he always maintained his grave demeanor. / Having made his confession, as I have described, he was immediately and publicly condemned, with more rigor than prudence, to being impaled alive and shot with arrows, but neither the prospect of death nor its excessive terms caused any alteration in his noble countenance. While the shifting faces of fortune never managed to change him, however, / God did so in a moment, his powerful hand working within so that in the light of faith and understanding he asked to be baptized and become a Christian. This caused both pity and great contentment among the assembled Spanish. Everyone was truly amazed, and fear ran through the watching barbarians. / On that sad but happy day he was immediately baptized in all solemnity, and in the little time left instructed in the true faith. Then, surrounded by a company of well-armed men, he was taken away to suffer a death to which he consented in hope of a better life. / Naked, barefoot, and bareheaded, dragging two heavy chains and surrounded by armed soldiers, the executioner led him forward by a heavily knotted rope around his neck. A throng of people followed, looking again and again to see if what was happening was possible, which even seeing with their own eyes they doubted. / Thus he came to the scaffold, a bowshot from the camp and half a pike's length above the ground, visible from all sides. With his usual energy and no sign of emotion he mounted the ladder as lightly as if he had been free of his shackles. / Reaching the top he turned his serene expression from side to side and stood there a moment looking at the vast numbers of the immense crowd, which stupefied by the incredible event watched every moment in rapt astonishment, aghast at what fortune had wrought. / He advanced on his own to the stake where the appalling sentence would be executed, from all appearances as though that terrible calamity was nothing at all. "Since fate and destiny have readied this death for me, " he said, "let it come. I ask for it and I want it, for no evil is great if it's the last." / The diligent executioner, an ill-clad black, immediately approached. Seeing him about to carry out the sentence, the barbarian, who with such patience had suffered every insult until now, could not endure this further one, even though it was the last, and raising his voice loudly said, / "How can an honorable Christian condone something so outrageous, where a man as important as myself is put to death at the hand of someone so vile? Dying alone should suffice for even the most guilty, who in the end pays for everything with his life, whereas using such measures with me is not punishment, but inhuman vengeance. / Isn't there a sword here among the many so frequently unsheathed against us, which familiar with our wretched throats can with one blow sever mine? Fortune may test its power on me today in many ways, but it won't succeed in having the hand of a brute touch the great general Caupolicán!" / With this he raised his right foot, even though it was encumbered by chains, and dealt the executioner a kick that sent him tumbling a good distance below, badly hurt. This impatient act rebuked and his sudden anger abated, they proceeded to seat him without resistance on the point of the sharply tapered stake. / However deeply the penetrating post dug

Canto 34

into his bowels, boring into his body, was not enough to make him give in to the intense pain, but with a serene expression, not moving a lip or an eyebrow, he remained as calm as if seated on his wedding bed. / Straight away six chosen archers, having readied themselves at thirty paces, slowly drew their bows one by one, and even though practiced in every evil they wavered in loosing their arrows, fearful of laying a hand on such a man, someone of such great authority and renown. / But cruel Fortune, having done so much already and with so little left to accomplish, sent the course of any erring shot straight ahead, and soon his chest, no part left intact, was pierced by a hundred arrows. Thus was that great spirit released, which fewer wounds could not have accommodated. /

[34.31] I sense the cruelest and most hardened listener moved to compassion upon hearing of this barbarous deed. I was not present for it, my Lord, having set out on a new conquest of a remote and never-visited people, but had I been there the brutal execution would have been stayed. / The victim's eyes remained open in such a way that the Indians looked at him as if still alive, for even now pale, grisly death could not disfigure him. Their fear was so great that they dared not fail to respect him, nor were there any among them so brave as to not be frightened in his presence. / Swift-flying Fame spread word of his unthinkable and ignominious death throughout the land, giving rise to agitation and disquiet. Incredulous throngs soon came running, dubious, anguished and bewildered, their hearts troubled, to see if it were true that he was dead. / The number of those coming down from the surrounding hills and neighboring districts was so great that they formed a vast, dense circle covering all that open area. Nor would they believe their own eyes without also touching him with their hands, and even after touching him it seemed to them like something from a dream or fantasy. / Neither the humiliating, senseless death, carried out to terrorize them, nor the loss of such an important figure, which is what we had hoped, either frightened or cowed the people. Instead, provoked by that injury they aspired to cruel satisfaction, filled with new rage and even greater wrath. / Some rabidly thirsted for vengeance because of the insult and dishonor received. Others, greedy with hope, were already laying claim to the authority and position of command, and before any lull could calm the excited people they fanned the flames of war, inciting the entire land to fury. /

[34.37] If I had to describe the boasting of Tucapel, Rengo, Lepomande, and Orompello, of Lincoya, Lebopía, Purén, Cayocupil, and Mareande, not even many pages would suffice and a longer book would be required, for each of them strove passionately to be chosen. / But the cacique Colocolo, seeing the danger of so many claimants and knowing few whose prudence and wisdom were equal to the great responsibility, interposed his venerable gravity, sending diligent messengers to each of the chieftains summoning them to council at a solitary, hidden location. / Those wanting to shorten the wait immediately prepared for the meeting, and many, worried about arriving late, hastened their preparations and travel. Others, even though they had other plans, did not refuse so as not to reveal them, and thus not a single man failed to follow the wise Colocolo's advice. / All agreed to come alone and without any commotion, bringing little, so that their enemies might have no indication of this new assembly. They also saw to it that Indians everywhere diligently and cunningly solicited the peace we had always offered them, adopting humble attitudes and feigned contrition. / A place and time having been set in a spacious, secluded valley, the warriors invited by the senate arrived at the location. Among them was

CANTO 34

Tucapel, determined to be chosen through good or ill, as well as others less qualified whose innermost thoughts were equally clear. / I hear new arguments breaking out among them, great discord arising, and hearts swelled with ambition. Old hatreds and rivalries erupt, and proposals and opinions differ with no sign of how they may be reconciled, each man's ranting based on his own inclinations and the strength of his arm. / Once they had entered into council, as I have noted, with all the caciques and nobles assembled with their insignia and accessories, armed according to ancient precedence, Colocolo, the wise and prudent elder, seeing their flushed faces, let some time pass and then began to speak. /

[34.44] If it will not tire you, my Lord, before I continue with what Colocolo said I want to change direction and take a different road toward the southern pole, for even though there remains much to tell you, the subject I embark on here will help inspire my flagging voice, wearied by everything demanded of it until now.[245] / Therefore if you will allow me to return to this matter later, although the way is long and roundabout I now will hurry after don García, who had been diligently reforming the kingdom's troubled towns so that justice and governance might be firmly reestablished. / After crossing Villarrica's fertile plain with its great volcano to the south, Vulcan's forge as they call it, which continually belches fire, he turned rightward, and having traversed that region came at last to the great channel and vast lake marking the furthest point reached by Valdivia.[246] /

---

245 The narration interrupted here resumes at Canto 36.43.
246 Valdivia's expedition into southern Chile in 1546 is described in the poem's opening canto (1.55.1 ff.); the Villarrica volcano, one of Chile's most active, made international news with eruptions in March, 2015.

Following in his footsteps and not resting a moment I went there as well, along with many others from the surrounding towns experienced in conquests and campaigns, until a warlike tumult arose, its deafening din echoing across the frightened region. / Carried on agile winds and dispersed far and wide by Fame, the harsh sound reached the ears of the most remote Indians, who were deeply troubled and fled this new clamor like fearful sheep scattered by the howls of wolves. / No gloomy veil of rapidly gathering clouds or sudden bolt of lightning that rends the heavens, wrapped in thunder and searing flames, not even an earthquake that shakes the ground, upset and frightened the people as much as the horrifying tumult of war now confounding the entire region. / Some say the Spanish are destroying herds and crops as they advance, some that they're pillaging towns and killing the caciques; others claim they're dishonoring noble wives and compelling their cloistered daughters, along with other insults and depravities regardless of status, sex, or age. / Disorder grows with every detail embellished by fame, and whatever their fear envisions they take as true. The only uncertainty is how they can save themselves, and this torments them. Some rush away amidst the cries; others turn back, believing the reports but resolved on nothing. / Later, when overpowering fear left room for reason, the bewildered people regained control of themselves, and contemplating utter destruction, gathered to consult about what might be done to remedy the situation. /

[34.53] Among the diverse assembly was an experienced soldier named Tunconabal, a man of courage and insight well-versed in Araucan ways. Exiled from his home because of some dispute, he had returned to private life and fled the tumult of war, / but now seeing the great fear and confusion of the agitated

CANTO 34

crowd, which without hearing a trumpet or seeing a single soldier was being frightened by its own hue and cry, he gathered them all in a suitably spacious location, and once the noise subsided began to speak to them as follows. / "Friends," he said, "I needn't tell you of the danger in which we find ourselves because of this perfidious enemy, who's already at our doors, nor of the great fear debilitating us all and driving us to relinquish our lands and liberty to the tyrant, to whom we offer free entry. / Behind what moated wall or parapet, or to what fort or citadel, which might last even one hour, can you retreat in this crisis? Yet if you turn and face him you'll be offering yourselves naked to his swords, for this sudden fury has caught us without weapons, discipline, or a leader. / These cruel and terrifying men with beards, usurpers of everything good, are stalwart, invincible, and victorious in all they undertake. Hurling bolts of lightning with a horrifying roar, they fight from the backs of great, swift beasts that are fearless, ferocious, and governed by thought alone. / As you have neither strength nor rampart with which to defend against such weapons, cleverness must compensate for weakness, protecting you from future ills. Make a show of timidity and meekness and promise them safe passage, as you would a neighbor or ally, for a promise made under threat means nothing. / Then, in the brief time that remains, quietly take your clothing, provisions, and herds to the furthest outposts in the mountains, leaving behind such a scant amount of food that they'll see the region as a sterile, intemperate place inhabited by a poor, wretched people. / Faced with such poverty and meager spoils, these insatiably greedy men will undoubtedly change their minds and renounce their useless enterprise, and once the lack of people and provisions makes them leave, we'll guide them through brambles and sheer slopes to a place from which they'll not easily return. / You have the narrow Ancud pass, closed on all sides by rocky crags and undergrowth with which nature hinders any contact with the outside world. Even animals cannot penetrate this vast, rugged forest, and birds of the sky find it difficult to cross in flight. / Led to this area, I've no doubt that seeing the dangerous high mountains will temper their desire and they'll hasten to turn back, and should they want to find a way around them they'll have to move on, leaving our apparently wretched region free of their intolerable insolence. / Even though such a journey endangers my life and liberty, I'm ready to set out with a destitute company to meet these men along the way, where clad in coarse clothes and feigning ignorance and joy, I'll give them some wretched gifts revealing our indigence. / Perhaps, seeing the great effort required and little fruit to be gained from this poor, sterile land, with its miserable tributes and rustic race of people, they'll alter their plan, which is to seek for wealth and riches, and be forced through our cunning to turn their weapons and attention in other directions." / The Indian had not yet finished speaking when voices arose in loud approval without a single dissent, and hastening to implement what the council had found fitting, they took away their belongings, provisions, and herds. / With his customary speed don García had already arrived at this final frontier, the last day's march bringing him to the boundary of the area known until then. Placing his foot on this line as he halted his rapid advance, he said, should hearing it not annoy you, what the next canto relates once the page is turned. /

CANTO 35

The Spanish set out to explore the new territory. Tunconabal meets them and advises them to return, but realizing they will not, provides them with a guide who leads them into rugged wilderness where they suffer terrible hardships.

What hills will hope of profit not make plane, what difficulties not overcome? What heart is so loyal or resolve so sound as not to be infected and corrupted by it? It destroys human relations, nor is there any harmony it will not disturb nor entrance so narrow or door so tightly shut it will not breach and leave ajar. / It loosens the tightest bonds of kinship and fraternity, turning friendship to enmity and delightful love to loathing. Source of calamity and evil, it overrules reason and alters fate, makes ice hot, fire cold, and rivers run uphill. / Thus it led so many soldiers down endless roads and through countless dangers, across deep gulfs and never-sailed seas, never stopping to rest, unto the farthest, unknown regions of the world. And wherever along these remote and barren byways the goad of gain brought them, they scrutinized whatever the earth's great globe might contain. /

[35.4] I told how don García arrived with a seasoned company at Chile's southern frontier, beyond which no one had ever passed. Setting his foot on the line that divided these two new worlds, he spoke the following words, which being present, I listened to attentively: / "Invincible people whose hearts remain undaunted by dangers or insufferable hardships, by angry seas, hostile winds, and a thousand other vexations, nor even by the elemental powers and stars, for having forced your way through them all you've now arrived at the end of the earth! / Behold here another new world which the heavens have kept hidden until now, the difficult way forward conceded to your efforts alone. See before you the certain prize for such great effort and how much Fortune promises, for being the authors of such a magnificent enterprise will make you lords without limits! / Garrulous Fame, racing to the ends of the earth, will assign your exploits first place when telling of ancient ones, for two vast worlds having failed to contain you, you now come to conquer a third where your mighty spirits can flourish without constraint! / As the occasion is so favorable and requires few words, I don't want to delay your fortune nor waste more time in speeches. Onward! All as one let us take possession of these new regions and realms upon whose entry the fates have readied such riches and glory!" /

Canto 35

[35.9] Scarcely restrained by his address, the throng of men instantly moved forward upon this new land untrod by outsiders, and at a regular but lively pace we began our first march, stretched out in a long, orderly line on a rarely-used trail. / We walked for some days without any clear direction, guided only by the course of the sun, and when our way was blocked we forged trails that frequently ended in precipitous cliffs. Our elusive, lying guides tricked us into areas where it seemed the largest giant could neither have pressed forward nor turned back. / The Prime Mover had already sped the sun westward in its track, warming humid Pisces as the earth completed four turns, when descending a steep slope we suddenly caught sight of a group of ten poorly clad Indians passing rapidly through the dense undergrowth.[247] / Weathered by the sun, wind, and rain, they wore long, thick fleeces and short pants cinched with rope. Broad in the chest, with muscular necks, they were rustic, brutish savages, fierce in attitude and appearance, with dark eyes and skin, their nails uncut and their hair in long tresses. / A robust elder was at their head, half of whose body was covered by a ragged mantle of coarse wool attesting to their wretched poverty. This man, as I noted earlier, was Tunconabal, who would try to change our minds and plans with feigned counsel and reasoning. / We immediately advanced on them, suspecting they were fugitives from the mountains, but cutting across our path they continued quickly up the slope and stopped at the base of a lofty crag near a twisting, tumbling stream. Here

---

247 In the Ptolemaic system, the outermost sphere or Prime Mover was seen as impelling the celestial bodies in their paths from east to west. Here the sun's annual passage through the sign of Pisces, which occurs in February, is described as having begun four days previously.

they awaited us without fear, placing their bows and arrows on the ground. / The elder called out in a loud voice, speaking a strange language our interpreter understood. "Unfortunate people," he said, "led by false reports to these mountains where serpents and wild beasts can scarcely keep themselves alive, and where even barbarians sustain themselves on nothing but wild roots! / What malicious report has incited your invincible spirits and what harmful counsel made the impossible seem easy? Control your acquisitiveness, however worthy, for the undertaking is dangerous, and once misled there's no doubt you'll all die a miserable death. / Even if you don't meet warriors obstructing your path, you'll find one mountain range after another, and one dense forest and then another and then a hundred more, as well as a landscape so harsh that the lack of pasturage and nourishment, together with the infected air, produce a sterility inhibiting all living things! / Although you see me here transformed into a brute and reduced to sylvan life, know that I was once a soldier and also wore armor. And thus by the regimen I once professed, seeing you lost like this prompts me out of pity to advise you to turn back and go no farther. / These barren clearings and dense forests, which continue all the way to the frigid south, will surely be the end and burial ground of all your successful expeditions. Behold the figures of these savage men who inhabit them like wild beasts and the scant provisions they provide, of which I present you with a pitiful offering." / From a bag of seaweed plaited into a kind of netting, he then took some native mountain fruits, tough, green, and tasteless, some dried meat of wild animals, and other rustic foods, including locusts and lizards cured in the sun and myriad kinds of filthy insects. /

[35.21] The strange spectacle of these barbaric people with their great rusticity, fierce appearance, and obstinate attitudes amazed us, as did the density and ruggedness of the mountains and the products of that wretched soil and barren, empty land, uninhabited and so far from any intercourse with neighbors. / We asked the old man if it would be mountainous ahead were we to continue that way. Smiling, he replied that it was even more rugged and precipitous and said that with the mountains growing so high it was both reckless and impossible to force one's way through such dense forests and undergrowth, placed there to protect nature's secrets. / But seeing our ambitious spirits, always ready to press forward, and realizing his maliciously offered advice would not make us turn around, he assumed a sorrowful expression and with a gentle, affectionate attitude, stopping to think for a moment, affirmed that nearby there was indeed another, more passable way. / On our right, toward the west, was a trail once used in ancient times that was now hidden by scrub. This route kept the mountains to the left, and while our men could safely follow it, the territory was so vast and uninhabited that he himself would provide us with an experienced interpreter and faithful guide. / We welcomed this proposal, for some of the men were already starting to hesitate, and having accepted his gracious gift we offered generous ones in exchange: a cotton mantle, dyed red, a bushy fox tail, fifteen beads of colored glass, and twelve tinkling bells. / These gifts having pleased the old man, such trinkets being admired among them, once the diligent guide arrived and everything was ready we made our departure. For two days the Indians followed us and then turned back by another trail, leaving their companion in charge. /

[35.27] The guide constantly assured us of great riches, herds, and villages, encouraging our beleaguered spirits with false reports. "When Phoebus has made six rotations bringing light to these regions," he said, "I promise you, on pain of my life, to satisfy your desires." / I cannot exaggerate our arrogance and lively, cheerful spirits, our hopes for wealth and treasure, our futile plans and vain talk. Mountains, cliffs, and rugged crags turned into pleasant, level roads, and dangers and exorbitant efforts no longer troubled our imaginations. / Unconcerned about food, we went on crossing summits and deep valleys, entire mountain ranges, fabricating lofty fantasies and chimeras in our busy minds. Thus complacent and contented we passed the first three days, but on the fourth, as the sun set behind the mountains, our lying guide abandoned us. / At this alarming sign, misgivings troubled even the bravest, seeing the scheme unmasked and our rigorous travails now multiplied. But finding ourselves in trackless wilderness and threatened by grave danger, hungry and exhausted, did not delay us even for a moment. / On we went, farther and farther into denser forests and thickets, forcing our way through the impassable growth with axes, machetes, and hatchets. Some of the men, using pickaxes and spades, broke up rocks and tore out deep-rooted scrub so that the shying horses, prodded forward, might steady their fearful hooves. / Never had nature thwarted man's passage with as many obstacles, with trees as high as the lofty heavens, nor had so many brambles and deep woods ever joined forces with as many crags and marshes as they did along this path hemmed in by woven underbrush and trees. / The sky conspired against us, as well, shedding a paltry, turbid light obstructed by foreboding clouds, turning day into murky night, and defending the way forward with hailstorms and cloudbursts of such ferocity that the heavens' war exceeded our earthly ills. / Buried deep in the undergrowth, some called for assistance; others, enmired in muddy swamps, cried out for help. Some climbed, others tumbled, skinning feet and hands and faces. Vain shouts could be heard here and there, with no one to come to their aid. / It was pitiful to hear the screams, to see the obstacles and obstructions, the horses that collapsed, exhausted, the mangled legs and broken arms. Our simple, frail clothes were torn to tatters by thorns, and ill-shod and ill-clad, protected only by our armor, we were covered in blood and sweat and mud. / In addition to these insufferable exertions, the lack of nourishment caused wretched, nagging hunger to tighten the bonds of our torment. The dubious benefit and all-too-obvious injury undermined our courage and strength, and a cold sweat sapped the vigor of our weary limbs. / Then, recalling the glory our efforts promised, our hearts would reinvigorate our bodies, and disdaining the difficulties fight back against the formidable obstacles, making everything yet to come seem easy. Thus does valor reveal itself most clearly as obstacles increase. /

[35.38] Fed by hope alone and forcing our way forward by sheer strength, the army finally emerged beneath the hidden skies for which we'd been searching. Thickets thinned; tree-locked forests, unweaving their interlaced branches, began to grant us easier passage. / First on one side and then the other precipitous cliffs and towering slopes lowered their lofty summits, allowing light to enter, and the thick, icy fog exhaled a dense wet vapor, thinning enough that vision could penetrate it. / For seven days we wandered, lost, using our swords to open a way forward, with no place to rest our weary bodies in all that time. Finally, one morning, we caught sight of the spacious, fertile plain of Ancud, and at the foot of the rugged mountain the long shoreline of an enormous lake. / Before us lay a vast archipelago scattered with innumerable charming islands, with gondolas and pirogues passing swiftly back and forth from side to side. A desperate sailor in the midst of tossing waves never saw a harbor with as much joy as we beheld the scene before us, / and instantly falling as one to our knees, filled with new joy and gratitude, we gave thanks to God for rescuing us from danger and misfortune. Forgetting our many hardships, we pursued this auspicious development, setting off with high hopes and in lively spirits toward the pleasant plain. / The sick, injured, and maimed, the lame and one-armed, the crippled, ill-clad, barefoot, tattered, and faint of heart, the emaciated and starving, all were encouraged and imbued with new strength and courage, the entire earth now seeming assailable and the conquest of heaven itself an easy matter. / In such high spirits, as we descended the rugged mountainside to the lakeshore, we came upon the little crowned fruits of the sweet myrtle, which even though a wild mountain plant and not yet ripe, at that moment were so delicious that heavenly manna and the fleshpots of Egypt could not have excited us more.[248] / Like a cloud of locusts sent to plague mankind, silently cutting their way through fertile fields of grain and not leaving behind a single kernel, just so, spreading out in small groups, our men moved across the broad plain, leaving the fullest myrtles despoiled of fruit and leaves and branches. / Some, goaded by tormenting

---

248 A number of early explorers describe the beneficial effects of myrtle berries, which were frequently made into wine; experiencing hunger during their exodus from Egypt, the people of Israel long for the "fleshpots" or cooking pots to which they had grown accustomed (16 Exodus 3).

hunger, ate the berries by handfuls. Others, not waiting to pick them one by one, devoured twigs and leaves. Some shunned sharing with their companions, seeking a hidden spot where they could consume the branch they had torn away, stripping it with rapacious fingernails. / Like a flock of hens that leave their pen for the field, where they diligently search all about for any wheat lost from the granary, and one of them, scratching and pecking, finds a buried morsel and runs off with it pursued by the rest, / just so the man with a full branch, pursued here and there by the others, immediately fled to a more secluded place where he could eat undisturbed. No one who found anything shared it, for that was not a time for sharing, nor was charity, even though they possessed it, extended to their neighbors. / Thus we were enjoying that rustic meal when a swift, curved gondola arrived, propelled by twelve long oars. Once it had run firmly onto the shore, the skilled rowers and other men leapt fearlessly to the ground in a frank show of friendliness. / But if you wish to know who these men were and what had brought them there, for the present I cannot tell you, since the long road has exhausted me. Therefore it will be best to pause my account and recover my strength, tiring you less as well. /

CANTO 36

A cacique comes ashore and offers the Spanish all they need for their journey, but the route ahead is soon blocked by a great channel of water. Don Alonso crosses this in a piragua, accompanied by ten soldiers, after which they return to their camp and follow a different road back to La Imperial.

Whoever sees many lands sees many things people consider fictions, the more marvelous they are the more prudent it is the less one speaks of them. Yet even though it's best to remain silent about improbabilities and avoid the danger of doubt, I declare that here on earth I found Truth, however much it is said to have risen to heaven.[249] / Shunned in all our lands, it had withdrawn to this remote region, where cunning, deception, and artifice had never yet found welcome. But leaving this aside, I return with the promptness I promised to the boat filled with men that beached itself on the sand. /

[36.3] A robust and gracious young man now approached us, accompanied by some fifteen others. The apparent leader of the group, he had black, curly hair and white skin, and as our scattered company gathered around he smiled and, greeting us courteously, began to speak in a grave, modest manner in his strange language: / "Men or pastoral gods born of these sacred groves and mountains, brought forth by celestial influence from their harsh, impenetrable bowels: what chance or fortune brings you by such unknown paths to our poor corner at the end of the earth, still free of strife and turmoil? / If your plan is to seek more ample lands and there's anything you need, you'll find every comfort and provision generously provided as you travel the country hereabout. / If you wish to settle here, we'll give you land where you can live; if the mountains delight you more, we'll safely escort you there. Whether it's friendship you want or you're looking for war, we can offer you either with equal ardor, so choose which you prefer. I myself would choose peace and friendship." /

[36.7] The grace, manner, and attire of the genteel young man were very pleasing, as were the eloquent speech he so gallantly addressed to us, his generous offers of hospitality, and the impressive stature and appearance of his men: light-skinned,

---

249 The poet is referring to the myth of Astrea, the goddess of justice, often associated with truth, who fled earth for the heavens, as recounted by Ovid in the *Metamorphoses* (1.150).

well-proportioned, and clad in cloaks and flowing tunics. / Their heads were covered by peaked caps of fine, curly fleece of varied hues, pulled low on the temples and hanging down behind, their richness a sign of the land's cold climate. / We thanked the youth for his offers and gracious good will, extending ours in return for his well-being, however we might be useful, and finally making known our needs, including the distress that hunger was causing us, asked for food and drink, for which we promised to pay. / Realizing our extremity, he immediately ordered his men to bring whatever was in the gondola, which he freely shared with our starving company, not only not asking for anything in return, but not even wanting our thanks. / Reinvigorated and our hope restored, we then set out along the shore in orderly ranks, and after proceeding for more than a league established our first camp close to the water at a site that appeared both spacious and protected. / We hadn't yet settled ourselves when a swift piragua approached, and then others from other directions, all cleaving through the frothy waters loaded with corn, fruit, and fish, which restored our destitute men without anything asked in exchange or any account being kept. / The sincere goodness and affection of these simple people made it clear that greed had not yet penetrated their mountains, nor had wickedness, theft, and injustice, the common sustenance of wars, made it here to corrupt natural law. / With our usual insolence, however, destroying everything we come into contact with, we soon opened the way for them, offering them ample entry and abundant space, and once the people's ancient customs were corrupted by new abuses, greed planted its standard here more firmly than anywhere else. / News of us spread through the islands that night. The next day two caciques arrived to congratulate us on our arrival, bringing magnificent gifts of refreshments and foods, as well as a fleecy sheep and two vicuñas, caught by hand in the mountains. / They were astonished to see men unknown to them, white, ruddy-faced, with thick hair and beards, who spoke and dressed differently from them. They stared at our spirited horses, controlled in their fury, but what frightened them most was the stupefying blast of gunpowder. /

[36.17] Setting out to the south, we followed the water's winding edge, making note of terrestrial degrees. The farther we went the broader the vast archipelago grew, revealing a great number of islands off in the distance. / Many caciques arrived to look at us as at something miraculous, none of them of such scant means as to appear without some kind of gift. One brought a fine, large mother-of-pearl bowl, another a curly sheep pelt. This one presented us with a bow and quiver, that one with a horn, another with a strangely colored shell. / Always inclined to inquiry and to learning about the unknown, and seeing that my star had already led me through so many perils, I boarded one of the agile gondolas accompanied by some of the young men and crossed to the nearby principal island, which appeared to be flat and populated by simple folk. / Here I saw Indians, dwellings constructed of simple walls and roofs, cultivated trees and plants, fruits, grains, and vegetables. I noted what was significant about the people, their rites and customs, dealings and occupations, and the laws under which they lived so dutifully. / I visited two other islands, walking along their fertile, green shores, and circled several more accompanied by small boats, whose occupants gave me detailed explanations of heretofore unseen marvels until darkness and a cool wind brought me safely back to shore. /

[36.22] The army pushed on the next day, the third of our journey, the end and furthest point of which we reached after marching three hours, for here the immense lake emptied into the sea through a deep, swiftly-moving channel, whose current and great breadth prevented our proceeding any further.[250] / A profound sadness and immense disappointment came over the soldiers' faces and spirits, seeing our route blocked by that vast waterway. Even led by their bridles the horses could not breast the powerful current by swimming, nor was a narrow piragua able to withstand its force. / As for returning the long way we had come, reason suggested it was impossible that a single man would survive the terrible hardships, while remaining in that place was unthinkable and the brash idea of pushing farther south against all advice and common sense. / Seeing our anguish, a young Indian who spoke some words of Spanish cheerfully offered to show us a different, better way back. The men could hardly contain their joy, and we resolved to set out immediately, having already seen signs of the frigid southern winter. /

[36.26] Since my cherished goal had always been to see this enterprise to its end, however, I outfitted one of the boats with rowers and crossed that great strait of churning water accompanied by ten companions, all bold and resolute men. Relying on the sheer strength of our arms and agile oars, we reached the opposite shore exhausted, / and having no interpreter or information set out haphazardly across the sandy soil. The rocks and areas of dense woods soon made walking difficult, and realizing the project was perilous and that pushing ahead would be folly, we returned to the piragua and crossed back over the

---

250 This waterway appears to be the Chacao Channel, which separates mainland Chile from Chiloé Island.

Canto 36

swirling channel. / To satisfy my desire to always advance ever farther, I then pretended I was going to leave a marker in that area, something important to explorers, and having gone some five hundred paces away and wanting to leave a suitable sign, in the bark of the largest tree I could find I used my knife to inscribe the following: /

> *Reaching this point, where no one had ever come before, don Alonso de Ercilla was the first to cross this channel in a small, unballasted boat with only ten men, in the year fifteen fifty-eight, on the last day of February at two o'clock in the afternoon, as he returned to companions who had stayed behind.* /

Arriving at the camp where the others were waiting to set out, with cruel winter already threatening the desolate countryside, we were led by the friendly, knowledgeable Indian in a rapid, cheerful march, along a trail that however obstructed seemed easy compared to our earlier one. / The barbarian islander, never wavering in his intentions, kept his promise and led us out of that region through the dense, deep forest I have described. I pass over this quickly to avoid being tedious, brevity being best in spite of the many hardships we endured. /

[36.32] Reaching La Imperial, we were welcomed by its generous residents with various foods to satisfy our ravening hunger, and with so many spirited young gallants in the town a tournament was organized where each might show his mettle. / An unexpected incident marred the festivities, however, and in a rush to judgment I found myself condemned to death and my throat exposed to the keen-edged axe. My heinous crime, exaggerated by rumors, had only been to lay my hand on the hilt of my sword, never once unsheathed without good reason. / This led to my being exiled, in amendment of the initial sentence, and to a long period of confinement, during which, armed with patience and hard steel, I served on the frontier night and day, for in spite of having been wronged I never missed an engagement.[251] / Here there were constant alarms and bloody skirmishes, deadly ambushes, fights, assaults, and pitched battles, and the clever cunning and singular strategies of our enemies, most of which were ineffective, although some caused difficulties for us. / But after the great battle at the Quiapo stronghold, where so much mail was destroyed and barbarian blood spilled, once the rampart was rebuilt I hastened my departure, for the affront I had suffered grew fresher each day, constantly agitating and gnawing at me.[252] / And thus it was, in a sturdy trading ship whose sails were hoisted for departure, I left that land and ungrateful realm which had cost me so much blood and effort, and with no surprises or delays and the Auster at our backs, sometimes skirting the coast and sometimes moving out to sea, we reached the celebrated Callao de Lima. / I was there when our soldiers began their campaign up the mighty Marañon, where Lope de Aguirre, more brutal than Nero or Herod, had put so many friends to the sword,

---

251 In the context of potentially rebellious soldiers, placing one's hand on the hilt of a sword in the presence of a senior officer was considered a capital offense. The situation described here, which arose from an argument between the poet and another soldier, was misread by the young commander, Garcia Hurtado de Mendoza, who on appeal commuted the original sentence to exile and a prison term.

252 Quiapo or Quipeo was a fortification that exchanged hands several times between the Spanish and Araucans.

including his own beloved daughter, for no other reason than that they might all die together.²⁵³ / And even though he was more than two thousand miles away, across uninhabited wilderness, being accustomed to long journeys I immediately headed there by ship, arriving in Panama on the very day news arrived of the tyrant's defeat and death, my hurried efforts proving in vain.²⁵⁴ / I was waylaid in Tierra Firme by a strange, lengthy illness, but after recovering I returned by way of the Azores to Spain, where I had only been a short time before traveling to France, Italy, and Germany, to Silesia, and to Moravia as far as Pozsony, a city on the Danube in Pannonia.²⁵⁵ / More than once I crossed these regions and many others on difficult roads, meeting and conferring with people of different nations, witnessing unusual events and situations, singular institutions, rare animals of the earth and sea, and lands never watered by heaven as well as others condemned to eternal rain. /

[36.42] How is it I have turned away so quickly from my intended route? How could I have forgotten my promise and the account of Arauco already begun? If your pleasure has not been sated, I want to resume that abandoned project, striving to speak of things whose enjoyment will excuse their telling. /

---

253 Aguirre was a conquistador who led a notoriously bloody rebellion against Spanish authority in Peru; he was killed and the rebellion suppressed in 1561, as the next octave recounts.

254 While Spanish forces set out to intercept Aguirre by way of Peru's Marañon river, Ercilla sailed to Panama, from where he planned to travel south.

255 The isthmus of Panama was known in colonial times as the Province of Tierra Firme; Pozsony is a former name for Bratislava, in present-day Slovakia; Ercilla's European travels were in service to Philip II.

I'll return to the council, which, as I said, had begun at the agreed-upon location with those notable caciques embroiled in disagreements and confrontations. I will tell of the election that proved so contentious, recounting how, in the end, they came to an agreement, and also of assaults and skirmishes and battles, all of which require more space. /

[36.44] But what am I doing? And why am I seeking out wars among unknown Indians in the farthest, hidden reaches of the world, exhausting my weary mind, when I constantly encounter armies here at home, war's strident tumult resounding in my ears as they consume the whole earth with their fury? / Here I see all Spain aroused, abristle with its victorious armies, and France, agitated and acrimonious, unfurling its resentful banners. In Italy and distant Germany I hear the loud beating of drums, and in every nation the assembling of men, equipment, and weapons. / In order to speak of such bellicose clamor and commotion, I need new strength and courage, my Lord, as well as your favor. Reckless daring has brought me to a great gulf, but with your help I have firm hope of bringing my weary ship to shore. / Should my humble style cause my timid voice to falter, the subject reassures me, promising to be heard with gracious attention. Therefore, my Lord, about to begin such a great journey, it will be prudent to marshal my troubled spirit as it gains vigor from my theme. /

CANTO 37

In this final canto war is discussed as a nation's right, and the war King Philip waged against the kingdom of Portugal is explained along with the warrants he provided the Portuguese justifying his armies.

I sing the wrath of the Castilian people, moved by justifiable anger and prerogative, and their right to the Lusitanian crown consigned to bloody arms: peace, unity, and the bonds between Christians transformed to raging discord, with both sides' angry lances hurled at kindred breasts. / War came from heaven, sent among mankind once our nature was corrupted by the forbidden fruit. Peace is conserved and human insolence constrained by war, which God uses to afflict the world from time to time in order to punish, admonish, and amend it, / oppressing and humbling the pride of insolent rebels, defeating and destroying the mighty, and setting limits on limitless ambition. War is the people's right, and the order and discipline of armies preserve and sustain states, maintaining civil law. / Yet war becomes unjust when peace is no longer its goal, or when it's begun in a blind rage or for vengeance or some private end. Concord being public, public must be the cause that disturbs it, and by no means can a single limb be allowed to destroy the peace and harmony of the whole body. / Just as we profess our brotherhood and fellowship in God, so earnestly commended by Christ in his eternal New Testament, peace and the bonds that bind us can only be dissolved by public purpose or dispute, and only through the authority of the king their defender.[256] / Then, like a faultless angel whose gaze is fixed on the common cause, a soldier may take up arms and inflict his wrath upon the enemy, and if some personal consideration or motive restrains him, not only does he imperil the enterprise but errs against and offends the public right. / Similarly, in a just and licit war the conquering army can injure, imprison, and kill the defeated, forcing those previously free into slavery and obedience: for he who is lord and master of a life is equally so of the person, doing whatever he wants with the loser since everything is conceded the winner. / And as in all times and places of common cause a man can blamelessly bear arms in skirmishes or formal battles, the same reasoning permits one-on-one combat on foot or on horseback, armed or unarmed, whether in open fields or in the lists. / In just war a challenge is just, being subject to the authority of the prince beneath whose hand and dominion rest public order. If it is a private or personal matter,

---

256 The passage references scripture such as John 13:12-17 and 15:12-13.

however, such combat is denounced and rebuked, for whether one provokes or accepts the provocation it is illicit, unjust, and condemned. / Christian princes should never favor nor authorize arms when raised in hatred, vengeance, or rivalry, which are proscribed, nor should they decide or test a case by relegating the judgment to force, since for unknown reasons the guilty sometimes emerge victorious. / Judgment by bloody arms is thus rightly condemned since its outcome is uncertain, as ordained by highest Providence. Whether an outcome is happy or sad is not what makes a cause good or bad, nor is the justice of anything ever to be left to chance or fortune. / A soldier has no obligation to inquire as to whether a war is legitimate and beneficial or justly or unjustly incited. As ruler of the state and the one who rightly receives the obedience and service of the army, it is for the king alone to examine the common cause. / And since the weight and grave responsibility for war rest upon the sovereign's head and whatever harm and evil issue from it fall squarely upon his shoulders, he should carefully consider whatever he undertakes, and before giving free rein to fury, justify the arms he has readied and not incite them out of avarice or ambition. /

[37.14] Thus it is in the present circumstance, where compelled by inescapable obligations and in support of the law, Philip has taken up licit arms. He does not base his right on strength nor is he driven by an avidity to rule, for his scepter and monarchy extend as far as the course of the sun. / Instead, free of ambition and avarice, which corrupt and contaminate even the healthy, and summoned by right and justice, he marches in person against a rebellious realm. Scornfully disdaining the malice that denies him and impedes his receiving the crown, he has resolved, sword in hand, to facilitate an entry denied to reason.[257] / Yet even though moved by just indignation he dissembles his power, justifying his claims and weapons with a prudent and patient spirit while restraining his arm raised high to strike, delaying the bloody cure that afterwards will brutally crush the rebels' haughty obstinacy. / With his mighty, wrathful hand he will bend the traitors' arrogant necks to the yoke, destroying the formidable armada of French pirates that protects them, and following the death of their leader, Filippo Strozzi, all those who have disturbed the peace will be put to the sword with righteous severity.[258] / This blood will not tarnish his mercy, being the blood of a perfidious enemy, for when crime and insolence are severe, he who punishes them is merciful and compassionate. Pardoning wickedness authorizes worse to come, and he who forgives everyone of everything is as cruel as someone who never forgives at all. / When rigor is fitting forgiveness is not merciful, and he who punishes a present evil avoids being cruel in the future. Whoever does not prevent wickedness consents to it and can be called its accomplice, just as those who excuse the wrongs of public officials pervert and corrupt the state. /

[37.20] I do not mean that clemency is not a fine quality and estimable virtue, for to forgive is a glorious victory, the more

---

257 The situation described arose after the death in August of 1578 of Sebastian I of Portugal, who left no heir; Philip's claim to the throne was based on his mother, Isabella of Portugal, being the eldest daughter of Manuel I (Sebastian's great-grandfather) and older sister to Henry, mentioned below; as the canto goes on to state, Sebastian was also the son of Philip's sister, Juana of Austria, and thus his nephew.

258 A Spanish fleet commanded by the Marquis of Santa Cruz defeated the French, led by Strozzi, in the Azores in 1582.

laudable the more powerful one is. But the common peace so beneficial to all cannot endure without justice, and the timely use of rewards and punishment sustains commonwealths and states. / Not all excess and evil that exist can be remedied or punished, for time and circumstances sometimes require that matters not be rushed or pursued. A prince who wishes to understand this should know that he is obliged to forgive a great deal, for it is a cruel and rigorous medicine that strips flesh from bone in every situation. / Clemency pacifies the hatred and indignation of enemies. It engenders devotion, produces friends, and wins the love and affection of a people, while continuous, harsh punishment defames the prince and makes him abhorrent. Thus comes the proper duty and attribute of kings to mitigate the sharp edge of the law. / There would be no reason to conceal past wrongs if the perpetrator didn't gain more courage for new offenses and misdeeds. Fear of punishment restrains harmful inclinations, and seeing a criminal hung from the gallows chastens wickedness and redresses evildoers. / But punishment should also not be applied as by an ignorant, unskilled surgeon, who when the illness is mild and the wound slight takes his knife to what is healthy, damaging with his festering incisions what would have healed without being touched. No treatment or cure is beneficial if worse than the ailment. / I want to be clear, since some will say I contradict myself: punishment is a virtue when required and should be public. But it is also virtuous for the powerful to forgive the offense when it is personal, or if amends can be made without punishment. / Little by little I am going astray, and time being short and my topic long, rather than make things easier I am taking a greater load upon my weary shoulders. Abridging what is least important and most burdensome, I will now turn my pen back to Portugal and provide a brief account of it. /

[37.27] What is this, oh Lusitanians? What delusion prompts you to interpose your obstinate chests, taking up forbidden weapons to violate laws and rights? Are your depraved spirits moved neither by collective peace nor the public good, nor by obligations, religion, or Philip's own power and grandeur? / Behold the generosity with which he has guaranteed your wealth, liberties, and exemptions, constrained not by necessity but at the head of a formidable army with its battalions, and how he has restrained the murmur of their weapons in order to persuade you with words, like a dutiful father leniently leading an unruly child to obedience. / What blind pretension or fantasy, what stubborn, foolish passion disturbs your reason, confounding your judgment to the point that a nation united by sacrament as symbolized in the Cross of Christ, having taken up cruel, murderous arms, does injury to its own entrails? / The same banners and insignia emerge from opposing camps, leading countless foreign nations to the spilling of innocent blood, introducing errors and the contagious habits of insolent vices, the spreading pestilence of which will leave all Catholic Spain infected! / Eternal, sovereign Father, I implore Your grace and beseech you to inspire my hand, since everything moves in and through You, so that I may impartially grant the Portuguese and Spanish what each is owed, without any personal consideration or other bias diverting me from what is just. / And since You know our hearts and the honorable zeal inspiring mine, and since all good intentions and actions have their beginning and end in You, grant me sufficient spirit, endowing me with the language to inform my reckless pen, which dares to undertake so boldly and with so little facility such a great enterprise. /

[37.33] Sebastian, the Lusitanian king, wanting in his juvenile ardor to invade the vast region of Africa and subdue its pagan impudence, quickly assembled his realm's treasure, strength, and soldiers, his lofty intentions promising an easy campaign. / King Philip, seeing his nephew incited so capriciously, opposed these wayward plans with a true father's counsel, and seeking to divert him from a route that led to such a great precipice, he arranged for them to meet in Guadalupe to discuss the matter. / The grave uncle's forceful arguments, pleas, and efforts at persuasion did not prevail, however, any more than the great multitude of obstacles, enough to reverse a river, or the exposing of so many men's necks at once to the whims of the inconstant goddess, always eager to turn the world upside down. / The arrogant youth made promises where well-founded fear saw difficulties, and brushing aside prudent arguments and ignoring all objections pursued his will, hastening his own death and destruction, for no counsel or warning could do anything against heaven's decree and fatal sentence. / Be their voice ever so agile, who will now sing the lamentable outcome, the bloody, wretched end of such a poorly-led enterprise and army, the irreparable ruin of a kingdom whose ancient fame was lost in just one day, all through the willfulness of an ardent youth governed by chance rather than reason? / Let someone else speak of that dismal day, whose wretchedness exceeds even the saddest, for even though my pen is bloodied it cannot recount so many misfortunes. If heaven on high grant me strength, I want to continue on the road I've begun, for here as well I sense a great, turbulent cloud beginning to form. / After the young monarch so impulsively attacked the African army and died fighting in blinding, dust-filled turmoil and chaotic confusion, as Fortune brought down four kings in one furious oscillation and extinguished the fame and renown of countless men, overwhelming the western armies, / Portugal immediately swore in Henry as its ruler, an ordained priest and cardinal, the brother of Sebastian's grandfather. A man of great religious zeal, the burden of his years and infirmities made him more fit for heaven than earth, however, and by offering him the kingdom, destiny left him with little life and no successor.[259] /

[37.41] Mighty Philip was deeply distressed by the death of the king and the realm's misfortunes, and as the nephew of and successor to the ailing Henry, a man of advanced age and ill-assured life, he wished to clarify his right of succession to the crown and its titles, being the closest relation by way of collateral descent. / With zealous and praiseworthy foresight he therefore assembled the most learned, Christian men, possessed of great intelligence and devoid of self-interest or ambition, so that in conformity with conscience and what was right, rather than by tortured reasoning or other routes, they might consider whether or not his relationship supported his claim to the kingdom. / For her part, Catherine, the duchess of Braganza, was claiming that as the daughter of prince Duarte the kingdom should rightfully pass to her. Don Antonio was also disputing the crown, and although the common people favored him, due to his illegitimate birth he

---

[259] Three kings are known to have perished in the battle of Alcácer Quibir, which took place on August 4, 1578: Sebastian I; Muhammad II, the former sultan of Morocco, who had fled to Portugal upon being ousted to seek assistance in recovering his kingdom; and Al-Malik I, Muhammad's uncle, who had overthrown him; as noted earlier, Henry was the brother of Isabella of Portugal, Philip II's mother.

was excluded.[260] / Once the investigation had been conducted as befitted such an arduous business, each of these men was to give his opinion freely, without regard to anything else. Having used this opportune period to prepare for greater difficulties, if the realm proved resistant to reason, Philip's powerful armies would then vindicate themselves. / All the councilors clearly saw that according to law and ancient privileges, the collateral line not following the father, the closest legitimate relative should succeed, the male preferred to the female and the older to the younger, such succession and prerogative being by right of blood rather than inheritance. / Don Antonio having been excluded and set aside by human law and divine rationale, the rights of Philip and Catherine were each examined with equal care. Both were descendants of equal degree from the same stock, he the nephew of Henry and she his niece, he male and she female, he a feared king, older and more highly born. / Attentive to these facts as well as to ancient privileges, customs, and many other arguments, all of which were adduced in an honorable, just, impartial, and wise spirit, they unanimously declared Philip the successor by right, and in keeping with the law adjudicated to him the realm with its lands, seas, and titles, along with any states conquered in the name of the crown. / The justice of his cause having been declared by so many worthy men did not fully dispel the hatred and ill-will of the emboldened commoners, in many of whose hearts was rooted an endemic and ancient enmity. The king therefore continued to assess the people's spirits and intentions, / and filled

---

260 Catherine of Guimarães, duchess of Braganza, was the daughter of Duarte, the sixth son of Manuel I (and thus Isabella's and Henry's younger brother); Antonio, prior of Crato, was the illegitimate son of Luis, Manuel's second son.

with compassionate zeal and desiring public calm and the good of the realm, pondered how he might douse the enkindled flames, seeking every possible way to quiet the widespread unrest that began to openly manifest itself in the absence of any constraint. / Toward this end he quickly chose Cristóbal de Moura, in whom he recognized so many of the requisite qualities for such an important matter: born in Portugal of noble blood and someone who as a vassal of the Portuguese king could instill in him an assurance, hope, and confidence equal to Philip's own. / Once fully informed of the honorable intentions the Spanish king had so frequently expressed, Henry would understand the basis and strength of his cause and declared right, advanced not by violent means nor by some disordered desire to rule, but by the rigor of justice itself, by law, reason, ancient privileges, and nature. / As one would expect of such a just ruler, once he recognized this and reflected on the great danger in which his fathers' realm and Christianity found themselves, he would consider himself well served to calm the disturbances among his own people and would declare in a fitting manner that Philip was his just and legitimate successor. / With this the emboldened citizenry would cease their tumult and scandalous disorder and his declaration would put an end to the great insults and to further injury, assuring that for the remainder of his happy years and in accordance with its statutes and customs, the realm would pledge itself to Philip as its legitimate heir apparent. /

[37.54] Upon making the embassy and setting forth Philip's proposed intentions, Cristóbal received a lukewarm hearing from Henry, who gave him a frivolous and ambiguous answer, and however clearly the manifest justness of the King was represented, tried to justify himself with pretexts rather than clarify the dispute or declare his position. / Faced with the prolongation of such a difficult and important issue, as a result of which popular impudence continued to gain strength, Philip then sent Pedro Girón, the duke of Osuna, together with the learned Guardiola, providing them with new proposals and sufficient authority and power to achieve a resolution. / Emphasizing the danger posed to the two realms' common peace and benefit by further delay, they were to make clear with greater insistence how essential it was amidst the discord for Henry to clarify his position in a decree, eliminating any pretext for a thousand plots.[261] / And in order that nothing remain undone and no expedient left untried, before the hidden rancor could erupt and blind passion upset the two states' peace and tranquility, Philip also sent two eminent and illustrious members of his royal council. / One was Rodrigo Vázquez, a man of prudence, rectitude, learning, and statesmanship, of great perspicacity and experience. The other, no less competent and famous among the learned, was the doctor Molina, both of them exceptional, distinguished, and held in the highest esteem.[262] / All this was done so that Henry, having been fully informed by them and all his doubts satisfied, might instruct the *Cortes*, already in session, of Philip's rights, and the obstinate and impassioned citizenry, made aware of the general advantages as well as the promised liberties and privileges, be brought to his devotion. / But while the aging, prudent ruler knew this to be in the common interest, the kingdom passing directly to his nephew by explicit law, he kept the issue in suspense by long, impertinent delays during which his subjects and states might gain greater advantage. / As the indecisive and procrastinating

---

261 Pedro Téllez-Girón; Juan Cristóbal de Guardiola.
262 Rodrigo Vázquez de Arce; Luis de Molina.

king was postponing any response or resolution, however, death's own swift resolution, established by the Author of all life, came to him. Due to the population's stubborn rebelliousness, the successor was then forced to assemble his armies, conjoining power and justice against their malicious intrigues, / and having previously sought every possible means to peace, to appeal further to their obstinacy and resistance with promises, privileges, and gifts. Despising the proffered benefits and making clear their enmity, the intractable people still closed the door against reason and what was right. / Who could describe for you the many scenes I see before me now: such clamor from sounding trumpets, so many standards trembling in the wind, the bloody weapons readied by the Portuguese and Spanish, their equipment and machines of war, the battles on land and at sea! / Amidst the ferocious arms are issues of right and justice, examples of mercy and grandeur, obstinacy and intractable enmity, magnanimous liberality and generosity that swelled the bags of the greedy, along with other vivid hues and colors that bring joy to writers. / Henceforth let those who are inspired continue to sing, enriching their harmonious verses, for Philip offers them abundant, fertile material and an open, spacious field. A favorable occasion and good fortune are worth far more than fruitless labor, labor as fruitless as mine, which has always led to barren emptiness. /

[37.66] How many lands and nations I've traveled, traversing the frozen north and conquering the antarctic's unknown antipodes below! The climates through which I've passed and the changing constellations, navigating innavigable gulfs, extending your crown, my Lord, all the way to the frigid austral zone! / And all the journeys you've made by land and sea on which I've never failed to follow you, to Italy, Augsburg, and Flanders, and to England, when that realm asked you to be their king. From there, to serve you further, war's furious clamor drew me to Peru, where so many swords had been unsheathed against you in unbridled fury. / Once the rebellious Indians were punished and the realm reduced to obedience, I moved on to remote Arauco, which had angrily shaken the yoke from its neck, and as soon as it was subdued by a lengthy war and subjected to odious domination, I immediately pursued the conquest of even more distant, heretofore unseen lands. / In order not to tire you I leave aside the immense hardships and all I suffered, the hunger and thirst, the heat and cold, the irremediable lack of clothing; the mountains I crossed, the mighty rivers, the empty, unexplored deserts; the risks and dangers, the crises and adversities still waiting to be told.[263] / Nor do I speak of how, in the end, owing to a young, impetuous captain, I was unjustly taken to the scaffold to be publicly beheaded, nor of the long and senseless confinement I was subjected to so unfairly, nor of a thousand other miseries more difficult to endure than death itself. / My will to serve you never wavered and is even stronger today, and yet my shattered hopes are foundering, finding myself always struggling against the current, and my weary ship, after such a long and arduous journey, still fighting adverse fortune as it comes to port so far from its goal. / Even though my stubborn star now has me discouraged and humbled, in the end the difficult course I have run, following the right road, will become clear, and while misfortune may press even harder, a reward lies in having been merited and honors not in being received but deserved. / The

---

263 The earliest edition of Part III of the poem did not include Cantos 35 and 36, which describe the hardships of the expedition to southern Chile.

cowardly disfavor that relegates me to such misery slows and suspends my hand, forcing me to halt my pen. Thus I bring this to an end, for another talent and voice and other accents are better suited to the vast, uncountable sum of your lofty thoughts and accomplishments. / Since my ship cannot be far from its last harbor, nor can the wisest pilot ever know his feared and final port, in the little time left I want to finish what I should, before my uncertain life's uncertain course, wandering and dissolute for so many years, comes to an end. / It has taken a long time and I've waited until the end to return, yet I know very well it is never too late at any time or place to come back to God, whose mercy is never artful, nor should the great sinner ever fear, having so good a God, whose nature is to forget the sin but not the service. / Having devoted the best years of my life to the world, pursuing vain hopes along rough roads, I now see how little benefit I've gained and how great the offense I've given God, and recognizing my error, henceforth have reason to weep and sing no more. /

END OF PART III

ERCILLA'S INDEX OF NOTABLE EVENTS IN THE POEM[264]

14 Spaniards come to join Valdivia	C. 4:9

A

Ali Pasha, commander of Turkish armada, speaks to his troops at Lepanto	C. 24: 28
Andrea:	
fights with Rengo	C. 14:46
fights with Orompello	C. 25:49
Andresillo, the *yanacona*:	
explains his deception to Captain Reynoso	C. 31:5

---

264 Ercilla attached an index of "*cosas notables*" or notable events with each installation of the *Araucana*. The three are combined here.

    promises to help Caupolicán and the Araucans   C. 31:21
    enters the Spanish camp with Pran   C. 31:26
Andalién river   C. 1:60
Angol, cacique, his death   C. 9:80
Arauco, the important valley of, from which the State
    derives its name   C. 2:16
Arauco and the Araucans:
    customs and practice of war   C. 1:12
    government   C. 1:10
    council of war in valley of Arauco   C. 8:11
    council of war in the valley of Ongolmo   C. 16.39
    their festivities and games   C. 10:11
    decision to burn their homes   C. 29:5
    the caciques gather to elect a leader to
    replace Caupolicán
        C. 34:38
Austria, don Juan de, his speech at Lepanto   C. 24:11

B

Barbarigo, Antonio, his death   C. 24:83
Battles:
    Andalicán   C. 22:9
    Tucapel fort   C. 2:68
    ambush in which Valdivia and his soldiers are killed   C. 3:22
    Andalicán hill   C. 5:9
    Concepción   C. 9:46
    Mataquito   C. 14:8
    Millarapué   C. 25:17
    Purén ravine   C. 28:53
    attack on Spanish camp in Tucapel valley   C. 31:45

Biobío, the famous river   C. 1:62

C

Cañete, Marqués of:
    aid sent to Chile   C. 13:15
    chastisement of Peru   C. 13:3
Cárdenas, don Bernardino de, death   C. 24:73
Carthage:
    its founding by Dido   C. 32:5
    the senate speaks to Dido   C. 33:21
Caupolicán:
    the unusual test by which he is elected general   C. 2:35
    speech to the senate   C. 16:42
    pacifies conflict between Peteguelén, Tucapel,
    and Rengo   C. 16:61
    reviews the Araucan army   C. 21:28
    challenges don García de Mendoza   C. 25:7
    sends Pran to spy on Spanish camp   C. 30:43
    speaks with Andresillo about attacking the Spanish   C. 31:12
    ruined, disbands the army and remains secluded   C. 32:24
    his capture   C. 33:67
    speaks to Reynoso; his confession   C. 34:5
    outburst on the scaffold   C. 34:25
    his death   C. 34:19
Chile:
    location and provinces of, along with the
    State of Arauco   C. 1. 6-11
Concepción:
    arrival of Spanish reinforcements from Peru   C. 16:18
    agitation among the citizens   C. 7:1-31

the Spanish abandon the city   C. 7:11
   sack of the city   C. 7:46
   burning of the city   C. 7:54
   the Spanish return to the fort   C. 9:38
Colocolo:
   his speech to the Araucan war council   C. 8:33
   reconciles Tucapel and Leucotón   C. 11:15
   mollifies the caciques during the election of
   a new General   C. 2:28
   his speech to the senate   C. 16:62
Crepino fights with Mareguano   C. 20:56

D

Dido, queen:
   her story as told by don Alonso de Ercilla   C. 32:54
   her lament over Sychaeus's ashes   C. 32:59
   flees her brother, Pygmalion   C. 32:70
   casts her wealth into the sea   C. 32:80
   speech to her brother's ministers   C. 32:84
   her response to the embassy sent by Iarbas   C. 33:28
   her death   C. 33:51
Duels, their universal condemnation by law   C. 30:1

F

Fitón:
   his cave and pharmacopeia   C. 23:48
   his garden   C. 26:46
   his tour of the globe   C. 27:6
Fresia, wife of Caupolicán, her barbarous behavior   C. 33:76

ERCILLA'S INDEX OF NOTABLE EVENTS IN THE POEM

G

Galbarino:
    amputation of his hands   C. 22:45
    his speech to the senate   C. 23:7
    his speech to the warriors prior to battle   C. 25:35
    his death   C. 26:37
Glaura:
    found by don Alonso de Ercilla   C. 27:61
    saved by Cariolán   C. 28:25
Gracolano:
    attacks the Spanish wall   C. 19:5
    his death   C. 19:12
Guaticolo, old soldier living in the wilderness, Fitón's nephew   C. 23:35

I

Itata, fast-flowing river   C. 12:43

L

Lauca, an important young woman, whom
    don Alonso de Ercilla finds badly wounded   C. 32:32
Lautaro:
    turns against the Spanish   C. 3:34
    named Caupolicán's lieutenant   C. 3:84
    takes Tucapel's part in his dispute with the caciques   C. 8:56
    the Spanish attack his encampment outside Santiago   C. 11:54
    his conversation with Marcos Veaz   C. 12:9
    returns to the Itata valley   C. 12:36
    his speech to his soldiers   C. 12:48
    his and his lover Guacolda's dream   C. 13:44

his death   C. 14:17
Lepanto, the naval battle of   C. 24:6
Father Lobo, his death   C. 9:76

M

Maule, the famous river   C. 1:60
Mallén, the cacique, his death   C. 15:55
Doña Mencía de Nidos, the famous woman   C. 7:20
Mendoza, don García de, speech to his soldiers   C. 21:52
Millalauco addresses the Senate   C. 17:6
Miracle witnessed by the Araucan army   C. 9:13

O

Diego Oro, father, death   C. 3:50
Diego Oro, son, death   C. 9:78
Ortiz, his death   C. 9:73

P

Penco:
   the Spanish build a fort on the hill there   C. 17:23
   attack on the fort   C. 19:3
Peteguelén's death   C. 19:36
King Philip:
   his right to and justification of force
   regarding Portugal   C. 37:14
   moves against Portuguese rebels   C. 37:61
Pran:
   reveals himself to the *yanacona* Andresillo C. 30:49
   his death   C. 32:15

Q

Quilacura, cacique, his death	C. 28:20

R

Rengo:
chases Juan and Hernando Alvarado and Ibarra	C. 9:93
wreaks havoc in the Spanish camp	C. 14:37
wrestles with Leucotón	C. 10:48
fights in the swamp at Andalicán	C. 22:34
reconciliation with Tucapel	C. 30:23

S

Saint Quentin, the attack on	C. 18:5

Storm at sea:
overtakes the ships coming from Peru	C. 15:68
aboard the *Capitana*	C. 16:5

T

Tegualda:
found by Alonso de Ercilla	C. 20:28
she tells don Alonso de Ercilla her story	C. 20:36
festivities held in her honor	C. 20:41
finds her husband's body	C. 21:7

Tucapel, the warrior:
kills the cacique Puchecalco	C. 8:44
fights the entire Spanish army	C. 8:47
disrupts festivities in the valley of Arauco	C. 11:17
his argument with Peteguelén and Rengo	C. 16:50
comes to Rengo's aid in battle	C. 25:67
attack on Penco	C. 19:31

fights with Rengo in the arena   C. 29:24
the fight with Rengo ends   C. 30:7
reconciliation with Rengo   C. 30:23
Tucapel, the fort:
   battle of   C. 2:68
   the Indians gain entry to   C. 2:65

V

Valdivia:
   his entry into Chile   C. 1:55
   his reluctance to engage the enemy, knowing, as a good
   captain, the danger involved; his speech to his soldiers   C. 3:11
   taken prisoner before Caupolicán   C. 3:64
   his death   C. 3:68
Villagrán, Francisco de:
   breaks through the roadblock with his horse   C. 6.41
   overwhelmed by his enemies   C. 5:54
   attacks Lautaro in his stronghold in the
   Mataquito valley   C. 12:65
Villagrán, Juan de, his death   C. 14:38

Villagrán, Pedro de, attacks Lautaro in his stronghold   C. 11:46

W

War as the people's right   C. 37:7

INDEX OF EXTENDED SIMILES

Like a hungry alligator that sees a school of fish (3.24)

Like a stag on a shimmering summer day (3.39)

Like a fleet-footed wolfhound,
    rushing through the undergrowth (4.36)

Just as a famished lion spots its prey from afar (4.49)

Like a skilled drummer preparing courageous
    soldiers for battle (4.63)

Like a fiery stallion that sees a rival draw near (5.6)

Like a herd of mountain goats driven into a
    narrow ravine (6.13)

Like a flock of crows scattered in flight across blue sky (6.26)

Like fearsome Typhon straining to throw off the massive
    mountain (6.48)

Like someone who dreams of being inside a vast arena (6.53)

Like bleating lambs separated from loving ewes (7.15)

Like a father who prudently tries to persuade his son (7.29)

Like a band of black starlings on a mound of golden wheat (7.45)

Like thrifty ants prudently preparing for winter (7.53)

Like a fencing master expertly wielding a
    two-handed sword (8.49)

Like opposing rivers that rush to meet (9.61)

Like a watchful tiger that sees a swift, muscular leopard (10.43)

Like a falcon on the bank of a river (11.9)

Just as when a wolfhound and ferocious mastiff bare
    their teeth (11.11)

Index of Extended Similes

Just as when bulls are about to come out fighting	(11.58)
Like some mighty river that bursts its floodgates	(11.66)
Like a storm that rather than slacken keeps growing in fury	(11.84)
Like criminals who never enjoy a moment's peace	(14.10)
Like timid deer that cautiously raise their necks	(14.21)
Like a valiant bear harassed by hunters	(14.49)
Like two mastiffs surrounded by small yapping dogs	(14.52)
Like fish in a draining lake	(15.46)
Like a great whale shaking its body	(15.74)
Just as birds, taught by necessity	(16.35)
Like the indomitable fury of a sudden flood	(18.11)
Like a shaggy Libyan lion bursting through a timid mob	(19.31)
Like a splendid soaring hawk that spies a heron high above	(20.14)
Like a sudden, terrible wind that comes sweeping across a dusty plain	(22.13)

Like a bristling wild boar that once it is wounded (22.38)

Like a shimmering comet bursting boldly
    through dense air (24.20)

Like an infuriated, hamstrung bull, bellowing with
    its tongue out (25.66)

Like a black, wind-swept cloud, which lashed by
    Zephyr or Vulturnus (25.74)

Just as when one sees the angry heavens (28.58)

Just as an experienced hunter, having scouted
    his prey and terrain (31.47)

Like a narrow, well-charged mine (32.9)

Just as when countless clouds begin to take shape (32.18)

Like a cloud of locusts sent to plague mankind (35.45)

Like a flock of hens that leave their pen for the field (35.47)

GENERAL INDEX

A

Actium 307
Adam von Dietrichstein 244
Aetna, Mount 73, 87
Africa xlii, 244, 302, 311, 428, 430, 432, 479
Albania 311
Alcácer Quibir 480
Alexander the Great 356
Alexandria 315
Algiers 310, 315, 323
Al-Malik I 480
Ancud 453, 461
Andalicán ix, 18, 23, 66, 69, 103, 282, 286, 295, 297, 453, 461, 488, 493
Andalién 17, 488
Andalot 240. *See also* François de Coligny
Antarctica xix, 8, 15, 37, 176, 356, 484
Apollonius, Rhodes 355

Argonautica 355
Arabs 311
Araucan women
  Fresia xx, 442, 490
  Glaura xiv, xx, 352, 368-71, 375, 491
  Guacolda xx, xxvii, 181-82, 186
  Lauca 420, 491
  Tegualda xii-xiii, xx, 251, 267, 273, 275-76
Araucans
  Ainavillo 17, 26, 282, 300
  Alcatipay 30
  Andicano 339
  Andresillo xv, 393, 401, 403-07, 409-11, 416, 487, 489, 492
  Angol 18, 24, 26, 60, 106, 120, 125, 488
  Bobadillo 40
  Brancol 267
  Brancolo 337
  Canio 75
  Caniomangue 120, 126, 282, 382

Cariolán 372, 374-75, 491
Caupolicán ix, xiii, xv, xx, xxix, xxxix, xli, 23, 27-32, 44-45, 47, 49-51, 64, 101-04, 106, 109-10, 112, 114, 118, 133-35, 138, 144-45, 219, 222, 232, 275, 279, 283, 295, 329-32, 341, 381, 384, 396, 399-404, 406-08, 413, 417, 138, 440, 442, 444-45, 448, 488-90, 494
Cauquenians 17, 281
Cauténians 283
Cayeguano 30, 32, 120, 136-37
Cayocupil 22, 24, 26, 126, 282, 450
Chilcán 120, 126, 159
Colca 192, 199
Colocolo viii, xx, xxxviii, 20, 22, 24, 26, 30, 106, 111, 145, 223, 278, 283, 300, 382, 450-51, 490
Corpillán 75, 188
Crepino 271-72, 490
Crino 134, 198
Cron 191
Curgo 283
Elicura 22-23, 27, 50-51, 54-55, 107, 120, 126, 225, 282
Eponamón 14, 108, 111, 115, 406
Fenistón 258
Fresolano 369-71
Friso 369
Galbarino xiii-xiv, xx, xxix, 285, 293-95, 334, 347-48, 491
Gracolano xii, 232, 252-55, 491
Guacol 281
Guacoldo 189
Guacón 58
Gualebo 268

Gualemo 22, 26, 280-81, 382
Guamán 81
Guampicolo 258, 283
Guancho 75
Guarcolo 300
Guarcondo 190
Guaticol 45, 192
Guaticolo 300, 327, 491
Lambecho 283
Lauco 191
Lautaro viii, ix-xi, xx, xxvii, xxxv, xli-xlii, 36, 50-52, 60, 64-67, 69-71, 73, 91-92, 94-96, 102-03, 105, 110-11, 119-23, 130, 141-42, 144, 146-50, 152, 155-68, 173, 180-87, 190, 223, 491, 494
Lebopía 22, 26, 120, 126, 258, 450
Lemolemo 22, 24, 27, 62, 112, 120, 126, 225, 280, 382
Leocán xli, 29, 48, 100, 107, 144
Leocato 47
Lepomande 120, 126, 134, 280, 450
Lincoya 22, 24, 27-28, 55, 57-58, 60, 105, 123, 225, 282, 288, 342, 344, 347, 382, 450
Llaucos 282
Longomilla 258
Mailongo 81
Mallén 201, 492
Mareande 40, 120, 126, 134, 280, 450
Mareguano 22, 66, 125, 268-70, 283, 490
Millalauco xii, 225-28, 230, 420, 492
Millalermo 280
Millo 283

GENERAL INDEX

Narpo 58
Nivequeténians 283
Nico 189
Ongol 22
Paicabí 22, 26
Palta 30, 76
Pantoja 76
Paynaguala 44
Penconians 17, 283
Peteguelén xii, 23, 105-06, 213, 220-22, 258, 383, 489, 492-93
Peycaví 282
Picol 189, 334
Picoldo 280
Pillán xli, 95, 146, 153, 157, 166, 181, 187
Pillo 75
Pillolco 120, 126, 134, 199, 279
Pilmaiquens 283
Pinol 254, 337
Pon 190-91, 337
Pran xv, 393, 400-01, 404-06, 408-11, 415, 488-89, 492
Puchecalco ix, 101, 108, 493
Purén xli, 22, 24, 26, 45, 106, 119, 126, 225, 382, 450
Quilacura 192, 281, 369, 493
Rengo xiii-xv, xxxvi, 127, 129, 137-41, 190-92, 194-98, 219, 222-23, 280, 285, 290-92, 329, 336, 339-40, 345, 380, 382-89, 393-95, 416, 450, 487, 489, 493-94
Renoguelons 283
Ron 76
Santillán 338
Surco 258
Talca 66
Talcaguano 30, 32, 66, 225, 232, 281
Talco 137-38, 189

Talcuén 199
Tambo 333
Teguán 283, 337
Titaguano 75
Tomé 23-24, 120, 126, 281
Torbo 75
Torquín 124, 136
Trulo 336
Trulos 282
Tucapel ix, xiii-xv, xxxvi, xli, 22-23, 27, 61, 101, 106, 108-111, 120, 123, 125, 135-36, 144-45, 198, 213, 221-23, 257, 260-64, 282, 288, 329, 334, 340-41, 380, 382, 384-89, 393-98, 416, 450-51, 489-90, 493
Tulcomara 280
Tunconabal xvi, 452, 455, 457
Tuncos 283
Zinga 199
Arauco, state of vii, xiii, xxvi, xxix, 7, 9, 16-18, 25, 34, 48, 50, 52, 66, 81, 116-18, 145, 158-59, 162, 166, 174, 177-78, 228, 231, 285, 299, 306, 329, 335, 365, 408, 471, 485, 488-89
Arauco, valley ix, 23, 101-02, 133, 297, 488, 493
Arctic 29, 235, 359, 441
Ariosto, Ludovico
Orlando Furioso xxv, xxxii, 194
Armor
Brassard 11, 387
Breastplate xxxiv, 32, 58, 65, 75, 88, 103, 105, 120, 123, 127, 157, 198, 258, 312, 323, 346, 377, 385
Corselet 103, 124, 282, 288
Gorget 11, 411

| 501 |

Greaves 11, 71, 377
Shield 57-58, 71, 76, 92, 117, 154-55, 187-88, 191, 194-65, 197, 233, 239, 257-59, 266, 280, 288, 319, 323, 333-38, 385, 387, 389
Astrology
  Aquarius 162
  Cancer 204
  Capricorn 230, 283, 364
  Gemini 204
  Scorpio 117, 162
  Virgo 231
Atacama 178, 180
Atlas mountains 234
Ausonian sea 306-07, 310
Austria 246
Austria, Anna of 247
Austria, Ernst, archduke of 244
Austria, Juan of 211, 246, 248, 312, 316, 488
Austria, Juana of 476
Austria, Maria of 244
Azores 471, 476

B

Balkans 311
Barbary pirates 315
Bazán, Maria de 250
Beylerbey 311
Biblical figures
  Ammon 9
  Iaculan serpent 94
  Lot 9
  Mary xxv, 354
  Moses 354
Bizerte xv, 429
Bombards 319
Braudel, Ferdinand 327
Bulgarians 311

Burgos 120

C

Callao de Lima 470
Camilla 276
Campus Martius 201
Canary Islands 362
Carthage xv, 231, 381, 422, 429, 431, 435-38, 489
Caspian Sea 124
Castile 247, 318
Cateau-Cambresis, treaty of 243
Charles V, Emperor xxii, 8, 35, 63, 74, 104, 168, 218, 229, 232, 235, 243-44, 246, 312, 358
Charles IX 243
Chauces 311
Chayllacano 298
Chincha Islands 179, 180
Christ 313, 474, 478
Christians and Christianity xxiv, xxv, xxx, xxxix, xlii, 12, 16, 43, 48, 56, 70, 83, 112-13, 218, 228, 232, 242, 248, 264, 296-97, 302, 311, 315-18, 322-25, 327, 330, 341, 348, 356, 361, 371, 373, 400, 447-48, 475, 480
Copiapó 203, 365
Cortés, Hernán 362
Croatia 246
Croats 311
Curzolari Islands 307
Cuzco 177
Cyprus 247, 324, 427

D

Dalmatia 246, 311
Danube 247, 471
Dido xv, xxviii, 124, 231, 276, 413,

420-23, 425, 427, 430-32, 434, 436, 438, 489-90
Djerba 430
Dyrrachium 231

E

Egypt 462
Elicura, valley of 50-51, 54, 107
Elissa 420, 425, 434. *See also* Dido
England xxii, 175, 178, 485
Europe xxix, 203, 290, 304
Eurytion 254
Exodus 354, 462

F

Famagusta 247, 324
Famous Twelve 56
Ferdinand I 244
Ferdinand II 361
Fitón xiii-xiv, xxv, xxviii, 249, 294, 299-300, 303, 307, 327, 343, 349, 351, 490
  miraculous orb xiv, xxv, xxvii, 305-06, 351-53
  pharmacopeia 303, 490
    Alacrans 303
    Amphisbaena 302
    Asp 302
    Basilisk 301
    Cenchris 302
    Cerastean serpent 302
    Chersydrus 302
    Dragon tails 303
    Echeneis fish 303
    Eye of Lynx 301-02
    Griffin 303
    Haemorrhois 302
    Harpy's wing 302
    Hyena hump 302
    Iaculus 302

    Nesting eagle stones 303
    Phoenix 303
    Rabid dogs 302
    Scorpion 303
    Scytala snake 303
    Seps 302
    Shark maws 303
    Vipers 303
Flanders 235, 246, 484
France xxii, xxvii, xxxi, 56, 227, 235-36, 240, 242-43, 471-72
Francis I, king of France 358

G

Gabriel, archangel 354
Ganges 316
Genoa 191, 247
Germany 247, 311, 471-72
Georgians 311
Granada 246-47
Greece 215, 306
Greed xxvi, xxxi, 19, 35-37, 44, 127, 229, 241, 296, 379, 422-23, 429, 466
Greeks 311
Guadalupe 479
Guardiola, Juan Cristóbal de 483

H

Henry, king of Portugal 476, 480-83
Henry II, king of France 243
Herradura 216
Holy League xxvii, 248, 306
Huánuco 177
Hungary 244, 246-47
Hyrcanian tiger 124

I

Iarbas 432-37, 490

| 503 |

Ibycus 156
Incas xxvi, 15-16, 364
Inquisition 244
Isabella of Portugal 476, 480
Islam 311, 315, 317
Italy 215, 248, 311, 471-72, 484

J

Janissaries 311, 317
Jarama 340
Jason 355

K

Knights Hospitaller 245, 323

L

Lampedusa 430
Lepanto xiii, xxvii, 211, 306-08, 310, 327, 487-88, 490
Lepanto personae
  Ali Pasha, Muezzenade 315-17, 322, 487
  Austria, Juan of 312, 316, 488
  Barbarigo, Agostino 314, 316, 324, 488
  Bazán, Álvaro de, marquis of Santa Cruz 314, 321, 326, 476
  Cara Bey, son of Ochalí 314
  Cárdenas, Bernardino de, marquis of Betata 323, 489
  Cardona, Juan de 324
  Colonna, Marco Antonio 318, 324
  Doria, Andrea 314, 326
  Leinì, Andrea Provana di 318
  Lomellini, Pier Battista 314
  Mehmed Pasha, Suluk 315
  Meghen, count 236
  Ochalí, Pasha of Algiers xiii, 310, 315, 323, 326-27

Pertau Pasha 324
Pius V 318
Requesens, Luis de 321
Rovere, Francisco Maria II della 318
Selim II 247, 315
Soto, Juan de 312
Spinola, Ettore 325
Strozzi, Filipo 476
Venier, Sebastiano 324
Libya 94, 302, 430
Libyan lion xxv, 257, 497
Licudia 430
Liguria 325
Lobera, Pedro Mariño de 63
  Crónica del Reino de Chile 63
Lombardy 247
London xxii, 178
Lucan xxiii, 76, 94, 215, 231
  Pharsalia xxiii, 76, 94, 215, 231, 302
Lusitania 473, 478-79
Lutheran 244
Lycia 311
Lyconians 311

M

Madrid xliii, 244, 340
Magellan 9, 365
Malta 245, 314, 323-24
Mantua 420-21
Manuel I 476, 481
Marañon river 470-71
Marmolejo, Alonso de Góngora 63
  Historia de Chile desde su descubrimiento hasta el año 1575 63
Mary Tudor 175
Mataquito 165, 219, 336, 488, 494
Mauritania 432-33

Maximilian II 244, 247
Mediterranean 306, 311, 314, 323, 327
Moors 245-47, 361
Moravia 471
Moura, Cristobal de 482
Mythological figures and references
  Acheron 307
  Alcides 140, 422
  Alecto 319
  Antaeus 140, 195
  Apollo 28-29, 96, 138, 185, 283
  Astrea 465
  Atropos 126
  Aurora 29, 185, 250
  Avernus 307
  Bellona xxv, xxvii, 31, 233, 235
  Cerberus 307
  Charon 307
  Clytie 185
  Cocytus 307
  Cyclops 33
  Daedalus 127
  Death 108, 187, 336, 346, 416
  Demogorgon 307-08
  Diana 27, 234
  Erinyes 308, 319
  Fame 65, 91-92, 232, 433, 449, 452, 456
  Fortune xxx, 21, 38, 44, 46, 73, 79, 102, 106, 108, 130-31, 145, 164, 171, 177, 180-81, 183, 187, 195, 204, 220, 223-24, 240, 243, 254, 267, 290, 304, 312, 314-15, 335, 342, 350, 368, 373, 401, 407, 415, 448-49, 456, 480
  Furies 233, 307-08, 319
  Gaia 140
  Gorgon 308
  Hecate 308
  Helios 29, 138
  Hercules 140, 195, 361, 422
  Ibycus 156
  Icarus 127
  Lethe 307
  Mars 8-9, 32, 46, 51, 74, 102, 108, 117, 131, 198, 240, 251, 262, 278, 283, 312, 319, 321, 338, 385, 407
  Medusa 302, 308
  Mercury 262
  Nereids xxiv, 219
  Orcus 307
  Parcae 437
  Phaeton 31
  Philomela 93
  Phlegethon 307
  Pluto 307
  Procne 93
  Reason xxv, xxvii, 298
  Styx 307
  Tartar 355
  Tisiphone 319
  Tithonus 29
  Tritons xxiv, 219
  Truth 464
  Typhon 87, 496
  Venus 9, 185
  Vulcan 34, 99
  Zeus 87

N

Naples 307, 358
Nazca 179, 180
Negroponte 315
New Testament 477
New Sea 8, 365. *See also* South Sea
Nihil ultra 361
Nile 357, 358

Ninus 355
Ninyas 356
Numidia 311

O

Orient, the 313, 354
Ottoman Empire xxvii, 245, 306, 310-11, 315, 324, 326-7
Ovid 464

P

Panama 175, 471
Pannonia 245, 471
Paris 242
Pasha 311
Peleus 78
Peñon de Vélez de la Gomera 244
Peru x-xi, xxii, xxvi-xxviii, xxxvii, xli, 3, 8, 16, 63, 156, 168-71, 174-75, 177, 180, 193, 471, 485, 489, 493
Peruvian towns
  Arequipa 177
  Charcas 177
  Chaule 202
  City of Kings x, 156, 168, 178
  Cuzco 177
  Guamanga 177
  Guarco 179
  Huánuco 177
  Jaén 177
  La Paz 177
  Loja 177
  Piura 177
  Quito 177
Petrarch xxv, 193
Philibert, Emmanuel, duke of Savoy 243
Philip II xii, xvi, xxii, xxv, xxix-xxx, xxxii, 8, 35, 63, 175, 231-32, 238, 240, 242-43, 245-47, 307, 310, 327, 361, 444, 446, 471, 473, 475, 479-84, 492
Philip III 247
Phoenicia 275, 420, 431
Pizarro, Francisco 18
Pliny the Elder 302
Pope, the xxxvi, 87, 248, 307, 314
Portugal xvi, xxxi, 444, 473, 476, 478, 480, 482, 492
Pozsony 471
Prester John 356
Prime Mover 457
Promaucaes 15-17
Protestantism 243-44
Ptolemy 262, 467
Puelche 128
Punic war, First 381
Punic war, Third 358
Purén, fort 34, 63, 445
Purén, valley xiv, 54, 117, 367-68, 376, 398, 488
Pygmalion 231, 422, 429, 490

Q

Quiapo 470
Quran 354

R

Rhodes 323
Rivers, Chilean
  Biobío xxvi, 16-17, 90, 280, 284, 286, 365, 397, 489
  Cauquén 365
  Claro 149
  Coquimbo 365
  Itata 17, 163, 216, 283, 365, 491
  Lauquén 373
  Maipo 16

Maule xi, 15, 17, 147, 154, 193, 283, 365, 397, 492
Maule xi, 17, 147, 154, 193, 283, 365, 492
Nivequetén 17, 280
Rauco 70, 248, 298
Romans
  Aeneas 124, 420-21
  Alcestis 276
  Amyclas 215
  Caesar Augustus, Octavian 67, 215, 231, 307, 381, 420, 445
  Cassius Scaevus 43
  Cato, the Utican 381
  Cloelia 276
  Cornelia 276
  Fulvia 276
  G. Mucius Scaevola 43
  Gaius Marius 381
  Herod 470
  Hippo 276
  L. Quintus Cincinnatus 43
  Longinus, Gaius Cassius 181
  Lucretia 276
  M. Atilius Regulus 381
  M. Claudius Marcellus 43
  M. Curius Denatus 43
  M. Furius Camillus 43
  Marcus Curtius 43
  Marcus Sergius 43
  Mark Antony 307
  Nero 201, 470
  P. Decius Mus 43
  P. Horatius Cocles 43
  Penelope 276
  Pompey 43, 76, 231, 381, 445
  Portia 276
  Q. Fulvius Flaccus 43
  Q. Publius Philo 43
  Scaeva 76
Sulla 201
Sulpicia 276
Titus 354
Tuccia 276
Virginia 276
Rome 43, 99, 381, 413, 422, 438
Rubicon 67
Rudolf II 244

S

Saint Elmo fort 245
Saint Quentin xii, xxvii, xxxii, 211, 227, 236-39, 242, 361, 493
Saint Quentin personae
  Cáceres, Alonso de 236, 240
  Coligny, Gaspard de 236
  Coligny, François de, Andalot 240
  Meghen, count 236
  Navarrete, Alonso de 236, 240
  Romero, Julian 236, 240
Sangallá Islands 202
Sanjak 311
Saracen 311, 325
Scythia 341, 359
Sebastian I, king of Portugal 476, 479-80
Segovia 247, 360
Semiramis 356
Silesia 471
Slavonia 311
Southern Cross 273
South Sea 10, 65. *See also* New Sea
Spain xxi-xxiii, xxv-xxvii, xxx-xxxi, xxxviii, 5, 41, 48, 71, 92, 104-06, 158, 231, 243-44, 247-49, 307, 317, 322-23, 360-62, 441, 471-72, 478
Spaniards
  Acebedo 375

Aguayo, Pedro de 77, 333
Aguilera, Pedro de Olmos de 75, 81, 260
Aguirre 333
Aguirre, Lope de 470-71
Alegría 338
Almagro, don Diego de 16
Almagro, Juan Gómez de 53, 55, 57-58, 61-64
Altamirano 337
Alvarado, Hernando 75, 127, 189, 333, 493
Alvarado, Juan 75, 120-21, 125-27, 129-30, 333, 493
Andía, Francisco de 260
Andrea xxxv, 191-92, 194-98, 336-37, 487
Aranda 287, 331
Arce, Rodrigo Vázquez de 483
Arias, Francisco 338
Ávalos 338
Avendaño, Miguel de 289, 333, 366
Avendaño, Pedro de 289, 333, 366
Barrios 338
Bastida 338
Bernal 76, 81, 289, 333
Berzocano 332
Cabrera, Antonio de 260, 338
Cáceres, Alonso de 288-89, 338
Campofrío 260
Carranza 333
Carrillo 260, 333
Castañeda 53, 58, 75, 289, 333
Castillo 333
Córdoba 53, 57, 59, 260, 289
Córdoba, Gonzalo Fernandez de 53
Coronado 338, 346
Cortés 53, 57-58, 61, 289, 333

Cortéz, Hernán 362
Crato, Antonio, prior of 481
Dorán 339
Elvira, Martín de 255-56
Escalona 53, 57, 61
Escobar 289
Espinosa 260
Esquivel, Florencio 339
Galdámez 338
Gamboa, Juan Lopéz de 289, 333
Garnica 260
Girón, Francisco Hernández 169
Girón, Pedro 483
Godoy 339
Guzmán, Martín de 260
Gutiérrez 260
Hernández, Gonzalo 53, 56-57, 59, 76, 339
Herrero, Diego García 53
Ibarra 338, 493
Juárez, Vasco
Jufré, Juan
Lago, 339
Lamas, Juan de
Lasarte 199, 260, 289, 333
Lira, Diego de 260, 338
Lobo, Father 125, 492
Maldonado 53, 57, 61, 75, 345
Manrique 345
Manrique, Leonardo 53, 57, 60
Mendoza, Andrés Hurtado de, marquis of Cañete x, 156, 168, 175-76, 489
Mendoza, Antonio de 169
Mendoza, García Hurtado de 175, 259, 338, 470, 489, 492
Mexía 260
Miranda 289, 333
Molina, Luis de 483
Monguía 333

Morán 53, 57, 59
Navarra, Pedro de 338
Nereda 53, 57, 61
Niño, Pero 53, 57, 60
Oro, Diego (father) 44, 492
Oro, Diego (son) 125, 492
Ortigosa 260
Osorio, Francisco 260, 288, 375
Pacheco, Alonso 199, 260
Pacho, Hernando 260
Pardo, Arias 260, 338, 345
Paredes 333
Peña 76, 289, 333
Peñas, Juan de 45
Peñalosa 53, 57
Pereyra, Simón 260, 273
Pérez, Diego 260, 333
Pérez, Hernán 288
Pero Niño 53, 57, 60
Pineda, Juan de 338
Pizarro Francisco 16
Ponce, Francisco 338
Quiroga, Rodrigo de 333
Remón, Juan 287, 289, 338, 345
Reynoso, Alonso de xv, 45, 76, 289, 333, 397, 404-05, 409, 443-45, 487
Ribera 338
Riberos 260, 338
Ronquillo 260, 333
Ruiz, Martín 76, 289, 333, 338
Segarra 338
Toledo, Luis de 333
Torres, Juan de 260
Ulloa 289, 333
Vaca 260
Valdivia, Pedro de viii, xii, 16-19, 34-42, 45-47, 49, 51-52, 54-55. 103, 107, 175, 190, 349, 365, 445, 451, 487-88, 494

Valenzuela, Julian de 258-29
Veaz, Marcos 10, 156
Vega 338
Vela, Blasco Nuñez de 169
Velasco, Miguel de 366
Verdugo 338
Vergara 53, 57, 339
Verrío 260
Viezma 338
Villagrán Francisco de xi, 65, 67, 70, 72, 75, 77, 79-81, 86, 148, 173, 180, 184-85, 190, 494
Villagrán, Gabriel de 190, 199
Villagrán, Juan de 190, 495
Villagrán, Pedro de x, 148, 156, 161, 166-67, 189-90, 200, 494
Villarroel, Andrés de 45, 339
Yanaruna, Juan 334
Zuñiga 260, 291, 333
Spanish Inquisition 241
Spanish towns
  Arica 200
  Cañete 365, 398
  Cautén xli, 107, 166, 366, 374
  City of Kings x, 156, 168, 178-79, 470. *see also* Lima
  Concepción ix-xii, xxiii, xli, 16-18, 35, 89, 96, 102, 113, 193, 211, 213, 216, 488-89
  Copiapó 203
  Coquimbo 18, 203
  Del Lago xli, 18, 107
  La Imperial viii-x, xiii, xvi, xli, 18, 35, 51-52, 54-55, 63-64, 101, 112-15, 166, 275, 279, 365-66, 398, 464, 469
  La Serena 105, 201
  Lima xxii, 156, 179, 364, 470. *See also* City of Kings
  Mapochó 107, 203

Mataquito 165, 219, 336, 488
Penco xli, 18, 31, 34, 65, 102, 117, 147, 163, 198, 204, 445, 492-93
Purén 376
Quillota 204
Santiago ix-x, xiii, xxxi, xli, 16, 18, 89, 94, 107, 111, 119, 141, 147, 165-66, 190, 491
Villarrica 18, 365
Spica, the star 231
Suleiman I 245-46
Sychaeus 420, 422-23, 426, 438
Syrians 311
Syrtes 430
Szigeth 246

T

Taboga 178
Tartars 311
Téllez-Girón, Pedro, duke of Osuna 483
Tercios 236
Thrascians 311
Tierra Firme 471
Toledo 353
Transylvania 246, 311
Tropic of Capricorn 283, 364
Troy 23, 76, 97, 319
Tucapel fort viii, xiv-xv, 20, 35-36, 51-52, 55, 349, 352, 404, 409, 488, 494
Tunis 430
Tunisia 311, 429-30
Turkey xiii, 244-45, 310-11, 314-15, 317-19, 322-25, 487
Tyre 231, 420, 422

V

Valois, Elizabeth of 243

Vega, Garcilaso de la xxv, 194
Venice xxvii, 23, 248, 363
Vienna xxii, 247
Virgil xxiii, 276, 421, 438
  Aeneid xxiii, xxviii, 124, 134, 203, 231, 254, 275, 420-21

W

Walloons 236
Weapons
  Bombard 319
  Cannon xxiv, xxxiv, 31, 34-35, 65, 70, 73, 76, 107, 119, 177, 179, 219, 230, 232, 253, 258, 309, 314, 317, 319, 411, 416
  Catapult 10, 76, 254
  Culverin 319
  Dart 10, 71, 109, 122, 155, 279, 334, 344
  Esmeril 323
  Falcon 179, 323
  Halberd 10
  Harquebus 107, 121-22, 256, 265
  Javelin xxxv, 10, 120, 192, 344, 377
  Lance xxiii, 14, 23, 40, 42, 72, 74-76, 83, 88, 122, 133-35, 142, 162, 188, 190, 222, 232-33, 256-56, 265, 280, 282, 335, 371, 377, 411
  Lasso 10
  Pike xxxiv, 24, 54, 56-57, 60, 71-72, 80, 96, 104, 120-22, 150-51, 157, 241, 253, 257, 280, 288-89, 331-32, 334-35, 348, 414
  Poniard 10, 334
  Saker 179
  Slingshot 10, 129-30, 377
Winds

General Index

Aeolus 203, 206
Aquilon 62
Auster xli, 179-80, 202-03, 359, 363, 470
Boreas xli, 62, 203-04, 206
Caurus xli, 151-52, 358-59
Eurus xli, 363
Garbino xli, 179
Mediodía 363
Notus xli, 179-80, 202, 362
Thrascias 99
Vulturnus xli, 341, 363, 498
Zephyr xli, 206-07, 214, 341, 498
World tour, Fitón's
Acaca 365
Africa 354, 356-57
Albania 355
Alexandria 358-59
Amhara 357
Apollonia 358
Arachosia 354
Aranjuez 360
Arauco 365
Arequipa 364
Arma 363
Armenia 355
Asia 353, 355, 359
Assyria 356
Atacama 365
Austria 359
Azores 362
Babylon 356-57
Bahama Channel 362
Baltic 359
Banda 365
Barcelona 360
Bayonne 358
Begmender 357
Bermeo 360
Biafrans 358
Biscay 360
Bithynia 353
Black Sea 353-55
Bogotá 363
Bohemia 359
Bohol 365
Bologna 358
Bordeaux 358
Bosporus 353
Brabant 358
Bracamoros 363-64
Bruney 365
Bulgaria 359-60
Burgos 360
Cabo de la Vela 363
Cadiz 361
Cairo 357
Cajamarca 363
Calchaqui 364
Cali 363
Candia 359-60
Cañete 365
Canta 354
Capira 363
Caria 353
Carmania 354
Cartagena 363
Cartama 363
Caspian Sea 355-56
Cathay 354
Ceylon 354
Chachapoyas 363
Chalcedon 353
Chiloé 365
China 354
Chuquiabo 364
Circassians 354
City of Kings 364
Coimbra 360
Colchis 355

| 511 |

Comechigone 364
Copiapó 365
Córdoba 361
Coronados 365
Corsica 358
Corvatia 359
Cremona 358
Cuba 362
Cuzco 364
Cyprus 359
Dacia 359
Danube 359
Dembiya 357
Denmark 359
Diaguitas 364
Dominica 362
Don, the river 359
Drangiana 354
Egypt 355
England 358
Escorial, San Lorenzo del 361
Ethiopia 356-57
Euphrates 353, 355
Europe 354, 359, 362
Ferrara 358
Flanders 358
Florence 358
Florida 362
Frisia 358
Fuenfría 358
Gaboto 364-65
Galatia 353
Galicia 360
Gambia 358
Ganges 354
Garamantes 354
Gedrosia 354
Genoa 358
Georgians 354
Germany 359

Gibraltar 358, 361
Gilolo 365
Gojjam 356-57
Gothia 359
Granada 361
Greece 359
Greenland 359
Guayaquil 363
Guelders 358
Guineans 358
Hibernia 358
Hierro 362
Holland 358
Hormuz, straits of 354
Huamanga 364
Huánuco 364
Hungary 359-60
Hyperborean peaks 359
Hyrcania 354
Iberians 354
Iceland 359
India 354
Indian Ocean 354
Iran 354-55
Ireland 358
Jalisco 362
Jamaica 362
Judea 359
Juries 364
Kura 355
La Imperial 365-66
León 360
Libyan desert's 357
Liguria 358
Lisbon 360
Lithuania 359-60
Livonia 359
Logroño 360
Loja 175, 363
Lucayas 362

Lycia 353
Lydia 353
Lyon 358
Macedonia 359
Machan 365
Madrid 360-61
Mandinka 357
Manikongo 357
Mantua 358
Matán 365
Mate 365
Media 356
Medina del Campo 360
Meroe 357
Mesopotamia 355
Mexico xli, 362
Michoacán 362
Milan 358
Mojos 363-64
Moldavia 359-60
Moluccas 354, 365
Moravia 359
Morea 359-60
Motir 365
Mountains of the Moon 356-57
Muscovy 359
Nazareth 353
New Spain 362
Naples 358
Nile 357-58
Nombre de Dios 362
Norway 359
Orient 354
Orleans 358
Osorno 365
Padua 358
Paita 363
Palestine 353
Pamphylia 353
Pamplona 360

Panama 362
Paphlagonia 353
Pardo 360
Paris 358
Parthia 355
Pasto 363
Pavia 358
Penco 365
Peronne 358
Persia 354
Persian Gulf 353-54, 356
Pharnacea 353
Piacenza 358
Piedmont 358
Pilcomayo 362
Piura 363
Plata 364
Podolia 359
Poitiers 358
Poland 359
Pontus Euxinus 353
Popayan 363
Potosí 364
Prussia 359
Puerto Viejo 363
Quito 363
Red Sea 354, 356
Rhodes 355, 359
Riphean mountains 359
Russia 359
Salamanca 360
Samogitia 359
San Juan 362
Santa Marta 363
Santo Domingo 362
Sardinia 358
Sarmatia 359
Savona 358
Savoy 358
Sceva 356

Scotland 358
Sebu 365
Segovia 360
Seville 361
Sicily 358
Siena 358
Silesia 359
Slavonia 359-60
South Sea 365
Spain 360-62
Sultania 355
Susiana 354
Sweden 359
Syria 353
Syrtes 358
Tagus 361
Tamerlane 355
Tartar 355
Tartary 355, 359
Tauris 355
Ternate 365
Thrace 353
Tidore 365
Tigris 355
Toledo 361
Toulouse 358

Transylvania 359
Trapesus 355
Trebizond 355
Tripoli 358
Troglodytes 357
Trujillo 363
Tucumán 364-65
Tulbiya 357
Tumbez 363
Tunis 358
Turkey 353
Tuscany 358
Valdivia 365
Valencia 360
Valladolid 360
Venezuela 363
Villarrica 365
Wallachia 359-60
Wolofs 358
Zapes 358
Zaragoza 360
Zarza 363

Y

Yanacona xv, 291, 333, 374, 393, 487, 492